INSIDE
COMPUTER
UNDERSTANDING:
Five Programs
Plus Miniatures

THE ARTIFICIAL INTELLIGENCE SERIES

A Series of Monographs, Treatises, and Texts
Edited by Roger C. Schank

SCHANK AND ABELSON • *Scripts Plans Goals and Understanding:
An Inquiry into Human Knowledge Structures, 1977*

LEHNERT • *The Process of Question Answering:
Computer Simulation of Cognition, 1978*

MEEHAN • *The New UCI LISP Manual, 1979*

CHARNIAK, RIESBECK, AND MCDERMOTT • *Artificial
Intelligence Programming, 1980*

SCHANK AND RIESBECK • *Inside Computer Understanding:
Five Programs Plus Miniatures, 1981*

INSIDE COMPUTER UNDERSTANDING:

Five Programs
Plus Miniatures

Edited by

ROGER C. SCHANK
CHRISTOPHER K. RIESBECK
Yale University

Routledge
Taylor & Francis Group
New York London

This edition published 2012 by Routledge

Routledge

Taylor & Francis Group   Taylor & Francis Group

711 Third Avenue   2 Park Square

New York, NY 10017   Milton Park, Abingdon

                              Oxon OX14 4RN

First Published by

Lawrence Erlbaum Associates, Inc., Publishers
365 Broadway
Hillsdale, New Jersey 07642

Library of Congress Cataloging in Publication Data

Main entry under title:

Inside computer understanding.

  Bibliography: p.
  Includes index.
  1. Artificial intelligence. 2. Programming
(Electronic computers) I. Schank, Roger C.,
1946-   II. Riesbeck, Christopher K.
Q336.I55 1981   001.64'2   80-18314
ISBN 0-89859-071-X

Contents

Preface   ix

1. **Our Approach to Artificial Intelligence**   1

   The Evolution of our Ideas or
       (Whatever Became of Margie?)   3

   The Future   8

2. **The Theory Behind the Programs:**
   Conceptual Dependency   10

   Representing Events   11

   The Scope of CD   25

3. **The Theory Behind the Programs:**
   A Theory of Context   27

   Causal Types   28

   Connecting Text   29

   Script Application   31

   Plans   33

   Goals   37

   Themes   39

4. LISP   41

Introduction   41
The Syntax of LISP   41
Expressions and Values   42
Defining Functions   44
Conditional Branching   45
Building and Using Lists   45
Iteration   50
Reference Section   54
Conceptual Dependency in LISP   60
Implementation Notes   64

5. SAM   75

Richard Cullingford
Introduction   75
An Overview of Sam   83
An Annotated Example   89
The Program Itself   101

6. Micro SAM   120

Introduction   120
Sample Output   126
Flow Chart   129
The Program   129
Exercises   132

7. PAM   136

Robert Wilensky
Introduction   136
Summary of PAM'S Behavior   141
The Program   145
A Technical Description of PAM   163

8. Micro PAM   180

Introduction   180
Sample Output   182
Flow Charts   184
The Program   187
Exercises   193

9. TALE-SPIN   197

James Meehan
Introduction   197
Overview of TALE-SPIN   203
Modules   210
Technical View of TALE-SPIN   220

10. Micro TALE-SPIN   **227**
Introduction   227
Sample Output   228
Flow Charts   233
The Program   234
Exercises   256

11. POLITICS   **259**
Jaime Carbonell
Introduction   259
Overview of POLITICS   270
A Detailed View of POLITICS   283
An Annotated Example of the POLITICS System   299

12. Micro POLITICS   **308**
Introduction   308
Sample Output   309
Flow Charts   310
The Program   311
Exercises   316

13. Conceptual Analysis of Natural Language   **318**
Lawrence Birnbaum and Mallory Selfridge
Introduction   318
Overview of the Analyzer   325
Theoretical Issues   331
A Detailed View of the Program   335
A Detailed Example   344

14. Micro ELI   **354**
Introduction   354
Sample Output   361
Flowchart   363
The Program   364
Exercises   369

Bibliography   **373**

Author Index   **379**

Subject Index   **381**

Preface

We have written this book for those who want to comprehend how a large natural language-understanding program works. The book had its beginnings as a result of a summer school we ran at Yale in June and July of 1978. During that winter, with the support of the Sloan Foundation's program in Cognitive Science, thirty-five professionals in Cognitive Science, mostly psychologists by training, were taught to grapple with the details of programming in Artificial Intelligence. As a part of the curriculum we designed for them, we created what we called "micro-programs." These micro-programs were an attempt to give students the flavor of using a large AI program without all the difficulty normally associated with learning a complex system written by another person. Thus, when we discussed our parser, ELI, or our story understanding program, SAM, we also gave students the micro versions of these programs, which were very simple versions that operated in roughly the same way as their larger brothers, but without all the frills. Students were asked to add pieces to the programs and otherwise modify them in order to learn how they worked.

Our feeling, and that of the students who used them, was that these micro programs were very useful pedagogically. We later used these same micro programs in our first year graduate course in AI. Further, we sent them out to other institutions where they were used and found to be helpful. From the positive response that we got, we decided it was time to put together a series of discussions and micro programs covering a number of the projects that we have done over the past few years.

In previous books, *Conceptual Information Processing* in 1975 and *Scripts Plans Goals and Understanding* in 1977, we have outlined what has come to be known as the "Yale view of AI". There, we have presented our theories of the language process in humans and how we can model that process on a digital computer. But, to a large extent, many of the theories and the programs that embody those theories have remained difficult to assess for psychologists, novices in AI, and others interested in Cognitive Science. This is partially due to the difficulty one has in describing any large computer program in anything approaching reasonable English prose. It is also due to the fact that comprehending AI programs is somewhat analogous to trying to understand a sport like baseball or football. It is hard to get the nuances right if one hasn't played the game. With respect to AI programs, it is often hard to assess their significance without having at some point tried to create one's own program.

We have also found that a great many people who have read our work and are interested in it, still ask us, "But how do the programs really work?" We feel that this is a question which is particularly important to answer at a time in academic history when computers are becoming more pervasive. A detailed look at our programs, as opposed to catchy input-output pairs, seems to be potentially valuable to many different kinds of readers.

This book is intended to give the student of AI a look at how some natural language comprehension programs work from the inside. It consists of detailed descriptions of five such programs. Four of these were written as Ph.D. theses at Yale under our supervision. We asked the students (who by this time have become professors) to write new descriptions of their programs with a student audience in mind, and to include with these descriptions micro versions of their programs. Micro-SAM, a script applier, already existed, written by Eugene Charniak as part of the Sloan summer program. Micro-ELI was written at the same time and is a simplification of our conceptual analyzer of three years ago. Our model of text analysis continues to evolve and our current analyzer differs in a number of ways from ELI. A description of the new analyzer, including its relationship to previous ones, precedes our account of Micro-ELI. That description was written by Larry Birnbaum and Mallory Selfridge.

The work described in Chapters 5 through 14 is based on the theory that we have outlined in our previous books. In AI research, the task frequently falls upon the Ph.D. student of taking a rough theory and "making it work". Rarely does this theory "work" right away. New theories have to be postulated and refinements made to old theories before anything can work at all.

In addition, successful Ph.D. theses have the pleasant effect of pointing towards where we are going next. In the cases presented in this volume, where they point seems clear. More work on goals, themes and memory will be required in the years ahead. In addition, programs that rely upon integrated knowledge sources that can handle large numbers of inputs seem of high priority.

We have tried, as editors of this volume, to impose a uniform style of description for each of the systems. Each descriptive chapter has been written according to the same outline, and the programs have been edited to use the same dialect of LISP, which is described in Chapter 4. The LISP programs form an important part of this book, since hands-on programming experience conveys better than anything else what the issues are and how we have approached them. The descriptive chapters do not depend on a knowledge of LISP, however, and we hope that everyone with an interest in AI will gain a better idea of how computational models of intelligence function.

For those who intend to try the micro-programs, first read Chapter 4 which describes the version of LISP that is used. We have tried to keep the set of functions small enough so that you will be able to use the programs no matter what dialect of LISP you have. However, our first concern was that the programs be readable, so we have used some features (such as looping functions and formatted printing) that may have to be added to some versions of LISP. Chapter 4 describes what needs to be done. Chapter 4 also contains a description of a simple pattern matcher which is used by the micro programs for testing inputs and retrieving information.

After reading Chapter 4, we recommend that you do Micro-SAM first. This has a detailed write-up of script application and shows how the pattern matcher plays a basic role. Micro-SAM's exercises guide the first-time programmer in a step-by-step fashion through some simple program modifications.

After Micro-SAM, try one of the other understanding programs, either Micro-PAM or Micro-POLITICS. These programs have much in common with Micro-SAM, because certain low-level functions are useful to any inferencing program. Doing a second micro-program will help teach what is the same and what is different among the various approaches to comprehension.

After doing two memory programs, you can try either Micro-ELI, which is a conceptual analyzer, or Micro-TALE-SPIN which is a story generator. After learning Micro-ELI itself, the next step is to interface it with the memory programs (i.e., Micro-SAM, Micro-PAM and Micro-POLITICS). Do not do Micro-ELI until you have a grasp of what the output of the analyzer will be used for.

If you do Micro-TALE-SPIN, you will find very little in common on the surface with the other programs. This is because Micro-TALE-SPIN is not a comprehension program. Also Micro-TALE-SPIN is a very large program, most of which is data that tells how goals and plans hook together, and how to express in English many different kinds of meaning forms.

All the work described in this book was done at the Yale Artificial Intelligence Project during the years 1975–1978. The research was supported by the Advanced Research Projects Agency of the Department of Defense and was monitored by the Office of Naval Research under contract N00014-75-C-1111.

We would like to acknowledge the contribution of Robert Abelson to the background ideas for many of the programs described here. The theoretical work behind these programs is described in *Conceptual Information Processing* (Schank, 1975) and *Scripts Plans Goals and Understanding* (Schank and Abelson, 1977). Chapters 2 and 3 give the theoretical claims and assumptions that are necessary for reading the ensuing chapters. For a fuller understanding of the theory involved, the 1977 volume should really be read in its entirety.

Many people worked on the original projects described herein, as well as the micro-programs. We as editors have done all the things that make editors so beloved by authors. We have reworded, rewritten, removed, reorganized, recoded and revised, repeatedly. Ann Drinan was our accomplice in these crimes. But the ideas themselves come from the authors, with a little help from their friends.

The center of the SAM project was Richard Cullingford. Gerald DeJong and Walter Stutzman modified Neil Goldman's conceptual generator for use in SAM. Wendy Lehnert and Janet Kolodner developed the question-answering routines. Anatole Gershman modified the parser to accept newspaper stories. Richard Granger wrote a module to enable SAM to guess at the meanings of unknown words in context. Richard Proudfoot and Mallory Selfridge worked on the module of SAM concerned with the properties of script roles. The Micro-SAM program and exercises were written by Eugene Charniak.

The major part of PAM was written by Robert Wilensky. The English generator used to answer questions and to tell stories from different viewpoints was written by Roderick McGuire and Richard Granger. The question answering routines were written by Janet Kolodner. Michael Lebowitz helped to extend PAM in its later stages. Micro-PAM was written by Robert Wilensky and Michael Deering at the University of California at Berkeley. The exercises were developed at Yale by Michael Lebowitz.

James Meehan was solely responsible for the original TALE-SPIN program. The development of Micro-TALE-SPIN was supported by a grant from the Committee on Instructional Development and by the Department of Information and Computer Science at the University of California, Irvine. Dan Eilers provided programming assistance.

The POLITICS program was also primarily a solo project by Jaime Carbonell, with assistance from Stephen Slade.

The CA (Conceptual Analyzer) was done by Lawrence Birnbaum and Mallory Selfridge. It is based on what they felt was good and bad in the ELI parser from the SAM system. ELI was in turn based on the conceptual analyzer of the MARGIE system. Both of these earlier programs were written by Christopher Riesbeck.

The Yale Artificial Intelligence Project is a large highly interactive group. Robert Abelson, Wendy Lehnert, and Drew McDermott all played an important role in inspiring and guiding much of the work described above.

Roger C. Schank
Christopher K. Riesbeck

INSIDE
COMPUTER
UNDERSTANDING:
Five Programs
Plus Miniatures

1 Our Approach to Artificial Intelligence

The goal of Artificial Intelligence (AI) is commonly considered to be making machines intelligent. In the beginning, two domains dominated AI: chess and problem solving (e.g., Greene, 1959; Minsky, 1961; Newell et al., 1958; Newell and Simon, 1961). It was felt that a reasonable approach towards creating intelligent computers would be to make computers do things that clearly exhibited intelligence. Automated chess playing and theorem proving attracted maximum interest, largely because they were instances of things that were especially hard to do, and thus that exhibited intelligence.

Early work in AI did not have a particularly psychological flavor. Questions about how *people* played chess were not of primary interest. Much of the work done by Newell and Simon (1961) on problem solving was oriented towards finding out how people do various tasks, but the motivation of getting machines to do hard things predominated in AI nonetheless. Current chess playing programs are very good but not because they have simulated expert human chess players. Although some research has been done in that area within AI proper (Berliner, 1974), most expert chess programs perform well because they compute quickly and cleverly.

A great deal of current AI research is in the area of Robotics, that is, the adding of eyes, hands, and feet (or wheels) to the computer. Automated vision work (Duda and Hart, 1973; Winston, 1975) has in general not put any great emphasis on getting computers to see the way people do. Indeed, the problems really are quite different. AI researchers must primarily concern themselves with interpreting noisy input from a television camera. This makes the psychologist's and AI researcher's problems fundamentally different. Here again the AI emphasis is not always on the simulation of cognition but on computational achievement.

Our orientation in AI is much more in the area of cognitive simulation. The fundamental barrier to the achievement of intelligent machines is, in our opinion, our lack of knowledge about what people know and how they use what they know. We believe that it will be impossible to achieve machine intelligence without first coming to understand how people think.

Increasingly, AI in general has become concerned with the issue of what kind of knowledge people have, how it is stored, accessed, applied and acquired. This new focus is a result of the realization that world knowledge is behind people's ability to do almost anything intelligent. An AI simulation of an expert chemist requires finding out what that chemist *knows*. Similarly, a simulation of a three year old's linguistic ability also requires finding out what he knows (among other things). AI has gotten into the knowledge business in a big way in the last few years, partially because of the success of MYCIN, DENDRAL and other programs (Buchanan et al., 1969; Feigenbaum, 1977; Shortliffe, 1976).

As work in natural language processing began, researchers realized that initial toy systems could not be extended in the absence of a theory. Thus they began to experiment with whatever theories were available. Implementations of various linguistic theories emphasizing syntax had their heyday in AI for a while, but meaning was the real issue for AI, whereas for a long time linguists were assiduous in avoiding meaning altogether. When linguists did begin to approach issues of meaning, they did not do so from a process point of view. The notion of process, that is the construction of step by step models with precise beginning and end points, is fundamental to the building of any computer program. Natural language researchers within AI thus had to come to grips with the fact that they would have to build their own theories of the linguistic process. Since people can easily perform those tasks that AI wanted machines to perform, the quest for a theory of language processing gradually has become identical with the quest for a theory of human cognition.

Computer programs that attempt to replicate understanding without simulating the human understanding process are doomed to failure when it comes to very complex processes. Nowhere has this been clearer than in natural language processing. The tendency in the early years of mechanical translation (e.g., see Oettinger, 1960; Locke and Booth, 1955) and computational linguistics (e.g., Hays, 1967), two fields that preceded the AI approach to natural language processing, was to write programs based on grammars that would do initial syntactic parses of a sentence. These syntactic parsers failed for three important reasons. First, they were incredibly complicated to write, often employing tens of thousands of grammar rules for only very small parts of English. Second, they totally ignored meaning considerations, attempting to resolve syntactic issues as if they were completely independent of meaning. Third, and most important, they attempted to create a process that had nothing in common with its human counterpart. People are good at predicting the content of what they will hear. However, they are not very good at remembering long sequences of words.

Because of these two factors, people do not wait until a sentence is finished before they begin to process it. Rather, they attempt to understand as much as they can of what they hear or read as the hearing or reading goes along.

It is our contention that computer models must model this process. That is, they must do a great deal more upon hearing the first few words of a sentence than simply attempting to find the syntactic relationships that hold between those words. They must also be processing the meanings, inferences, and general world knowledge related to those words, just as people do. That processing significantly alters the remainder of the processing that will be done in any given sentence.

Language has evolved through people's efforts to ease communication, given limitations of memory and time. Natural languages are not like programming languages. They have been built for speech and for quick reading, not for logical completeness and exactness. Because people are good at supplying missing information in what they read or hear, natural language leaves out a great deal of information. This explains why elliptical utterances, anaphoric references, and highly ambiguous words are so common. If you know what's being talked about, you only need to be given a few verbal clues to aid your understanding.

Thus, the Yale view of AI is that people are the best models of intelligent behavior that we have. We must attempt to simulate them before even considering improving upon the human algorithm. However, while all the work presented here was done with the above viewpoint in mind, it does not necessarily follow that we regard each program we have written as a psychologically correct model subject to empirical test. Frequently we will write a program in order to learn from it, never fully believing that our program was psychologically plausible in the first place.

THE EVOLUTION OF OUR IDEAS
or
(WHATEVER BECAME OF MARGIE?)

When we write an AI program we are attempting to walk the narrow line between human cognitive models and intelligent machines. We want our programs to serve two purposes. They should work, and thus extend the capabilities of computers, and they should tell us something about how people might work. Frequently we make trade offs between one or another of our goals. While we want our programs to work, they will have little value if they only do some limited task using a method which lacks generality. An AI program should tell us something of fundamental importance about cognition, either mechanical or human.

The programs that are described in this book are all intended to model one or another aspect of human cognition. None of them model every aspect, of course, and in that sense they are all rather artificial. One of the trade-offs that we must make is the decision to process language in what is a fairly artificial situation, usually lacking full background knowledge and full context. We make such trade-offs so that we can continue to test our ideas. Thus, for us, theory creation is a process of thought, followed by programming, then by additional thought, with each serving the other. Thus AI really operates under a novel view of science. Normal scientific method holds that first a theory is postulated, and then tested and found to be right or wrong. But in AI our theories are never that complete, because the processes we are theorizing about are so complex. Thus our tests are never completely decisive. We build programs that show us what to concentrate on in building the next program. Our theories evolve in this manner. This evolutionary way of thinking is a virtual requirement in AI and probably in any science whose domain is so complex as to make isolated testing of little use.

MARGIE

The fundamental problem that is addressed by the programs that are presented in this book, and by the work we did prior to these programs, is the problem of the representation of knowledge. Initially our work focused on the problem of the representation of the meaning of sentences. We developed Conceptual Dependency (CD) theory (the basics of which are described in Chapter 2) as the basis for our meaning representations. The purpose of our first computer program was to test the usefulness of CD as a meaning representation language. Our theory was that a meaning representation language for use in a computer program must provide the same representation to different inputs which mean the same thing, regardless of what input language or phraseology is used. For example, "John kissed Mary" and "Mary was given a kiss by John" should have the same meaning representation. Thus CD had to be capable of allowing us to do simple paraphrase and translation of sentences with inputs and outputs that varied considerably in syntactic form as well as in the selection of lexical items. To do this, we had to develop a program that would decode inputs into CD (i.e., a parser) and encode CD's back into a natural language (i.e., a generator).

As we were doing this, we began to realize the importance of inference in the understanding process. Accounting for inference processes in a general way was thus added to our requirements for CD.

MARGIE (Schank et al., 1975) was designed to test out the usefulness of CD and to serve as a prototype for an understanding system. MARGIE was an attempt to demonstrate that language can be mapped into a deep-level, language-independent conceptual base, and then mapped back out into either the same or another language without losing any essential information.

The MARGIE system had three separate modules: a conceptual analyzer or parser, which mapped the input sentences into Conceptual Dependency; a generator, which mapped the meaning structures back into natural language; and a memory and inference program, which determined the referents for new inputs and made inferences about this input.

MARGIE worked in two modes: Paraphrase and Inference. The paraphrase mode produced over 100 paraphrases of an input sentence. These were not simple transformations of the original sentence, but rather they were newly generated expressions based upon the meaning of the original sentence as determined by the analyzer. For example, the following is a sample of MARGIE in paraphrase mode:

INPUT: John killed Mary by choking Mary.
OUTPUT 1: John strangled Mary.
OUTPUT 2: John choked Mary and she died because she could not breathe.
OUTPUT 3: Mary died because she was unable to inhale some air and she was unable to inhale some air because John grabbed her neck.

In inference mode, many of the possible inferences that could be made from the input sentence were produced and then generated. The inferencer speculated about the possible uses of an object, the possible goals of an actor, and the possible results of an action The following is an example of MARGIE in inference mode:

INPUT: John gave Mary an aspirin.
OUTPUT 1: John believes that Mary wants an aspirin.
OUTPUT 2: Mary is sick.
· OUTPUT 3: Mary wants to feel better.
OUTPUT 4: Mary will ingest the aspirin.

MARGIE was our first attempt to model the understanding of natural language on a computer. The program was, however, rather unrealistic in that it worked with isolated sentences which had no overall context. This caused difficulties for the analyzer because it could not disambiguate input sentences with multiple meanings without a context to guide it. More importantly, the lack of context created a very serious problem for the inferencer. Because the inference mode created as many inferences as possible, both from the input sentence and from each successive level of inferences, there quickly arose a problem of the combinatorial explosion of inferences.

Clearly people do not make all possible inferences from what they hear; they make only the relevant ones. How people determine what path will be fruitful in inference-making thus became a serious issue for research.

MARGIE convinced us that Conceptual Dependency could function as a meaning representation language. Since we were able to generate sentences in languages other than English in MARGIE, we also had reason to believe that we had an interlingual representation language. MARGIE was the first computer program that made inferences from input sentences in the context of an overall theory of the inference process.

The major theoretical problem that resulted from the MARGIE system was that of unlimited inferencing. We decided to look at language in a more natural context. We believed that context held the answer to the inference explosion problem.

SAM

As part of our attack on the problem of irrelevant inferences, we began to design SAM. The purpose of SAM was to extend the work done in MARGIE to stories and to attack the problem of context.

To approach this problem, we worked on developing a theory of causal connectedness of text. The rudiments of this theory are presented in Chapter 3. We were able to control inferences partially by connecting sentences in a text by their causal relatedness. It was not always easy to do this, since causal relationships between sentences do not always exist or are often obscure and difficult to determine.

To solve this problem we examined certain simple stories on the most mundane of situations to determine how causal relations were likely to be computed by people engaged in story understanding. We came up with the notion of a script, which is basically a prepackaged chain of causal relations between events and states. In actual use, scripts represent a knowledge structure composed of stereotyped sequences of events that define some common everyday occurrence, such as eating in a restaurant, taking a bus ride, or going to a museum. (Scripts are described more fully in Chapter 3.)

At this point we began the construction of SAM, a computer program that read simple script-based stories. To do this, SAM constructed a representation of the meaning of each sentence that it read, and connected it to its place in the script that it had found to be active at that point in the story. Thus, the SAM system augmented MARGIE's inference capability by supplying detailed knowledge about all the usual events in a standardized situation. In this way the inference process was constrained by the context of the story, and only those inferences relevant to the events in the story were generated.

SAM was a major advance over the MARGIE program, because its use of scripts allowed it to understand real stories, such as newspaper accounts of traffic accidents, without getting mired in a series of irrelevant inferences. SAM demonstrated that an understanding system has to be context-based in order to function effectively.

However, SAM did have its own set of problems. It was built as a model of a person reading a story in great detail; its paraphrases of newspaper stories were quite laborious in explaining every minor detail. Obviously, people do not concern themselves with every script-based inference applicable when reading a story. Furthermore, the processing time involved in SAM's understanding a story was extremely large. To remedy these and other problems, we built FRUMP

(DeJong, 1979). FRUMP is, at this writing, still under development at Yale. FRUMP is an extremely robust program, which can process stories it has never seen before that are taken directly off a news wire, in a time frame which is actually faster than that of a human reader.

PAM and TALE-SPIN

SAM demonstrated that knowledge is at the root of understanding. In order to understand texts, we had to build in knowledge of the world, in the form of a script, to help "fill in the blanks", i.e., the gaps in the causal inference chain between events in a story. Representing a text, then, required knowledge of the real world. Thus, it was no longer possible to separate the problem of language from the problem of knowledge in the representation and understanding of text.

Script-based knowledge, while useful, could not be the only kind of knowledge available to an understander. In particular, a script-based understanding system was not intended to process stories about novel situations or unexpected events. Since the majority of interesting stories we read describe novel situations (stories that do not deviate from scripts are usually extremely dull and boring), this is a very real limitation. Obviously, there was a need to build a program which used some other type of knowledge structure which was less restrictive than scripts.

In Schank and Abelson (1977), we began to explore the use of goals and plans in story understanding and generation. We postulated that there was a small set of goals that most people have. Each of these goals was achieved by a combination of actions that we called plans. In our view, the task of the understander is to track the goals of every character in any situation that he hears about, so as to be able to determine how the actions of a particular character might relate to the achievement of his goals. Much of understanding is the charting of people's motivations and their methods for satisfying their goals in a given situation. Representation of a text, then, must involve a complete representation of the goals and plans of each character and how these affect each other.

After our representational work on goals and plans, we began to design a program, PAM, that could construct these now exceedingly complex representations in order to understand stories, and another program, TALE-SPIN, that could generate such representations in order to tell stories.

While goal-based stories are far more interesting than script-based ones, PAM is still limited in the kinds of stories it can understand, as was SAM.

The natural successor to SAM and PAM, namely a program that can account for extremely complex stories involving many kinds of knowledge structures, many with competing demands, is currently being designed at Yale. In this program, we are also attempting to account for various human memory issues. Specifically, we wish to account for the fact that people frequently misunderstand what they hear or read, often confusing their own prior knowledge and beliefs with the new information being presented. Further, we are attempting to automatically construct the knowledge structures that are necessary in understanding, so that the memory representations that we use can become more parsimonious by sharing knowledge from various sources.

POLITICS

Of course, there are other forms of human communication besides the reading of texts. Since our goal is to create effective models of understanding, we are also studying these other areas. The most significant of these is conversation. Conversational models require everything that was necessary for text understanding. However, one additional issue comes up in conversation almost as soon as one begins to consider the subject, namely the issue of subjectivity and belief. People bring their prejudices and the force of their beliefs and personalities into the conversational situation. (See Schank and Lehnert, 1979, for a discussion of some of these issues.)

POLITICS (Carbonell, 1979a) is a program which simulates a conversation with a United States Senator on a politically sensitive issue. POLITICS adopts a political perspective in the conversation, either conservative or liberal, and evaluates the import of any news event on the basis of this viewpoint. The program has its own belief system (see Abelson, 1973; and Colby, 1973), and a series of goal trees which rank political goals (or beliefs) into a hierarchy of relative importance.

THE FUTURE

The programs that are discussed in this book represent what we have done in natural language processing as of the end of 1978. They can be evaluated in three ways: as computer programs, as psychologically plausible theories of language, and, perhaps most importantly, as the basis of future work.

As computer programs their value is very limited. Only FRUMP has any possible use in the near future. The percentage of stories it understands from the news wire is increasing rapidly, and the prognosis for the practical usability of FRUMP in the near future is good.

What of the theories that these programs have sought to test? The facts are only beginning to come in from psychologists, linguists and others. It does seem, however, that scripts are an important memory structure (e.g., see Bower et al., 1979; Graesser et al., 1979; Nelson and Gruendel, 1978; Smith et al., 1978). SAM showed us that script-based processing was possible and it taught us quite a bit about building large understanding programs. PAM and TALE-SPIN showed us how to represent and use plans and goals in story understanding and generation. In one sense, their construction taught us what we already knew: real story understanders and story generators do not rely exclusively on any one type of knowledge structure, but instead use all of them together whenever necessary.

On the other hand, we learned a great deal from all these programs about the actual use of the concepts we had developed. Each of the programs elaborated upon and changed our original view of the theory they started out to test. For example, POLITICS and PAM explored issues in complex goal analysis, planning and counterplanning, all of which we had barely considered before but which we had to confront directly in the construction of the programs.

One of the biggest contributions of these programs has been the destruction of our assumption that constructing large independent modules was the right way to build big knowledge-based programs. Just as parsing turns out not to be usefully separable into a syntactic module and a semantic module, so also understanding turns out not to be separable into a parsing part and an inferencing part. Big programs like SAM were cumbersome because of the weakness of the link between the parser and the memory. Both FRUMP and POLITICS used specially designed parsers that were integrated with the rest of their component parts. Thus, information from the highest memory levels in both FRUMP and POLITICS is used to help in the parse. These programs functioned much more effectively because of this integrated approach. We have now started to construct all our programs in this way. Two new understanding programs, IPP (Schank et al., 1978) and BORIS, currently under development at Yale, use this integrated approach to understanding.

However, even more important than the need for integration, we learned, was the need for a reasonably organized memory in our programs. Such a memory capacity would enable our programs to use prior relevant experience in the actual processing of new inputs. We are now working on memory issues in CYRUS (Schank and Kolodner, 1979), a program that remembers what FRUMP tells it, and in IPP and BORIS.

2 The Theory Behind the Programs: Conceptual Dependency

All of the programs presented here are based on a theory of language and language processing that we have been developing over the last twelve years. The theory has undergone many changes during that time. What we shall present here is intended to emphasize the main points of our current thinking as well as to give some historical perspective on why the ideas evolved at the time that they did and in the way that they did.

Language is a medium whose purpose is communication. Thus, the primary focus of any study of language must be to determine what kinds of things can be communicated. Our emphasis must be on the content of the communication rather than on its form.

This may not seem like a very radical position, and indeed it is not, within the framework of AI. But, until very recently, the main body of thought in linguistics was oriented in the opposite direction. The study of form over content made the study of syntax paramount, with issues of meaning and knowledge considered only secondarily, if at all.

When we were first beginning to develop our theory, there was very little interest, either among linguists or computational linguists, in theories whose focus was not syntax. In putting Conceptual Dependency (CD), our representational theory, up against such syntactically-oriented positions, we were frequently ascribed the position of being anti-syntax, or that language could be understood without the use of syntax. Actually we never held any such position. Our belief was that meaning was the primary issue, and that the study of syntax should be guided by the demands of a theory of understanding. All the parsers we developed had a great deal of syntactic information available to them. However, none of them used that information except as an aid in obtaining a meaning from an input. Our point was that there should be no initial independent syntactic pass in understanding. We still do not believe that one can, or would want to, process any part of language using syntactic information exclusively or primarily.

In order for a theory of language to have relevance in AI it must provide a representation of meaning as well as the means to map into and out of that representation. As AI is an experimental science, we have constantly been modifying both our representations and our means of getting into and out of them. We do not claim that we have the definitive representation. However, we have learned a great deal about what kinds of things must be present in meaning representations from our experience in designing programs that use those representations.

REPRESENTING EVENTS

In attempting to get at what the correct representation of meaning should look like we must first understand that there are a great many different things that must be represented. These include: physical events, mental events, intentions, physical causes, mental causes (i.e., reasons), known clusters of related events and intentions, and predictions of consequences or repercussions of events.

At the heart of any meaning representation system is the representation for events. CD uses a simple structure to represent the core of an event, that is invariant across descriptions. That is, no matter what form an utterance describing that event may take, the form of the CD used to represent it is always the same. This works as follows:

Every EVENT has:
    an ACTOR
    an ACTION performed by that actor
    an OBJECT that the action is performed upon
    a DIRECTION in which that action is oriented

This formal structure of events is at the heart of CD. Its use forces you to postulate actors, objects, and so on that may have not been explicitly mentioned in a sentence describing an event, but which nevertheless must exist. This is so because, by definition, an event contains all of the elements described above. When parsing into CD, then, as well as when inferring from a CD, one of the prime motivators of the system is "slot-filling". Unknown elements are replaced by items gotten from the sentence being parsed or from world knowledge at large. (This notion of slot-filling was used later by Minsky (1975) in his frame theory.)

Representing a sentence is thus very much dependent on what we mean by the idea of an actor and an action. An actor is a concrete object (called a Picture

Producer or PP) that can decide to act upon some concrete object (i.e., another PP) in some way. An action is what an actor does to a concrete object. By these definitions, a rock is a PP but it can never be an actor because it can never decide to do anything. Nouns are not necessarily PP's. For example, "honesty" can be the subject of a sentence but it is not a PP and hence cannot be an actor.

Some examples will serve to illustrate the representation issue:

John went to New York.

Here, the OBJECT is missing. It can be filled in by using a rule attached to a sense of the word "go" which says that the object is the same as the item that fills the ACTOR slot. (That is, in CD we would have "John went John to New York" which is bad English but good CD.)

John likes to drink.

In this sentence, we have a state of John that is caused by a partially completed CD. (States and causation will be dealt with later on.) We have an action for the CD ("drink"), and need to fill in the other elements. The ACTOR is inferred from the fact that the English verb "like" requires that the actor be the same as the subject of the verb "like" if not explicitly stated otherwise (i.e., "John likes Mary to drink"). The DIRECTION comes from the meaning of "drink" and is something like "towards the mouth of John." The OBJECT must be inferred from what we know about drinking. Something like "alcoholic beverage" is the default filler for that slot.

John fell.

Here, it would seem that "John" is the filler of the ACTOR slot. But careful thought shows that John has not really acted. Something has acted on him. John is the OBJECT here. The ACTION is a force applied to him. "Fell" has a default DIRECTION of "towards the ground". The missing actor is "gravity" or some other natural force.

John amazed Mary

Here John is the ACTOR, but the rest of the fillers for the CD here are not so clear. To say that John did the ACTION "amaze" totally disregards the fact that "amaze" does not refer to any particular action. Rather, it refers to a state of Mary that was caused by whatever action John did. The actual ACTION is unknown. John could have done a great many things that might have amazed Mary. Perhaps he hit a ball a long distance, or perhaps he said he was sorry. Thus, the ACTION, OBJECT, and DIRECTION of the CD of which John was the actor are all unknown. What is known is that the unknown ACTION caused a state change in Mary.

What is the point of looking at language this way? Consider the sentence "John likes to drink". A person hearing this sentence knows a lot of information about John derived from the inference that alcoholic beverages are ingested by John frequently and from other inferences about the effects of such repeated actions. To get a computer to understand English, it is necessary to get the computer to make the same inferences. This can only be done by forcing the machine to seek to fill in missing slots in a CD and by giving it some methods of doing that. Without the rigid format of CD, an understanding mechanism would not know what it did not know. Knowing what information you need to know is a crucial part of understanding.

This general issue can be further illustrated by the example "John fell". Here it is the combination of an OBJECT having a force applied to it in the DIREC-TION of another object that causes us to speculate on the effects of those two objects coming in contact with each other. The rule that dense objects forcefully contacting each other can damage one of the objects must be activated whenever such a situation occurs. In this example, that rule causes us to speculate on whether John was hurt. Such speculations are an important part of understanding and are facilitated by CD.

If the example above had been "John threw a rock at Mary", the same rule about force applied to objects and their potential collision would still be applicable. However, this time it is the item in the DIRECTION slot that is the one that is potentially damaged. We worry about Mary being hurt, not the rock. To make the same rule apply in each case, with the variable being the relative densities of the objects involved, we must write such rules using a starting point of something other than words. It was just such a realization that caused us to begin the search for primitive actions.

The Primitive Actions

Originally (Schank, 1969) CD used English words to fill the slots in an event representation. Those who have seen CD only since the time that primitives were a part of it tend to identify the theory behind CD as being identical with the theory behind primitives. But these two theories, while dependent upon each other, cover quite different ground.

The significant tenets of CD can be stated as follows: the representation of events is done apart from the words used to encode those events; the task of the understander is to represent the events underlying sentences rather than to represent the sentences themselves; such representations are governed by a set of rules regarding the fitting of inputs into a predefined representation scheme; and finally, the rules for filling in the slots of those representations are the rules which are the basis of language understanding.

The need for primitives comes from a desire to have rules work in the most general way possible with no duplication of information. When two sentences describe the same event in such a way that these descriptions have the same overall meaning but quite different forms, we expect our CD representations to be identical for both descriptions. To do this requires using a vocabulary inside CD that expresses meanings and that can be mapped into very different linguistic forms (even different languages). The search for this interlingual vocabulary is the search for primitives, or basic meaning elements that can combine to produce complex meanings in much the way that atoms combine to make molecules.

The easiest way to explain primitives is to start with an example. Consider the sentences:

> John gave Mary a book.
> Mary took a book from John.
> Mary received a book from John.
> John sold Mary a book.
> John bought a book from Mary.
> John traded a cigar to Mary for a book.

Clearly there is a common meaning element in all these sentences that underlies the verbs that we see on the surface. As we have said, in CD an event is always described by a combination of actor, action, object, and direction. Thus, in attempting to analyze "John gave Mary a book" we can begin with the empty event:

> actor:unknown
> action:unknown
> object:unknown
> direction:unknown

Of course all of these roles are not known. The actor is clearly John and the object is clearly the book. In the early days of CD and in most linguistic theories, the action would be considered to be "give". "Giving" takes an animate direction, (i.e., we give things to animate objects, usually humans). So a simplistic analysis is:

> actor:John
> action:give
> object:book
> direction:Mary

Now consider "Mary took a book from John". The actor here, of course, is Mary, the object is again "book", and the direction would seem to be "John".

But there is something quite different about direction "from" and direction "towards". If we write the direction as "John" here, we will certainly have lost information.

The problem is that directions have to have two parts in order to be completely specified. If the direction is "from John" then it has to be "to somebody else" as well. Similarly, in the earlier sentence, just because we heard only about the "to Mary" part does not mean there is not a missing "from" part lurking about somewhere to be discovered in the remainder of the sentence, or to be figured out for ourselves. Making the assumption that "take" is the action, let us revise our analysis of the direction role to account for what we have said for both of these sentences. This leaves us with:

actor		John	actor		Mary
action		give	action		take
object		book	object		book
direction	TO	Mary	direction	TO	unknown
	FROM	unknown		FROM	John

Although we had expected our analyses of the meaning of these sentences to look somewhat alike, there really does not seem to be any obvious similarity here. The problem is that we have not really dealt with the meanings of "give" and "take" yet. To consider what their meanings might be we can attempt to fill in the blank slots in the direction roles. We can figure out who the book was "given from" because the meaning of "give" specifies that "John" was the "giver". The actor is the same as the beginning direction (or donor) of the object. Similarly, in the latter sentence, we know that Mary now has the book. The actor of a "take" is the same as the "to direction" (or recipient) of the object.

actor		John	actor		Mary
action		give	action		take
object		book	object		book
direction	TO	Mary	direction	TO	Mary
	FROM	John		FROM	John

These analyses look a little more alike, but something is still missing. Let us consider what the difference is between these two sentences. Clearly they have different actors. But what else is different? They both involve an event whose overall consequence is the same. The effect of this event is to transfer possession of a book from John to Mary. The only difference at all between them is the person focused on as actor in the event.

Instead of talking about actions such as "give" or "take", we should consider the action in both these events to be the one most clearly associated with the intention and overall effect of the event, namely "transfer of possession". Once we have done this, our analysis will treat these sentences as having a meaning differing only in terms of the actors involved, as follows:

(1)			(2)		
actor		John	actor		Mary
action		TRANSFER POSSESSION	action		TRANSFER POSSESSION
object		book	object		book
direction	TO	Mary	direction	TO	Mary
	FROM	John		FROM	John

It is important to consider the overall net loss and net gain from such an analysis. Clearly, if we lose information, then we have not effectively captured all of the meaning. But have we actually lost information? If we inform our generator that whenever it finds a TRANSFER POSSESSION where the actor and the TO direction are the same, it should express that information by using the verb "take" and that it should use the verb "give" when the FROM direction and the actor are the same, then we will lose nothing by this analysis. What do we gain?

First of all, we gain economy. Every time memory sees TRANSFER POS-SESSION it can apply appropriate inference rules. If these inference rules were written in terms of words (i.e., if you give someone something they have it, if they take it they have it, and so on), they would involve tremendous duplication for every verb that referred to TRANSFER POSSESSION. This loss of economy would be considerable as it is not only a case of "give" and "take" here but hundreds of other verbs that involve transfer of possession as well.

Secondly, we capture the similarity of meaning that is so crucial to our understanding. People can express the same event by either sentence (or by some of the others given above in the right circumstances.) Our perspective is slightly different in each case and that difference is captured by the difference in actors in the analyses. But the overall meanings are very close (as they should be, since they refer to the same event) and our meaning representation must reflect this.

In CD, TRANSFER POSSESSION is called ATRANS, which is a primitive action. Whatever we call it, that name has no real meaning in an understanding system apart from what happens in that system as a result of its occurrence. In other words, the actual meaning of ATRANS in the system is the set of inference rules that fire off because of its presence, no more and no less.

To consider further the use of ATRANS, let us examine "John bought a book from Mary". What is the proper analysis of the meaning of the verb "buy"? There are actually two ATRANSes taking place. The first involves the book. The second, which is causally related to the first, also involves an ATRANS. But this time, the participant's roles are switched and money is the object.

```
actor          John                      actor          Mary
action         ATRANS    <- - - - - - -  action         ATRANS
object         money     CAUSED   object                book
direction  TO  Mary      - - - - - - ->  direction  TO  John
           FROM John                                FROM Mary
```

(The double arrow here indicates that the two events caused each other.) What is the analysis of "Mary sold a book to John" then? It seems obvious that its meaning is identical to the meaning given above. Thus the analysis of each of them is the same. (It is possible to argue that the meaning of these sentences as slightly different. This problem arises from taking sentences out of context. The role of context is discussed in Chapter 3. The point here is that no matter what the context, *at least* the above elements are present.)

Perhaps the most important case to look at in arguing for the use of ATRANS is a sentence like "John traded a cigar to Mary for a book", This sentence seems a lot like the two above in meaning, yet there is considerable difference in the structure of the sentences. "Money" is implicit in the meanings of "buy" and "sell". It is thus the job of the parser to put "money" in the appropriate place in the analyses. But with the verb "traded", the objects of both ATRANSes are specified by the use of the word "for". An analyzer will thus make use of a rule that says that "for" following "trade" fills in the second ATRANS. Thus the meaning analysis of this sentence is identical to that of those above, with "cigar" replacing "money".

Primitive Action Issues

The most controversial thing about the primitive actions that we use in CD has not been the usefulness or reasonableness of any one of them, but the fact that we have consistently maintained that an extremely small set of them will account for what needs to be represented in the physical world. The reason that it is possible to maintain such a position is that the primitive actions combine in fairly complex ways. Furthermore, a large number of verbs in English do not refer to actions at all. Words like "amaze" refer to unnamed actions that result in state changes. So, although we commonly say that people can "hurt", "comfort", "please", or "annoy" other people, none of these verbs qualify as actions.

In CD we currently use eleven primitive actions. These are:

ATRANS	MTRANS	SPEAK	INGEST
PTRANS	MBUILD	GRASP	EXPEL
PROPEL	ATTEND	MOVE	

Since we have written about CD extensively elsewhere, (Schank, 1972; Schank, 1973; Schank, 1975) there is little point in duplicating all the arguments for and explanations of each of these. For our purposes here we need only explain some of the philosophy behind these primitives, their practical use in the programs we write, and their completeness or lack of it in any comprehensive theory of language.

CD has a large number of features that we have not discussed here. One of these is the possibility of having one CD dependent on another. There ، ‑e two ways that this can happen. One is by causal relationship, which we shall discuss later. The other is by instrumentality. In this case, one CD fills in details about the achievement of another. Some of the primitive actions are used almost exclusively in this capacity. For that reason we will not focus on them here, but will describe them as they relate to more fundamental actions. The instrumental acts are: GRASP, MOVE, SPEAK, ATTEND, and EXPEL. The other six are the actions actually used by our computer programs.

The Remaining Six Primitive Actions

A very important primitive actions is MTRANS. MTRANS means to transfer information from one person to another, or from one part of one's mind to another. There are hundreds of verbs whose main meaning element is MTRANS: "read", "tell", "see", "hear", "remember", "forget", "teach", "suggest", "promise", and so on. The important thing about each of these verbs is that they all have as their main focus, a transfer of information. Let us consider, the verbs "read", "tell", "see", and "promise".

First, we can see that "see" and "read" are close to each other, as are "tell" and "promise". That is, while all of these verbs have the common element of MTRANS, the analyses we expect to find for "see" and "read" should be quite similar, as should be the ones for "tell" and "promise".

To "see" is to MTRANS information from one's eyes to one's consciousness. This is usually done by ATTENDing one's eyes to whatever is to be seen. So, we need to represent two new things in order to analyze "see". First, we need some representation for consciousness. For this we do not need a technical explanation of how the brain works. We are trying to represent how people think about how they think. Therefore we only need represent what a naive person thinks about when he hears a sentence using the word "see". We call the part of the brain (i.e., the mental location or MLOC) that receives incoming information the Conscious Processor (CP). Whether such a thing actually exists physically is quite irrelevant. It is simply a label to help describe how people talk about thinking.

We also need an instrumental action that specifies the ATTENDing. ATTEND's object is any sense organ and its direction is some concrete object.

Thus the meaning of "John saw Mary" is represented as:

actor:John
action:MTRANS
object:image of Mary
direction TO:MLOC (CP of John)
FROM:eyes of John

instrument:

actor:John
action:ATTEND
object:eyes
direction TO:Mary
FROM:unknown

That is, "seeing" is MTRANS to the MLOC(CP) by means of ATTEND eyes.
Now let us look at "reading" as in the sentence "John read a book". This is
represented as:

actor:John
action:MTRANS
object:information in a book
direction TO:CP of John
FROM:book

instrument:

actor:John
action:ATTEND
object:eyes
direction TO:book
FROM:unknown

Notice that in this analysis "seeing" and "reading" are nearly identical. In fact,
"seeing a book" and "reading a book" would be exactly identical except for one
important thing: the object of MTRANS for "see X" is "the image of X". The
object of MTRANS for "read X" is "the information in X".

Now we consider the verbs "tell" and "promise". "Tell" is very simple. It
is an MTRANS of information between people by speaking.

Now consider the sentence "John promised to give Mary a book":

actor:John
action:MTRANS

```
       object:      actor:John
                    action:ATRANS
                    object:book
              direction TO:Mary
                    FROM:John
                       time:future
   direction TO:unknown
        FROM:John
```

The above representation has several interesting properties. First, we notice that there is no instrument. The above sentence does not specify how the communication took place. "Promises" can be made verbally, by letter, and by intermediaries. Since "promise" doesn't say anything about instruments, we leave the instrument out.

Second, there is an unknown TO direction. We might assume that Mary received this promise, and indeed this would be a good inference, but the sentence does not actually say so, and someone else could have in fact been the receiver of the promise.

The most interesting part of "promise" has been left out of our representation. "Promise" as we have it here is indicated as meaning something like "to say that you will do something". (Note that we have added a time to our event in this example to express the future nature of promise. Times are actually present in all events, but we have been leaving them out for simplicity's sake.) But "promise" is really much more than "tell that you will do". The assumption of "promise" is that the speaker believes that the overall effect of the event referred to will be good (presumably for Mary, though possibly for himself). Thus we have a new element here, namely the belief of the speaker. This is represented as:

```
      state: in the mind of the speaker
   object:  actor: John
           action: MTRANS
           object: book
   direction TO: Mary
        FROM: John
          time: fugure
             |
             | CAUSE
             |
       object: Mary or speaker
       state: benefitted
```

Thus, we are saying that "promise" refers to an attitude on the part of the speaker which expresses his belief that the event referred to will be beneficial to either himself or Mary. This ambiguity is tilted in one direction or the other by context.

There are three primary physical actions: PTRANS, INGEST and PROPEL. Consider the sentence "John went to New York". "Going" is simply transfer of location. So far, we have required that all events have certain slots, but here there is no obvious candidate for the object slot. What was transferred? The answer is that since we are prone to speak of self-locomotion, the verb "go" does not take a syntactic object. All actions have a conceptual object, however, so while it seems quite funny to say: "John walked himself to the store", conceptually this is just what we do mean. Thus the conceptual actor for "go" is usually the same as its conceptual object. Our representation for the example above is thus:

John went to New York.

        actor: John
       action: PTRANS
       object: John
direction TO: New York
        FROM: unknown

Now consider "John took a plane to New York". We might imagine, if we were extremely naive, that since "take" was used before to mean ATRANS, that ATRANS is the primitive action being used here. But, consider the following sentences that also use "take":

John took a plane.
John took an aspirin.
John took Mary.
John took a beating.
John took the job.
John took the match.
John took the food.
John took the picture.
John took my advice.

We could go on indefinitely. It is obvious that "take" only sometimes means ATRANS. To get the correct meaning of a verb such as "take", it is necessary to examine the syntactic object of "take" and see what its properties are. If it is an object whose function is to PTRANS, then one strong possibility (though certainly not the only one—context is the ultimate determiner) is that "take" means "PTRANS by means of". Thus most probable analysis of "John took a plane to New York" is:

actor: John
action: PTRANS
object: John
direction TO: New York
FROM: unknown

instrument

actor: plane
action: PROPEL
object: plane
direction TO: New York
FROM: unknown

and

actor: John
action: PTRANS
object: John
direction TO: plane
FROM: unknown

What we have given here is a very complex instrument that says that John got himself into the plane and the plane propelled itself through the air to New York.

The above analysis is really not wholly correct. If we have John going on to the plane, why not have him sitting and reading a magazine as well? Where do we stop? This problem will be discussed in Chapter 3 on scripts.

Consider the sentence: "The rock hit the boy."

Sentences such as this are understood by people in a form different from the way they are spoken. Since we understand that rocks never really act, we do not see "the rock hit the boy" as being like the sentence "the man hit the boy". Rather we recognize immediately that rocks are inanimate concrete objects, and that inanimate concrete objects ordinarily function as objects of an action. Conceptually, then, the rock in this sentence must be an object of someone or something else's action. Who, then is the actor? What slot does "the boy" fit in? As understanders we must also concern ourselves with determining what the action in this event is. What really happened? In order for a rock to hit a boy certain things must be true. First of all the rock must have been in motion. Since rocks cannot put themselves in motion, something must have put the rock in motion. In order to set something in motion it is necessary to apply a force to it. We call the action of applying a force PROPEL. Not all PROPELs lead to "set in motion" (imagine pushing the Empire State Building with your hand).

In our analysis of this sentence then, we have an action—PROPEL; an object—the rock; and an unknown actor. "The boy" is the direction of the

PROPEL of the rock (and therefore of the rock itself). We also know that if the rock hit the boy a contact occurred between the rock and the boy. Furthermore, we know that this contact occurred as a result of the PROPEL event. Thus we can represent the meaning of the sentence "The rock hit the boy" as:

```
      actor:unknown
      action:PROPEL
      object:rock
   direction:boy
           |
           |  CAUSED
           |
      state:contact
   object 1:rock
   object 2:boy
```

PROPEL underlies any action that involves force. Thus "to shoot" is to PROPEL bullets; "to kick" is to PROPEL one's foot; "to throw" is to PROPEL an object. "Throw at" is PROPEL with the intention of "making contact". "Throw to a person" on the other hand is also a PROPEL, but it is primarily an ATRANS. PROPEL here serves merely as an Instrument for the ATRANS.

The inferences that derive from PROPEL come mainly from knowledge we have about the function, weight, density, and fragility of the objects being PROPELled and about the objects these PROPELled objects come in contact with. Thus, PROPELling an egg is understood quite differently from PROPELling a rock or PROPELling a ball. Similarly, PROPELling bullets depends strongly on the means (i.e., the Instrument) of the PROPELling, since if they are thrown by hand, they are of little consequence.

"Drinking", "eating", "breathing", and so on are all examples of INGEST. We represent these by using what we know about each event from our experiences. For example:

John drank a glass of milk.

```
        actor: John
       action: INGEST
       object: milk
 direction TO: mouth of John
         FROM: glass
```

instrument:

```
        actor: John
       action: PTRANS
       object: glass containing milk
 direction TO: mouth of John
         FROM: table
```

instrument:

>   actor: John
>   action: MOVE
>   object: hand of John
>   direction TO: glass
>   FROM: unknown

instrument:

>   actor: John
>   action: GRASP
>   object: glass of milk
>   direction TO: hand of John

Here we see a case of infinite expansion of instruments. The analysis reads, "John drank the milk by getting the milk to his mouth by moving his hand to the milk and grasping the glass." Do people really think of all this every time they hear the verb "drink"? The answer is "yes" and "no". Since it happens this way nearly every time, it would be a waste of time to think about it. But nonetheless, people do have available to them the possibility of accessing this information if they should need it for some reason. (For example, if John is known not to have the use of his hands, we would wonder how he managed to drink. Such wondering cannot be explained unless "using hands" somehow explicitly presents itself as instrumental information in the meaning of the sentence.)

The sentence "John shot up heroin" also adds an instrument for INGEST, but this time it does it explicitly. Thus we have:

>   actor: John
>   action: INGEST
>   object: heroin
>   direction TO: vein of John
>   FROM: hypodermic needle

instrument:

>   actor: John
>   action: PROPEL
>   object: hypodermic needle
>   direction TO: bodypart of John
>   FROM: unknown

The last action we shall discuss, MBUILD, requires a different conceptual object than the rest of the actions. MBUILD is a process that receives an input either from memory or from outside, and produces an output which it places in the CP. Thus the representation for MBUILD will contain an "object IN" slot and an "object OUT" slot to account for the problem to be considered, and the solution reached by the MBUILDing process.

John figured out where the money is.

          actor: John
         action: MBUILD
   object IN: LOC(money) is place?
        OUT: LOC(money) is place X
direction TO: CP
     FROM: Memory

John wondered who ate the cheese.

          actor: John
        action: MBUILD
   object IN: actor: ?
            action: INGEST
            object: cheese
            direction TO: mouth of?
                 FROM: unknown
        OUT: none
direction TO: CP
     FROM: Memory

The problem of representing the mental operations of people is, of course, as complex as figuring out just how it is that people think.

THE SCOPE OF CD

CD has been developed both as a theory of language and as a representational language that enhances our ability to construct computer programs that understand language. We are frequently in the position of attempting to serve two masters at once: Is it ultimately correct? Will it work? It has been our philosophy not to bother ourselves with designing features in our representational language that will never actually be used. For this reason, we are sometimes challenged by more theoretically minded linguists about issues such as quantification or pseudo cleft raising. We believe these issues to be important. However, we also believe that the solutions to such complex problems depend on solutions to simpler problems. It does not make sense to concentrate research on the subtleties of language until some progress has been made on the more obvious issues of representing simple meanings or designing algorithms for understanding and generating simple sentences.

We do not concern ourselves with arguing for the correctness or full theoretical extent of any concept we have introduced. In this experimental science of AI, the computer programs we present are realizations of our theories at this stage.

One final word about CD needs to be said. CD has been very useful for us as a common language that all our programs can use for communicating with each other. As such, the eleven primitive actions and various other aspects of CD have served us well. However, we are well aware that for domains beyond those of simple physical events and human interactions, CD is often inadequate, or at least non-optimal. To augment CD, we invented scripts, plans, goals and themes as additional methods of representing information.

In Schank and Carbonell (1978) we introduced a set of "social ACTs" that represent "social meanings" such as AUTHORIZE or PETITION. For example, a policeman's giving a person a speeding ticket is indeed an ATRANS, but the event is more appropriately viewed as a legal authorization to begin prosecution.

We currently believe that we are still at the beginning of the solution to many of the representational issues that confront a theory of language. We believe CD, in some form or other, to be at the bottom of all of the representational forms. However, since CD is at times too low level and specific to represent the full meaning of complex ideas, people, and computer programs, must have higher more meaningful representations available to them. Nevertheless, whatever the representation scheme used, those involving English words are entirely misdirected. Meanings are entities that existed prior to, and will exist long after, English.

3 The Theory Behind the Programs: A Theory of Context

CD is a theory of how to represent sentences with respect to the information that they convey about events and states of the world. Traditional linguistic theories have limited their scope to considering sentences out of context. However, any reasonable theory of the representation of events and the sentences describing those events must consider those sentences within a context. Two questions arise when we consider the nature of a theory of context:

How do sentences connect together?

What kinds of knowledge do people have that enable them to discover a context in which to put sentences (and events) together?

Before we begin to consider how sentences are put together, however, we must consider how events and states can be put together within a sentence. Consider the following sentence:

John cried because Mary said she loved Bill.

This is a meaningful, well constructed English sentence. Yet, it is literally quite silly. John didn't cry because of the event of Mary's speaking. What her "speaking" did cause was "thinking", which can cause "sadness" which can be a reason for "crying".

In order to fully comprehend such sentences, we must compute the causal relationships that hold between the events and states in the sentence. To do this requires a model of the world that contains knowledge of what can cause what.

27

To see this better, consider the following sentences:

John's leg was broken because Mary tripped him.
John's leg was broken because Mary yelled at him.

In the first sentence we have no trouble figuring out the causality because we know that "tripping someone" can cause a broken leg and this is consistent with what we have been told explicitly in the sentence. However, this is not the case in the second sentence. Here again, we must figure out what really happened. We must create in our minds a scenario that explains the possible connection between "breaking a leg" and "yelling". Perhaps Mary's yelling distracted John while he was walking and he walked into a wall or fell into a hole. As understanders we are just guessing here, of course. What is important is that this causal completion process is an integral part of understanding. To see that this is so, we need only look at a sentence where we can't imagine a reasonable causal connection. For example, consider:

John couldn't laugh because Mary ate ice cream.
John broke his leg because Mary read to him.

These sentences are nonsensical because we cannot figure out the causal connections. In the sentences above we could. What makes sentences understandable then? They must lend themselves to an analysis by the understander which allows him to make the proper causal connections.

CAUSAL TYPES

The rules for the establishment of causal connections within a sentence are the same as those we use to make causal connections among sentences describing an event. Mostly these connections depend on determining what actions result in what states, and what states enable what actions. There are four causal links that we use to connect together events and states: result causation, enable causation, initiation causation, and reason causation.

Result Causation

An event can have a *result* that changes some state of an object involved in the event. Thus "the lamp broke because John hit it" is an instance of result causation.

Enable Causation

When a state change occurs it may change the conditions of the world in such a way as to enable an event to take place that could not have taken place before.

This is called *enable causation*. These state changes only enable potential events. That is, they do not directly cause the event to take place but only enable its potential occurrence. Thus "John ate because there was food on the table" is an instance of enable causation.

Initiation Causation

Whenever an event or state change occurs, or whenever a state or a potential event exists, it is possible that an actor may be made aware of it, and thus made to think about it. This is called *initiation causation*. Initiation causation accounts for people's thinking about things. Thus if we have, "John realized that Mary was unhappy because he saw her crying", we have an instance of initiation causation.

Reason Causation

Once people have started thinking about things, they are likely to decide to do something. (This is the primitive action MBUILD.) Deciding to do something is the *reason* for doing it. Thus when we say that "John ate fish because he was hungry" we have an example of reason causation.

CONNECTING TEXT

When we first began to work on units of discourse larger than the sentence, we noticed that the causal connections that we had been developing appeared quite frequently in texts. In fact, a great many texts could be seen, after an analysis that linked together all the causal connections, implied or explicit, to be one enormous causal chain of events and states. Furthermore, there was a great advantage to viewing a text in this manner. It made explicit what was implicit, it focused attention on key events in a story by virtue of their being more closely connected to other parts of the story, and it provided a mechanism whereby paraphrase and summary of those texts was facilitated. All this is described in more detail in Schank (1973) and Schank (1975).

We began to attempt to build computer programs which would analyze texts in this manner and ran into a serious problem. Frequently texts seemed to make long "leaps of faith". That is, you often could not determine the causal connectedness because you needed a great deal of detailed knowledge about a situation in order to determine the causal relationships involved.

For example, consider the following story:

> John was hungry. He went into Goldstein's and ordered a pastrami sandwich. It was served to him quickly. He left the waitress a large tip.

People are capable of responding rather easily, and with a fair amount of certainty, to the following questions:

> What is Goldstein's?
> What did John eat?
> Who made the sandwich?
> Who took John's order?
> Who served the sandwich?
> Why did John leave a large tip?

The knowledge that people have that enables them to understand stories such as the one given above is organized around standard situations. We call these standard situations *scripts*.

Scripts serve to organize the knowledge that people must have in order to understand. In addition, scripts point out what behavior is appropriate for a particular situation. Knowing that you are in a restaurant script enables you to know that if you ask a waitress for food, it is likely that she will get it for you.

We use our knowledge of everyday situations to help us understand stories or discourse about those situations. We need not ask why somebody wants to see our ticket when we enter a theater, nor why one should be quiet, nor how long it is appropriate to sit in one's seat. Knowledge of specific situations such as theaters allows us to interpret the remarks that people make about theaters.

People ordinarily leave out the detailed and uninteresting parts of the causal chain in a story they are telling. A script encodes these details in a causal chain that is, in essence, entered into the understanding process as a block whenever that script is activated. For example, a story that refers to a script with ten events in it may explicitly state only the first and last of those events. However, once the script has been activated, all the other events are readily accessible to the understanding process because of the completed causal chain.

Understanding a story that relies upon scripts requires first deciding what script is being referred to in the story. This is called *script instantiation*. Next, that script is used to fill in the important details in the causal chain being built. We call this process *script application*. Script application fills in the gaps in a causal chain between two seemingly unrelated events.

These two understanding processes have their counterparts in the generation of language. When someone decides to tell a story that references a script, he recognizes that he need not (and because he would otherwise be considered rather boring, should not) mention every detail of his story. He can safely assume that his listener is familiar with the referenced script and will understand the story as long as certain crucial items are mentioned.

A restaurant script contains a tremendous amount of information that encompasses the enormous variability of what can occur in a restaurant. We thus have a "fast food restaurant" track, a "cafeteria" track, etc., in the restaurant script, each of which includes the entering, ordering and paying scenes, but with a different set of possibilities than the "fancy restaurant" track. In the "fast food" track, paying can occur immediately after ordering and before eating; eating may occur inside or outside the restaurant; the person who takes the order must be approached by the patron, etc.

(Our recent research on memory has made the notion of a "track" within a script somewhat obsolete. We currently view scripts to be part of a larger memory structure. See Schank (1979) for a detailed discussion of our theory of memory organization. We include a discussion of "tracks" here because they were an integral part of the SAM program.)

Every script has associated with it a number of roles. When a script is instantiated, the actors in the story assume the roles within the script. If an actor has not been specifically mentioned in a story when a particular script is being used, his presence is assumed. This explains the use of the definite article in reference to "*the* waitress". She has been implicitly mentioned before by virtue of the fact that the restaurant script is being used.

SCRIPT APPLICATION

To see how scripts can come into play in a story, consider the following:

> John took a bus to New York. In New York he went to a museum. Then he took a train home.

In this story, the names of scripts are mentioned and it is presumed that each script proceeded normally. (Alternatively, it is possible that some abnormal things happened which were considered unworthy of narration by the author of the story.)

Here we have three explicitly stated scripts: $BUS, $MUSEUM-GOING, and $TRAIN. It is unlikely that people would actually think about all the details of each of these scripts if they heard the above story. What is more likely is that they would simply remember that the script occurred.

But, the presence of the script is important, because understanders of this story are capable of answering questions such as: Did John go through the door of the museum?, or Did John pay bus fare? Although we cannot be absolutely certain of the accuracy of our answers to such questions, the fact is that we do answer questions like these all the time. We can do so because we have the appropriate scripts available to us. However, we do not usually think of all these details consciously without being specifically asked.

The nature of the detail to be consciously inferred depends upon what script details (i.e., events in the script) are actually found in the story. Consider this story:

> John went to a restaurant. He ordered chicken. He left a large tip.

A script is divided into pieces called *scenes*. The action of ordering instantiates the ordering scene of the restaurant script. Because the entering scene lies on the path to the ordering scene, we assume that it has already taken place. The events between ordering and tipping as well as the final exit scenes will also be assumed. That is, we will have understood the story as if it had actually been:

John went to a restaurant.
He sat down.
He read a menu.
He ordered chicken.
He ate the chicken.
He left a large tip.
He paid the check.
He left the restaurant.

We fill in, as if we had actually heard them, the events of the script that was referenced. As long as we are simply filling in the events from "ordering" to "tipping", it is safe to assume "sitting", "reading", and "eating" also. Since "tipping" is a prelude to "paying" and "leaving", we also assume these two actions.

But an understander does not want to assume too many steps when he is told of events that are far apart in the script. Thus the story, "John went to a restaurant. He left." is a little odd. Do we want to assume that he ate? It is possible that John did eat in this story, but we might not want to simply assume it because only the first and last scenes in a very long script have been mentioned.

So, an understander's job is to figure out from the script what steps have been left out. We must fill in the steps that surround the events that we were specifically told about by explicitly inferring them and treating them as if they had been actually said.

An important aspect of scripts in the understanding process is their inferential effect. The very fact that a deviation in a script has occurred can have repercussions for later understanding that relies upon scripts:

John was robbed on the train.
At the restaurant he couldn't pay the check.

The robbery is an unpredicted event in the train script. It does not affect the normal completion of the train script, but it will affect any script that follows whose entering conditions involve money. In order to eat in a restaurant it is necessary to have money. An understander recognizes the potential problem here as soon as he sees the restaurant script starting because the robbery causes him to make the inference that "the customer has no money". This state is known to be important and is thus remembered for future use. The violated entry condition of the restaurant script sets up an expectation that the part of the restaurant script that deals with people who can't pay will be used. Thus if we ask an understander what may happen next in the story above, we might expect him to answer, "The police will be called" or "John will have to wash dishes." These answers are inferences which come from that part of the restaurant script which was activated by the violated entry conditions.

In Chapter 5, Cullingford describes in detail the processes of script instantiation and script application. In Chapter 11, Carbonell discusses the role of scripts in the POLITICS program.

PLANS

Of course, people can adapt to situations with which they have no previous experience. This adaptability comes from knowledge of plans and goals. These entities contribute to understanding much the way scripts do. People need a great deal of knowledge in order to understand. That knowledge can be of two kinds: specific and general. Scripts are intended to account for the specific knowledge that people have. But not all stories we understand are so commonplace and mundane that they can be comprehended solely by the use of scripts. When a script cannot help a person make sense of new input, he must turn to his knowledge of what we call *plans*. Since people themselves can plan how to act in a new situation, they can also rely on their knowledge of planning to help them understand other people's plans. In general, plans help people solve new problems or deal with unexpected information. But, more importantly for the problems we have been discussing here, a knowledge of planning helps an understander to comprehend someone else's plan.

Many stories (particularly the more interesting ones) are about entirely new situations for which we have no available script. When we hear such stories we rely on our knowledge of how to plan out an action that will lead to the attainment of a goal. We use this knowledge to reconstruct the planning process used by the character we are hearing about. This reconstruction helps us to make sense out of what is going on. Once we have figured out the plans and goals of a character in a story, we are then capable of making guesses about the intentions of an action in an unfolding story, which helps us make sense of the story.

Let's look at a sample story:

John needed money for a down payment on a house.
He called his sister.

How are we to make sense of such a story? It makes no use of the standard situational scripts we have been discussing. There probably isn't a "paying for a house" script available to us since most of us don't do that sort of thing too often.

Even if we have done so, how many of us used our sister? While it is not too likely that a script would be available to help us here, the situation is not entirely novel either. Understanding this paragraph would not be very different if "down payment" were changed to "son's education" or "paying off a bookie". In each case there is the general problem of raising a lot of money. In order to understand such stories, people have available to them knowledge about goals and the actions that can achieve those goals. This kind of knowledge is more general than scripts but not so general as to be entirely novel for any given individual.

Let's look at another story:

John wanted to become foreman.
He went to get some arsenic.

When we hear this story we assume that the second sentence is a step in a plan the main actor has to achieve the goal stated in the first sentence. We assume this without having to hear a statement such as "Now I am going to tell you about the plan that John used." As understanders we have come to believe that actions which follow a stated goal are somehow related to the achievement of that goal. In the first sentence of this story we are told of John's goal. We therefore assume that the second sentence tells us a step in his plan. However, many possible second sentences in this story would not have been a step in his plan. The problem in understanding this story, then, is first to recognize that the second sentence is potentially a step in some plan, and then figure out what that plan is. Here we must realize that getting arsenic is a step in some plan, and then try to figure out how this fits into a plan for becoming foreman.

We really have not understood this story until we have done that simple analysis. Understanding stories involves understanding the relationship that one sentence has to another. If this relationship is in terms of goals, and plans to carry out goals, then an understander must be equipped with knowledge about the kinds of goals and plans that people normally have.

Goals can be of long term importance such as those referred to above or they can be very short term goals, as in the following example:

Mary wanted to cut her steak.
She called to John in the kitchen.

In the above story, we again have a goal followed by a first step in a plan to achieve it. The problem is recognizing that that is what we have. Consider another example:

John was hungry.
He took out the Yellow Pages.

Most readers realize that John was using the Yellow Pages to find a good restaurant. But suppose the story had been:

John was hungry.
He took out some ground beef.

A rule that is appropriate for understanding the second story would, if applied too generally, predict that John is about to cook and eat the Yellow Pages in the first story. But no one really ever considers such a possibility. Why not?

To understand the first story we must recognize that "hungry" means that a plan will (or should) be generated whose goal is to gain control of food. One means for gaining control of food is going to a restaurant. This requires changing your location from where you are now to where the restaurant is. This in turn requires knowing where you are going, which may require a plan to determine what restaurant you want to go to and where it is. If we understand that the Yellow Pages contains a list of restaurants, the inference necessary here is easy to make. Suppose we had heard instead:

John was hungry.
He took out Popular Mechanics.

We might wonder if there were some kind of restaurant guide in the back or an appropriate advertisement in the magazine. We would have trouble understanding this story because we have difficulty linking up the stated goal (hunger) with what seems to be the plan to achieve that goal (getting Popular Mechanics).

Now let's consider how we follow the plans and goals that we hear about. Consider:

John was lost. He pulled his car up to a farmer who was standing by the road.

The above story shows how the knowledge of plans (or the lack of that knowledge) can make the difference in the understandability of the text. The first sentence of the story identifies a goal (becoming not lost), which in turn tells us about a related goal (which we call D-KNOW). This second goal predicts that actions that result in gaining new knowledge will be attempted.

One standard method of acquiring knowledge is to ASK. In this story we have a second sentence that can be understood as preparing for ASKing to take place. We can then expect that the next event in the story should be the ASKing itself or an event that implicitly assumes the ASKing.

ASK is what we call a *planbox*. It is a rather stereotypical method of attempting to achieve a desired goal. A planbox has a set of preconditions, or states of the world, that must be made true in order to use that planbox. It also has an ACT associated with it (MTRANS here), and a goal that a successful planbox will fulfill (here D-KNOW or the acquisition of new information).

Consider the following story:

> John saw a menacing figure approach his store. He unlocked the drawer where he kept his gun.

In this story we could imagine that the understander had a "reaction to robbery" script available. However, it is simpler and more realistic to understand that when someone tries to satisfy his goal of D-CONTROL of your property, one of the actions available to you to try to prevent that is OVERPOWER or THREATEN. These two actions are both planboxes. When we infer that a character has a goal (D-CONTROL) here, we attempt to understand how his subsequent actions relate to the planboxes that we know to be standard methods of achieving that goal. Here, we understand that a gun is a means by which we can THREATEN and OVERPOWER, and thus we can reasonably predict that one of these actions is being attempted. Such predictions are what understanding is all about.

There is a logical progression in the choice of planboxes which can be used. For example, suppose you want a book that someone else has. What can you do about it? You have a number of alternatives; which one you choose depends on your particular personality and on your relationship with the current owner of the book. The first and simplest possibility is simply to ASK for the book. You might try this in the circumstance where the current owner is your friend and the book is not too available. Another alternative is to EXPLAIN to the owner why you want or need the book. This might work if the reason were good enough. Still another possibility is to BARGAIN for the book. This can be done by offering money or another equally valuable object, or by offering to do a favor for the current owner as a kind of repayment.

Then there are the nastier means of getting the book. You could THREATEN the owner with physical harm if he doesn't give you the book. You could carry through with the threat or simply not bother threatening and just OVERPOWER the current owner and take the book. Also, you could sneak around and STEAL the book while the owner was unaware of what was going on.

The six planboxes written in upper case above are the standard methods available for achieving the plan D-CONTROL. When we attempt to D-CONTROL of something we have these methods available. Similarly, when we attempt to understand a story that involves someone else attempting to D-CONTROL of something, we can interpret his actions as attempting to satisfy one of the conditions necessary for using one of the above methods or as being the actuation of one of those methods.

D-goals are the simplest kind of goals, ones that are used in the service of higher level, more grandiose goals. The three most common D-goals are:

D-KNOW, D-PROX (change location), and D-CONTROL. We will now discuss some of the details involved in using planboxes to achieve D-goals.

D-KNOW is the goal that involves the plan of getting to know X, where X is always a fact. The actor for D-KNOW is always the same as the person who has the goal. The object of D-KNOW is the same as the actor. That is, a D-KNOW goal for John means that John wants John to know X.

If John wants Mary to know X, none of the above subplans will work. Threatening Mary if Mary doesn't know X is silly. If John knows X and wants Mary to know X, he must simply MTRANS X to Mary. If there is an obstacle, he must get around that obstacle. Otherwise, if John does not know X but wants Mary to know X, the subplans available to him are the same as those for D-KNOW, because John will have to act as if he were obtaining the knowledge for himself.

The next D-goal is D-CONT. The planboxes of D-CONT are organized aorund the idea that you might persuade whomever has Z to give it to you. Thus the planboxes for D-CONT are those discussed above: ASK, EXPLAIN, BAR-GAIN, and THREATEN. Two more planboxes arise from the possibility that you might gain control of the object without either the knowledge or permission of the owner (STEAL), or with his knowledge but without his permission (OVERPOWER).

Of all D-goals, D-PROX is the most "physical". That is, there are special mechanics involved in getting somewhere. Something other than mere persuasion is involved in changing proximity states. Some planboxes for D-PROX are: RIDE ANIMAL, USE VEHICLE, USE PUBLIC TRANSPORTATION, and USE SELF. D-PROX requires an actor A, and a desired location L. Often the location L is desired because a desired object X is located at L.

A variant of D-PROX occurs when actor A wishes to be near another actor B rather than an object. In that case, A could go to B by any of the standard planboxes, but could also persuade B to come to him, or could arrange to meet B at a third location.

GOALS

The key theoretical issue underlying the process of planning is the problem of goals. We cannot effectively consider how people's actions can be seen as steps in plans to achieve goals without a good understanding of the kinds of goals that people ordinarily pursue. In Schank and Abelson (1977) we consider the problem of goals at some length. Since that time, Wilensky, Meehan, and Carbonell have done considerable work on the subject.

One of the first things we can say about goals is that every person both has his own idiosyncratic set and also shares a large number of his goals with the community he lives in. In attempting to understand a person's goals, we expect him to do what we would do in the same situation, but we are not entirely shocked if he does not.

To begin our look at goals, consider the following stories:

> John was walking in the park with his sweetheart, Mary. Suddenly, some boys jumped out from behind the bushes and held a knife to Mary's throat. They asked John for all his money. He gave it to them and they ran away.
>
> John was walking in the park with his sweetheart, Mary. Suddenly, some boys jumped out from behind the bushes and held a knife to Mary's throat. They asked John for all his money. John laughed. The boys killed Mary and ran away. John picked up another girl in the park and went to the circus.

The first story is easy to understand. We do not even realize what assumptions we are making in reading it. In the second story, however, our assumptions are quite clear because they have been violated. When we are told that John loves Mary and knows she is in danger, we want to be able to assume that he has the goal of saving her. When we hear that someone has threatened Mary and demanded his money, we know that two goals are in conflict: preserving the health of Mary and preserving his own possessions. We expect John to have a value system that ranks the HEALTH of a loved one over his own POSSESSIONS (although we cannot be sure to what extent John believes that Mary's health is actually in danger). This knowledge is what allows us to interpret an input such as "He turned around and hit the robber" as a decision that indicates that preservation of possessions is very important to John (or that he thought the risk to Mary was slight). When we are asked, "Why did John do that?" we can answer, "Probably because he thought he could protect himself this way and he didn't want to lose his wallet." This answer would come from a reliance on the standard goals we assume for most people. In the second story above, we are upset as readers because all the expectations we have for how people should act (what goals they have) are violated. The second story indicates the extent to which we use goals in processing stories without being very aware of it.

Here are some of the goal types we have found useful:

Satisfaction Goals

There exists a set of goals that we can safely assume all people (and animals) to have. They come from biological needs and have a certain frequency with which they must be satisfied. The most obvious examples are Satisfy-Hunger, Satisfy-Sex, and Satisfy-Sleep. There is a standard set of goal objects, or instruments used for achieving a goal (i.e. hamburger, lover, etc.), associated with each Satisfaction goal (except for sleep). If a person is trying to satisfy a Satisfaction goal through a particular goal object which becomes unattainable, we expect that some new goal object will be substituted for the first one.

Enjoyment Goals

Sometimes, people do things simply because they think they will enjoy doing them. We call such goals Enjoyment goals; typical Enjoyment goals are: Travel, Entertainment, Exercise, Competition. The activities involved in Satisfaction goals can also be pursued primarily for enjoyment, as in Enjoy-Eating or Enjoy-Sex. There are various goal objects associated with Enjoyment activities, but the primary way to plan for them is to arrange to be present at the site where they occur.

Achievement Goals

People also have the goal of achieving certain positions or of owning certain properties. Some common Achievement goals are: Possession, Power Position, Good Job, Social Relationship, Skill. When Achievement goals are satisfied, they typically guarantee the future satisfaction of bundles of Satisfaction goals and Enjoyment goals. Thus, if you are rich or powerful, higher goals are much easier to satisfy.

Preservation Goals

People actually spend a good deal more of their time preserving or maintaining what they have than they do attempting to achieve new goals. One of the most important kinds of goals, therefore, is a Preservation goal. Preservation goals are set up by people to maintain the health, safety, or good condition of people, positions, or properties once such positions or states have been attained. When you have achieved something of value, you act so as to keep it. This is also true for things you may have possessed all your life, such as good eyesight.

THEMES

If we ask ourselves where goals come from, we are left with a very difficult question. Why do people do what they do? Frequently people pursue a course of action because they can see no other options; they are often blinded to other possibilities by their background, their jobs, their social status, or their view of what is moral or what is "right". We call all of these things *themes*.

Once we identify the theme that a person is operating under, we can predict the pattern of goals that he will pursue. Also, and equally important, once a theme is identified, we can stop asking ourselves why a person is doing what he is doing. The garbageman collects the garbage because it is his job. The robber robs because he believes that is the best method he has of getting money and he does not have strong moral beliefs about honesty. The debutante "comes out" because that is what girls of her class do.

Of course, each of these explanations is superficial. But the important point is that once a theme about which we have knowledge is identified, an understander can decide not to seek further explanations. An understander need only identify a familiar theme and then use that theme as a source of predictions about what goals will be pursued.

Themes are a very important area for future research. None of the work shown here depends heavily on them, although they all use the concept in one way or another. See Schank and Abelson (1977) and Schank (1979) for further details.

4 LISP

INTRODUCTION

It is not possible in a book that is already too long for comfort to include a full introduction to the LISP programming language. Therefore the interested reader is referred to *Artificial Intelligence* (Winston, 1977), which contains a number of useful exercises but is unfortunately based on a different dialect of LISP; *The New UCI Lisp Manual* (Meehan, 1979), which is a good reference manual to the dialect used here; and *Artificial Intelligence Programming* (Charniak et al., 1980), which covers explicitly in greater detail many of the techniques referenced here.

The purpose of this chapter is to describe briefly the set of LISP functions used by the micro programs presented later, and in particular to explain the special forms we have created to improve the looks of the LISP programs.

THE SYNTAX OF LISP

A LISP expression is either an atom, or a list of atoms, or a list of atoms and lists. Atoms can be:

1. numbers, such as 0, 24, or −6. A number is any sequence of digits, starting with a digit, a plus sign, or a minus sign, and ending with any character that is not a digit.
2. strings, such as "Have a nice day" or "*** Error: no field ***". A string is any sequence of characters beginning and ending with a double quote.

41

3. identifiers (also called literal atoms, and sometimes just atoms, when no confusion will result), such as FOO, A, or TAG26. An identifier is any sequence of characters (except the special ones listed below) not starting with a digit, plus sign, or minus sign. Note that digits and signs can appear with the identifier. TRY-RULE is an identifier.

The special characters are left parenthesis ("("), right parenthesis (")"), left bracket ("["), right bracket ("]"), blank (" "), tilde ("~"), and period ("."). Such characters can be used as letters if preceded by a slash ("/") but we do not use this feature in the micro programs.

A list is written as a left parenthesis, followed by any number of atoms or lists, separated from each other by one or more blanks or ends of lines, followed by a right parenthesis. For example:

(1 2 3)   is a list of three numbers.
(PLUS 2 3)   is a list of an identifier and two
                                                   numbers.
(JOHN GAVE MARY A BOOK)   is a list of five identifiers.
(APPEND (CAR FOO) (CDR BAZ))   is a list of one identifier and two
                                                   lists.
(IF (SPANK PARENT CHILD)   is a list of an identifier, a list,
   THEN (NOT (LIKE PARENT CHILD)))   an identifier, and a list.

The LISP interpreter ignores the blanks and ends of lines, except for using them to terminate atoms. Therefore, you should indent freely to make your programs and data readable.

Note that parentheses are not optional in LISP. If you want a list, you must use parentheses. If you don't want a list, you must not use them. The one exception is that at the very end of a list, you can use a right bracket ("}") to represent an arbitrary number of right parentheses. The right bracket forces the LISP interpreter to finish any lists it is building.

Comments in LISP are introduced with the tilde character ("~"). A comment stars with the tilde and goes to the end of the current line. Any character can be put in a comment.

EXPRESSIONS AND VALUES

In LISP every expression has a value. The LISP interpreter is a program that repeats the loop of reading an expression, evaluating it, and printing the result. Evaluating an expression in the LISP interpreter is equivalent to what running a program does in other languages. Understanding how the value of each kind of expression is calculated is the key to understanding LISP.

The value of a number is that number. For example, the value of 1 is 1. In our version of LISP, the value of a string is that string. For example, the value of "Go" is "Go". In some other versions of LISP, strings have no value. Strings are normally used only for printing purposes, not for calculation, so this difference doesn't matter.

Identifiers need to be assigned values. If they are not given a value, asking the LISP interpreter to evaluate them will cause an error. Certain special identifiers already have values assigned. The two most important are T and NIL, which are assigned to themselves. NIL represents two things. First, NIL is used to represent "false". Anything not NIL is "true" by definition. (T is a special case of a true expression.) NIL is also used to represent the empty list, or the list of no elements. Note that NIL is an atom not a list. *The empty list is the atom* NIL. Another way to write NIL is (), which shows this use of NIL more clearly.

Most other identifiers have to be explicitly assigned values in one of several different ways. One way to assign a value is to use the function SETQ. Functions in LISP are called by telling the LISP interpreter to evaluate a list with the function name as the first element and the arguments to the function following. Thus to assign the value 5 to the identifier X we have the LISP interpreter evaluate the expression (SETQ X 5). Then if we have the LISP interpreter evaluate the identifier X we get the answer 5. If we had told the LISP interpreter to evaluate X before assigning a value, an error would have resulted.

The evaluation of (SETQ X 5) actually involved two evaluations. First, the LISP interpreter tried to evaluate the list. The function SETQ says that the first argument, X, is to be given the value resulting from evaluating the second argument, 5. The LISP interpreter therefore evaluated 5, and the result, 5, was assigned to X.

Suppose we now typed (SETQ Y X). Again, SETQ will tell the LISP interpreter to evaluate the second argument, which is X. The value of X has been set to 5, so SETQ will set Y to 5 also. Note that Y is not set to the identifier X but to the value of X. If we wanted to set Y to the identifier X then we would write (SETQ Y (QUOTE X)). QUOTE is a special function that just returns its argument. It is used to prevent an evaluation. A single quote mark ("'") can be written in front of any expression instead of using QUOTE. The effect is exactly the same. For example, we could set Y to the identifier X with (SETQ Y 'X). In some versions of LISP, an at-sign ("@") is used instead of the single quote mark.

The evaluation of arguments of functions allows us to do several things in one expression. For example, if X is set to some number, then the following expression will return 3 plus X squared:

(PLUS 3 (TIMES X X))

First, the LISP interpreter tries to evaluate the whole expression. Since it is a list, the LISP interpreter will apply the first element, PLUS, to the arguments. PLUS is the built-in function for addition. PLUS, like most functions in LISP, has all of its arguments evaluated. (SETQ is an exception, along with certain other basic functions which will be described in the next few sections.) Therefore, to do the desired addition, the expressions 3 and (TIMES X X) have to be evaluated first. 3 evaluates to 3. TIMES is the built-in function for multiplication. In order to evaluate (TIMES X X) the LISP interpreter has to evaluate X. If X has been assigned the value 5, then the value of (TIMES X X) will be 25. Hence the arguments to PLUS will be 3 and 25, so the whole expression will evaluate to 28.

DEFINING FUNCTIONS

Programming in LISP is primarily a matter of defining new functions to augment the built-in ones. To define a new function we use a special built-in one called DE. For example, we could define SQUARE to be a function that squared a number by telling the LISP interpreter to evaluate this:

(DE SQUARE (X) (TIMES X X))

This defines SQUARE to take one argument, which has the internal, local name X, and which does only one thing: it multiplies X by X. The result of this multiplication is the value returned when SQUARE is called with an argument. For example, (SQUARE 5) will return 25.

X is called a *local variable*. That means that the X inside SQUARE is independent of any other use of X. When SQUARE is called, X is temporarily assigned the value of SQUARE's argument. When SQUARE is finished, X is automatically reassigned to whatever value (if any) it had before.

The general format for defining functions is:

(DE name (list of identifiers) expression expression . . .)

This defines a function with the first argument of DE as its name. The second argument is the list of local variables. This list may be empty, in which case we use () or NIL. The length of the list determines how many arguments the function takes. Thus, if the list is three items long, then the function takes three arguments. The function, when called in a list with arguments, sets the identifiers to the values of the corresponding arguments. Then the expressions are evaluated from left to right and the value of the last one is returned as the value of the function call. Note that some versions of LISP do not allow more than one expression in the body of the function. Such versions of LISP use the function PROGN (defined in the reference section of this chapter) to collect several expressions into one.

The value returned by the function DE is the name of the function defined.

CONDITIONAL BRANCHING

All programming languages have to have some kind of conditional form to allow the programs to do different things in different situations. In LISP the function COND is used to do this. For example, the following expression defines ABS to return the absolute value of a number.

```
(DE ABS (X)
   (COND ((MINUSP X) (MINUS X))
         (T X)))
```

This definition says that if X is a negative number, then return the negative of it (i.e., a positive number), otherwise return X. The function MINUSP is a built-in LISP function that returns T if the value of its argument is negative and returns NIL otherwise. MINUS is the built-in function which returns the negative of its argument. The COND uses MINUSP to test X and, if X is negative, it calls MINUS. If MINUSP returns NIL then COND tests T (which is true by definition) and so COND returns X.

COND is different from most other functions in that its arguments are not expressions, but lists of expressions. The general format of COND is:

```
(COND (expression expression . . . expression)
      (expression expression . . . expression)
      . . .
      (expression expression . . . expression))
```

The lists are sometimes called the "branches" of the conditional. COND evaluates the first expression in the first branch. If the result is true (i.e., not NIL), then COND evaluates the rest of the expressions in that branch, and returns the value of the last expression evaluated. It does not evaluate any of the other branches in this case.

However, if the value of the first expression in the first branch is NIL, then COND ignores the rest of that branch and goes to the next one, testing its first expression, and so on. If none of the branches have a true first expression, then COND returns NIL. Often we make the first expression of the last branch T, which means that the last branch catches anything that the previous branches did not.

Some versions of LISP allow only one expression after the test in a branch. In such versions of LISP, use PROGN to put several expressions into one.

BUILDING AND USING LISTS

Our examples of LISP functions have all been arithmetic ones, but actually such functions are not the central ones in LISP. More important are the functions that build and use the list data structure. We will show how these functions work by an extended example.

First, let us make the following assignments:

```
(SETQ ANIMALS '(DOG CAT PIG MULE))
(SETQ EXOTICS '(LLAMA AARDVARK WARTHOG))
(SETQ PLANTS '(ROSE TOMATO GRASS))
```

ANIMALS is a list of four identifiers, each one the name of a common animal. EXOTICS is a list of less common animals, and PLANTS is a list of common plants. Note that the LISP interpreter does not really know anything about dogs or llamas. It just has the above lists with the identifiers given.

We can find out whether or not something is in a list with the function MEMBER. For example, if we type

```
(MEMBER 'PIG ANIMALS)
```

the interpreter will return the list (PIG MULE). That is, it returns that portion of the list starting with PIG. If we type

```
(MEMBER 'DOG ANIMALS)
```

then the whole list of animals will be returned, since DOG is the first element in the list. But if we type

```
(MEMBER 'HORSE ANIMALS)
```

the interpreter will return the atom NIL which is used to say that HORSE is not in the list. Notice that we do not QUOTE the atom ANIMALS because we want value of ANIMALS, not the atom ANIMALS itself.

Some versions of LISP return only T if an element is in the list. In such cases, you will probably find it useful to define another function, say IN-LIST, which does what the above function does.

We can add things to the list ANIMALS in several ways. The function CONS takes an expression and a list and returns a new list which contains the old list, plus the added expression in front. For example, to make a list of animals which includes horses, we would type

```
(CONS 'HORSE ANIMALS)
```

which would return the list (HORSE DOG CAT PIG MULE). This has not changed the list ANIMALS. To update ANIMALS, we need to type:

```
(SETQ ANIMALS (CONS 'HORSE ANIMALS))
```

(SETQ identifier (CONS expression identifier)) is a common expression in LISP programs, the list-building equivalent of "X = X + 1". Therefore we have defined a special function called PUSH which adds an element to the front of list. With PUSH we would have added horses to the animal list with the expression:

(PUSH 'HORSE ANIMALS)

PUSH is not built-in in most versions of LISP so we have put its definition at the end of this chapter. PUSH returns the expression added, i.e., HORSE in this example.

The second argument of CONS (and PUSH) should be either a list or the atom NIL, the empty list. If you CONS an expression onto NIL, you get a list of the expression. For example:

(CONS 'HORSE NIL)

returns the list (HORSE).

The function APPEND is used to merge two lists together. For example, to merge the exotic animals with the common ones:

(SETQ ANIMALS (APPEND ANIMALS EXOTICS))

which constructs the list:

(HORSE DOG CAT PIG MULE LLAMA AARDVARK WARTHOG)

Note that the APPEND did not change the value of either EXOTICS or ANIMALS. It just returned a list of this form. The SETQ reset ANIMALS to be the new list.

Another function is LIST, which takes one or more arguments and makes a list of them. For example, we could make a super-class of living things, keeping the sub-classes distinct, with:

(SETQ LIVING-THINGS (LIST PLANTS ANIMALS))

which would set LIVING-THINGS to the list

((ROSE TOMATO GRASS)
 (HORSE DOG CAT PIG MULE LLAMA AARDVARK WARTHOG))

This makes LIVING-THINGS a list of lists. Its first element is the list of plants and its second is the list of animals.

The two fundamental functions used for looking at the elements of lists are CAR and CDR. CAR returns the first element of a list. For example:

    (CAR PLANTS)

returns ROSE.

    (CAR LIVING-THINGS)

returns the list (ROSE TOMATO GRASS).
    CDR returns the rest of a list, after the first element. For example:

    (CDR PLANTS)

returns the list (TOMATO GRASS).

    (CDR LIVING-THINGS)

returns the list of lists

    ((HORSE DOG CAT PIG MULE LLAMA AARDVARK WARTHOG))

Note that the CDR of a list is always a list (perhaps empty). A common confusion is to think that CDR returns the next element of a list. It does not. To get the second element in a list, use CAR and CDR together like this:

    (CAR (CDR PLANTS))

returns TOMATO. A built-in function is CADR which does the same thing. That is, (CADR PLANTS) returns TOMATO. Most versions of LISP have the functions CADR (which is the same as CDR then CAR), CDDR (which is the same as two CDRs), CADDR (which is the same as two CDRs then a CAR), and so on, up to some interpreter-specific limit, such as four CARSs and/or CDRs.
    The CDR of a list with one element (or the CDDR of a list with two elements, and so on) is the empty list, NIL. That is,

    (CDDDR PLANTS)

returns NIL because PLANTS has only three elements.
    Note that CDR does not change any lists. To remove the first element from ANIMALS we would type:

    (SETQ ANIMALS (CDR ANIMALS))

This form, setting a list to the CDR of itself, is a kind of inverse to CONS. The function POP does a similar thing. That is,

(POP ANIMALS)

removes the first element from ANIMALS. The difference is that CDR returns the remaining list and POP returns the element removed. POP is not built into most versions of LISP and so we have included its definition at the end of this chapter.

The functions CAR, CDR, POP, PUSH, and so on, expect lists as arguments. To check whether the value of something is a list or not we can use the functions ATOM and CONSP. The function ATOM takes one argument and returns the atom T if its argument is an atom and NIL if its argument is a list. CONSP is almost the opposite of ATOM. It returns NIL if its argument is an atom and it returns the argument itself if it is a list. For example,

(ATOM 'A) returns T
(ATOM '(A)) returns NIL
(CONSP 'A) returns NIL
(CONSP '(A)) returns (A)

We can tell if two expressions are the same with the predicate EQUAL. EQUAL takes two arguments and returns T if they have the same value and NIL if they don't. For example,

(EQUAL 1 1) returns T
(EQUAL 1 2) returns NIL
(EQUAL '(A B) '(A B)) returns T
(EQUAL '(A B) '(B A)) returns NIL

We could tell if a list were empty by seeing if it were equal to NIL. For example, we could tell that PLANTS only had three elements because

(EQUAL (CDDDR PLANTS) NIL)

returns T. Since we often want to know if a list is empty, LISP has the function NULL. That is,

(NULL (CDDDR PLANTS))

also returns T.

The predicate NOT takes an expression and returns T if that expression is NIL and NIL if it is not NIL. For example, we could define CONSP as:

(DE CONSP (X) (NOT (ATOM X]

Because NIL is both false and the empty list, it turns out that NOT and NULL are really just two names for the same function. However NULL is the better name to use when testing for the empty list, and NOT is the better name to use when testing whether some predicate returned false or not.

Lists are one important way to represent facts. Another way is to attach information directly to identifiers. This is done with the function PUTPROP. For example:

    (PUTPROP 'DOG 4 'NUMBER-OF-LEGS)

saves with the identifier DOG the property name NUMBER-OF-LEGS with the value 4. Things saved with PUTPROP can be retrieved later with the function GET. For example:

    (GET 'DOG 'NUMBER-OF-LEGS)

returns the number 4 if the PUTPROP has been done. If no property has been saved, then NIL is returned. Property names must be identifiers and properties can only be saved with identifiers. The values saved can be any expression. Properties are very handy, especially when there are a lot of facts about a lot of identifiers that need to be saved. Our version of LISP, for example, uses properties to store function definitions and variable values.

ITERATION

We have already seen how to define functions and put in conditional branches. The other basic thing we need to know is how to do loops, that is, how to cause certain expressions to be evaluated until some condition becomes true.

Recursion

LENGTH is a built-in function that takes a list and returns its length—how many elements the list has. We could define it with the following:

    (DE LENGTH (L)
    (COND ((NULL L) 0)
            (T (PLUS 1 (LENGTH (CDR L]

To see how this works, suppose we call LENGTH with the list (A B). L is set to (A B), so (NULL L) is false. This means that LENGTH returns one plus the length of the CDR of L, which is (B). In order to calculate this, LENGTH is called again, with L set to (B). Again L is not empty, so the length of (B) is one plus the length of the CDR L, which is NIL. LENGTH is called with L set to

NIL, which means that LENGTH returns zero. Since the length of (B) was one plus zero, the length of (B) is one. Since the length of (A B) was one plus the length of (B), the length of (A B) is two.

The definition above is called a *recursive* definition because the definition of LENGTH refers to LENGTH. Recursion is often considered to be an exotic technique, but it should not be. It is in fact often the most appropriate way to do certain tasks. Recursion does however take getting used to. If you have never tried recursive definitions before, experiment with them. Some good functions to try defining recursively are MEMBER, APPEND, LAST and REVERSE. They are all described in the reference section.

LOOP

Another way to define the function LENGTH is to use the LOOP function. LOOP is not built into most versions of LISP. Therefore we have included its definition at the end of this chapter. Using LOOP, the definition of LENGTH is:

```
(DE LENGTH (L)
    (LOOP (INITIAL COUNT 0)
          (WHILE L)
          (DO (SETQ COUNT (PLUS 1 COUNT))
              (POP L))
          (RESULT COUNT)
```

This definition says that while L is not NIL (i.e., not empty), increment a counter by one and remove one element from L. The counter is initialized to zero, so at the end the counter will be set to the length of the list. The counter is returned as the value of the LOOP and hence as the value of LENGTH. LOOP, like COND, takes lists of expressions as its arguments. For LOOP, each list starts with a keyword saying what LOOP should do with the rest of the expressions in the list. In the above definition, INITIAL says that COUNT is a local variable that is initialized to zero. WHILE says that the LOOP should repeat itself as long as L is not NIL. DO says that on each cycle of the loop, COUNT should be incremented by one and L should be shortened by one element. RESULT says that the final value of COUNT should be returned. In general, LOOP is called with the following format:

```
(LOOP (INITIAL identifier expression identifier expression ...)
      (WHILE expression)
      (DO expression expression ...)
      (UNTIL expression)
      (RESULT expression))
```

All of the clauses are optional. INITIAL and RESULT, if used, should appear at the beginning and end, respectively. If there is no RESULT clause then LOOP returns NIL when it finishes. You can have as many DO, UNTIL and WHILE clauses as you want, in any order. The order determines when each clause is executed in the loop. Thus you can have WHILE-DO, UNTIL-DO, DO-UNTIL-DO, and so on. As another example of LOOP, we could define the LISP interpreter with:

```
(DE INTERPRET ()
 (LOOP (DO (PRINT (EVAL (READ]
```

PRINT is the built-in LISP function for printing expressions, EVAL is the built-in function that evaluates expressions, and READ is the built-in function that reads expressions. Since there is neither a WHILE clause nor an UNTIL clause to tell LOOP when to stop, it repeats the DO clause forever.

FOR

While LOOP is general enough to do all our iterations, it is a little clumsy when we want to do the same thing to every element in a list, and very clumsy if we want to save the results of what we do to each element. For example, suppose we had a list of numbers and wanted to make a list of the same length but with 1 in place of every positive number, −1 in place of every negative number, and 0 for every 0. That is, if the list of numbers were "(4 5 0 −2 12)", then the new list would be "(1 1 0 −1 1)". If we call the function SIGNUM, then a LOOP version would be:

```
(DE SIGNUM (L)
 (LOOP (INITIAL R NIL X NIL)
       (WHILE L)
       (DO (SETQ X (POP L))
           (PUSH (COND ((MINUSP X) −1)
                       ((EQUAL X 0) 0)
                       (T 1))
                 R))
       (RESULT R)))
```

There is an easier (and usually faster) way to write this however. The function FOR is especially designed to evaluate expressions for every element in a list, saving selected results if desired. A FOR version of SIGNUM would be:

```
(DE SIGNUM (L)
 (FOR (X IN L)
      (SAVE (COND ((MINUSP X) −1)
                  ((EQUAL X 0) 0)
                  (T 1)))))
```

The COND expression is still the same but the FOR takes care of everything else. The subexpression "(X IN L)" tells FOR to set X to each element of L. We don't have to use POP or CAR or CDR. The "(SAVE . . .)" tells FOR to save the results in a list.

The FOR loop becomes even more useful when we want to go through a list and do some action only when some test is true. We do this with the WHEN keyword. For example, suppose we wanted a function that took a list of numbers and returned a list of the negative ones. If we called the function NEGATIVES, then one way to write it would be:

```
(DE NEGATIVES (L)
  (FOR (X IN L)
    (WHEN (MINUSP X))
    (SAVE X)))
```

Note that we don't need a COND. The WHEN keyword says that when X is less than 0, save X. If L has no negative elements, then the result is NIl   (As an exercise, try writing this function with LOOP.)

Instead of SAVE, we can also use the keyword DO. DO tells FOR to ignore the results and just return NIL. For example, to print the square of every element of a list of numbers, without bothering to save anything, we would write:

```
(FOR (X IN L)
  (DO (PRINT (TIMES X X))))
```

We can use WHEN with DO to control evaluation. Thus, to print the squares of only the negative numbers, we would write:

```
(FOR (X IN L)
  (WHEN (MINUSP X))
  (DO (PRINT (TIMES X X))))
```

There is one more special use of FOR. The keyword EXISTS, which should not be used with WHEN, DO or SAVE, tells FOR to stop processing as soon as the expression following the EXISTS is not NIL for some element of the list. FOR-EXISTS returns the list from that element on. This is mostly used to test whether anything in a list fits a certain condition, without having to go through the whole list. For example, the following expression will return a true value if at least one element of a list is negative:

```
(FOR (X IN L)
  (EXISTS (MINUSP X)))
```

Note: you can have more than one expression after a DO, WHEN, SAVE or

EXISTS. The expressions are evaluated from left to right and the value of the last is used.

The general format of FOR loops is:

```
(FOR (identifier IN list)
     (WHEN expression expression...)
     (<keyword> expression expression...))
```

where <keyword> is either DO or SAVE. The WHEN can be left out, in which case another possible <keyword> is EXISTS.

FOR is not built into most versions of LISP. Therefore, we have included a definition of it at the end of this chapter.

REFERENCE SECTION

We now turn to a very brief run-through of the more important LISP functions. Functions are given in expression format. All arguments are evaluated when the function is called unless otherwise specified. The presence of three dots in the argument list indicates that an arbitrary number of arguments may be given. Upper-case is used to represent what must be included. Lower-case is used to represent the arguments to a function. The functions are listed alphabetically.

(AND expression expression...)

AND evaluates the expressions from left to right. If one returns NIL, then AND stops evaluation and returns NIL. Otherwise, AND returns the value of the last expression. Note: in some versions of LISP, AND only returns T or NIL.

(APPEND list list...)

Each of the arguments should be a list. APPEND returns the list formed by joining these lists together. For example
(APPEND '(A B) '(C D) '(E F)) returns (A B C D E F)

(CONS-END list expression)

This returns a copy of the list with the expression added to the end. It is not built into most versions of LISP, so we have included its definition at the end of this chapter.

(APPLY name list)

The first argument should be the name of a function, and the length of the list should be the same as the number of arguments that the function named requires. The function is called with its arguments taken from the list. For example,
(APPLY 'CONS (LIST 1 '(2 3))) returns (1 2 3)

(ASSOC identifier list)
>   The second argument should be a list of pairs, such as ((A B) (C D)...).
>   ASSOC returns the first pair whose CAR is equal to the identifier. If none
>   is found, NIL is returned.

(ATOM expression)
>   This returns T if the expression is an identifier, number or string, otherwise
>   it returns NIL.

(CAR list)
>   CAR returns the first element of the list.

(CDR list)
>   CDR returns the list minus its first element.

(COND (expression expression ... expression)
>   (expression expression ... expression)
>
>   ...
>
>   (expression expression ... expression))

>   COND is the branching function. It is described in detail in the first part
>   of this chapter.

(CONS expression list)
>   CONS returns a list starting with an expression and continuing with the
>   elements of the second argument.

(CONSP expression)
>   CONSP returns the expression if it is not an atom, otherwise it returns NIL.

(DE name (list of identifiers) expression expression ...)
>   DE defines functions. It is described in the introductory section. Name is
>   returned.

(DEFPROP identifier expression identifier)
>   None of the arguments are evaluated. The expression is stored under the
>   first identifier, with the property named by the second identifier. The first
>   identifier is returned.

(DF name (identifier) expression expression ...)
>   This defines a function that does not evaluate its arguments. Note that only
>   one identifier is given as a local variable. When the function is called, this
>   identifier is set to the list of arguments as they appear in the call. The
>   function can then evaluate them or not as it wishes. For example, we could
>   define DEFPROP with:
>   (DF DEFPROP (L) (PUTPROP (CAR L) (CADR L) (CADDR L)))

(DIFFERENCE number number ...)
>   DIFFERENCE returns the first number minus the sum of the rest.

(DM name (identifier) expression expression . . .)
This defines a function called a *macro*. Like DF, the function does not
evaluate its arguments. However, there are two important differences. First,
the identifier is set to the whole expression, not just the list of arguments.
Second, the result of this function is evaluated a second time by the LISP
interpreter. Normally a macro builds some other expression which is the
thing you actually want evaluated. At the end of this chapter there are macro
definitions for FOR, LET, LOOP, POP and PUSH. Macros are very
useful, although unfortunately not all versions of LISP have them.

(DRM character (LAMBDA () expression expression . . .))
This is a function for defining *readmacros*. A readmacro is not a function
but a character which the LISP interpreter expands into an expression when
it reads it. That is, the character becomes a shorthand for the longer expression. The value of the readmacro is constructed by evaluating the expressions in the LAMBDA body from left to right and returning the value of
the last one. For example, the micro programs frequently use the form
(*VAR* identifier), so they define ? to be a readmacro, such that ?X
becomes (*VAR* X) when it is read. This is done with:
    (DRM ? (LAMBDA () (LIST '*VAR* (READ))))
When the LISP interpreter reads the ?, the readmacro reads one more
expression and returns the list (*VAR* expression). To the LISP interpreter
it is just as if we had typed the *VAR* form instead.
Not all versions of LISP have readmacros. If yours does not, then whenever
we use them you will have to write the equivalent long form instead.

(EQUAL expression expression)
This returns T if the two expressions look the same, otherwise it returns
NIL.

(EVAL expression)
This evaluates the expression. For example:
    (EVAL '(PLUS 1 2)) returns 3.

(EXPLODE expression)
This returns a list of the characters that are used when printing the expression. It is used mostly to get at the letters in an identifier. For example
    (EXPLODE 'ATOM) returns (A T O M).

(FOR (identifier IN list)
(WHEN expression expression . . .)
(<keyword> expression expression . . .))
where <keyword> is either DO or SAVE. The WHEN can be left out, in
which case another possible <keyword> is EXISTS. This is an iteration
function which evaluates the expressions after <keyword>, when the last

WHEN expression is true, with the identifier set to successive elements of the list. It is described in the first part of this chapter.

(GET identifier identifier)

GET returns the value attached to the first identifier under the property named by the second identifier. If none is found, NIL is returned. Note that NIL is also returned if NIL is the value stored.

(LAST list)

LAST returns a list of the last element of the list.

(LENGTH list)

LENGTH returns the number of elements in the list.

(LET (identifier expression identifier expression...)

expression expression...)

This makes the identifiers in the first argument into local variables and assigns each one to the value of the expression that follows it. Then the expressions after the first argument are evaluated from left to right. The value of the last expression evaluated is returned.

For example,

```
(LET (X 1 Y 2)
  (MSG T "X is " X " and Y is" Y)
  (LIST X Y))
```

will print "X is 1 and Y is 2" and return the list (1 2).

(LIST expression expression...)

LIST makes a list of the expressions.

(LOOP (INITIAL identifier expression identifier expression...)

(WHILE expression)
(DO expression expression...)
(UNTIL expression)
(RESULT expression))

This is described in detail in the introductory section. The INITIAL clause initializes local variables. Then the DO expressions are evaluated repeatedly as long as the WHILE expression is true and the UNTIL expression is false. When the loop stops, the RESULT expression is evaluated and returned.

(MEMBER expression list)

MEMBER returns the portion of the list starting with the expression, if any, in the list; otherwise it returns NIL.

(MINUS number)

MINUS returns the negative of the number.

(MINUSP number)

MINUSP returns T if the number is negative; otherwise it returns NIL.

(MSG form form . . .)

MSG is used for formatted printing. It takes three different kinds of arguments. The identifier T causes a new line for printing to be started. A string is printed directly, without the quotes. Variables and other expressions are evaluated and the value is printed. For example, if X were set to 144 and Y were set to 28, then

(MSG T "The sum of " X " and " Y " is " (PLUS X Y))

prints

The sum of 144 and 28 is 172.

MSG always returns NIL. If your version of LISP does not have MSG, you can either define it with DF or use a series of PRINT statements instead.

(NOT expression)

This returns T if the expression is NIL; otherwise it returns NIL. This is just the function NULL with a different name.

(NUMBERP expression)

This returns T if the expression is a number; otherwise it returns NIL.

(NULL expression)

This returns T if the expression is NIL; otherwise it returns NIL.

(OR expression expression . . .)

OR evaluates the expressions from left to right. If one returns a value that is not NIL, then OR stops evaluation and returns it. Otherwise, OR returns the value of the last expression. Note: in some versions of LISP, OR only returns T or NIL.

(PLUS number number . . .)

PLUS returns the sum of the numbers.

(POP identifier)

The value of the identifier should be either a list or NIL. POP removes the first element from the list, changing the value of the identifier. The first element is returned.

(PRINT expression)

PRINT prints the expression and returns it.

(PROG1 expression expression . . .)

PROG1 takes up to five arguments, all of which are evaluated, and the value of the first is returned. See the definition of the macro POP for an example.

(PROGN expression expression . . .)

PROGN takes any number of arguments, all of which are evaluated, and the value of the last is returned. PROGN is especially useful in versions of LISP that do not allow more than one expression in a function body or after the test in a COND branch.

(PUSH expression identifier)

The value of the identifier should be either a list or NIL. PUSH adds the expression to the front of the list, changing the value of the identifier. PUSH returns the expression.

(PUTPROP identifier expression identifier)

The expression is stored under the first identifier, with the property named by the second identifier. The expression is returned.

(QUOTE expression)

The expression is returned unevaluated. QUOTE is the same function as when a single quote ("'") is typed.

(READ)

READ takes no arguments. When evaluated it causes the interpreter to read one expression from the input device. This expression, unevaluated, is returned as the value of READ.

(REMOVE expression list)

REMOVE returns all the elements in the list except those equal to the expression. Only top level elements are removed.

(REMPROP identifier identifier)

The property named by the second identifier—and any value stored under it—is removed from the first identifier. REMPROP returns T if there is such a property; otherwise it returns NIL.

(REVERSE list)

REVERSE returns a new list which has the elements of the old list in the opposite order.

(SELECTQ expression

          (expression expression expression . . .)
          (expression expression expression . . .)

      . . .

expression)

SELECTQ is a special kind of COND; it evaluates the first expression and then looks through the lists that follow for the first one whose CAR, *unevaluated,* is equal to the value of the expression. If one is found, then the remaining expressions are evaluated and the value of the last is returned. If none are found, then the last expression is evaluated and returned. For example, the following expression will print 1, 2, or 3, depending on whether (CAR X) is A, B, or neither:

    (SELECTQ (CAR X)
        (A (PRINT 1))
        (B (PRINT 2))
     (PRINT 3))

(SET identifier expression)

>SET is like SETQ but the first argument is evaluated and should return an identifier, which will be assigned the value of the expression. The value assigned is returned.

(SETQ identifier expression)

>The first argument is not evaluated. The value of the expression is assigned to the identifier and returned.

(SPRINT expression number)

>SPRINT is what is called a "prettyprinting" function. If more than one line is needed to print the expression, then the succeeding lines are indented to indicate how the parentheses balance, just as we indent by hand the code we wrote in the text. The second argument sets the left margin. SPRINT is used when the expression being printed will be large and we want it to be readable. SPRINT always returns NIL. If your version of LISP has no such function, use PRINT instead.

(SUBST expression expression list)

>SUBST copies the list, but wherever the second expression occurs in the list, it uses the first expression. That is, the first expression is substituted for the second expression in the list. This substitution occurs at all levels of the list, not just the top level. For example:
>
>>(SUBST 'Y 'X '(DE FN (X) (CAR X)))
>
>returns (DE FN (Y) (CAR Y)).

(TIMES number number . . .)

>TIMES returns the product of the numbers.

(ZEROP number)

>This returns T if the number is zero; otherwise it returns NIL.

CONCEPTUAL DEPENDENCY IN LISP

All of the micro programs use the Conceptual Dependency representation system described in the previous chapters. They all use the same format for coding Conceptual Dependency forms in LISP and also share a number of functions for building and using these forms.

CD Forms in LISP

The micro programs in this text all use the same syntax for representing Conceptual Dependency expressions. A CD expression has the form:

>(predicate (role filler) (role filler) . . .)

where the predicate (which is an identifier) is the central act, state, or cause; and the roles (which are also identifiers) give names to the slots for the act, state, or cause. The fillers (which can be either identifiers or whole CD expressions) fill in those slots. For example, "John gave Mary a book" would be represented:

```
(ATRANS (ACTOR (PERSON (NAME (JOHN)))) (OBJECT (BOOK))
        (TO (PERSON (NAME (MARY))))
        (FROM (PERSON (NAME (JOHN)))))
```

The main predicate is ATRANS. The first role pair is

```
(ACTOR (PERSON (NAME (JOHN))))
```

with the role being ACTOR and the filler being (PERSON (NAME (JOHN))). The predicate of this filler is PERSON and it has the role pair (NAME (JOHN)), and so on.

When mental acts or causals are involved, then one or more of the fillers will be a CD, as in "John told Mary Bill went to the store":

```
(MTRANS (ACTOR (PERSON (NAME (JOHN))))
        (OBJECT (PTRANS (ACTOR (PERSON (NAME (BILL))))
                        (OBJECT (PERSON (NAME (BILL))))
                        (TO (STORE))))
        (TO (CP (PART (PERSON (NAME (MARY)))))))
```

The order of role names is not important and roles can be left out, which is equivalent to having NIL fillers for those roles.

CD Patterns

It is often important to tell whether or not two CD forms in LISP are the same. The function EQUAL is not sufficient for this task, because it would say that the following two CDs are not the same:

```
(PTRANS (ACTOR (PERSON)) (TO (STORE)))
(PTRANS (TO (STORE)) (ACTOR (PERSON)))
```

But in fact they are the same because the order of roles does not matter in CDs. Therefore, we have defined another function especially for CDs, called MATCH. MATCH applied to the two CDs above would return true. MATCH in fact is quite lenient. It says that (PERSON) matches (PERSON (NAME (JOHN))), because extra roles do not matter. However, (PERSON (NAME (JOHN))) does not match (PERSON (NAME (MARY))) because, if a role is present in both CDs, then the fillers must match.

MATCH is defined to be more flexible than just comparing two CD forms. It is actually a *pattern matcher* that takes a CD *pattern* and a normal CD and says whether they match. A CD pattern is a CD form containing *pattern variables*. A pattern variable is indicated by a pair of the form (*VAR* identifier). When MATCH compares a pattern with a regular CD, it allows a variable in the pattern to match anything in the corresponding position in the CD. For example, MATCH says that the following pattern and CD match:

    (PTRANS (ACTOR (*VAR* X)) (TO (STORE)))
    (PTRANS (ACTOR (PERSON)) (TO (STORE)))

Because pattern variables are used a lot, we have defined the question mark to be a readmacro such that "?identifier" returns "(*VAR* indentifier)". Hence we could write the pattern above as

    (PTRANS (ACTOR ?X) (TO (STORE)))

It is important to remember that the actual variable name is just the identifier, not the "?identifier". The question mark is used to tell MATCH that the variable is there, but the question mark is not part of the name of the variable.

When MATCH finds that a pattern matches a CD, it returns a list of the form:

    (T (variable value) (variable value) . . .)

which says that the match occurred and the variables in the pattern were matched to the corresponding values in the CD. The result of MATCH applied to the above pattern and CD would be:

    (T (X (PERSON)))

which says that the pattern matched the CD and the variable X was matched to the CD form (PERSON). Notice that if we match a regular CD with a regular CD, then the result of a successful match will be just the list (T), since there are no variables. An unsuccessful match always returns NIL.

The form that MATCH returns is called a *binding list*, because it gives the bindings for the pattern variables. MATCH uses this list while it is matching the pattern with the CD to enforce the following rule:

    IF a variable in a pattern is in the binding list,
    THEN it can only match a CD that matches the value it is bound to.

This means that if the same variable appears twice in a pattern, then the pattern will only match CDs where the same filler appears in both places. For example, the pattern

(PTRANS (ACTOR ?X) (OBJECT ?X) (TO (STORE)))

will match

(PTRANS (ACTOR (PERSON)) (OBJECT (PERSON)) (TO (STORE)))

but not

(PTRANS (ACTOR (PERSON)) (OBJECT (KITE)) (TO (STORE)))

because in the second case X can not match both PERSON and KITE.

Finally, the function MATCH allows us to tell it in advance what values certain variables must have. This becomes important in story understanding. Suppose we have the variable MAIN-CHARACTER and some knowledge structure, such as a script or a plan-goal hierarchy, that consists of a lot of patterns, many of which use that variable. Suppose also that after understanding the first line of a story we know that MAIN-CHARACTER is (PERSON (NAME (JOHN))). Then we would want to remember in all later patterns matching that John is the main character. We do this by giving the binding list

(T (MAIN-CHARACTER (PERSON (NAME (JOHN)))))

to MATCH whenever we ask MATCH to compare a pattern with a CD. A call to the function MATCH in general looks like this:

(MATCH pattern CD binding-list)

The pattern can have zero or more variables. The second argument, the CD, should never have variables. The binding list should either be NIL, which means there are no initial restrictions on the pattern variables, or else a list of the same form that MATCH returns when a successful match occurs. If the pattern matches the CD, then a new binding list is returned, which consists of everything in the original binding list, plus any new bindings that occurred during the match.

The use of binding lists for story understanding is described for a particular example in Chapter 6.

CD Functions

(FILLER:PAIR pair)

This takes a pair of the form (role filler) and returns the filler.

(FILLER:ROLE role CD)

This looks for a pair of the form (role filler) in the CD form and returns the filler. If there is no such pair, then NIL is returned. Since binding-lists are in the same format as CD forms, FILLER:ROLE can be used to find out what a variable is bound to in a binding-list by saying:

(FILLER:ROLE variable-name binding-list)

(HEADER:CD CD)

This returns the main predicate of a CD form.

(INSTANTIATE pattern binding-list)

This takes a CD pattern and a list of variable bindings and returns a regular CD where all variables (i.e., the (*VAR* identifier) forms) have been replaced with the bindings they have in the binding list. If a variable in the pattern is not in the binding list, then it is replaced with NIL.

(IS-VAR CD)

This returns true if the CD is a pattern variable.

(MATCH pattern CD binding-list)

If the pattern matches the CD, then the binding-list is returned, with any new variable bindings added. If the match fails, then NIL is returned. MATCH is a described in detail in the previous section.

(NAME:VAR pattern-variable)

This takes a pattern variable of the form (*VAR* identifier) and returns the identifier.

(ROLE:PAIR pair)

This takes a pair of the form (role filler) and returns the role.

(ROLES:CD CD)

This returns a list of the role pairs in a CD form.

(SETROLE role filler CD)

This returns a copy of CD with the pair (role filler) added. If the CD already had a filler for the role, the old pair is removed.

IMPLEMENTATION NOTES

This section gives the LISP definitions of those functions that are not part of standard versions of LISP. If your LISP interpreter supports macro definitions (as most good versions of LISP do), then these definitions should be included with whatever micro programs you want to run. If your LISP interpreter does not support macros but does support functions with unevaluated arguments, then macros can be imitated with the functions in the section "Adding macros to your LISP interpreter." If even this is not possible, then you should use the macro definitions as guidelines for fixing the code in the micro programs so that you can run them.

Underlying Functions in LISP

The following functions are used to implement FOR, LOOP, and LET. They are not used in the micro programs explicitly. We have found that students learn how to program in LISP much faster if they never have to learn about such things.

(FUNCTION expression)
> FUNCTION is the same as QUOTE, but is used when the expression is a function name or LAMBDA form to tell LISP that the expression can be compiled (for those versions of LISP that have compilers).

((LAMBDA (identifier identifier . . .) expression expression . . .)
> arg-expression arg-expression . . .)
> This is the same as
> (LET (identifier arg-expression identifier arg-expression . . .)
>   expression expression . . .)

(MAPC (FUNCTION (LAMBDA (identifier) expression expression . . .))
>   list)
> This is the same as
>   (FOR (identifier IN list)
>   (DO expression expression . . .))

(MAPCAR (FUNCTION (LAMBDA (identifier) expression expression . . .))
>   list)
> This is the same as
>   (FOR (identifier IN list)
>   (SAVE expression expression . . .))

(MAPCAN (FUNCTION (LAMBDA (identifier) expression expression . . .))
>   list)
> MAPCAN is like MAPCAR but it appends the results into a list. For example,
>   (FOR (X IN L) (WHEN (FOO X)) (SAVE (BAZ X)))
> is equivalent to
>   (MAPCAN (FUNCTION (LAMBDA (X)
>   (COND ((FOO X) (LIST (BAZ X))))))
>   L)
> though the latter is not as clear.

(PROG (list of identifiers) expression expression . . .)
> If you know ALGOL or PL/I, then you should think of PROG as a block, with local variables, labels, GO-TOs and RETURNs. LOOP expands into a PROG form before execution. For example, this LOOP form:
>   (LOOP (INITIAL X '(A B C))
>   (WHILE X)

```
              (DO (PRINT X)
                    (SETQ X (CDR X)))
              (RESULT 'DONE))
```
expands into this PROG form:
```
      (PROG (X)
                    (SETQ X '(A B C))
      LOOP (OR X (GO EXIT))
                    (PRINT X)
                    (SETQ X (CDR X))
                    (GO LOOP)
      EXIT (RETURN 'DONE))
```
The first argument of PROG is a list of local variables. When the PROG starts, it sets these variables to NIL. The remaining arguments are either identifiers or expressions. Identifiers are labels for the expressions that follow them. PROG evaluates the non-atomic statements in order. If a (GO identifier) is evaluated, then PROG moves to the expression immediately following that identifier and continues evaluation from there. If a (RETURN expression) is evaluated, then the PROG immediately stops, and the value of the PROG is the value of the expression. If the last statement is evaluated and there is no RETURN, then the value of PROG is NIL.

```
(SOME (FUNCTION (LAMBDA (identifier) expression expression ...))
      list)
```
This is the same as
```
      (FOR (identifier IN list)
              (EXISTS expression expression ...))
```
SOME is not found in all versions of LISP. If your version of LISP does not have it, you should use the LOOP function instead.

LISP Definition of LOOP

A general version of the LOOP function is defined in Charniak et al. (1980). The version below is slightly simpler, and sufficient for the micro programs in this text.

```
LOOP appends together pieces from the LOOP clauses to form a PROG
body of the form (PROG (...) ... LOOP ... EXIT (RETURN...))
— (WHILE...) becomes (OR ... (GO EXIT))
— (UNTIL...) becomes (AND ... (GO EXIT))

(DM LOOP (L)
 (LOOP1 (CDR L)
          (GET-KEYWORD 'INITIAL L)
          (GET-KEYWORD 'RESULT L)
```

```
(DE LOOP1 (CLAUSES I-BODY R-BODY)
 (APPEND (LIST 'PROG (VAR-LIST I-BODY))
         (SETQ-STEPS I-BODY)
         (CONS 'LOOP (APPLY 'APPEND (MAPCAR 'DO-CLAUSE CLAUSES)))
         (LIST '(GO LOOP) 'EXIT (CONS 'RETURN R-BODY]
```

`GET-KEYWORD is used by both LOOP and FOR—it returns a list
`of expressions—NOTE: if your version of LISP says that
`(CDR NIL) = NIL, then the LAMBDA can be replaced with a simple
`(CDR (ASSOC . . .))

```
(DE GET-KEYWORD (KEY L)
 ((LAMBDA (X) (CDR X))
  (ASSOC KEY (CDR L)
```

`DO-CLAUSE takes a keyword clause and generates the appropriate
`code—INITIAL and RESULT are taken care of separately

```
(DE DO-CLAUSE (CLAUSE)
 (SELECTQ (CAR CLAUSE)
          ((INITIAL RESULT) NIL)
          (WHILE (LIST (LIST 'OR (CADR CLAUSE) '(GO EXIT))))
          (DO (CDR CLAUSE))
          (UNTIL (LIST (LIST 'AND (CADR CLAUSE) '(GO EXIT))))
          (MSG T "unknown keyword" CLAUSE]
```

`VAR-LIST: (v1 e1 v2 e2 . . .) => (v1 v2 . . .)

```
(DE VAR-LIST (L)
 (COND ((NULL L) NIL)
       (T (CONS (CAR L) (VAR-LIST (CDDR L)
```

`SETQ-STEPS: (v1 e1 v2 e2 . . .) => ((SETQ v1 e1) (SETQ v2 e2) . . .)
`—omits cases where ei (i = 1, 2, 3, etc) is NIL

```
(DE SETQ-STEPS (L)
 (COND ((NULL L) NIL)
       ((NULL (CADR L)) (SETQ-STEPS (CDDR L)))
       (T (CONS (LIST 'SETQ (CAR L) (CADR L))
                (SETQ-STEPS (CDDR L]
```

LISP Definition of FOR

A general version of the FOR function is defined in Charniak et al. (1980). The
version below is a little different (the EXISTS keyword is new), but is sufficient
for the micro programs in this text.

`The different forms of FOR loops are expanded as follows:
`(FOR (X IN L) (DO (FOO X))) =>
`(MAPC (FUNCTION FOO) L)

`(FOR (X IN L) (SAVE (FOO X))) =>
`(MAPCAR (FUNCTION FOO) L)

```
'(FOR (X IN L) (WHEN (FOO X)) (DO (BAZ X))) =>
'(MAPC (FUNCTION (LAMBDA (X) (COND ((FOO X) (BAZ X))))) L)

'(FOR (X IN L) (WHEN (FOO X)) (SAVE (BAZ X))) =>
'(MAPCAN (FUNCTION (LAMBDA (X) (COND ((FOO X) (NCONS (BAZ X))))))
          L)

'(FOR (X IN L) (EXISTS (FOO X))) =>
'(SOME (FUNCTION (LAMBDA (X) (FOO X))) L)

(DM FOR (L)
 (FOR1 (CADR L)
       (GET-KEYWORD 'WHEN L)
       (GET-KEYWORD 'DO L)
       (GET-KEYWORD 'SAVE L)
       (GET-KEYWORD 'EXISTS L]

(DE FOR1 (IN WHEN DO SAVE EXISTS)
 (CONS (FOR-MAPFN WHEN DO SAVE EXISTS)
       (CONS (FOR-LAMBDA (CAR IN) WHEN DO SAVE EXISTS)
             (CDDR IN]

(DE FOR-MAPFN (WHEN DO SAVE EXISTS)
 (COND (DO ' MAPC)
       (EXISTS 'SOME)
       (WHEN 'MAPCAN)
       (T 'MAPCAR]

(DE FOR-LAMBDA (VAR WHEN DO SAVE EXISTS)
 (LIST 'FUNCTION
  (CONS 'LAMBDA
   (CONS (LIST VAR)
    (COND (WHEN (FOR-WHEN WHEN DO SAVE))
          (T (OR DO SAVE EXISTS]

(DE FOR-WHEN (WHEN DO SAVE)
 (LIST (LIST 'COND
             (APPEND (ADD-PROGN WHEN)
                     (OR DO (LIST (CONS 'NCONS (ADD-PROGN SAVE]

(DE ADD-PROGN (L)
 (COND ((CDR L) (LIST (CONS 'PROGN L)))
       (T L]
```

LISP Definition of LET

LET can be defined with:

```
'(LET (I1 V1 I2 V2...) X1 X2...) =>
'      ((LAMBDA (I1 I2...) X1 X2...) V1 V2...)

(DM LET (L) (LET1 (REVERSE (CADR L)) NIL NIL (CDDR L]
```

```
(DE LET1 (L VARS VALS BODY)
 (COND ((NULL L) (CONS (CONS 'LAMBDA (CONS VARS BODY)) VALS))
       (T (LET1 (CDDR L)
                (CONS (CADR L) VARS)
                (CONS (CAR L) VALS)
                BODY]
```

LISP Definition of PUSH, POP, and CONS-END

PUSH can be defined with:

```
(DM PUSH (L)
 (LIST 'CAR (LIST 'SETQ (CADDR L) (LIST 'CONS (CADR L) (CADDR L]
```

Its inverse, POP, can be defined with:

```
(DM POP (L)
 (LIST 'PROG1
       (LIST 'CAR (CADR L))
       (LIST 'SETQ (CADR L) (LIST 'CDR (CADR L]
```

CONS-END can be defined with:

```
(DE CONS-END (L X) (APPEND L (LIST X]
```

LISP Definitions of CD Functions

A CD form is represented in the micro programs with the form (predicate role-pair role-pair . . .). The functions defined below are used to get information from this data structure. The function names follow a convention established in Charniak et al. (1980): a function name of the form "x:y" means that the function applies to a data structure of type "y" and returns a data structure of type "x". For example, ROLE:PAIR applies to pairs, such as (ACTOR JOHN), and returns the role, in this case ACTOR.

```
¯HEADER:CD gets the head act of a CD form.
¯ROLES:CD gets the list of role-pairs of a CD form.

(DE HEADER:CD (X) (CAR X))
(DE ROLES:CD (X) (CDR X))
```

```
¯Role-pairs have the form (role filler)—ROLE:PAIR returns the role
¯and FILLER:PAIR returns the filler.

(DE ROLE:PAIR (X) (CAR X))
(DE FILLER:PAIR (X) (CADR X))
```

¨A filler for a role is found by looking for the role name in the CD,
¨and returning the filler if a pair is found.

```
(DE FILLER:ROLE (ROLE CD)
  (LET (PAIR (ASSOC ROLE (ROLES:CD CD)))
    (AND PAIR (FILLER:PAIR PAIR]
```

¨SETROLE Makes a new CD form with (ROLE FILLER) added or replacing
¨ the old (ROLE . . .) pair.

```
(DE SETROLE (ROLE FILLER CD)
  (CONS (HEADER:CD CD)
          (APPEND (FOR (PAIR IN (ROLES:CD CD))
                        (WHEN (NOT (EQUAL (ROLE:PAIR PAIR) ROLE)))
                        (SAVE PAIR))
                  (LIST (LIST ROLE FILLER]
```

¨Variables, which are used by the pattern matcher, start with a
¨question mark ("?"), as in ?FOO.
¨This is converted internally to (*VAR* role-name), so ?FOO
¨becomes (*VAR* FOO).
¨The DRM defines ? to convert itself to *VAR* when it is read.
¨This DRM must be evaluated before any CDs with ?s are read.
¨IS-VAR returns true if X is a variable.
¨NAME:VAR returns the name of a variable—e.g., the name of
¨(*VAR* FOO) is FOO.

```
(DRM /? (LAMBDA () (LIST '*VAR* (READ]
(DE IS-VAR (X) (AND (CONSP X) (EQUAL (CAR X) '*VAR*]
(DE NAME:VAR (X) (AND (CONSP X) (CONSP (CDR X)) (CADR X]
```

LISP Definition of the Pattern Matcher

The pattern matcher is used by all the micro programs except micro-ELI. It is a
very important function, but also a difficult one to understand if you have never
tried to write a pattern matcher before. Therefore, besides the code for MATCH,
we have also included an informal flow chart. You should read the code and
comments carefully, and then try executing MATCH by hand on some examples.

¨MATCH takes three (predicate role-pair . . .) forms as arguments:
¨1) a CD pattern which may contain variables;
¨2) a CD constant which has no variables;
¨3) a binding form which specifies any bindings that the variables
¨   in the pattern may already have.
¨   The predicate of the binding form doesn't matter, so T is used.
¨   For convenience, MATCH also takes NIL as a binding form and
¨   converts it to (T), which is a binding form with no variables
¨   bound.
¨MATCH returns NIL only if the match failed. A match that succeeds
¨but which involved no variables returns (T).

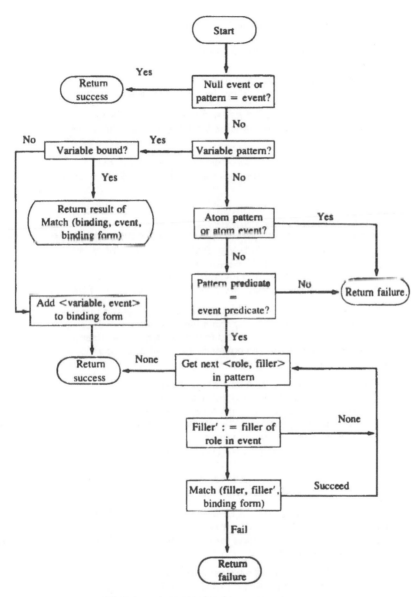

FIG. 4.1. MATCH (pattern, event, binding form).

For example, if the arguments were
pattern = (PTRANS (ACTOR (*VAR* SHOPPER)) (TO (*VAR* STORE)))
constant = (PTRANS (ACTOR (PERSON)) (TO (STORE)))
binding = (T (SHOPPER (PERSON)) (STORE (STORE)))
then the variables in the pattern are SHOPPER and STORE and the

binding form says that these variables are bound to PERSON and
STORE.
The pattern matches the constant if the predicates are equal and if
all of the roles in the pattern are matched by roles in the constant
—a variable matches if its binding matches;
—roles in the constant that are not in the pattern are ignored.

MATCH returns either NIL if the match failed or an updated binding
form that includes any new variable bindings that may have been
made.

A NIL constant always matches—this means that the pattern
(PERSON (NAME (JACK))) matches the constant (PERSON) even though the
NAME is missing.

```
(DE MATCH (PAT CONST BINDINGS)
  (LET (BINDING-FORM (OR BINDINGS (LIST T)))
    (COND ((OR (NULL CONST) (EQUAL PAT CONST)) BINDING-FORM)
          ((IS-VAR PAT) (MATCH-VAR PAT CONST BINDING-FORM))
          ((OR (ATOM CONST) (ATOM PAT)) NIL)
          ((EQUAL (HEADER:CD PAT) (HEADER:CD CONST))
           (MATCH-ARGS (ROLES:CD PAT) CONST BINDING-FORM]
```

MATCH-ARGS takes a list of role pairs (a role pair has the form
(role filler)), a constant CD form, and a binding form.
It goes through the list of pairs and matches each pair against the
corresponding role pair in the constant form—all of these must
match.

```
(DE MATCH-ARGS (PAT-ARGS CONST BINDING-FORM)
  (LOOP (INITIAL PAT-ARG NIL CONST-VAL NIL)
        (WHILE (SETQ PAT-ARG (POP PAT-ARGS)))
        (DO (SETQ CONST-VAL (FILLER:ROLE (ROLE:PAIR PAT-ARG) CONST)))
        (WHILE (SETQ BINDING-FORM
                     (MATCH (FILLER:PAIR PAT-ARG)
                            CONST-VAL
                            BINDING-FORM)))
        (RESULT BINDING-FORM]
```

MATCH-VAR takes a variable, a constant, and a binding form—
if the variable has a binding then the binding must match the
constant—otherwise the binding form is updated to bind the
variable to the constant.

```
(DE MATCH-VAR (PAT CONST BINDING-FORM)
  (LET (VAR-VALUE (FILLER:ROLE (NAME:VAR PAT) BINDING-FORM))
    (COND (VAR-VALUE (MATCH VAR-VALUE CONST BINDING-FORM))
          (T (CONS-END BINDING-FORM (LIST (NAME:VAR PAT) CONST]
```

Instantiating Patterns

The function INSTANTIATE takes a CD pattern and a binding list, such as the
one produced by MATCH, and returns a CD form with the variables in the
pattern replaced by their bindings.

```
(DE INSTANTIATE (CD-FORM BINDINGS)
        (COND ((ATOM CD-FORM) CD-FORM)
        ((IS-VAR CD-FORM)
         (INSTANTIATE (FILLER:ROLE (NAME:VAR CD-FORM) BINDINGS)
                      BINDINGS))
        (T (CONS (HEADER:CD CD-FORM)
                 (FOR (PAIR IN (ROLES:CD CD-FORM))
                      (SAVE (LIST (ROLE:PAIR PAIR)
                                  (INSTANTIATE (FILLER:PAIR PAIR)
                                               BINDINGS)
```

Expanding Macros

The functions FOR, LET, LOOP, POP and PUSH were implemented as macros
in the UCI LISP interpreter. Macros are the best way to do such things (see
Charniak et al., 1980, for reasons why) but they are inefficient. Every time a
macro is called, it has to build a new expression which is then evaluated. Some of
the programs, such as McELI, which have LOOPs inside of LOOPs, run many
times faster if the macros are expanded once and for all. An easy way to do this is
to redefine the functions DE and DF as follows:

```
(DE DEFFN (L TYPE)
 (LIST 'DEFPROP (CADR L)
       (EXPANDMACROS (CONS 'LAMBDA (CONS (CADDR L) (CDDDR L))))
       TYPE)

(DE EXPANDMACROS (X)
  (COND ((OR (ATOM X) (EQUAL (CAR X) 'QUOTE)) X)
        ((GET (CAR X) 'MACRO)
         (EXPANDMACROS ((GET (CAR X) 'MACRO) X)))
        (T (CONS (EXPANDMACROS (CAR X))
                 (EXPANDREST (CDR X)))

(DE EXPANDREST (L)
  (COND ((ATOM L) L)
        (T (CONS (EXPANDMACROS (CAR L)) (EXPANDREST (CDR L))

(DM DE (L) (DEFFN L 'EXPR)
(DM DF (L) (DEFFN L 'FEXPR)
```

where the function EXPANDMACROS is defined to take an expression and
return a new expression with all the macros expanded.

Adding Macros to Your LISP Interpreter

If your LISP interpreter does not support macros but does support FEXPRs, then
use the following, to allow the macros given above to be defined:

```
(DF DM (L)
 (PROGN
  (PUTPROP (CAR L) (CONS 'LAMBDA (CDR L)) 'MACRO)
  (PUTPROP (CAR L)
            (LIST 'LAMBDA '($$$L)
                  (LIST 'MACHAC (LIST 'QUOTE (CAR L)) '$$$L))
            'FEXPR)
  (CAR L)))

(DE MACHAC ($$$FN $$$L)
 (EVAL ((ISMACRO $$$FN) (CONS $$$FN $$$L))))
```

The unusual variable names are used to avoid variable name conflicts. The above code means that macros are really FEXPRs but defined in such a way that all the other functions used in this text, such as EXPANDMACROS, will work without change.

5 SAM

Richard Cullingford

INTRODUCTION

SAM (Script Applier Mechanism) is a system of computer programs written to investigate how knowledge of context can be used to aid in understanding stories. The basic knowledge source SAM applies is the script. Using scripts of varying degrees of complexity, SAM can read (by the process of script application) not only simple stories, but also newspaper articles referring to domains as diverse as car accidents and state visits. Each of these types of texts involve certain invariant components, such as what can happen, the order in which things happen, and who is involved. This consistency of form and content enables the script-based model of reading to be used.

The reasons for building SAM were both practical and theoretical. First, of course, we had a practical desire for a functioning, complete story understander. At the time when work began on SAM (mid-1975), there were no running programs capable of ''intelligently'' reading stories, although several theoretical proposals had been made (e.g., Charniak's 1972 ''demons'' and 1978 ''frames'' models of story comprehension). Already in existence, however, were a conceptual analyzer, ELI, the English Language Interpreter (Riesbeck and Schank, 1977), and BABEL, a Conceptual Dependency-to-English generator (Goldman, 1975). Both of these programs were incorporated into SAM.

While clearly recognizing that script application is not the whole solution to the problem of story understanding, the resulting program successfully models certain key aspects of human reading. SAM processes stories, in English, from ''left-to-right'' a sentence at a time, in one pass, making a number of necessary inferences as it goes. It can then show that it has achieved a reasonable depth of comprehension of what it has read, by generating English or other natural language summaries or paraphrases of the story, and by answering questions about it.

Scripts in SAM are collections of *episodes* with *turning-points*. The episodes are collections of events linked into *causal chains*. Each event causes one or more states which in turn cause further events. Turning points are places in a script where several different actions might follow. In a restaurant, for example, one may take a seat or wait to be taken to a seat by an employee. Turning points also include "interference" and "resolution" activities, in which the flow of action departs slightly from the "usual". For example, all the tables may be occupied when someone arrives at a restaurant (an interference in the restaurant script), but a patron may choose to wait until a table becomes available (a resolution).

In dealing with the complicated activities found in newspaper articles, we needed a way of organizing the simple scripts of the Schank and Abelson theory (Schank and Abelson, 1977) so that they could be accessed as needed by the understander. Otherwise, the understander ran the risk of being swamped by the host of potentially relevant scripts it possessed. The entities that organize simple scripts are called *situations*. Each situation gives access to a knowledge domain in a hierarchical manner, from the most important activities to the most detailed (DeJong's 1979 "issue skeletons" embody a similar idea). For example, SAM contains situations for motor-vehicle accidents, state visits, and oil spills. People read each of these types of stories to find radically different kinds of information. In a car accident story, we usually want to find out first whether anyone was killed or hurt, then what the police did, and finally the extent of the property damage. Stories about oil spills, though they also begin with an "accident," lead to a different set of questions: Did any oil escape? If so, how much? What beaches, flora and fauna are threatened by the spill?

The ranking of events within situations is governed by the concept of *instrumentality*. Certain events or actions are performed only as a means to support or implement more important, higher-level activities. Consider, as a simple example, the very common situation known as "taking a trip". Starting a car (a very rigid, simple script) is a precondition for driving it (a somewhat more complex script). Driving a car, in turn, is a possible "instrument" for taking trips of various kinds, since a person may use it to get to a place where more significant activities can take place. The "trips" themselves (very flexible, high level scripts) may involve going to the store, on a vacation or business trip, or (in the case of a Very Important Person) a state visit.

The process of script application involves several kinds of inferences. SAM reads stories in a top-down, predictive manner. Each script provides prestored expectations about what will be read, based upon what has already been seen. We identified the need for three important types of inference: causal-chain completion, role instantiation, and role merging. Causal-chain completion refers to the process of inferring the intervening events which must have taken place between two events explicitly mentioned in a story, in a manner which maintains both *causal* and *situational* continuity. Role instantiation refers to the assignment of specific references to the variables in a script, while role merging is recognizing when multiple references refer to the same specific role filler. The following example will illustrate these three different types of inferences:

John walked into a subway station. He went to the express platform.

Causal-chain completion inferences enable us to fill in all the events which must have occurred which are not mentioned explicitly in the story. Here, our knowledge of what happens in subways tells us that John went through a turnstile (after perhaps having acquired a token from a cashier) before going to the platform. We assume that he used steps or an escalator (i.e., he did not magically fly to the platform), and we never consider that he might have gotten a ticket at a ticket window, as would be the case for a train ride. Role instantiation inferences cause us to associate "John" with the role of "rider" in the subway script, and "create" a turnstile for him to go through. Role merging inferences enable us assume that the "He" in the second sentence refers to John, because the "he" is doing something that the script *predicts* a rider will do at this point, and the role instantiation inference has already established that John is the rider.

SAM is a prediction-based understander attempting to deal with stories expressed "naturally" in English. One of the things we learned in working with a large variety of stories is the variety of subtle, little noticed inferences that are necessary. These inferences are needed to reconcile expectations from causal chains with the real inputs, which often differ from these expectations in "unimportant" ways. For example, suppose we had the following story:

John entered a movie theater, went over to the ticket counter, and asked for a ticket.

The problem here is to identify that the input "... went over to the ticket counter" in fact validly instantiates the expectation which arises from the causal chain, namely "patron goes to *cashier*." The inference needed to instantiate this expectation is quite simple: Things near to the same thing are near to each other (or transitivity of proximity). SAM combines this inference with scriptal information about the cashier role (i.e., "the cashier stands near the counter") in order to conclude that in fact "(John) went over to the counter" and thus that the expectation has been satisfied.

Scripts, constructed and organized as sketched above, together with the inference processes involved in script application, appear to be necessary components for any understander operating in a predictive manner on realistic story inputs. However, aside from its intrinsic interest as an "understander" of texts of a certain kind, SAM also provides a model of one kind of processing that more general understanders of the future will have to perform.

Input/Output Examples

The following examples of input and output illustrate the level of story under-standing SAM achieved. In each case, English input is mapped into a Conceptual Dependency representation by the conceptual analyzer, ELI; and natural language output is created by the generator, BABEL.

Input Text:

JOHN WENT TO A RESTAURANT. HE ORDERED A HOT DOG. THE WAITER SAID THEY DIDN'T HAVE ANY. HE ASKED FOR A HAM-BURGER. WHEN THE HAMBURGER CAME, IT WAS BURNT. HE LEFT THE RESTAURANT.

Question-Answering Output:

Q1: DID JOHN SIT DOWN IN THE RESTAURANT?
A1: PROBABLY.

Q2: DID JOHN ORDER A HOT DOG?
A2: YES.

Q3: DID JOHN EAT A HOT DOG?
A3: NO, THE WAITER TOLD JOHN THE MANAGEMENT WAS UNABLE TO GIVE IT TO HIM.

Q4: WHAT DID THE WAITER SERVE JOHN?
A4: THE WAITER SERVED JOHN A HAMBURGER.

Q5: WHY DIDN'T JOHN EAT THE HAMBURGER?
A5: BECAUSE THE HAMBURGER WAS OVERDONE.

Q6: DID JOHN PAY THE CHECK?
A6: NO JOHN WAS ANGRY BECAUSE THE HAMBURGER WAS OVERDONE AND SO HE LEFT THE RESTAURANT.

This story, which was processed by an early version of SAM, contains several examples of the "understanding" power provided by a simple script, "going to a restaurant". In reading this story, SAM has constructed a "trace" or scenario through the script, which contains not only the events that were explicitly men-tioned, but also those that reasonably could have been inferred to have happened. An example of such a causal-chain completion inference is to be seen in the answer to Question 1, which asks about an event which usually occurs between a patron's entering a restaurant and his placing an order.

Question 4 also shows SAM's ability to *analyze in context*. The story input "(when) the hamburger came" has been identified as referring to the "serving" event. Note that the role merging inference has identified "the waiter" as the active entity in this event, given that hamburgers obviously cannot move by themselves.

In addition to inferring what happened while reading the story, SAM is also capable of making inferences at the time of *question-answering*. This arises with questions about events that did not happen. In Question 3, the non-occurrence of the highly expected "eating" event is attributed to an "interfering" condition: the restaurant was out of hot dogs. Similarly, in Questions 5 and 6, SAM infers that the reason for the second non-occurrence of "eating," followed by the customers' refusal to pay the check, is a second "interfering" condition: the hamburger was burnt. (The theory embodied in SAM's question-answering subsystem, QUALM, was developed by Wendy Lehnert, and is described in Lehnert, 1978.)

Input:

Friday evening a car swerved off Route 69. The vehicle struck a tree. The passenger, a New Jersey man, was killed. David Hall, 27, was pronounced dead at the scene by Dr. Dana Blauchard, medical examiner. Frank Miller, 32, of 593 Foxon Rd., the driver, was taken to Milford Hospital by Flanagan Ambulance. He was treated and released. No charges were made. Patrolman Robert Onofrio investigated the accident.

English Summary:

AN AUTOMOBILE HIT A TREE NEAR HIGHWAY 69 FOUR DAYS AGO. DAVID HALL, AGE 27, RESIDENCE IN NEW JERSEY, THE PASSENGER, DIED. FRANK MILLER, AGE 32, RESIDENCE AT 593 FOXON ROAD IN NEW HAVEN, CONNECTICUT, THE DRIVER, WAS SLIGHTLY INJURED. THE POLICE DEPARTMENT DID NOT FILE CHARGES.

Spanish Summary:

UN AUTO CHOCO CONTRA UN ARBOL CERCA DE LA CARRETERA 69 EL VIERNES AL ANOCHECER. DAVID HALL, DE 27 ANOS, QUE VIVIA EN NEW JERSEY, EL PASAGERO, SE MURIO. FRANK MILLER, DE 32 ANOS, QUE VIVIA EN 593 CALLE FOXON EN NEW HAVEN, CONNECTICUT, EL CHOFER, QUEDO UN POCO HERIDO. EL DEPARTAMENTO DE POLICIA NO ACUSO A NADIE.

Question-Answering Output:

Q1:   Was anyone killed?
A1:   YES, DAVID HALL DIED.

Q2:   Was anyone hurt?
A2:   YES, FRANK MILLER WAS SLIGHTLY INJURED.

Q3:   Why was Miller hurt?
A3:   BECAUSE THE AUTOMOBILE HIT THE TREE.

Q4:   Did Miller go to the hospital?
A4:   YES, HE WAS IN THE MILFORD HOSPITAL.

Q5:   How did Miller get to the hospital?
A5:   THE FLANAGAN AMBULANCE COMPANY TOOK HIM TO
       THE MILFORD HOSPITAL.

This story, a simplified version of an actual account from the *New Haven Register*, is processed by SAM using the motor-vehicle-accident situation, which contains simpler scripts for "car crash", "ambulance ride", "hospital treatment", and "police investigation". Since SAM is intended to model an average person's understanding of these knowledge domains, the latter scripts are relatively sketchy by comparison with, say, the restaurant or movie-theater script. Nevertheless, as the summary and question-answering output shows, they give SAM a reasonable level of "understanding".

The basic strategy SAM uses in reading newspaper stories is the same as that used for simpler stories. It attempts to locate the events mentioned in the story in the situation. The structure of the situation then tells SAM how to select a causally connected chain of episodes. For example, SAM must connect the input concerning a crash with the one about a person being taken to the hospital. It uses its knowledge about car accidents and the function of ambulance companies (the ambulance script) to infer the probable events that someone saw the crash and called an ambulance, that the ambulance came to the scene, that the ambulance attendants placed the person on a stretcher, etc. It also makes the crucial connection, never stated in the story, that the person who was taken to the hospital must have been *injured* in the crash. As it fills in these causal relations, it makes inferences about the script roles involved in the events. For example, it asserts that the "vehicle" which struck the tree is the "car" that left the road, and that the "New Jersey man" must be "David Hall".

SAM also has a limited capability to use the time/place setting of a story for inferences about where things are happening and how long they take. For example, the use of locational information in the car crash script leads to the conclusion, expressed in both the English and Spanish summaries, that the crash must have happened "near Route 69". Similarly, the crash must have occurred on the same day as the "swerve", namely Friday evening.

Note that the process of role instantiation may be delayed in certain cases until enough information is provided by the story. For example, the story does not give explicit information about the severity of the injuries to the man who went to the hospital. SAM delays its decision concerning this script "role" until the sentence about "treated and released" is read, at which point it concludes that he must have been "slightly injured".

Summary of SAM's Behavior

The version of SAM which was constructed for reading newspaper articles contains situations describing motor vehicle accidents, plane crashes, train wrecks, oil spills, and state visits. In each of these domains, SAM has processed at least one story, ranging from 2 to 10 input clauses, completely from English text input to English summary or question-answering output. It has also "understood" at least four other stories from each domain, using hand-coded analyses of the text.

Each of the stories processed by SAM is "distinct" in the sense that a slightly different inference process is required by each. In one story, for example, all the role merging inferences were concerned with pronominal references. In another, the merging of multiple references involved matching totally different identifications of the same person (e.g., "a New Jersey man" vs. "David Hall, 27"). More complicated inferences were also studied which involved determining when enough information had been accumulated to justify a role instantiation.

Input events are located in the script by comparing them with *patterns* from the causal chains comprising the scripts. Since the patterns are the Conceptual Dependency units of SAM's scripts, the amount of knowledge SAM possesses can perhaps be best characterized by the number of patterns it uses. The simplest situation, "train wreck", contains roughly 40 patterns, while the most complicated, "motor-vehicle accidents", contains more than 100.

SAM runs as a collection of from three to six intercommunicating modules, the number depending on the task. The modules were written in UCILISP and MLISP for a DEC System-10 computer (KA-10 central processing unit, 192K words of main memory). They range in size from about 35K words for the smallest module to 75K words for the largest, ELI. In each module, roughly half the memory was comprised of free space for working storage; the rest was assigned to "permanent" code and data.

Processing time for story understanding varied from about 20 seconds to over a minute of CPU time per input clause, of which more than half was typically consumed by the conceptual analyzer. "Logistical" reasons for the slow rate of understanding include the interpretive processing of the system's code, overhead incurred during communication between modules, and the raw speed limitations of the host computer. Little effort was expended in making SAM as small or as fast as possible.

Issues

SAM was a pioneering effort in story understanding, an attempt to directly confront the messy, but real, problems associated with reading connected texts, as opposed to isolated sentences. It was also the first system which brought enough knowledge to bear on a domain that certain interesting problems in summarization, question-answering and machine translation could be attacked.

SAM embodies a theory about the nature and use of the essential contextual component of reading. In the beginning, we looked at simple contexts, starting SAM off with simple, made-up stories about eating in restaurants and riding in subways. None of these stories were particularly interesting for a human listener, even a child. Nevertheless, the techniques developed for making causal connections, handling reference problems, using time-and-place setting, and organizing expectations were invaluable when we eventually adapted SAM to the task of reading newspaper stories. This is because, in a sense, understanding a text about a plane crash or a state visit is no harder than reading about a bus ride. The context is "bigger", but not essentially different.

The process of designing a script for a new domain is now well-understood, though tedious. SAM's approach to script management appears to be efficient enough to allow reasonable access to any piece of information a script-based system might need. Therefore, SAM and its successors are extensible. Each new script is constructed and applied in the same way as existing ones.

SAM, of course, was never a practical system, being vast, slow, and as is especially the case with multi-module programs, fragile. It is slow, however, because it tries to do the job right by understanding every word it reads at a depth that makes it possible to produce a variety of outputs that a human would find reasonable and appropriate. In a research effort directed at an area as large as text understanding, the only reasonable way to proceed is to design a system which, like SAM, consists of a community of experts, each accessing its own specialized knowledge base, as it tries to contribute to the problem at hand (cf. the "knowledge sources" of the Hearsay-II speech processing system, Erman and Lesser, 1975).

Natural language processing research has advanced to the point where a number of plausible proposals have been made describing the sources of knowledge which are needed for story understanding. To name a few, we have story grammars (Rumelhart, 1975), frame-based knowledge (Minsky, 1975; Charniak, 1972), causal/mechanical knowledge, e.g., "commonsense algorithms" (Rieger, 1975), scripts, plans, goals, and belief systems (Abelson, 1973; Schank and Abelson, 1977). The key research problem in the coming years will be to build a system capable of using these diverse sources of knowledge.

To see what some of the problems might be with such an integrated system, consider the following made-up detective story, which has elements of script-based processing in it:

> Spillane strolled into the Cafe Budapest. While the waiter was taking his order, the owner, a notorious Mafia figure, approached them threateningly.

The first sentence and the beginning of the second are clearly accounted for by the restaurant script. However, the restaurant script offers no information about the threatening approach of the owner. It simply explains what he is the owner of. Other types of knowledge structures must be employed to account for the owner's unexpected behavior. Scripts are necessary, however, to set the scene, and to indicate what is unusual or unexpected in the story. A theory of integration is clearly needed to control the interplay of knowledge sources such as is needed to understand this story. Such a theory, based on a mechanism called a *hierarchical task manager,* is under development (Cullingford, 1979), but a description of it is well beyond the scope of this book.

AN OVERVIEW OF SAM

SAM is configured as a set of three modules: ELI, which analyzes the text into a meaning representation; PP-MEMORY, which tags and identifies references to Picture Producers (PPs); and APPLIER, which applies scripts.

Control is passed around among the modules of SAM in a co-routine fashion. One program may run for a while, send elsewhere for some information it needs to continue, and eventually regain control. Since SAM is designed to read stories by making heavy use of scripts, the basic job of understanding is performed by the Script Applier. However, script knowledge can be, and is, exploited by the other modules as well.

Transforming the English text of a story into a CD meaning representation is the job of the Analyzer, ELI (English Language Interpreter). This is an extremely complicated program whose operation is described in Riesbeck (1975) and Riesbeck and Schank (1976). Script application works using the language-free output of ELI. Although ELI is an integral part of SAM, we will not discuss it in any detail here. A few comments about its function in the story understander may be helpful, however.

ELI is the only module of SAM that is concerned with linguistic knowledge, and it is the only one that worries about the particular ways that English indicates meaning via the choice of word senses, the order of words, the inflection of words, etc. ELI's job in SAM is to extract from an English sentence only the

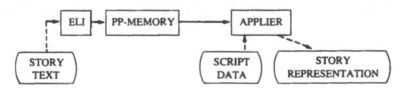

Rectangles represent processes.
Ovals represent stored information
Solid lines represent flow of control.
Dotted lines represent flow of information.

FIG. 5.1.   SAM understanding phase.

conceptual elements which are there explicitly, *avoiding inference as far as possible*. In SAM, we deliberately reserved the task of inferring the things which an input leaves out for the "memory" routines (PP-Memory and the Script Applier), rather than for ELI. This is because making inferences of this type depends on the use of world knowledge, rather than on the superficial semantic information ELI possesses as part of its knowledge of English.

ELI builds only conceptual entities which are present explicitly in the input. It constructs its meaning representations by filling slots in conceptual structures which are usually derived from the surface verb. A particular sentence invoking a conceptual structure will fill in some, but not all, of its slots. As an illustration of conceptual slots which may or may not be filled, consider how ELI would handle the following simple story:

> John took the BMT to Manhattan to see a play. At the theatre, he walked over to the ticket counter and asked for a ticket. The usher took it from him and showed him to his seat. The play was so offensive that John decided to leave. The threatre refused to refund his money.

When analyzing the first sentence, the Analyzer would not make any inference about where John came from. Similarly, in parsing ". . . asked for a ticket," it would not make any assertion about the recipient of the communication, other than the default assumption that this must be some "higher animate". Finally, ELI would not attempt to specify references, pronominal or otherwise. The inferences needed to fill empty slots or to make reference specifications depend on detailed world knowledge, and so are more properly performed by the "memory" routines.

ELI maps the surface text into a conceptualization: a piece of data expressing the "inference-free" meaning of the sentence. From this point on SAM deals directly with the meaning representation. The details of the sentence as it actually appeared in the story are lost. This mode of operation is consistent with our claim that understanding is language-free, in a deep sense. This claim is supported by many psychological experiments on the recall of text (e.g., Bartlett, 1932; Johnson-Laird, 1974; and Kintsch and Monk, 1972) which indicate that the representation of stories in memory is "conceptual" or "propositional". What is remembered are the ideas in a text, not the actual words used. ELI sends its results to PP-Memory, the second module of SAM, which is a memory for Picture Producers (PPs).

Conceptualizations are built out of two ingredients: PPs, and propositions about PPs whose central elements are the primitive ACTs and STATEs of Conceptual Dependency. (Chapter 2 introduces the meaning representation. Conceptual Dependency; for a detailed description of CD, see Schank et al., 1975.) PP-Memory's job is to find the PPs in the conceptualization and assign tokens to them. The tokens are tags or handles for the PPs which will be used by all the other parts of SAM. This module also supplies tokens for roles which the Script Applier has encountered in the course of instantiating a script path, but which were not mentioned in the input. In the above story, the Applier would tell PP-Memory to create a token for the cashier who is implicitly introduced by the conceptualization for "... asked for a ticket."

A PP in an ELI conceptualization may refer either to something SAM has seen before or something "new". Therefore, PP-Memory has to deal with the problem of *reference:* is a new PP in a conceptualization an instance of one already seen, a reference to a "permanent" token known to the system, or a pointer to someone, something, someplace, etc., not seen before? The data structures possessed by PP-Memory encode "time-invariant" facts about PPs such as the "conceptual class" they belong to (human, physical object, organization, etc.), what roles they have in different script contexts, and certain assertions about them which are true in any context. For example, the PP "chair" denotes a "physical object" which people sit on in a variety of contexts. It is realized as "chair" in a restaurant environment, and as "seat" in the bus or subway environment (since it presumably can't be moved). Attached to "chair" in a real human memory would be additional things such as its "visual image" (perhaps the chair at the person's desk), and facts such as "a chair usually has legs, a seat and a back." SAM's memory for PPs does not have much in the way of the latter kinds of information because we frankly don't yet know how to represent images and quantified assertions very well. What it does have is data about how PPs are used in script contexts. PP-Memory is a memory for scriptal roles and props.

At any point in understanding, then, SAM has a list of tokens already identified, and a set of new tokens from the current conceptualization. Some of the new tokens correspond to pronouns in the surface sentence, thus confronting us with the well-known problem of pronominal reference (e.g., in the above story, the word "he" is used to refer to John several times). A more difficult reference problem is created by the occurrence of "it" in "the usher took it from him ..." Here, recourse to detailed world knowledge from the theater script about the duties of ushers is needed to enable the correct assignment of "it" to the "ticket" John presumably got from the cashier. In each of these cases, the reference problem is solved by the Script Applier.

Another class of tokens refers to well-known people and things in the world. These are called "permanent" tokens. Examples of permanent tokens in this story are "the BMT" and "Manhattan". Although permanent tokens are identified as such immediately by PP-Memory, they may have differing script roles in different stories. "Chairman Mao", for example, might be the head of state who extended the invitation in a "visiting-dignitary" story, or the deceased VIP in a "state-burial" story. As in the case of pronominal reference, therefore, PP-references of this kind can only be settled by detailed examination of context: the PP with its associated conceptualization, and what has been read before. The reference problem is always solved cooperatively in SAM, by PP-Memory and by the Script Applier, the module which knows about contexts and what can be a role in a context.

When PP-Memory is finished processing ELI's output, it sends the result to the Script Applier. This program has three fundamental problems to solve as it processes a new conceptualization: (1) locating a new input in its database of scripts; (2) setting up predictions about likely inputs to follow; and (3) instantiating the appropriate segment of the script up to the point referred to by the input. Of these three problems, the first one, which we call the *script-management problem*, is the most important. To solve this problem, we had to answer questions such as: Which pieces of SAM's episodic knowledge are relevant at any given point in processing? When should a context be removed, and what should take its place?

The Script Applier controls the comprehension process by consulting its collection of scripts. Each script has several important parts. First, there are the script's characteristic event-chains, or episodes. Since an event in a script may be realized in the world in many ways, the events in script episodes are *patterns*. These are data structures containing constant parts which are expected to appear exactly in an input, and variable parts which define a range of alternative inputs.

A special set of patterns is found in the script "preconditions", or those global facts which SAM assumes to be true when a script is entered for the first time, unless it reads something to the contrary. When the restaurant script is activated, for example, the Script Applier will assert that the restaurant patron is hungry and has money to pay for the meal. If the text has indicated that the patron does not have any money (if, for example, he left his wallet at home), the violation of the precondition will trigger a prediction that the patron will have trouble when it comes time to pay the bill.

An important part of each script is the information which is always in active memory. This includes static data such as an initial list of those patterns which activate the script, how related episodes are combined into chunks or "scenes", time- and place-setting data for the script, and how other, simpler scripts may be used as units in the main script.

The Script Applier's control structure is sketched in Fig. 5.2. The three main procedures are a Pattern-Matcher, a Predictor, and an Instantiator. All the procedures run under an Executive, and all have access to script data. The Pattern-Matcher consists of a routine which sets up desired script contexts one at a time, the Matcher proper, and a set of auxiliary inference processes. The Predictor adds and removes event-patterns based on the pattern currently active and what has gone before.

An "active" script in SAM defines a context which consists of:

1. A list of patterns which predicts what inputs will be seen at a given point in a story.
2. A binding list which links the tokens for PPs produced by PP-Memory with script variables.

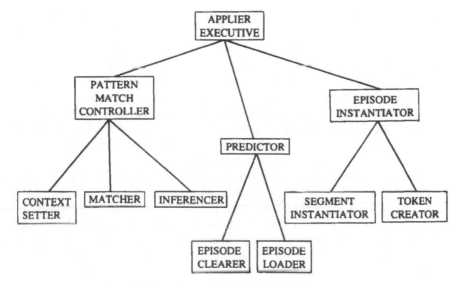

FIG. 5.2.   Script applier control structure.

3. A record of the script scenes which are currently active.
4. A list of scriptal inferences—events which have happened which interfere with the normal flow of activity in the script—which are currently outstanding.
5. A script-global "strength" indicator which SAM uses to flag how strongly it "believes" in its inferences.

The Script Applier's basic cycle is to call in these script contexts one at a time, and attempt to locate an input in the context invoked. Candidate scripts are brought into active memory in the following order: first are those script contexts which were explicitly referred to by the input or which were indirectly accessed via a PP or sub-conceptualization in the input; next are the currently active scripts; last are the scripts the system possesses but which have not been invoked.

The Applier uses its Pattern Matcher to decide which script is being referenced by an input. The matching process has two distinct phases. First the "backbone" of the pattern, i.e., the ACTs, STATEs and other constants, is matched against the backbone of the input. If the input backbone is of the right type, then the features of the PPs appearing in the input are checked against the features of the corresponding script variables.

Script variables referred to by an input may either be ones which were previously bound, or ones which have not been accessed. The feature-checking process is slightly different in each case. If the script variable is a "new" one, a process called Rolefit determines whether the candidate PP can be an instance of the variable. Since script variables are really defined by *function*, the two primary features used in Rolefit are: (1) the conceptual "class" the object belongs to, e.g., human, animate, physical object, organization, etc., and (2) any indicator of the function the PP might have. If the PP is a person, for example, Rolefit would look for an occupation, title or associated script.

If the variable is an "old" one, there already exists a PP-token which has to be compared to the new one. The comparison is carried out by a procedure called Rolemerge. This looks at the conceptual class and function of the input, as before, then checks secondary features of the input PP and the previous one (e.g., residence, age, etc.) looking for contradictions. The Rolemerge process is SAM's method of doing reference specification.

A form of pattern-directed function invocation (Hewitt, 1970) is used to check on special features of the input which SAM may be interested in at any given point. Suppose, for example, the system is reading a story about a car accident and comes to a description of injuries. When the pattern in the script for "someone was hurt" is matched, the Script Applier automatically calls a function to check to see how hurt the person was, i.e., was the person "slightly hurt," "seriously injured" or even "dead". The result of this function call would be to modify predictions about future inputs, e.g., how long the subsequent stay in a hospital is likely to be.

Once an input has been located in a script, the instantiator links it up with what has gone before in that script, and then checks on the effect this may have on other active scripts. If a script is being referenced for the first time, the Applier checks on the script Preconditions to see whether a script is being entered normally, or whether some unusual events are to be expected in the new context because of a previous event. If more than one script is active, the Applier may be able to update the story representation on the basis of the static information that is always available for the scripts. For example, the bus script contains the information that this script is "sequential" with the train script. That is, if the bus script is active when the train script is first invoked, the instantiation of the bus script must be completed before the train script is started. On the other hand, the train script contains the information that a reference to the restaurant script context via "dining car" in an existing train script context defines a "parallel-nested" relationship. Inputs to follow may refer to either script, but the restaurant script should be completed before the train script.

Many transactions between component scripts are handled by the more complex scripts which define the "global" context of the story. For example, taking a bus, train, plane, etc., are known to be "instrumental" means of reaching or leaving the place where the "goal" activity of a trip takes place. The global trip script may be explicitly introduced, as in "John went to Miami on a business trip", or implicitly referenced by one of its instruments, as in "John took a train to Miami." Script situations, as these global scripts are called, provide the most important machinery for the solution of what we have called the script-management problem.

When the linking process has been completed, SAM updates its predictions about the context, based on the new input and what has gone before, by merging the specific incremental predictions associated with the pattern that was matched with the script global search list. The updated context is then stored, and the next round of processing is started with a call to ELI. After the whole text has been absorbed, the Script Applier constructs a representation of the story that is used by all the postprocessing routines. The representation is a network of causally connected conceptualizations: both those which were explicitly accessed by an input, and those which could be inferred to have happened. "Header" information is also provided which the summarizing and question-answering modules use to get at the important events in the network, the global structure of the story in terms of the scripts which were referred to, and the details of the script role bindings.

SAM's summary and paraphrase methods are discussed in Schank et al. (1975) and Schank and Abelson (1977). Briefly, these routines access the story representation and pick out the "interesting" events recorded there. Since the CD structures SAM deals with internally are interlingual, output can be generated in any language which incorporates the requisite world knowledge. As a machine translation system, SAM can express summaries or paraphrases in Mandarin Chinese and Spanish, or simulate "simultaneous translation" of an English story into Chinese (Stutzman, 1976). The generators used by SAM are modifications of Goldman's BABEL program (Goldman, 1975).

The summary/paraphrase task is one of choosing what it seems appropriate to say. Even if we have the means for expressing any conceivable conceptualization memory may have access to, there is the prior problem of deciding which ones are the best response in a given situation. That is, the summary/paraphrase process has to answer these two questions: (1) which of the conceptualizations marked by the Script Applier as being important are "interesting" enough to be expressed? and (2) what time- or place-setting information should be included to formulate the result into a connected whole?

The ability to answer questions about a story that has been read is in many ways the most crucial test of whether the story has really been understood. The theory underlying SAM's question-answering (Q/A) capability is provided by Lehnert's QUALM, discussed in detail in Lehnert (1978).

AN ANNOTATED EXAMPLE

This section presents some excerpts from the processing log SAM kept as it read a three-line story about a state visit of the Premier of Albania to China.

Our sample story is understood by SAM as referring to the VIP-visit script situation, which has component scripts for travelling, parades, banquets, etc. The first output is from the understanding phase of SAM. Then a summary for the story is expressed in English and Spanish. Finally, SAM answers several questions about the story.

The text of the story is as follows:

> Sunday morning Enver Hoxha, the Premier of Albania, and Mrs. Hoxha arrived in Peking at the invitation of Communist China. The Albanian party was welcomed at Peking Airport by Foreign Minister Huang. Chairman Hua and Mr. Hoxha discussed economic relations between China and Albania for three hours.

Though superficially quite simple, this story contains very real problems of analysis, inference and generation, as will be indicated below. Although the log contains output from every module of SAM, the emphasis will be on the interactions of the "deep-memory" modules, viz., PP-Memory and the Script Applier, rather than on the internal workings of the other modules. The Conceptual Analyzer, in particular, carries a large processing load in SAM. Except for the most complex stories, it uses the most CPU time of all the routines. However, the log will contain only the sentences input to it and the LISP CD representations it computes.

The log from which these excerpts were taken was made under a DEC System-10 utility program called OPSER, which has facilities for starting up and controlling several jobs, and sending any output from the jobs to a single terminal. Lines beginning with a "!" are OPSER messages indicating the module from which succeeding lines of output came. PARSER is the Conceptual Analyzer, TOK is PP-Memory, and APPLY is the Script Applier.

SAM starts up with the Script Applier in control:

```
!(APPLY)
SCRIPT APPLIER MECHANISM ... VERSION 4.1 ... 12 JULY 1976
PROCESSING NEWSPAPER TEXT (TEXT . V3)
AVAILABLE SCRIPTS:
($TRAINWRECK $VIPVISIT $VEHACCIDENT)
GETTING NEW INPUT
```

The version of the Script Applier shown here processes newspaper stories about train wrecks, state visits and motor-vehicle accidents. It contains special procedures for handling lead sentences, making predictions from what it finds in them, and taking care of the reference problems that the complicated noun groups found in these stories often cause.

PARSER gets control and analyzes the first sentence. The conceptualization for "arrived" says that a group consisting of Premier and Mrs. Hoxha PTRANSed themselves into the city of Peking, and that the arrival happened in some temporal relation to an invitation by Communist China. (PTRANS is the

CD action primitive for events which contain a change in physical location. The MODE specifier on the conceptualization indicates that the PTRANS ceased ("arrived" vs. "went") in Peking.)

Next TOK replaces references to PPs in the conceptualization with tokens which name the property-list structures that the memory modules use. If the PP is a "permanent token", a well-known person or place in the world, TOK also copies the information from the permanent token onto the new token created for this story. "Enver Hoxha", "Peking", and "Albania" are examples of permanent tokens.

```
!(PARSER)
Sunday morning Enver Hoxha, the Premier of Albania, and Mrs. Hoxha arrived in Peking at
the invitation of Communist China.

CONCEPT. GN1
((ACTOR TMP32 <=> (*PTRANS*) OBJECT TMP32
                    TO (*INSIDE* PART (#POLITY POLTYPE  (*MUNIC*)
                                                POLNAME (PEKING)))
                    FROM (NIL) INST (NIL))
MODE (MOD1) TIME (TIME2))

MOD1 = (*TF*)

TIM2 = ((WHEN TMP7)(DAYPART MORNING)(WEEKDAY SUNDAY))

TMP7 = ((<=>($INVITATION INVITER (#POLITY POLTYPE  (*NATION*)
                                            POLNAME (COMMUNIST CHINA))
                        INVITEE (NIL)
                        INVITOBJ (NIL))))

TMP32 = (#GROUP MEMBER (#PERSON GENDER (*FEM*)
                                    LASTNAME (HOXHA))
                MEMBER (#PERSON GENDER (*MASC*)
                                FIRSTNAME (ENVER) LASTNAME (HOXHA)
                                TITLE (PREMIER)
                                POLITY (#POLITY POLNAME (ALBANIA)
                                                POLTYPE  (*NATION*))
                        REF (DEF)))

!(TOK)
top level PARSER atom is: GN1

processing PP:
(#GROUP MEMBER TMP24 MEMBER TMP28)
creating new token: GROUP0

processing PP:
(#PERSON GENDER TMP25 LASTNAME TMP26)
creating new token: HUM0

processing PP:
(#PERSON GENDER TMP11 FIRSTNAME TMP12 LASTNAME TMP13 TITLE TMP19
            POLITY  TMP20 REF TMP23)
creating new token: HUM1
```

```
processing PP:
(#POLITY POLNAME TMP21 POLTYPE TMP22)
creating new token: POLIT0

processing PP:
(#POLITY POLTYPE TMP59 POLNAME TMP60)
creating new token: POLIT1

processing PP:
(#POLITY POLTYPE TMP74 POLNAME TMP75)
creating new token: POLIT2

PERMANENT TOKEN IDENTIFIED:
POLIT2 IS !POL101
PERMANENT TOKEN IDENTIFIED:
POLIT1 IS !POL100
PERMANENT TOKEN IDENTIFIED:
POLIT0 IS !POL103
PERMANENT TOKEN IDENTIFIED:
HUM1 IS !HUM100

top level TOK atom for GN1 is MEM0

!(APPLY)
NEW INPUT: MEM0
```

At this point, the Script Applier has received the conceptualization with tokens added, representing the meaning of the first sentence of the story. It is important to note what the PARSER and TOK have done, and what they did not do. The PARSER has not attempted any inferences about where the Hoxhas came from, or how they got to Peking, although world knowledge suggests that they probably flew from their homeland, Albania, to China. Furthermore, though we know that invitations characteristically precede the invited person's actually going somewhere, PARSER has suggested only that there is some temporal relation between the inviting and arriving events. The surface string or input does not directly state who was invited or what the reason for the invitation was, so the PARSER leaves the corresponding slots in the conceptualization empty.

TOK has provided tokens for the PPs appearing in the conceptualization, e.g., the Premier and his wife. It has also recognized that the Premier, Peking, Albania and China are permanent tokens. Like PARSER, however, TOK does not have the knowledge required to infer that the group that arrived is the one that was invited, so it leaves this slot alone. Finally, TOK has not been able to suggest a possible script that the PPs in this conceptualization may be participating in. This is because people, cities and nations are associated with so many contexts that it is impossible to make a processing suggestion.

APPLY searches first for the imbedded "invitation".

```
!(APPLY)
FINDING IMBEDDED CDS: (MEM6)
```

SEARCHING FOR MEM6 IN SCRIPT $TRAINWRECK
SEARCHING FOR MEM6 IN SCRIPT $VIPVISIT

LOCATED AT VAR1
BOUND SCRIPT VARIABLE: &INVGSTATE TO POLIT2
TRACK $VIP1 of $VIPVISIT ACTIVATED

SETTING PARSER WORD-SENSES FOR $VIPVISIT

APPLY searches for the input in the trainwreck script and fails. Invitation is found in the VIP-visit script. The pattern found also says that China fills the role of the state which extended the invitation.

Now the system is primed to read more about events from the VIP-visit script domain. APPLY was able to identify the nature of the invitation from the fact that a nation, China, was doing the inviting, rather than a private citizen. Since SAM now assumes that it knows which context is active, it biases the Analyzer to check first on words and phrases which are appropriate for the state-visit context.

APPLY now looks for the "arrival" that was mentioned in the input:

SEARCHING FOR MEM0 IN SCRIPT $VIPVISIT

PATTERN BACKBONE MATCHED AT VAR3
VARIABLE BINDING CONTRADICTION IN (&PTRORG . GROUP0)
TRYING INFERENCE TYPE CONVEY ON VAR3
PATTERN BACKBONE MATCHED ON DERIVED PATTERN:
((ACTOR &INVDGRP <=> (*PTRANS*) OBJECT &INVDGRP TO
            (*INSIDE* PART &INITDEST)))
SUCCCESSFUL MATCH ON DERIVED PATTERN

LOCATED AT VAR3
BOUND SCRIPT VARIABLE:
&INITDEST TO POLIT1
&INVDGRP TO GROUP0

GETTING NEW INPUT

Now that the first sentence has been read, a number of predictions about what will come next have been made, and some of the script's variables have been identified. The pattern-match on the "arrival" event contains a typical example of the auxiliary inferencing processes SAM uses to reconcile small differences between an input and a pattern which encodes a specific expectation about what will be read. One of the predictions which is active when the top-level conceptualization is accessed is for a journey by the invited person, specifically, a pattern for an organization such as an airline company or a passenger shipping line to move this person, or a group containing this person, to the country making the invitation. What SAM gets instead is a conceptualization in which a VIP party moves itself there. In this circumstance, SAM infers that the VIPs were moved by an organization which wasn't mentioned. If this pattern were instantiated for inclusion in the story representation at this time, APPLY would assume that an airline was, in fact, the organization that did the moving.

SAM now starts on the second sentence of the story. PARSER interprets this as a "state welcome" since it is the VIP-visit script which is active:

```
!(PARSER)
The Albanian party was welcomed at Peking Airport by Foreign Minister Huang.

CONCEPT: GN7
((<=> ($VIPWELCOME WELCOMER (#PERSON TITLE (FOREIGN MINISTER)
                                            LASTNAME (HUANG))
                   WELCOMEE TMP55))
TIME (TIM3) MODE (MOD7))

TMP55 = (#GROUP RESIDENCE (#POLITY POLTYPE (*NATION*)
                                   POLNAME (ALBANIA))
                REF (DEF))

TIM3 = ((WHEN TMP72))

TMP72 = ((ACTOR TMP55 IS (*LOC* VAL (*PROX*
                 PART (#LOCALE LOCTYPE  (*AIRPORT*)
                               LOCNAME (PEKING))))))
```

As in the first sentence, the top-level conceptualization for "welcomed" is related to another conceptualization by a temporal link. The modifying conceptualization states that "the Albanian party" (a group pronoun) was in the proximity of "Peking Airport". After TOK has processed PARSER's output, APPLY looks for the latter event:

```
!(APPLY)

SEARCHING FOR MEM15 IN SCRIPT $VIPVISIT

TRYING INFERENCE TYPE IMRES ON VAR4
PATTERN BACKBONE MATCHED ON DERIVED PATTERN:
((ACTOR &INVDGRP IS (*LOC* VAL (*PROX* PART &PTRTERM))))

SUCCESSFUL MATCH ON DERIVED PATTERN
LOCATED AT VAR4

ROLE INSTANTIATED: &PTRORG

!(TOK)
creating new token: ORGO

!(APPLY)
GOT TOKEN ORGO FOR &PTRORG
BOUND SCRIPT VARIABLE:
&PTRTERM TO LOC0
```

This sequence illustrates a typical interaction between APPLY and TOK in the process of inferencing during pattern-matching. APPLY is looking for a pattern where the VIP group comes to the arrival point (e.g., an airport), while the story talks about their already being "at Peking Airport". Thus SAM must make the inference that because the group is already at the airport, they must have arrived there previously. Also, because an airport has been mentioned, APPLY now knows the identity of the transporting organization. It calls TOK to obtain a token of the right type, and binds it to the appropriate script variable.

Now APPLY searches for the "welcoming" event:

```
SEARCHING FOR MEM11 IN SCRIPT $VIPVISIT
PATTERN BACKBONE MATCHED AT WEL4
CHECKING GROUPS: (GROUP1 GROUP0)
POSSIBLE REFERENCE FOUND: GROUP1 IS GROUP0
LOCATED AT WEL4

MERGING TOKENS ((GROUP1 . GROUP0))
```

Here we see the first case of a reference that needs to be filled in. When TOK identified the Hoxhas as permanent tokens, it copied the information it had about these individuals onto the tokens created for them in this story. Additionally, the Hoxha family group was marked as having the same residence as its members, Albania. The group for "the Albanian party" is merged with the original group on this basis. Since SAM keeps only one token around for each script variable, it tells TOK to copy any new information available from the second token it made for the Hoxhas onto the first, and throw the second one away.

This TOK does, and SAM starts on the final sentence of the story:

```
!(PARSER)
Chairman Hua and Mr. Hoxha discussed economic relations between China and Albania for
three hours.

CONCEPT: GN13
((ACTOR TMP171 <=> (*MTRANS*)
 MOBJECT (*CONCEPTS* REGARDING
              (#CONTRACT
                  TYPE (*ECONOMY*)
                  PARTY (#GROUP MEMBER (#POLITY POLTYPE  (*NATION*)
                                               POLNAME (ALBANIA))
                        MEMBER (#POLITY POLTYPE  (*NATION*)
                                               POLNAME (CHINA)))))
 INST ((ACTOR TMP171 <=> (*SPEAK*)))
   FROM (*CP* PART TMP171) TO (*CP* PART TMP171))
 TIME (TIM7) MODE (MOD3))

TMP171 = (#GROUP MEMBER (#PERSON GENDER (*MASC*)
                           LASTNAME (HOXHA))
            MEMBER (#PERSON TITLE (CHAIRMAN)
                           LASTNAME (HUA)))
```

PARSER interprets this event as a dual-MTRANS involving a group consisting of Hoxha and Hua, about an "economic contract" (agreement of some sort) between the countries of Albania and China. After TOK has finished, APPLY searches for the event in $VIPVISIT:

```
!(APPLY)
SEARCHING FOR MEM20 IN SCRIPT $VIPVISIT
PATTERN BACKBONE MATCHED AT TALK2

LOCATED AT TALK2

BOUND SCRIPT VARIABLE:
&INVITOBJ TO CNTRCT0
&GRP1 T8 GROUP2
```

Now all three sentences have been recognized within the VIP-visit script. The final conceptualization about an economic agreement has realized one of the main conceptualizations (Maincons) of the script, since this is a possible reason for the state visit. Other possible reasons, not instantiated in this story, include the signing of a treaty or the issuance of an official communique. APPLY is prepared at this point to hear about other official ceremonies, or about the VIPs leaving Peking for home.

There are no more story inputs, so APPLY builds a memory representation for the story:

```
BUILDING STORY REPRESENTATION FOR (TEXT.V3)

MAKING STORY SEGMENT FOR SUBSCENE $VARRIVE1 IN $VIPVISIT
MAKING STORY SEGMENT FOR SUBSCENE $VWELCOME1 IN $VIPVISIT
MAKING STORY SEGMENT FOR SUBSCENE $VTALK1 IN $VIPVISIT

BINDING SCRIPT VARIABLE &MTGPLC TO POLIT1

EVENT GRAPH:
((EVNT1 EVNT2 EVNT3 EVNT4)
 (EVNT5 EVNT6 EVNT7)
 (EVNT8 EVNT9))
```

This story has instantiated three episodes from the VIP-visit script: (1) an episode in which a VIP group travels to Peking; (2) an official-greeting episode, acted out, in this case, at Peking Airport; and (3) an instance of the "official talks" episode. APPLY uses the script-variable bindings it has accumulated during the recognition part of the run to instantiate the events in these episodes. Along the way, it has made inferences about variables which the story did not explicitly mention. For example, the place where Hua and Hoxha met for their talks was not explicitly stated, so APPLY assumes it was in the city where the Hoxha party arrived. The result of the instantiation process is the "event graph" of instantiated, interconnected episodes. The event graph, the details of the script variable bindings, and other information about the story are stored in permanent memory.

At a later time, this information is loaded by the summary postprocessor of SAM, which selects events of interest and passes them to a Generator for expression. In the output shown below, ENGLSH is the English generator, and SPANSH is the Spanish generator. (The summarizer SAM uses was programmed by Jerry DeJong. The Spanish output was obtained from a modification of Goldman's BABEL, programmed by Jaime G. Carbonell.)

!(ENGLSH)

CONSTRUCTING SUMMARY FROM STORY (TEXT . V3)

PREMIER ENVER HOXHA, THE ALBANIA GOVERNMENT HEAD, AND
CHAIRMAN HUA KUO-FENG, THE CHINA GOVERNMENT HEAD, DISCUSSED
ALBANIA/COMMUNIST-CHINA ECONOMIC AFFAIRS IN PEKING, CHINA
TWO DAYS AGO.

For this simple story, the summarizer has chosen to express only the script Maincon. The Maincon has been augmented by setting information provided by the Script Applier. For example, APPLY has inferred that the official discussions took place in Peking, China. The information that TOK had as part of its knowledge of the permanent tokens ''Enver Hoxha'' and ''Chairman Hua'' has been reflected in the summary by the additional information about their names and occupations that ENGLSH has been instructed to express.

Now the Spanish generator expresses the summarizer output:

!(SPANSH)

CONSTRUCTING SUMMARY FROM STORY (TEXT . V3)

EL JEFE DEL GOBIERNO DE CHINA, HUA, Y EL PRIMER MINISTRO
DE ALBANIA, HOXHA, DISCUTIERON UN TRATADO SOBRE ASUNTOS
ECONOMICOS EN PEKING.

Finally, SAM answers some questions about the story it has read. In the Q/A configuration of SAM, PARSER, TOK and ENGLSH are the Analyzer, PP-Memory and English Generator, as before. QA is the question-answering module. The details of the Q/A strategies incorporated in SAM can be found in Lehnert (1978).

PARSER analyzes the first question:

!(PARSER)
Who went to China?

CONCEPT: GN1002
((ACTOR TMP8 <=> (*PTRANS*) OBJECT TMP8
    TO (*PROX* PART (#POLITY POLTYPE (*NATION*)
                                   POLNAME (CHINA)))
    FROM (NIL) INST (NIL))
MODE (MOD0) TIME (TIM2))

TMP8 = (*?*)

!(TOK)
top level PARSER atom is: GN1002

processing PP:
(#POLITY POLTYPE TMP39 POLNAME TMP40)
creating new token: POLIT101

top level TOK atom for GN1002 is MEM101

PARSER interprets this as a question, marked by (*?*), about the ACTOR of
a PTRANS which ended up in the vicinity of China. TOK assigns a token to
China in the usual way. Then QA gets control:

!(QA)
NEXT QUESTION:
((ACTOR (*?*) <=> (*PTRANS*) OBJECT (*?*)
              TO (*PROX* PART POLIT101)))

(QUESTION TYPE IS CONCCOMP)
(SEARCHING $VIPVISIT-SCRIPT STRUCTURE)
(FOUND AT SCRIPT STRUCTURE LEVEL)

THE ANSWER IS:
(GROUP0)

!(ENGLSH)
PREMIER ENVER HOXHA AND MRS. HOXHA

QA takes the conceptual question, identifies it as a query about a role in a
conceptualization, and searches the story representation for an answer. It finds
the needed role-filler, Premier Hoxha and his wife, and instructs ENGLSH to
express this answer.

The answer to the question "Who went to China?" depends, as is usually the
case, on an inference. First of all, the story does not explicitly say that anyone
went to China, only that an official party arrived in Peking. The answer depends
on the causal-chain inference that an arrival in the capital of a country (or
anywhere else in the country) must be preceded by entering that country. The
Script Applier, as part of its world knowledge about official visits, built this

information into the top level of the story representation. Why the top level? The VIP-visit script is a special case of the trip script. People, especially VIPs, are always taking trips, using standard means of transportation (that is, scripts whose Maincons are based on a PTRANS) to get to and from the places they want to visit. The VIP-visit script has the general structure of a trip. Therefore, the Script Applier keeps a record of the "going" part of the trip, which the question-answering module accesses to find the answer to the question "Who went to China?"

```
!(PARSER)
How did they get to China?

CONCEPT: GN1008
((ACTOR TMP103 <=> (*PTRANS*) OBJECT TMP103
                    TO (*PROX* PART (#POLITY POLTYPE (*NATION*)
                                             POLNAME (CHINA)))
               FROM (NIL) INST (*?*))
MODE (MOD1) TIME (TIM5))

TMP103 = (#GROUP MEMBER (#PERSON) REF (DEF))

!(QA)
NEXT QUESTION:
((ACTOR GROUP101 <=> (*PTRANS*) OBJECT GROUP101
TO (*PROX* PART POLIT102) INST (*?*)))

(QUESTION TYPE IS INSTPROC)
(SEARCHING $VIPVISIT-SCRIPT STRUCTURE)

THE ANSWER IS:
((ACTOR ORG0 <=> (*PTRANS*) OBJECT GROUP0
                TO (*PROX* PART POLIT2)))

!(ENGLSH)
MRS. HOXHA AND PREMIER ENVER HOXHA FLEW TO COMMUNIST-CHINA
```

The answer to the question "How did they get to China?" depends on three crucial inferences that the Script Applier has made. First, "they" must be recognized as the Hoxha party. This is a reference problem which TOK and QA solve by using the same methods that the Script Applier used to determine the reference for "the Albanian party" in the story input. Secondly, "China" was recognized as "Communist China" by the Script Applier, rather than "Nationalist China", on the basis of its knowledge of where "Peking" is. Finally, the instrumental means that enabled the Hoxhas to get to China was determined by a role-instantiation inference that the Script Applier made when the phrase "... welcomed at Peking Airport" was read. As in the answer to "Who went to China?", the answer to "How did they get there?" is stored in the story representation as the instrument of the conceptualization which summarizes the "going" part of the State-Visit Trip.

!(PARSER)
Why did Enver Hoxha go to China?

CONCEPT: GN1015
((CON (*?*) LEADTO
    ((ACTOR TMP160 <=> (*PTRANS*) OBJECT TMP160
            TO (*PROX* PART
                     (#POLITY POLTYPE (*NATION*)
                          POLNAME (CHINA)))
            FROM (NIL) INST (NIL))
            MODE (MOD2) TIME (TIM6))) MODE (NIL))

TMP160 = (#PERSON GENDER (*MASC*) FIRSTNAME (ENVER)
                            LASTNAME (HOXHA))

!(QA)
NEXT QUESTION:
((CON (*?*) LEADTO
    ((ACTOR HUM102 <=> (*PTRANS*) OBJECT HUM102
            TO (*PROX* PART POLIT103)))))

(QUESTION TYPE IS CAUSANT)
(SEARCHING $VIPVISIT-SCRIPT STRUCTURE)

THE ANSWER IS:
(BECAUSE ((CON ((ACTOR GROUP2 <=> (*MTRANS*)
                     INST ((ACTOR GROUP2 <=> (*SPEAK*)))
                     MOBJECT (*CONCEPTS* REGARDING CNTRCTO)
                     FROM (*CP* PART GROUP2)) TIME (TIME10))
         IS (*GOAL* PART (GROUP2))) TIME (TIME10)))

!(ENGLSH)
BECAUSE CHAIRMAN HUA KUO-FENG AND MR. ENVER HOXHA WANTED TO DIS-
CUSS CHINA/ALBANIA ECONOMIC AFFAIRS.

This concludes our sample computer run of SAM on a newspaper story. Let's highlight once more some of the important inference processes which actually came into play as SAM read this story.

As the first sentence is processed, a procedure called Rolefit checks to see that at least one member of the group that arrived is a Very Important Person. This is done to establish that this event fits into VIP-visit script rather than some other script, such as the tourist script. An allied process, Rolemerge, is used in the second sentence to determine that "the Albanian party" is the same group as the one mentioned in the first sentence, namely Premier and Mrs. Hoxha. Note that in the second sentence, a special sense of "welcome" is used which typically involves bands, speeches, etc. This sense of "welcome" is itself a script imbedded in the VIP-visit script, and is analyzed as such by SAM within the state-visit context.

Other inferences which SAM makes can be seen in the outputs produced for the story. The need for time- and place-setting information can be seen in the summary, which asserts that the meeting between Hua and Hoxha occurred in

Peking on the same day as the arrival, even though the story does not explicitly say this. (SAM inserts the phrase "two days ago" because it is arranged, by convention, to be reading newspaper articles on Tuesday.) The answer to "Who went to China?" depends on a causal-chain inference, that going to Peking must be preceded by entering the country that Peking is part of. Finally, a role-instantiation inference is required in answering the question "How did they get to China?", which assumes that visiting VIPs who are greeted at airports were transported by plane. This is a typical useful, but only "probably" true, natural inference that story understanders make all the time.

THE PROGRAM ITSELF

Script Structure

This section describes some of the important features of script structure. We will return to the subway script as an illustration.

What does a "standard" trip on the subway look like (in New York, for example)? A patron enters the station and goes to a turnstile. Next, the patron puts a token in, passes through, and goes to the appropriate platform. Eventually, the train comes. The patron enters and finds a seat. After a number of stops, the destination is reached, the patron leaves the train and exits from the station.

This stereotyped sequence of events is the "backbone" of the subway script, $SUBWAY, as understood and used by millions of commuters in New York, and, with minor variations, in other cities as well. In each case, what we have is an organization (the subway company or Authority) providing a certain kind of transportation to a member of the public in return for money. In the fundamental subway script, there is a cast of characters ("roles"); the objects they use while going about their business ("props"); and the places ("settings") where the script's activities happen. The roles, props and settings of a script taken together make up the script *variables*, which are matched up against the real-world people, places and things that a story contains. (Upper case names preceded by "$" indicate a script, and names preceded by "&" indicate a role from a script. Thus, DRIVER would be the "driver" role from the bus script, $BUS.)

Below is a list of the roles of the subway script:

&PATGRP	a group of subway riders
&CASHIER	the cashier
&CONDUCTOR	the conductor
&DRIVER	the person controlling the train
&SUBORG	the subway organization

Picture Producers (PPs) which fill script roles must belong to one of the "primitive", higher-animate PP-classes of Conceptual Dependency. For example, the patron role in $SUBWAY must be filled by a PP of the class "person" or "group", since we want to be able to accept both "John Smith" and "Mr. and Mrs. Smith" as role fillers. The subway company providing the service, for example, "the BMT", must belong to the class "organization".

The settings of a script are the places where the script's events happen. Settings belong to the PP-class "locale". In $SUBWAY, the three most important settings are the originating station, the inside of the car the patron selects, and the destination station.

The props of a script are associated either with the script's roles or its settings. Examples of the former are small objects, such as tokens and coins (PP-class "money"), which people handle and carry around. The latter props have the function of "furniture" in a setting. For example, the cashier's booth and the turnstile are furniture in the subway concourse; seats and bubble gum machines are furniture on a platform. (These PPs have the class "physical object".) A special prop in $SUBWAY is the train itself. This is an example of a "structured" physical object whose parts, the cars, are important locations for script activity in their own right. The props of $SUBWAY include:

&TOKEN	a token
&FARE	money paid for a token
&TURNSTILE	a turnstile
&PLATSEAT	a seat on the platform
&SUBWAY	the train itself
&SUBWAYCAR	one of the cars
&CARSEAT	a seat on the car
&STRAP	a strap for the patron to grasp
&EXITGATE	the gate leading from the platform at the destination station

The most important components of $SUBWAY are its events, involving the roles, props and settings. An example is the patron's giving money to the cashier at the cashier's cage. The events in all of SAM's scripts are based on a single CD ACT or STATE primitive, with appropriate script variables filling the slots in the conceptual structure. The event described above would look like:

```
((ACTOR &PATGRP <=> (*ATRANS*)
  OBJECT &FARE TO &CASHIER))
```

This uses the CD action primitive ATRANS, which signals an abstract transfer of possession or control.

Several things need to be emphasized about events in scripts. First of all, they are *language-free*. The CD representation of an event provides a canonical form into which SAM's Analyzer maps the many surface strings or inputs which are conceptually "equivalent". We would use the same form whether the sentence were "John gave 50 cents to the cashier," "The cashier got 50 cents from

John," or "50 cents was received from John by the cashier." The use of CD representation thus cuts down tremendously on the size of the script, since only the conceptual content of sentences need be considered. It also reduces the amount of processing SAM needs to do, since the needed inferences can be tied directly to the conceptual events, rather than having to be duplicated for each "equivalent" surface string.

Another point about script events is that they contain both "constant" parts (e.g., ACTOR and *ATRANS* in the example given above) and "variable" parts (e.g., &PATGRP and &FARE). Each event, therefore, is really a *pattern*—a data structure designed to match an arbitrary range of real-world events. For example, any member of the public can ride on the subway, so the corresponding slot in the script's events cannot be fixed but must accept any person or group that comes along in a story. In the "paying the cashier in the subway" activity, we need a way to specify the things which are always true. For example, this event has a person handing over an amount of money to another person who is an agent of the subway organization. We also have to provide for things which can vary in small details. The fare may be expressed as "fifty cents" or a "half dollar", "John" may pay the cashier, or "John and Mary" may pay.

In one common form of pattern matching, a script role is compared with a person or organization mentioned in a story. The following is a definition of a typical person as it would exist in property-list format in PP-Memory:

"Dr. Marcus Welby, 53, of 45 Orchard St., New York"

HUM0:
      CLASS (#PERSON)
      TITLE (DOCTOR)
      OCCUPATION (*MD*)
      (PERSNAME (MARCUS)
      SURNAME (WELBY)
      AGE (53)
      GENDER (*MASC*)
      RESIDENCE (LOC0)

LOC0:
      CLASS (#LOCALE)
      LOCTYPE (*ADDRESS*)
      STREETNUMBER (45)
      STREETNAME (ORCHARD STREET)
      POLITY (POL0)

POL0:
      CLASS (#POLITY)
      POLTYPE (*MUNIC*)
      POLNAME (NEW YORK)

(We're assuming that "Marcus Welby" is a permanent token known to PP-Memory. This is the basis for the specification of "medical-doctor" under the OCCUPATION property. Similarly, "New York" is known to be a city.)

Suppose that Marcus Welby is taking a ride on the subway. At some point, the token HUM0 might be matched up against the script variable for the patron role, &PATGRP. This script variable has the following property-list definition:

&PATGRP:
    CLASS (#PERSON #GROUP)
    DUMMY T
    SFUNCTION (*NONE*)

This means that the atom &PATGRP is a dummy variable to be bound to PPs belonging to either the PP-class "person" or "group". Since Welby is a person, so far so good. The property SFUNCTION states that a PP which can fill this role in the script must not have some other function in the script (i.e., a subway patron can not be the same person as the subway train driver). Indicators of the functions people can have are to be found on the OCCUPATION and FUNCTION properties of the corresponding token. Here, the occupation *MD* is not one which is internal to $SUBWAY, so again the PP checks out. If, however, the PP were "Marcus Welby, the driver", the token would contain a FUNCTION (*DRIVER*) flag, and the possible role of Welby as the "driver" of the subway would prevent the acceptance of the PP as an instance of the patron role.

This simple example of the relation between a script variable and the real PPs that may instantiate it illustrates two basic facts about roles and props in scripts. First is the observation that they are "abstract" or "generalized". It doesn't matter that Welby is a masculine adult, since all kinds of people ride on subways. This leads to a second fact, namely, that script variables are really defined by *function*. Concentrating on what people do and what objects are for (this might be called an "episodic" approach), rather than on the details of their structure as bundles of features representing various abstract classes (a "semantic" approach) makes psychological sense. When asked what a waiter is, for example, people invariably reply on some functional basis such as "a person who takes orders in a restaurant and brings people their food."

The basic idea in defining a pattern is to include only the minimum amount of information needed to uniquely identify the event. Consider, for example, the pattern for:

"Patron enters station"

((ACTOR &PATGRP <=> (*PTRANS*)
           OBJECT &PATGRP
           TO (*INSIDE* PART &STATION1)))

This pattern would be matched by the conceptualizations corresponding to inputs such as:

(a) John and Mary went into a subway station.
(b) John walked into a subway station.
(c) John strolled out of a restaurant up the street into a subway station.
(d) John went into the BMT.

Example (a) would instantiate the pattern because, as we explained above, John and Mary form a group undistinguished by function. In example (b), the pattern would consider the fact that John "walked" to the subway as insignificant; it would create the same conceptualization if John had "sauntered", "rambled", "ran", or even "come in on a skateboard". In (c), where John came from is of no interest to $SUBWAY, although in this case, it would constitute a signal to $RESTAURANT (presumably active at this point) that this script should be closed before $SUBWAY is opened. Finally, (d) would instantiate the pattern because PP-Memory would contain a permanent token for "BMT", which is marked as a subway organization.

An important class of patterns which will serve to illustrate all of them is that of *headers* of scripts. A script header is a collection of patterns for those events which will "invoke" or "initiate" a script. Each header has a set of predictions about what should happen next in a particular context; these patterns (and thus these predictions) are the only ones present in active memory if the script has not been accessed by the conceptualizations read so far.

The basic rule in defining a script header is that a complete event is needed to bring the script into play. That is, in order for a script to be instantiated, a conceptualization must be recognized rather than just a PP. For example, $RESTAURANT should not be invoked just because "a restaurant" is mentioned. This is not to say that script-related information should be completely suppressed, because it may be useful in later stages of understanding. For example, in "I met a truck driver in a diner", remembering the role the person had in $TRUCK may be crucial to understanding what he might say or do later.

Conceptualizations can be produced not only by surface clauses, but also by certain kinds of prepositional phrases. Such phrases can act as complete thoughts by modifying the time- or place-setting of the main event. Consider the following sentence:

Mary was killed in an accident.

The above sentence can be paraphrased roughly as "When ther was an accident, Mary was killed." The top-level event of Mary's being killed is placed into some temporal relation to the "accident". Thus just the prepositional phrase "in an accident'' is sufficient to create a conceptualization which can invoke the entire accident script.

Script headers come in four varieties, which are ranked on the basis of how strongly they predict that the associated context will be instantiated. The first type is called a *precondition header* (PH) because it triggers a script on the basis of a main script precondition being mentioned in the text. (A precondition is an important global condition which SAM assumes to be true when a script is activated, unless the text says otherwise.) As an example, the sentence "John was hungry" is a PH for $RESTAURANT because it is an enabling condition for the main conceptualization (INGEST food) of the script. A story understander having access to both scripts and plans would make the prediction (a relatively weak one, to be sure) that $RESTAURANT would come up because this is known to be a common means (i.e., a plan) of getting fed. A related PH would be an actual statement of the goal that the script is normally assumed to achieve, or one from which that goal could easily be inferred. In "John wanted to eat a hamburger" or "John wanted some Italian food", the inference chain to the script precondition is relatively straightforward. Patterns for PH's are explicitly stored in the script, since SAM does not have the ability to use plans.

A second type of header, which makes stronger predictions than a PH about the associated context, is the *instrumental header* (IH). An IH commonly comes up in inputs which refer to two or more scripts, at least one of which can be interpreted as an "instrument" for the others. For example, in "John took the subway to the restaurant", both $SUBWAY and $RESTAURANT would be predicted, since subsequent inputs about either make perfectly good sense. Here, the reference to $RESTAURANT is anticipatory, and $SUBWAY is a recognized instrumental means of reaching locales in which more important script goals can be expected to be accomplished.

The notion of a time-place setting for a script leads to the third and most strongly predictive type of header, the *locale header* (LH). Many organizations have a "residence" or "place of business" in which they characteristically carry on their activities. They may have distinctively designed ornaments or buildings (e.g., a pawn shop's sign, a barber's pole, or McDonald's Golden Arches) which signal their script to the world. When an understander reads that an actor is in the proximity of the residence, or, better yet, inside the residence, its expectations about the occurrence of the script are correspondingly reinforced. Examples of LH's are "John went to the soccer field" and "John went into the Museum of Modern Art."

The final type of header is a flat assertion that the script occurred. Examples include:

There was a car accident.
An earthquake struck.
John went on vacation.
Mary went sailing.

Such a *direct header* (DH) is the top-level pattern in a script. DHs are always the first patterns to be checked in a context, since they have the maximum predictive power. They are always checked, since sentences (especially from newspaper stories) may use them to fill in a role or other attribute of the script. Consider, for example, phrases such as "a two-car crash", "a violent hurricane", "a three-day state visit."

Here are the headers of the subway script:

```
SBIN1:                        [Direct Header]
   ((<=> ($SUBWAY MAIN &PATGRP PTRORG &SUBORG
                   ORIG &ORIG DEST &DEST)))

SBIN2:                        [Locale Header]
   ((ACTOR &PATGRP <=> (*PTRANS*)
      OBJECT &PATGRP
      TO (*INSIDE* PART &STATION1)))

SBIN3:                        [Instrumental Header]
   ((ACTOR &SUBORG <=> (*PTRANS*)
      OBJECT &PATGRP
      TO (*PROX* PART &DEST)))

SBIN4:                        [Precondition Header]
   ((CON ((ACTOR &PATGRP <=> (*PTRANS*)
      OBJECT &PATGRP
      TO (*PROX* PART &DEST)))
         IS (*GOAL* PART &PATGRP)))
```

The DH is intended to handle conceptualizations corresponding to inputs such as "John took a subway ride to Coney Island." The LH takes care of sentences such as "John walked into the Boro Hall subway station." The IH will handle conceptualizations such as "The IRT took John to Shea Stadium." Finally, the PH would match conceptualizations for sentences such as "John wanted to go downtown."

Activities in scripts are stereotyped. Events follow one another in one of a small set of recognized ways. On entering the subway, for example, the patron may either proceed directly to the turnstile, or stop to buy a token. A chain of event-patterns describing one of these well-understood activities is called an *episode*. "Buying a token" is an episode consisting of the events: "enter the station", "see the cashier's cage", "go to it", "ask for a token", "be told the fare", and "pay the fare". Note that the script demands that the fare be paid *before* the token is handed over. This is how this episode is always structured in the subway script, although the actions can be reversed in other scripts, such as when a person is buying an ice cream cone.

Every episode has a main conceptualization, or Maincon, which is the goal, or point, of the episode. The episodes (marked with "E") and Maincons (marked with "M") of $SUBWAY are shown in Figure 5.3.

In Fig. 5.3, the branching of paths at (1) leads to the subsequent episodes E2 and E3, which describe alternative ways of arranging to get through the turnstile. A branch of this type is called a *turning point*. The "loops" at points (2) and (3) are for the *cyclic* episodes E5 and E7, that is, for episodes which may happen several times in succession. At (2), several trains may arrive before the one the patron wants, and so the patron must continue to wait.

One could make a single episode out of all the events from entering the subway to leaving the destination station. If we did this, however, we would clearly be ignoring important facts about the structure of $SUBWAY. Some parts of the subway ride are more important, more central to the situation, than others. Getting a token, for example, is an important activity in $SUBWAY because without one a patron can't get through the turnstile to get his ride. Taking a seat on the platform, on the other hand, is not so important because it doesn't really have any effect on whether the patron can get on the train. Another fact is that sometimes different ways to do the same thing may be available. Having a token before the ride, asking for one at the counter, or showing the cashier a special

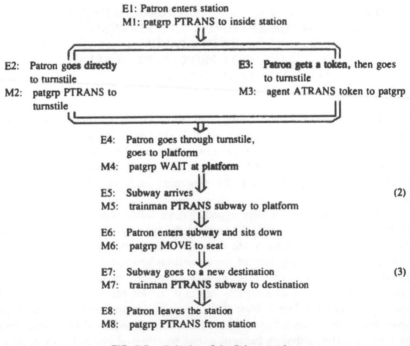

FIG. 5.3.   Episodes of the Subway script.

pass are all possible ways of procuring a ride. In this case, we have a set of episodes which seem to go together.

The activities of a script which always have to occur for us to recognize that the script has in fact been instantiated are called its *scenes*. The scenes of $SUBWAY are:

$SUBWAYENTER   enter the station and wait at the platform
$SUBWAYRIDE   enter the train and ride to destination
$SUBWAYEXIT   leave the station at destination

"Entering", including buying and using a token, is a scene of the subway script because it is necessary to procure a ride. "Riding" is a scene because this is the transporting activity that the script is all about. "Leaving" is a scene because we can't be sure that the ride is over until the patron exits from the station (he might otherwise just be transferring between subway lines). Each scene of a script is defined by a set of episodes which (1) describes the different ways in which the important activity of the scene can happen, and (2) describes other, less important, actions, such as sitting down on the platform, which can be interlinked with the main episodes, but which don't contribute directly to their accomplishment. The use of "$" before scene names is meant to suggest that each scene (and each component episode) shares some of the features of the script it belongs to.

Applying Scripts

The Script Applier attempts to understand a story by introducing the "largest", most inclusive script it possesses which is initiated by the first conceptualization in the story. As each input conceptualization is recognized in the script, predictions are made by the Script Applier about future inputs. This cycle continues until the system receives an input which does not refer to a predicted event. At this point, it again brings in the largest script which the input initiates, matches roles and props across the script interfaces, checks the preconditions, if any, for the new script, and starts matching inputs in the new context.

As an illustration of the Script Applier's cycle of pattern-matching, instantiation, and prediction, consider SAM's processing of this simple story:

John Smith decided to go to a museum. The subway took Smith to Manhattan. He strolled up Fifth Avenue and entered the Metropolitan Museum. He gave the cashier fifty cents. He looked at some sculpture. Then he looked at some paintings. Later he went home.

The first step in understanding a story is to internalize a conceptualization that the Analyzer has produced. This means that SAM will give the conceptualization the internal labels (such as "GN" below) which are used by memory, and will fill in any known tokens. Thus after analysis, the first sentence of the above story looks like this:

"John Smith decided to go to a museum."

GN0:
    ((ACTOR GN1 <=> (*MBUILD*) to (*CP* PART GN1)
             MOBJECT GN2))

GN2:
    ((ACTOR GN1 <=> (*PTRANS*) OBJECT GN1
            TO (*PROX* PART GN3)))

GN1:
    (#PERSON PERSNAME (JOHN) SURNAME (SMITH))

GN3:
    (#ORGANIZATION ORGOCC ($MUSEUM) REF (INDEF))

PP-Memory replaces the list structures (#PERSON...) and (#OR-GANIZATION...) with tokens having the appropriate properties:

"John Smith"   HUM0:
               CLASS (#PERSON)
               PERSNAME (JOHN)
               SURNAME (SMITH)

"a museum"   ORG0:
               CLASS (#ORGANIZATION)
               ORGOCC (MUSEUM)
               REF (INDEF)

Then, PP-Memory attempts to identify the tokens just created with tokens already present in its memory: "permanent" tokens for well-known PPs which are always around; and tokens created in the course of reading the story thus far. Assuming that "John Smith" is not a special person known to SAM, PP-Memory can't identify either PP at this point. The REF (INDEF) marker is left by the Analyzer to tell PP-Memory not to look for a referent for the PP among existing entities.

Next, PP-Memory flags the museum script ($MUSEUM) as a suggested script to be tested by the Script Applier. The tokenized conceptualization is then passed to the Script Applier. The Script Applier decomposes the conceptualization into sub-conceptualizations containing only a single CD ACT or STATE. The result of this process is a list of simple conceptualizations which preserve the temporal or causal ordering between events.

Simple conceptualization-patterns are needed to calculate causal-chain results of connections. For example, the causal result of a PTRANS is a change in the location of the OBJECT PTRANSed. Common sentences in any language clump simple conceptualizations together in arbitrarily complex ways. Consider, for example, the CD structure built by the Analyzer for the following sentence:

Mary Jones died Tuesday of head injuries received in a car accident on Sunday.

((CON GN1 LEADTO GN2))

GN1: ((ACTOR GN5 TOWARD (*PSTATE* VAL (*NEGVAL*))
          REL GN3))

GN2: ((ACTOR GN6 TOWARD (*HEALTH* VAL (−10))) TIME (TIM2))
TIM2: ((WEEKDAY TUESDAY))

GN3: ((CON GN4 LEADTO GN1))

GN4. ((<=> ($VEHACCIDENT VEHICLE GN7)) TIME (TIM4))
TIM4: ((WEEKDAY SUNDAY))

GN5: (#BODYPART TYPE (*HEAD*))
GN6: (#PERSON PERSNAME (MARY) SURNAME (JONES) GENDER (*FEM*))
GN7: (#PHYSOBJ TYPE (*CAR*))

This conceptualization basically says that a negative change in the physical state of a bodypart (belonging, by inference, to Mary Jones) caused a terminal change in her state of health, and that the physical change was caused by $VEHACCI-DENT. The process of decomposition would produce the ordered list of simple conceptualizations: "There was a car accident", "A head injury occurred", and "Mary Jones died." In a story containing the above sentence, SAM would try to locate each unit event in the indicated order. Putting the simple conceptualizations into "narrative order" takes advantage of the natural causal/temporal order of the script. Each new conceptualization is expected to be found on the basis of predictions set up by earlier inputs.

In the course of understanding a story, the Script Applier maintains data structures which describe the state of each script present in the system. This information forms a *script context* which, if the script is active, is updated whenever a new conceptualization is found to fit within the context. Each script context is defined by: the list of patterns from that script which are currently in memory; an association-list of tokens bound to script variables; the name of the last pattern matched in the script; the list of script episodes currently in memory; the header for this incarnation of the script; and a script-global inference-strength indicator which the Applier uses to flag how probable its inferences appear to be.

The most important data structure is the *story representation* being constructed by the Script Applier for the current text. This structure provides access to the final record of the story, from the most general information about the story to the most specific.

Initially, the record of the script contexts contains only the headers for the scripts in the system, and the variables keeping track of the active contexts are null. When the Script Applier receives the tokenized conceptualization for the first sentence of the museum story above, it will look at the museum script, $MUSEUM, because of PP-Memory's suggestion. Because this is the first input, the high-priority search queue of scripts is simply a list of suggested scripts which so far contains only $MUSEUM.

The input is matched successively against the headers. The input matches a Precondition Header of $MUSEUM ("main actor decides/wants to go to a museum"), and $MUSEUM is activated. More predictions from the script are loaded, and $MUSEUM is added to the list of active scripts and the script search list. It is also marked as being the most recent script accessed by an input.

In addition, the setting of the museum script has the property that other scripts can take place there. These scripts (e.g., $BATHROOM and $RESTAURANT) are added to the search list. Next, the Analyzer's handling of lexical and phrasal information is changed. For example, ELI is given special definitions of museum-related words such as "exhibit" and "painting".

Finally, the information that $MUSEUM is usually imbedded in a trip-situation is used. $TRIP is a higher level trip script situation which consists of a sequential arrangement of three sub-scripts: $GOTRIP, $GOALTRIP, and $RE-TURNTRIP, or travelling to some destination, doing whatever is the goal or point of the trip, and returning home again. $MUSEUM is an appropriate part of the "goal" segment of $TRIP (i.e., MUSEUM is a part of $GOALTRIP which in turn is a part of $TRIP). Because $TRIP is a script situation, it therefore ranks above $MUSEUM in the hierarchy of scripts, and so it takes control of processing.

The current story representation is the variable !STORY. SAM has now set !STORY to $TRIP, which is the most global script currently active, and has added $TRIP to the active script list. The goal-segment ($GOALTRIP) of $TRIP is set to $MUSEUM. Since $MUSEUM was initiated by a precondition header ("desired"), we may hear about the going-segment of $TRIP, $GOTRIP. At this point, SAM has the patterns ready for $GOTRIP as well as for $MUSEUM. $GOTRIP is set to a list of scripts which are appropriate for moving people around, i.e., scripts involving persons and organizations whose Maincons contain a PTRANS. "John Smith" is assigned the role of main actor in both $MUSEUM and $TRIP.

At this point, a number of processing structures have been partially built. At the top level, the story is assumed to be a $TRIP. $TRIP is currently in the go-segment. The go-segment is as yet unspecified, but is expected to be instantiated by a sequential connection among PTRANS-scripts. The goal-segment is expected to consist of a sequential instantiation of $MUSEUM and, perhaps, some other scripts which are appropriate "goal" activities of a trip. The return-segment will also be a sequential arrangement chosen from among the PTRANS-scripts. Finally, the instantiation of $MUSEUM may contain instantiations of $BATHROOM and $RESTAURANT as well. Thus the global story representation, !STORY, has the following property-list structure:

!STORY: (SEQ SCLAB1)

SCLAB1:   (SEQ SCLAB2 SCLAB3 SCLAB4)
     scriptname: $TRIP
     scriptseg: $GOTRIP

SCLAB2:   (SEQ)
     scriptname: $GOTRIP
     scriptq: ($BUS $SUBWAY $TRAIN $DRIVE $WALK)

SCLAB3: (SEQ SCLAB5)
     scriptname: $GOALTRIP
     scriptq: ($MUSEUM $RESTAURANT $MOVIE $THEATER
             $VARIETYSTORE)

SCLAB4: (SEQ)
     scriptname: $RETURNTRIP
     scriptq: ($BUS $SUBWAY $TRAIN $DRIVE $WALK)

SCLAB5:
     scriptname: $MUSEUM
     scriptq: ($BATHROOM $RESTAURANT)

This method of introducing $TRIP partly "hides" the activities appropriate to $MUSEUM. The active script list is currently ($TRIP $GOTRIP $MUSEUM). Since the global search list which guides the selection of contexts is built up from the active-script global, the patterns appropriate for $TRIP will be looked at first, then those for $GOTRIP, and finally those for $MUSEUM. The script search list thus has this structure:

$TRIP
    $BUS $SUBWAY $TRAIN $DRIVE
    $MUSEUM
             $BATHROOM $RESTAURANT

The pattern for the precondition header matching the conceptualization underlying the first sentence of the story is:

```
((ACTOR &MGRP <=> (*MBUILD*) TO (*CP* PART &MGRP)
                MOBJECT
                    ((ACTOR &MGRP <=> (*PTRANS*)
                            OBJECT &MGRP
                            TO (*PROX* PART &MORG)))))
EXPLICIT (&MORG)
```

The variable &MGRP is the main actor of $MUSEUM, that is, a group of people (perhaps only one) who don't have a function in $MUSEUM and who will perform as the "public" in this script. &MORG is a variable standing for the museum organization, the "actor" providing this service to the public. The property EXPLICIT on the pattern indicates that the museum organization must explicitly appear in the input conceptualization. This avoids a spurious match on an input such as "John decided to go."

The first phase of matching consists of a comparison of the "constant" parts of the conceptualization for the sentence with the constant parts of the pattern. The full form of the conceptualization for the first sentence of the story, after PP-Memory has finished with it, is:

"John Smith decided to go to a museum."

MEM1:
    ((ACTOR HUM1 <=> (*MBUILD*)
                TO (*CP* PART HUM1)
                FROM (NIL)
                INST (NIL)
                MOBJECT MEM2)
            TIME (TIM1) MODE (NIL) MANNER (NIL))

TIM1: ((BEFORE *NOW* X))

MEM2:
    ((ACTOR HUM1 <=> (*PTRANS*) OBJECT HUM1
                TO (*PROX* PART ORG1)
                FROM (NIL)
                INST (NIL))
            TIME (TIM2) MODE (NIL) MANNER (NIL))

TIM2: ((VAL GN0))

HUM1: "John Smith"

ORG1: "a museum"

Note that many "slots", such as the INSTrument of the PTRANS (how John went), have been left unfilled (NIL), because the sentence did not explicitly refer to them.

The basic rules in the backbone match are: (1) "literal" roles and fillers specified by the pattern must appear in the input; (2) extra roles and fillers in the input are ignored; (3) a dummy must be matched against the same conceptual cluster each time it appears in the pattern; and (4) an empty filler slot in the input matches anything, unless the pattern, using the EXPLICIT property, demands that the filler be explicitly present.

Since the pattern does not contain instrumentals, and doesn't care where John is deciding to leave FROM, these roles are not examined. Since the OBJECT to be PTRANSed is the same as the ACTOR of both the PTRANS and the MBUILD, we avoid a spurious match on a sentence such as "John decided to throw a ball at the museum." Finally, because of the EXPLICIT marker on &MORG, the backbone match will fail if the corresponding slot is (NIL). This would abort the match if the sentence were "John decided to go."

The result of a successful backbone match is a list of bindings of candidate PPs to script variables. The next step in the matching process is checking that the candidates can in fact be instances of the variables. The general process of fitting variables to PPs is called Rolefit. When a variable has been previously bound to a token by Rolefit, the fitting process must be augmented by checks to be sure that the new PP can be an instance of both the variable *and* the old token. This process is the manifestation in SAM of Reference Specification, and is called Rolemerge.

Rolefit in this example involves an intersection of the conceptual class markers of PP and token, and a check that the *function* specified by the variable can be performed by the PP. &MGRP can either be a person or a group, since we want the script to handle cases such as "John and Mary went to a museum." "Museum" matches the class specified for &MORG exactly. The point of this initial check on PP-class is to find out quickly if the candidate PP obviously cannot fill the specified role.

The checking of function is also facilitated by the existence of the PP-classes. One feature of each class is that the indicators of function it may contain are to some extent unique to the class. For people, a title or occupation marker strongly suggests the function the person will have in a context. For organizations, the associated script (and the sub- and super-scripts it points to) is the main indicator of function. Physical objects, however, often have a function in more than one script. A car, for example, can figure as a "vehicle" in a driving situation, or as the "object of sale" in a car-showroom situation. A input reference to "a car" maps into a conceptual structure of the form (#STRUCTURE TYPE (*CAR*)), where the reference to *CAR* is a shorthand for the cluster of functions and other information that PP-Memory possesses about cars in general:

```
*CAR*: CLASS (#STRUCTURE)
       SCRIPTROLES ((&VEHICLE1 . $DRIVE)
                    (&SALE-OBJ . $AUTOSHOWROOM))
```

Picture Producers fit into scripts on the basis of function. Because of this, a simple comparison of features may not be sufficient to determine whether a PP can be an instance of a variable. This is the case, for example, with the "obstruction" role in $VEHACCIDENT, and the role "group of visiting dignitaries" in $VIPVISIT. When faced with complex functions such as these, the Script

Applier resorts to a form of pattern-directed function invocation, to examine the input and the association-list of tentative variable bindings for applicability. In a state-visit context, for example, there is a header pattern looking for the arrival of a VIP. If a group of people actually arrived, this pattern would call a function to search among the members of the group to see if one of them qualifies as a VIP. This is the only way to distinguish $VIPVISIT from other manifestations of the trip situation, such as $VACATION or $BUSINESSTRIP. A characteristic of functions invoked at match time is that they have no real side-effects. If the match fails, all is as before.

The process of fitting new PPs to script variables bound to PPs from previous conceptualizations is called Rolemerge. Note that Rolemerge can, in fact, be implemented in two different places in SAM: in PP-Memory or in the Script Applier itself. The primary reference processor, however, is the Script Applier, since this module may have to act as a "backstop" for PP-Memory in cases where too little information is available in the PPs alone to make the decision. The Applier can make the needed reference in these latter cases because it has additional information from the predicted pattern that was matched.

When the Analyzer reads a definite reference such as "he" or "the man", it produces a PP with the note (REF (DEF)) attached. This is the signal to do a Rolemerge. For example, "he" is mapped into (#PERSON GENDER (*MASC*) REF (DEF)).

This processing note is first seen by PP-memory, which looks for the referent among the tokens already in existence, those created during the processing of the current conceptualization, or in its collection of permanent tokens. If the PP is a permanent token, PP-Memory makes the connection and turns off the processing suggestion. The Script Applier then searches for the PP as though the reference were indefinite. Suppose, for example, the second sentence of our story referred to "the BMT" rather than to "the subway". The PP for BMT will match the predicted subway PP.

Each time a pattern is matched, the "window" on the associated script must be moved to conform with the script's expectations about what will happen next. The prediction process has two distinct phases: (1) clearing patterns from active memory which refer to events which occurred before the presently matched pattern; and (2) bringing in episodes containing the patterns predicted by the present one. The removal of unneeded patterns is accomplished by consulting the permanent memory structures for the script to determine which scenes currently in memory precede the currently active scene.

In the above story, $TRIP is active after the first sentence is read. $TRIP is a linear sequence of going-, goal- and returning-segments, with appropriate events filling the segments. The "conceptual" structure of the story is:

                    $TRIP
    $GOTRIP $GOALTRIP $RETURNTRIP
    $SUBWAY $MUSEUM $SUBWAY

The processing of this story will involve, at various points, predictions from its component scripts: $SUBWAY and $MUSEUM. But there are predictions from situations, over and above what the component scripts provide. The $TRIP situation, for example, predicts that only certain scripts will be used in each of its segments. For example, it initially prescribes that only personal and organizational PTRANS scripts will be referenced. You have to get to the place where something "important" is happening before you can participate in it. Furthermore, a text can refer to a trip in general without filling in too many details. Consider, for example, what it means to "take a train trip", "go on vacation", or "return from Miami".

In SAM, when a story is read with the aid of a situation, its predictions are the first to be looked at. After the first sentence of the story is processed, the $GOTRIP segment of $TRIP is active.

When a predicted pattern has accepted the current input, the input has been "recognized" within the script, and a causal chain is constructed which connects the last input to the new one. This chain contains events which can be plausibly inferred to have happened given the inputs that were read. The Script Applier builds up causal chains by examining the episode structure stored in permanent memory for the active script. Suppose, for example, we read:

Smith went into the BMT. He took the train downtown.

The first sentence instantiates an event from the entering scene, $SUBWAYENTER of $SUBWAY, and activates the script. The second sentence realizes the Maincon of $SUBWAY, which is part of $SUBWAYRIDE. If the episodes are in the same scene, then the Applier searches the causal successors of the earlier event, remaining on the main paths of the episodes, until the later event is found. While looking at any given main path event, the Applier also checks immediate inferences (forward or backward) from it.

If the original events are in different scenes, the Applier connects the earlier event to a "default" Exitcon from the earlier scene, connects the later event to a default Entrycon for the later scene, and connects the two scenes with the default paths for the scenes in between. Since $SUBWAYENTER and $SUBWAYRIDE are adjacent scenes, only the Exitcon and Entrycon are needed.

The mainpath connection between events that is built is a list of uninstantiated patterns. The Applier takes this list and replaces the occurrences of script variables in the patterns with the PP-tokens bound to them. For example, in the pattern for "patron goes to cashier":

$$((ACTOR \ \&PATGRP <=> (*PTRANS*) \ OBJECT \ \&PATGRP$$
$$TO \ (*PROX* \ PART \ \&CASHIER)))$$

the variable &PATGRP would be replaced by the token for Smith (e.g., HUM0). The above pattern contains a variable, &CASHIER, which is not bound to a PP, because the role was not mentioned. When this happens, we have a need for a Role-Instantiation inference, in which the Applier asks PP-Memory for a token having properties which are appropriate, in default, for this role. At the time $SUBWAY was activated, PP-Memory was informed about the properties of all the variables having a place in the script. It uses this information to supply the Instantiator with a token for "cashier" in which the PP's place in the script is recorded under the SROLES property:

HUM1:
  CLASS (#PERSON)
  SROLES (($SUBWAY . &CASHIER))

With this token supplied, the realized form of the pattern is:

((ACTOR HUM0 <=> (*PTRANS*) OBJECT HUM0
   TO (*PROX* PART HUM1)) TIME (TIME5))

where TIME5 defines an appropriate temporal relation between this conceptualization and the other events in the causal chain.

When the second sentence of the story is read, $SUBWAY is activated under control of the $GOTRIP segment of $TRIP. This means that the bindings for "person(s) taking trip", "conveyance", and "destination" are copied from $GOTRIP to $SUBWAY, and various parts of $SUBWAY are realized. The instantiation of $SUBWAY up to the point referred to by this conceptualization has several parts. First, the preconditions of $SUBWAY are realized. For example, the Script Applier assumes that Smith has a token to get through the turnstile, and wants to go somewhere on the subway. The "main character" is "Smith" and the "destination" is "a museum", which both already exist, so only "a token" has to be created by PP-Memory. Next, the Script Applier constructs a causal chain from the default Entrycon to the Maincon (which the second sentence instantiates), obtaining tokens from PP-Memory for "cashier", "turnstile", "platform", etc., as it goes. The first part of the third sentence instantiates an Exitcon from $SUBWAY, so a path consisting of the default episodes of $SUBWAYRIDE and $SUBWAYEXIT is constructed, and $SUBWAY is closed.

The conceptualization for the second part of this sentence (". . . he entered the Metropolitan Museum.") activates $MUSEUM using the locale header. At this point the situation moves into the goal-segment, $GOALTRIP, because this is the goal activity that was predicted at the beginning of the story. The specification of the reference for "he" in this clause is made on the basis that the main character in a change of location which is part of a trip is required to be the same as the global main character, &TRPGRP. Activation of $MUSEUM results in the prediction of a possible "admission" event, in which a member of the public pays to get into a museum. This pattern matches the next sentence from the story: "He gave the cashier fifty cents." Now that the main character is inside the museum, the script predicts museum episodes. One of the most important of these is the "cyclic" episode in which the patron goes to an exhibit of some sort, and studies the things on display there. The Maincon of this episode matches the conceptualizations for the next two sentences, where each instance of matching predicts another possible instantiation of the episode.

The last sentence of the story fails to match the outstanding predictions in either $GOALTRIP or $MUSEUM. It does, however, fit the prediction associated with the returning-segment of $TRIP. This pattern has as one of its roles the conveyance that the main character used to get back to where he started from. The conveyance is not mentioned in the last sentence, so $RETURNTRIP assumes that the conveyance that was instantiated in $GOTRIP (the subway) is the one that Smith used to get home.

6 Micro SAM

INTRODUCTION

McSAM is a very limited script applier. McSAM initially knows about shopping in a store—i.e., McSAM has a script with patterns describing five important events that occur during shopping: going to a store, picking out the object, buying it by giving the store money, and leaving the store.

When McSAM is given a story, such as:

Jack went to the store.
He got a kite.
He went home.

it first determines that the shopping script is relevant, and then it matches the individual events of the story against the patterns in the shopping script. In doing so, it fills in the events that were not explicitly mentioned in the story, such as Jack's giving money to the store.

McSAM takes Conceptual Dependency forms as input. It matches these forms against a pre-defined, predicted event sequence called a script. If the form matches one of the events in the script, then the form has been understood, i.e., it has been placed in a context. If the form does not match any of the events (or if there is no script active at the moment), then McSAM tries to find some other script to activate. Only one script at a time is kept active.

An Example of Script Application

In McSAM, the SHOPPING script is the following pre-defined sequence of events:

1. Someone goes to a store.
2. He picks up an object.
3. The store transfers possession of the object to him.
4. He transfers possession of some money to the store.
5. He leaves the store.

Suppose no scripts are active, and McSam gets the Conceptual Dependency representations for the following story:

Jack went to the store.
He got a kite.
He went home.

Then the following sequence of processing will occur:

1. "Jack went to the store"—since there are no active scripts, this does not match any predicted events. Attached to the concept underlying "the store" is the SHOPPING script. Therefore the SHOPPING script is activated by McSAM. "Jack went to the store" matches line 1 of this script.
2. "He got a kite"—this is analyzed as "possession of a kite was transferred to him." This matches line 3 of the active script. McSAM infers that line 2 must already have occurred.
3. "He went home"—this matches line 5 of the script. McSAM infers that line 4 must have occurred.

McSAM's final understanding of the story is:

Jack went to a store.
Jack picked up a kite.
The store transferred possession of the kite to Jack.
Jack transferred possession of some money to the store.
Jack left the store.

A script in McSAM is an ordered sequence of events. McSAM assumes that stories will refer to these events in the same order. Therefore McSAM keeps track of what script is active, and what event was last referred to by the story. Input CD forms are checked against only those events in the script that come after what has been already seen.

Scripts and Script Bindings

We said that a script contains a stereotyped sequence of events. Obviously it cannot be totally explicit about these events, because then the script would apply to only one story. We need to have variables (also called *script roles*) in scripts, so that we can say things like "X went to store Y."

In McSAM, the SHOPPING script happens to have four roles or variables: the shopper (SHOPPER), the store (STORE), the object bought (BOUGHT), and where the shopper goes when he leaves (ELSEWHERE).

We define a script by putting the property EVENTS under its name (e.g., SHOPPING). The value of this property is a list of CD forms which describe the events in the script. These CD forms use the script roles. For example, we define the SHOPPING script by:

```
(DEFPROP SHOPPING
    ((PTRANS (ACTOR ?SHOPPER) (OBJECT ?SHOPPER) (TO ?STORE))
     (PTRANS (ACTOR ?SHOPPER) (OBJECT ?BOUGHT) (TO ?SHOPPER))
     (ATRANS (ACTOR ?STORE) (OBJECT ?BOUGHT)
             (FROM ?STORE) (TO ?SHOPPER))
     (ATRANS (ACTOR ?SHOPPER) (OBJECT (MONEY))
             (FROM ?SHOPPER) (TO ?STORE))
     (PTRANS (ACTOR ?SHOPPER) (OBJECT ?SHOPPER)
             (FROM ?STORE) (TO ?ELSEWHERE)) )
EVENTS)
```

The question mark in front of the roles indicates that these items are variables (see the section on Readmacros). You do not have to explicitly declare script roles for a McSAM script. Compare these five CD forms with the five English sentences describing the SHOPPING script given in the previous section.

When a script is activated, a *script binding form* is created. A script binding form consists of a script name plus a list of the roles that have been given values. Script forms are written in CD syntax.

For example, when McSAM processes

```
(PTRANS (ACTOR (PERSON (NAME (JACK))))
        (OBJECT (PERSON (NAME (JACK)))) (TO (STORE)))
```

it activates the SHOPPING script and binds two of its roles to particular values: SHOPPER is bound to (PERSON (NAME (JACK))) and STORE is bound to (STORE). The script binding form is therefore

```
(SHOPPING (SHOPPER (PERSON (NAME (JACK)))) (STORE (STORE)))
```

A script is activated when an input CD form does not match any pattern in the currently active script and some predicate or subpredicate of the CD form is linked to a script. STORE, which is a subpredicate in the OBJECT slot of the PTRANS, is the only predicate in our initial McSAM data base that is linked to a script. The link is made using the property ASSOCIATED-SCRIPT.

```
(DEFPROP STORE SHOPPING ASSOCIATED-SCRIPT)
```

This says that the STORE predicate is linked to the SHOPPING script. McSAM then tries matching the PTRANS form against the CD patterns in that script.

Script Roles and Pattern Matching

When McSAM gets an input CD form (which does not have any variables), it uses a *pattern matcher* to compare the input with the script patterns. The pattern matcher has two purposes:

1. To tell whether an input matches a pattern or not
2. If a match does occur, to tell how the variables in the pattern have to be bound

For example, the input CD form

```
(PTRANS (ACTOR (PERSON (NAME (JACK))))
        (OBJECT (PERSON (NAME (JACK)))) (TO (STORE)))
```

matches the pattern

```
(PTRANS (ACTOR ?SHOPPER) (OBJECT ?SHOPPER) (TO
?STORE))
```

with the role SHOPPER bound to (PERSON (NAME (JACK))) and STORE bound to (STORE).

When McSAM looks for a match for an input, it uses the script binding form to determine what roles have been bound so far. When a script is first entered, the binding form is just (script-name). For example, after "Jack went to the store", the script binding form would be (SHOPPING). This says that SHOPPING is the script but that no variables have been bound yet.

The input must match with whatever bindings are in effect. Thus in the story "Jack went to the store. Janet got a kite..." the analysis of the second line would *not* match line 3 of the script because SHOPPER would be bound to Jack and Jack does not match Janet.

If a variable is not bound when a match is being done, then the variable immediately matches—and becomes bound to—the corresponding element in the input CD form. This binding is kept if the match does not fail elsewhere. For example, if SHOPPER and STORE are unbound, then matching the CD form

```
(PTRANS (ACTOR (PERSON (NAME (JACK))))
        (OBJECT (PERSON (NAME (JACK)))) (TO (STORE)))
```

against the pattern

(PTRANS (ACTOR ?SHOPPER) (OBJECT ?SHOPPER) (TO ?STORE))

will bind SHOPPER and STORE to (PERSON (NAME (JACK))) and (STORE) respectively.

The pattern matcher only checks those role-pairs that are given in the pattern. It ignores role-pairs in the input CD that are not in the pattern. Furthermore, the pattern matcher assumes that a role-pair in the pattern which does not appear at all in the input CD will match. Thus the input CD form

(PTRANS (ACTOR (PERSON (NAME (JACK)))))

matches the pattern

(PTRANS (OBJECT (BALL)))

because the input does not have an OBJECT role-pair, and the pattern does not have an ACTOR role-pair. Thus neither CD form contradicts the other and a match occurs. Since the pattern doesn't say who PTRANSed the ball, the pattern matcher, in effect, is saying that it might have been Jack. In order to avoid such unexpected pattern matches, always store complete CDs in memory, with as many roles filled in as possible.

Any new bindings that occur during a successful match are added to the script binding form, so that later inputs must be consistent with the accumulated set of bindings.

Instantiation

After McSAM matches an input CD with a script event pattern, it knows how far the script has progressed. McSAM then adds to the data base all the events in the script that were skipped over, plus the one just read.

McSAM does this by taking the script events and replacing all occurrences of script variables with their bindings, if any. This is called *instantiation*. The CD form produced by removing the variables is then added to the data base.

For example, the CD form for "Jack got a kite" is

(ATRANS (OBJECT (KITE)) (TO (PERSON (NAME (JACK)))))

which matches line 3 of the script:

(ATRANS (ACTOR ?STORE) (OBJECT ?BOUGHT)
(FROM ?STORE) (TO ?SHOPPER))

so McSAM binds **BOUGHT** to **(KITE)** in the script binding form:

```
(SHOPPING (SHOPPER (PERSON (NAME (JACK))))
         (STORE (STORE)) (BOUGHT (KITE)))
```

Line 2 of the script was skipped over ("He picked up a kite"):

```
(PTRANS (ACTOR ?SHOPPER) (OBJECT ?BOUGHT) (TO ?SHOPPER))
```

McSAM instantiates lines 2 and 3 of the script, adding to the data base

```
(PTRANS (ACTOR (PERSON (NAME (JACK)))) (OBJECT (KITE))
        (TO (PERSON (NAME (JACK)))))
```

and

```
(ATRANS (ACTOR (STORE)) (OBJECT (KITE))
        (FROM (STORE)) (TO (PERSON (NAME (JACK)))))
```

Note the input CD only said that Jack got a kite, but the form added to the data base (the instantiated versions of line 3) says that the *store* gave Jack the kite.

McSAM Versus SAM

McSAM has much too limited a structure for scripts. In SAM, scripts are sequences of scenes which in turn are made up of sequences of events. Scripts can have alternative sequences of events, such as seating yourself in a restaurant as opposed to being led by a hostess to a seat. Scripts can have optional events, and also different *tracks*, which are similar but not identical sequences of scenes, such as going to a diner as opposed to going to a fancy restaurant.

In Ms. Malaprop (Charniak, 1977b), scripts (which are called frames) are extremely modular. Frames are broken up into subframes, which in turn are broken up into other frames. A large frame, therefore, can share significant amounts of information with other frames, abrogating the need for tracks. The frames also indicate *why* things are done in the indicated manner. This allows the program to figure out optional versus obligatory parts of the frame.

McSAM does not build any structured representation of the meaning of a story. That is, the data base that McSAM generates contains the events that happened, but gives indication of how the events relate to each other, no labelling of events with the scenes they belong to, and so on.

McSAM also has too limited a view of how stories are told. It assumes that a story will relate events in the same order that they appear in a script. This is not always the case. For example, newspaper stories discuss events such as automobile accidents in a very specialized way. First, a one line summary is given of the whole event, then details of the people involved, then the outcome—i.e., who went to the hospital and what condition they were in—then details about how the accident happened, and so on. SAM has information about how such stories are written, which is used to predict which script events are likely to be seen next. McSAM just has the simple list *POSSIBLE-NEXT-EVENTS*. In a somewhat different manner, Ms. Malaprop's frames contain explicit time ordering statements. This makes that program less sensitive to input order than either McSAM or SAM.

McSAM at several points blurs the distinction between script binding forms and CD forms. They have the same format, and many of the programs (IN-STANTIATE, MATCH) do not distinguish between them. Ms. Malaprop carries this further by defining script-like entities for all predicates, including the "primitives" of the system.

Finally, it should be pointed out that McSAM does more work than it has to, by adding instantiations of every script event to the data base. Since the script binding form contains all the information needed to construct these CD forms, this is all that McSAM really needs to add. Thus you could remove the call to INSTANTIATE in ADD-SCRIPT-INFO and not lose any information. (You would, however, still have to update *POSSIBLE-NEXT-EVENTS*.) When people argue as to whether or not activated scripts are copied into memory, they are arguing—in McSam terms—as to whether or not INSTANTIATE is applied to every script pattern. Ms. Malaprop in particular does not automatically fill out the script events but computes them when asked. Removing this instantiation phase from McSAM would make it more like Ms. Malaprop.

SAMPLE OUTPUT

The following is a log of the McSAM program, applied to the CD forms for "Jack went to the store. He got a kite. He went home."

```
[PH: Initiation. 14-Jan-80 10:48AM]

(PROCESS-STORY KITE-STORY)

Input is
    (PTRANS (ACTOR (PERSON (NAME (JACK))))
            (OBJECT (PERSON (NAME (JACK))))
            (TO (STORE)))

New script SHOPPING
Matches
    (PTRANS (ACTOR (*VAR* SHOPPER))
            (OBJECT (*VAR* SHOPPER))
            (TO (*VAR* STORE)))
```

Adding script CD
    (PTRANS (ACTOR (PERSON (NAME (JACK))))
          (OBJECT (PERSON (NAME (JACK))))
          (TO (STORE)))

Input is
    (ATRANS (OBJECT (KITE)) (TO (PERSON)))

Matches
    (ATRANS (ACTOR (*VAR* STORE))
          (OBJECT (*VAR* BOUGHT))
          (FROM (*VAR* STORE))
          (TO (*VAR* SHOPPER)))

Adding script CD
    (PTRANS (ACTOR (PERSON (NAME (JACK))))
          (OBJECT (KITE))
          (TO (PERSON (NAME (JACK)))))

Adding script CD
    (ATRANS (ACTOR (STORE))
          (OBJECT (KITE))
          (FROM (STORE))
          (TO (PERSON (NAME (JACK)))))

Input is
    (PTRANS (ACTOR (PERSON)) (OBJECT (PERSON)) (TO (HOUSE)))

Matches
    (PTRANS (ACTOR (*VAR* SHOPPER))
          (OBJECT (*VAR* SHOPPER))
          (FROM (*VAR* STORE))
          (TO (*VAR* ELSEWHERE)))

Adding script CD
    (ATRANS (ACTOR (PERSON (NAME (JACK))))
          (OBJECT (MONEY))
          (FROM (PERSON (NAME (JACK))))
          (TO (STORE)))

Adding script CD
    (PTRANS (ACTOR (PERSON (NAME (JACK))))
          (OBJECT (PERSON (NAME (JACK))))
          (FROM (STORE))
          (TO (HOUSE)))

Story done—final script header
    (SHOPPING (SHOPPER (PERSON (NAME (JACK))))
          (STORE (STORE))
          (BOUGHT (KITE))
          (ELSEWHERE (HOUSE)))

Data base contains
((PTRANS (ACTOR (PERSON (NAME (JACK))))
          (OBJECT (PERSON (NAME (JACK))))
          (TO (STORE)))

```
(PTRANS (ACTOR (PERSON (NAME (JACK))))
        (OBJECT (KITE))
        (TO (PERSON (NAME (JACK)))))
(ATRANS (ACTOR (STORE))
        (OBJECT (KITE))
        (FROM (STORE))
        (TO (PERSON (NAME (JACK)))))
(ATRANS (ACTOR (PERSON (NAME (JACK))))
        (OBJECT (MONEY))
        (FROM (PERSON (NAME (JACK))))
        (TO (STORE)))
(PTRANS (ACTOR (PERSON (NAME (JACK))))
        (OBJECT (PERSON (NAME (JACK))))
        (FROM (STORE))
        (TO (HOUSE)))

(SHOPPING (SHOPPER (PERSON (NAME (JACK))))
          (STORE (STORE))
          (BOUGHT (KITE))
          (ELSEWHERE (HOUSE))))
```

[PH: Termination. 14-Jan-80 10:52AM. PS:<RIESBECK>SIX.LOG.4]

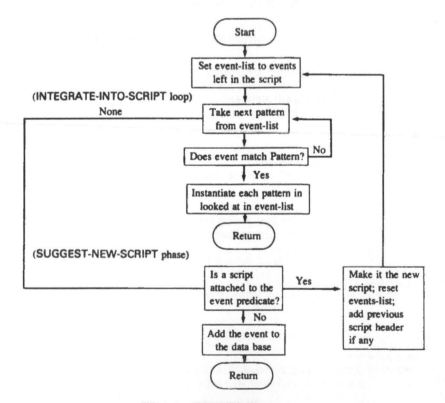

FIG. 6.1.   PROCESS-CD(event).

FLOW CHART

The flow chart in Fig. 6.1 shows one of the central functions in McSAM: PROCESS-CD. The flow chart includes the flow of control for its two subparts: INTEGRATE-INTO-SCRIPT and SUGGEST-NEW-SCRIPT.

THE PROGRAM

```
;************************************************************************
;                         MICRO SAM PROGRAM
;************************************************************************
;PROCESS-STORY takes a list of CDs and hands each one to PROCESS-CD
;which is the main function. At the end of the story, the current
;script is added to the data base and the data base is pretty-printed.

(DE PROCESS-STORY (STORY)
 (CLEAR-SCRIPTS)
 (FOR (CD IN STORY)
      (DO (MSG T "input is") (PRINT-CD CD)
          (PROCESS-CD CD)
          (MSG T)))
 (MSG T "Story done—final script header")
 (PRINT-CD (ADD-CD *CURRENT-SCRIPT*))
 (MSG T "Data base contains")
 (SPRINT *DATA-BASE* 1]

;PROCESS-CD takes one CD of the story at a time. Either a statement is
;predicted by the current script or it is in the data base or it
;suggests a new script.

(DE PROCESS-CD (CD)
 (OR (INTEGRATE-INTO-SCRIPT CD)
     (SUGGEST-NEW-SCRIPT CD)
     (PROGN (MSG T "Adding")
            (PRINT-CD (ADD-CD CD))
            (MSG "—not linked to any script" T]

;*DATA-BASE* is the pointer to the data base.
;*CURRENT-SCRIPT* is the script currently active. It is a statement
;with the script name as the predicate and the script variables and
;their bindings as the arguments.
;*POSSIBLE-NEXT-EVENTS* is a list of the events in *CURRENT-SCRIPT*
;that have not been seen yet.

;CLEAR-SCRIPTS resets these globals to NIL.

(DE CLEAR-SCRIPTS ()
 (SETQ *DATA-BASE* NIL)
 (SETQ *CURRENT-SCRIPT* NIL)
 (SETQ *POSSIBLE-NEXT-EVENTS* NIL]
```

The data base is simply a list of the statements we wish remembered.
New items are added to the end of the list.

```
(DE ADD-CD (CD)
  (SETQ *DATA-BASE* (CONS-END *DATA-BASE* CD))
  CD]
```

To integrate an incoming statement into the currently active script,
find the first event in *POSSIBLE-NEXT-EVENTS* that matches the
statement. If one is found, update the data base.

```
(DE INTEGRATE-INTO-SCRIPT (CD)
  (LOOP (INITIAL NEW-BINDINGS NIL
                 EVENT NIL
                 EVENTS *POSSIBLE-NEXT-EVENTS*)
        (WHILE (SETQ EVENT (POP EVENTS)))
        (DO (COND ((SETQ NEW-BINDINGS
                         (MATCH EVENT CD *CURRENT-SCRIPT*))
                   (SETQ *CURRENT-SCRIPT* NEW-BINDINGS)
                   (MSG T "MATCHES")
                   (PRINT-CD EVENT)
                   (ADD-SCRIPT-INFO EVENT))))
        (UNTIL NEW-BINDINGS)
        (RESULT NEW-BINDINGS]
```

ADD-SCRIPT-INFO is given an event in a script (the one that matched
the input in INTEGRATE-INTO-SCRIPT). Each script event up through
POSITION is instantiated and added to the data base.

```
(DE ADD-SCRIPT-INFO (POSITION)
  (LOOP (INITIAL EVENT NIL
                 EVENTS *POSSIBLE-NEXT-EVENTS*)
        (WHILE (SETQ EVENT (POP EVENTS)))
        (DO (MSG T "Adding script CD")
            (PRINT-CD (ADD-CD (INSTANTIATE EVENT *CURRENT-SCRIPT*))))
        (UNTIL (EQUAL EVENT POSITION))
        (RESULT (SETQ *POSSIBLE-NEXT-EVENTS* EVENTS]
```

SUGGEST-NEW-SCRIPT takes a CD form, adds it to the data base, and
checks the predicates of the form and its subforms until a link
to a script is found (if any). Thus in (PTRANS (ACTOR (PERSON))
(OBJECT (PERSON)) (TO (STORE))) the first script found is under STORE
If there was a previous script, add it to the data base before
switching to another script, but do not instantiate any events
that were left in *POSSIBLE-NEXT-EVENTS*.

```
(DE SUGGEST-NEW-SCRIPT (CD)
  (LET (NEW-SCRIPT (FIND-SCRIPT CD))
    (COND (NEW-SCRIPT
           (AND *CURRENT-SCRIPT* (ADD-CD *CURRENT-SCRIPT*))
           (MSG T "New script" NEW-SCRIPT)
           (SETQ *CURRENT-SCRIPT* (LIST NEW-SCRIPT))
           (SETQ *POSSIBLE-NEXT-EVENTS* (EVENTS:SCRIPT NEW-SCRIPT))
           (INTEGRATE-INTO-SCRIPT CD]
```

```
(DE FIND-SCRIPT (CD)
 (COND ((ATOM CD) (ASSOCIATED-SCRIPT CD))
        (T (OR (ASSOCIATED-SCRIPT (HEADER: CD CD))
               (LET (SCRIPT NIL)
                (FOR (PAIR IN (ROLES:CD CD))
                     (EXISTS (SETQ SCRIPT
                                  (FIND-SCRIPT (FILLER: PAIR PAIR)))))
               SCRIPT]
```

`PRINT-CD prints a CD form, indented, left margin in column 4.

```
(DE PRINT-CD (CD)
 (SPRINT CD 4) (MSG T]
```

```
- ****************************************************************************
-                 DATA STRUCTURES AND ACCESS FUNCTIONS
- ****************************************************************************
```

`A story is a list of CDs. A CD is a predicate (PTRANS, PERSON, etc.)
`plus zero or more (role filler) pairs. Here is a story in CDs:

```
(SETQ KITE-STORY
     '( `Jack went to the store.
        (PTRANS (ACTOR (PERSON (NAME (JACK))))
                     (OBJECT (PERSON (NAME (JACK)))) (TO (STORE)))
        `He got a kite.
        (ATRANS (OBJECT (KITE)) (TO (PERSON)))
        `He went home.
        (PTRANS (ACTOR (PERSON)) (OBJECT (PERSON)) (TO (HOUSE]
```

`Script names are atoms with an EVENTS property of the atom pointing
`to a list of events.

```
(DE EVENTS:SCRIPT (X) (AND X (GET X 'EVENTS]
```

`For example, this is the shopping script:

```
(DEFPROP SHOPPING
 ((PTRANS (ACTOR ?SHOPPER) (OBJECT ?SHOPPER) (TO ?STORE))
  (PTRANS (ACTOR ?SHOPPER) (OBJECT ?BOUGHT) (TO ?SHOPPER))
  (ATRANS (ACTOR ?STORE) (OBJECT ?BOUGHT)
          (FROM ?STORE) (TO ?SHOPPER))
  (ATRANS (ACTOR ?SHOPPER) (OBJECT (MONEY))
          (FROM ?SHOPPER) (TO ?STORE))
  (PTRANS (ACTOR ?SHOPPER) (OBJECT ?SHOPPER)
          (FROM ?STORE) (TO ?ELSEWHERE)) )
 EVENTS)
```

`Some predicates have associated scripts. For example, the SHOPPING
`script is associated with STORE. The script is stored under
`the ASSOCIATED-SCRIPT property of the predicate.

```
(DE ASSOCIATED-SCRIPT (X) (GET X 'ASSOCIATED-SCRIPT]
```

ˉFor example,

(DEFPROP STORE SHOPPING ASSOCIATED-SCRIPT)

ˉsays that SHOPPING is the associated script for STORE.

ˉClear the data base.

(CLEAR-SCRIPTS)

EXERCISES

1. a. Write a restaurant script to include the following events:

   > Go to restaurant.
   > Order meal.
   > Eat meal.
   > Pay.
   > Leave restaurant.

   It should have the roles RESTAURANT, DINER, and MEAL.
   b. Set the variable RESTAURANT-STORY to a list of the CD forms for "Jack went to a restaurant. He ate a lobster. He left."
   c. Run McSAM on RESTAURANT-STORY. Afterwards, the data base should contain instantiations of all the CDs in your restaurant script.
2. Right now we have a data base (*DATA-BASE*) and a function to add things to it (ADD-CD) but no function to retrieve things from it.
   a. Define a function FETCH that takes a pattern as an argument and returns the first CD in the data base that matches it, or NIL if there are none. Thus,

   > (FETCH '(PTRANS (ACTOR ?X) (OBJECT ?X)))

   should return the first CD where someone went somewhere.
   b. Define a function FETCH-ALL that takes a pattern as an argument and returns all the CDs in the data base that match it.
3. If FETCHING becomes an important operation, and the data base becomes larger, then storing everything in one big list would be very inefficient. You can improve things by breaking the data base up into many smaller data bases, one for each predicate. That is, there would be a data base for PTRANS, for ATRANS, and so on. To find out if

   > (PTRANS (ACTOR (PERSON (NAME (JACK)))) (TO (STORE)))

   is true, FETCH would only have to look at the PTRANS data base.
   This can be implemented by putting a property on each predicate—call it DATA-BASE—whose value would be a list of all the CDs with that predicate.

Modify FETCH and ADD-CD to include this improvement. You will probably also want to define functions to initialize and display this new data base format.

4. Assume that the sentence "A coin rolled into the store" is analyzed as

   (PTRANS (OBJECT (MONEY)) (TO (STORE)))

   a. What will happen if we gave this line to McSAM? What could be done to change the results?
   b. Suppose the sentence were "A dog walked into the store." Does your solution still work?

   The general problem is one of giving semantic knowledge to the pattern matcher, so that it will know that people are the appropriate actors in the SHOPPING script.

   c. Add to each script a VARS property which is a list of the form:

      ((var-name property) (var-name property) . . .)

      For example, under SHOPPING would be:

      ((SHOPPER (ANIMATE ?SHOPPER)) (STORE (STORE ?STORE)) . . .)

   d. Replace MATCH in INTEGRATE-INTO-SCRIPT with SUPER-MATCH. Define the function SUPER-MATCH to take a pattern, a CD, and a script binding form. It should return an updated binding form if the pattern matches the CD *and* the new bindings satisfy the constraints given by VARS. Note that the functions like ANIMATE and STORE will have to know how to get at the bindings of pattern variables.

5. When understanding "Jack went to the store" we know that Jack was at the store, but this inference is probably not one we want to make unless someone asks us to. That is, if McSAM processes something like

   (PTRANS (ACTOR (PERSON))
           (OBJECT (PERSON)) (TO (STORE)))

   we don't want it to always add

   (AT (ACTOR (PERSON)) (OBJECT (STORE)))

   but if the PTRANS form is in the data base, then

   (FETCH '(AT (ACTOR (PERSON)) (OBJECT (STORE))))

   should succeed. To do this we want an inference rule like "To find out if a person was at a location, find out if he went to that location." In this exercise we will add such a capability.

a. Define the FEXPR DEF-INFERENCE so that we can define an inference rule by typing

(DEF-INFERENCE pattern1 pattern2)

This should add the pattern-pair (pattern1 pattern2) to the list *INFER-ENCE-RULES*, which will be used to replace a search for pattern1 with a search for pattern2. For example, our AT rule would be:

(DEF-INFERENCE
(AT (ACTOR ?PERSON) (OBJECT ?LOC))
(PTRANS (ACTOR ?PERSON) (TO ?LOC]

b. Next modify FETCH to use the inference rules if it fails to find anything in the data base. For example, if FETCH does not find the CD:

(AT (ACTOR (PERSON (NAME (JACK)))) (OBJECT (STORE)))

then FETCH should try matching the CD against the first element of each pattern-pair in *INFERENCE-RULES*. If the CD matches a first element, then FETCH should instantiate the second element with the bindings returned by the match. Then it should search for the CD formed by this instantiation. Since the AT CD form matches the first element of the AT rule, FETCH should now look for the PTRANS CD form built by instantiating the second element of the pattern-pair, with PERSON bound to (PERSON (NAME (JACK))) and LOC bound to (STORE).

Your solution should allow a chain of inferences, so that a search for A could lead to a search for B which in turn could lead to a search for C. Furthermore, if using one inference rule for a CD does not pan out, FETCH should be able to try other inference rules. Beware of infinite loops!

6. McSAM ignores unfilled script roles. For example, assume the SHOP-PING script has a CD for physically giving some money to a cashier:

(PTRANS (ACTOR ?SHOPPER) (OBJECT ?PRICE)
(FROM ?SHOPPER) (TO ?CASHIER))

In the shopping story we have been using, neither price nor cashier are mentioned, so these roles are not filled, and McSAM instantiates the above CD pattern as the rather useless form:

(PTRANS (ACTOR (PERSON (NAME (JACK))))
(FROM (PERSON (NAME (JACK)))))

Clearly, we want to be able to specify default values for script roles, such as that a cashier is some person.

a. Add to the SHOPPING script a DEFAULTS property with the value:

    ((CASHIER (PERSON)) (PRICE (MONEY)))

This says that the default for CASHIER is (PERSON) and for PRICE is (MONEY).

b. Fix ADD-SCRIPT-INFO and INSTANTIATE so that a default CD form is generated to fill in an unbound script role, using the appropriate predicates from DEFAULTS.

For example, if SHOPPER is (PERSON (NAME (JACK))) but neither CASHIER nor PRICE are bound, then the form

    (PTRANS (ACTOR ?SHOPPER) (OBJECT ?PRICE) (TO ?CASHIER))

should instantiate as

    (PTRANS (ACTOR (PERSON (NAME (JACK))))
          (OBJECT (MONEY))
          (TO (PERSON (FUNCTION (CASHIER)))))

7. Add the McELI parser to the McSAM program. It already has the definitions needed to do KITE-STORY and an exercise for adding the restaurant story of Exercise (1). Write a top-level function which will take a list of sentences, parse them into CD, and then pass the results to McSAM for interpretation.

7 PAM

Robert Wilensky

INTRODUCTION

Stories often contain elements that do not conform to a stereotype, yet such stories are perfectly comprehensible to human readers. Since people can understand situations that they have not experienced, they must have an understanding ability beyond that obtainable from simple script or frame application. PAM was undertaken to investigate the source of this ability.

Previous understanding systems, such as SAM (Cullingford, 1978) and Ms. Malaprop (Charniak, 1977b) used highly structured forms of knowledge to direct the inference process—scripts (Schank and Abelson, 1977) in the case of SAM, and frames (Minsky, 1975) in the case of Ms. Malaprop. These systems demonstrate the role that knowledge about mundane situations plays in the inference process.

The original idea behind PAM (Wilensky, 1978) was provided by Schank and Abelson (1977). They pointed out that much of story understanding involves understanding the intentions of the characters in the text. This is particularly important when stories are about non-stereotypical situations.

Thus story understanding involves reasoning about people's intentions. In particular, reasoning about intentions is needed to find *explanations* for a character's actions. A reader involved in processing a text is engaged in the task of constructing an explanation for each event in that text. The reader makes inferences for the purpose of finding an explanation.

In order to build a system that can find explanations for events, it is necessary to have a theory of common sense explanation. This theory must specify what the components of an explanation are, how an explanation is to be inferred from a text, and how an understander can know when an inferred explanation is adequate. Schank and Abelson (1977) provided a set of plans and goals that comprised the components of the explanations initially used in PAM. The first step in creating PAM involved the application of these plans and goals to the construction of explanations.

A story understander needs to use its knowledge to interpret a sentence in context. Knowledge used in such a manner is said to have a *predictive* value. A reader uses what he knows and what has just been read to help understand what is going to be read next. However, stories that are not stereotypical are not totally predictable. Since the idea behind PAM was to build an understander with more flexibility than previous programs, it could not be expected to work mainly by prediction.

For example, consider the following story:

> John wanted to impress his date. He called up his friend Bill and asked him if he could borrow his Cadillac.

A reader of this story must infer that John was going to use the Cadillac to pick up his date. Making this inference requires that the reader use knowledge about what may impress someone; this knowledge is keyed by the first sentence and is used predictively to help understand the second. However, it is unreasonable to expect a reader to have predicted the exact form of behavior exhibited by John, namely, that he would call up a friend and ask to borrow something. The problem here is how to store the knowledge needed for this example so that it can be used predictively enough to effect contextual understanding, but not so predictively that it makes the understander inflexible. In other words, we need a mechanism that can predict something just a little.

Problems of a more theoretical nature also arose in building PAM. Many stories do not conform to the type of planning structures provided by Schank and Abelson. The problem is that most stories involve situations in which a number of goals appear at once. While the Schank and Abelson intentional structures are useful in finding explanations for stories in which a character pursues a single goal, a great deal more theoretical apparatus is necessary to understand the interrelationships between goals.

What is needed is a theory of goal interactions and an understanding of the story situations that they give rise to. The following goal interactions were found to be at the basis of many common story situations:

1. *Goal Subsumption*—A situation in which many recurrences of a goal are planned for at the same time. For example, consider the following story:

> John enjoyed drinking hot coffee. He bought a thermos.

Here John has the recurring goal of enjoying hot coffee, and keeping the coffee hot is instrumental to this goal. Using a thermos can be a plan for achieving this goal, and to use this plan, possession of a thermos is necessary. John's purchasing the thermos can be explained as a way of *subsuming* this recurring goal by establishing a state (namely, ownership of a thermos) that meets this precondition and endures over a period of time.

2. *Goal Conflict*—An inimical relationship among the goals of a single character. As an example, consider the following:

> John's friends asked him to go bowling. John had promised Mary he would take her out to dinner, but his friends persuaded him to come with them. The next morning, Mary told John she was going to divorce him.

Mary is probably angry at John because he didn't take her to dinner. To infer that John didn't take Mary out, a reader of this story must understand that John had two goals that were in *conflict* with each other, and that because he pursued one goal, the other goal was neglected. Thus the reader must be able to recognize the presence of a conflict and understand how it can influence a character's behavior.

3. *Goal Competition*—An inimical relationship among the goals of different characters. For example, consider

> John wanted to watch the football game, but Mary said she was going to watch the Bolshoi ballet. John punched Mary in the mouth and put on the ball game.

To understand why John struck Mary, a reader must realize that Mary had a goal that *competed* with John's goal. Thus John's punching Mary is explained as a plan to eliminate one's opposition rather than fulfill one's own goal. To find this explanation, a reader must be able to recognize the competition and understand the situations that it may give rise to.

4. *Goal Concord*—A coincidence of goals among different characters. Consider

> John and Bill were partners playing golf. Bill hit a shot into the rough. John sneakily moved the ball into a better position.

To understand why John helped Bill, a reader must understand that their goals were in *concord* with one another. Thus a reader must determine when characters have concordant goals, and how they may act in such circumstances.

These goal relationships provide a basis for a theory of planning about real world situations. That is, much of the intentional behavior described in story situations conforms to a situation involving a goal relationship. Understanding how a person might act when confronted by such a situation is a necessary step in building a program capable of understanding that person's behavior.

The goal relationships listed above give rise to a classification of story situations. Each type of situation has a set of knowledge and inference processes associated with it. By equipping PAM with knowledge about how to identify these situations and how to reason about them, PAM is able to understand many stories about complex and interesting dramatic situations.

Input/Output Examples

The following examples are actual input to PAM and output produced by PAM:

****

INPUT TEXT:

> John wanted money.
> He got a gun and walked into a liquor store.
> He told the owner he wanted some money.
> The owner gave John the money and John left.

INPUT: Why did John get a gun?
OUTPUT: Because John wanted to rob the liquor store.

INPUT: Why did John threaten the shopkeeper?
OUTPUT: Because John needed to get some money.

INPUT: Why did the shopkeeper give John the money?
OUTPUT: Because the shopkeeper didn't want to get hurt.

INPUT: Why did John leave?
OUTPUT: Because John didn't want to get caught.

OUTPUT:

STORY FROM JOHN'S POINT OF VIEW:

> I needed to get some dough. So I got myself this gun, and I walked down to the liquor store. I told the shopkeeper that if he didn't let me have the money then I would shoot him. So he handed it over. Then I left.

OUTPUT:

STORY FROM THE OWNER'S POINT OF VIEW:

> I was minding the store when a man entered. He threatened me with a gun and demanded all the cash receipts. Well, I didn't want to get hurt, so I gave him the money. Then he escaped.

****

This story demonstrates PAM's explanation-driven understanding mechanism. When PAM reads that John got a gun, it must infer that John was probably going to use the gun to rob someone. PAM constructs an explanation for this event by inferring that John got the gun so he could use it, that he planned to use it to threaten or overpower someone, and that he planned to do so to get some money from someone. This explanation is then used to infer an explanation for John's telling the shopkeeper he wanted some money—namely, that this was an attempt to threaten him.

These inferences are expressed through the paraphrases and question-answering session that follow the understanding process. Some other inferences that PAM must make in order to understand this story include the following: After threatening the shopkeeper, John had an additional goal of getting away safely; the store keeper gave John the money because he was afraid John would hurt him; John left the store to avoid subsequent capture.

The following computer example, while it appears simpler, requires more sophisticated reasoning. The story demonstrates PAM's use of its knowledge about goal relationships:

****

INPUT TEXT:

John wanted to win the stockcar race.
Bill also wanted to win the stockcar race.
Before the race John cut Bill's ignition wire.

INPUT: Why did John break an ignition wire?
OUTPUT: Because he was trying to prevent Bill from racing.

****

This story contains an instance of goal competition between John and Bill. To explain why John cut Bill's ignition wire, PAM must first recognize that John and Bill have competitive goals, and that one of them may therefore undertake a plan directed against his opponent. This is an example of an *antiplanning* situation, in which a character's action cannot be explained in terms of his own goals alone, but must be explained as it relates to the undermining of an opponent's goal.

The question and answer exchange above reflects PAM's understanding of the motivation behind John's action. Some other inferences PAM must make to understand this story are that John and Bill have competing goals because both of them cannot win the race, and that damaging the ignition wire is a way of making the car unfit for racing.

Another computer example that demonstrates PAM's knowledge of goal relationships is the following:

****

INPUT TEXT:

> John wanted to watch the football game,
> but he had a paper due the next day.
> John watched the football game.
> John failed Civics.

INPUT: Why did John fail a course in Civics?
OUTPUT: He failed to hand in an assignment.

****

Here PAM must infer that John has two goals that conflict with each other due to a limitation of time resources. The recognition of this conflict is needed to infer that John didn't hand in an assignment: He pursued a goal that conflicted with getting the assignment done, and thus John must have abandoned this latter goal. The question asked after the understanding phase demonstrates that PAM has inferred the reason why John failed his course. Another inference PAM had to make along the way is that writing the paper was instrumental to passing the course.

SUMMARY OF PAM'S BEHAVIOR

PAM currently understands 16 different classes of stories, ranging in length from 2 to 9 sentences. A class is distinguished by the kinds of inference processes that are needed to understand the stories in that class. For example, one class of stories involves inferring one character's goal bottom-up from a description of an action. Other classes include more complicated goal relationship situations, such as goal subsumption termination and goal conflict leading to goal abandonment. In each case, the stories in one class differ from those in another by more than a substitution of one plan or goal for another. For example, the story

John wanted a book. He asked Bill for one.

is in the same class as

John wanted a book. He told Bill he would buy one from him for a dollar.

Most of PAM's knowledge is encoded using a form of rule called a request. The exact format of a request will be explained later. For the time being, they may be thought of as condition-action pairs. An informal example of such a pair would be:

> If
>
>> a character has the goal of possessing a functional object,
>
> then
>
>> that character probably wants to use that object for its intended purpose.

There are approximately 180 such rules in PAM at the present.

Much of the knowledge PAM possesses is about plans and their relation to goals, actions, and each other. PAM currently has knowledge relating to 32 different planboxes (basic units of planning). These include such diverse plans as THREATEN, a general method of persuasion, and UNDO-PRECONDITION, a method to obstruct someone else's plan.

PAM is written in UCILISP and MLISP on a DEC System 20/50. The program currently runs in 177 pages (90k words). This includes 40k words of free storage used for building story representations and the like. The question-answer and English generator fit into this space, but ELI, the English Language Interpreter, does not.

It takes PAM an average of 5.58 CPU seconds to process a sentence. The processing time per sentence ranges from .9 to 15.2 seconds. This figure does not include the time required to analyze an English sentence into its Conceptual Dependency representation. ELI averages about 3–4 CPU seconds to perform this task.

Little attempt has been made to make PAM as fast or as small as possible. There are a number of straightforward modifications that could reduce the above figures somewhat. For example, all of PAM's code is interpreted. Compiling this code would probably cause a speed-up of about a factor of three. The total size of the program could be reduced considerably by garbage collecting working structures. PAM currently saves these for debugging purposes.

Issues

The primary purpose in building PAM was to gain some insight into the kinds of knowledge and processes needed for natural language understanding. The construction of PAM gave rise to a number of considerations.

Explanation Versus Frame-finding

One view of understanding that has gained attention recently is often referred to as the *frame hypothesis* (Collins, 1978). This hypothesis claims that understanding an input is equivalent to finding a frame into which the input can be integrated. Building PAM has caused us to question this idea.

There are two problems with the frame hypothesis.

1. Often, there is no one single frame into which coherent inputs will fit.
2. There will usually be a number of frames into which a given input can fit, but finding most of these will not necessarily amount to understanding the input.

The first point is applicable when an understander is reading a story for which he does not possess a pre-constructed frame. In this case, it is necessary to find a sequence of frames that can be connected together to provide coherency. This is exactly what is done by the explanation-driven understanding scheme used in PAM.

The second difficulty arises in knowing when a frame is suitable. For example, consider the following sentences:

John painted his car white.
John painted his terminal screen white.

The first sentence appears to be an instance of the painting frame. (See Charniak, 1977a, for a detailed examination of this particular situation.) Once a frame that fits the input has been found to be readily available, it can be instantiated and the input can be said to be understood.

The problem is that this algorithm does exactly the same thing for the second sentence above. However, it is undesirable that processing cease at this point in the second example, because an intelligent reader would wonder why John might have done such a strange thing. That is, in this case, as in most cases, the reader must decide if the frame he has found explains the input. But then the main question any understander must ask is whether the input has been explained.

Thus the notion of explanation-driven understanding is to some degree in competition with the frame-hypothesis. A reader tries to account for an input by constructing explanations. The process of constructing an explanation may entail finding one or more suitable frames, fitting a number of frames together, and deciding when the resulting structure is adequate. Finding frames is certainly an important part of the process, but it is only instrumental to the understander's true goal of building an explanation.

A Theory of Planning

Constructing PAM demonstrated the need for a theory of planning that is much more complex than previous theories. Although PAM itself does not do planning but rather uses plans to generate explanations, it still requires more knowledge about planning than was necessary for most previous problem solvers or robot planners. The basic problem is that most planning in the real world is concerned with situations in which a number of goals are present at once, whereas most work on planning has been concerned with single goal situations. Thus it was necessary to develop a theory of planning based on goal relationships. While this theory has so far only been applied to story understanding, it would seem that a robot planner will also need this knowledge if it is to act intelligently in complex situations.

The Integration of Prediction and Recognition

The type of stories PAM is meant to understand made it necessary that PAM have both recognition and prediction capabilities. Previous natural language understanding systems tended to avoid the issue of integrating the two. For example, SAM and Ms. Malaprop assumed that the appropriate script or frame would be available to the understander—that the program would not have to worry about what the frame was. Since PAM is designed to understand stories without having a particular frame in mind, it had to face the problem of hypothesizing appropriate frames (usually plans, in the case of PAM) and integrating them into existing structures.

One result indicated by PAM is that the cost of hypothesizing a frame is probably quite small. The amount of time required for PAM to find knowledge applicable to an unexpected input is a tiny fraction of its total run time (about 3 percent). Since the access method used by PAM (actually a simple discrimination net) causes the access time to grow logarithmically with the size of the knowledge base, it does not appear that the efficiency of a recognition algorithm is a major problem.

Of course, the question of what keys to base frame indexing on is still problematic. PAM's indexing is based on its explanation algorithm. However, the need to find frames occurs in other circumstances where this indexing is inadequate.

PAM has formulated the problems of story understanding in terms of explanation and planning in complex situations. Within this framework, PAM has offered solutions to a number of problems. However, many gaps still remain.

The Notion of Explanation

PAM's idea of explanation is based on its notion of planning—an explanation is in effect a sensible set of plans and goals. However, it is clear that not all explanation is intention-based. For example, consider these stories:

> John hit Bill. He cried.
> John hit Bill. He fell back.

Explaining the second sentences of the two stories above requires recourse to affective and physical knowledge, respectively. The concept of explanation should be extended to deal with situations such as these.

Knowledge Encoding

Most of PAM's knowledge about planning is encoded in the form of requests, which are highly procedural in character. That is, PAM's knowledge about plans and goals is stated in a form that is particularly useful for understanding stories and finding explanations, but not very useful for other purposes, such as generating plans or finding solutions to problems. It should be possible to represent some of this knowledge in a more declarative format that would have greater generality than PAM currently has.

The basic point of doing this would be to separate out knowledge about plans and goals from knowledge about how to use it. This latter kind of knowledge would include knowledge about explanations or knowledge about planning. Probably most of a person's knowledge about plans and goals is the same for both these tasks, and thus a uniform representation is desirable. Just how much the process of explanation and the process of planning can be separated from the knowledge about plans still remains to be seen. A version of PAM aimed at incorporating this modularity is now under construction.

Story Knowledge

One basic problem in PAM is that it really doesn't know what a story is about. PAM is willing to accept any goal-based sequence of sentences as a story. Real stories are not so arbitrary. A story understander has some notion of what stories tend to be about, and uses this notion to forget unimportant details and make inferences about story events.

Thus PAM needs a theory of story content. This theory should describe the type of events that comprise most stories, and should have a predictive value in suggesting what a reader is likely to hear about next in the story. In addition, such a theory would be extremely useful for explaining how we summarize stories and forget irrelevant details—an ability that will be of increasing importance as the amount of text that is processed increases.

THE PROGRAM

PAM's purpose is to find explanations. To do so, it must combine a top-down predictive ability with a bottom-up recognition mechanism. The overall flow of control in PAM is summarized in Fig. 7.1:

Figure 7.1 presents the order in which PAM processes an input. First, it checks to see if a specific prediction exists that is confirmed by the input. If there is one, then that prediction should explain the input. Otherwise, inferences must be drawn to hypothesize bottom-up explanations. Then the predictions must once again be consulted to see if any of them are met by one of these inferences. When an inference is found that meets a prediction, the input and any inferences that have been made in the process of explaining it are added to the story representation.

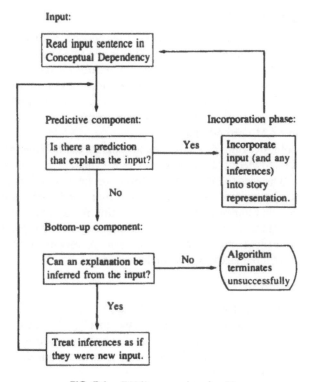

FIG. 7.1.   PAM's processing algorithm.

By having the appropriate predictions present and by making the correct bottom-up inferences, PAM will eventually infer an explanation for a reasonable input. The content of these predictions conforms to the theory of explanation incorporated in PAM. The essence of this theory is shown in Fig. 7.2:

Figure 7.1 may be thought of as a way to implement Fig. 7.2. For example, STEP 1 of Fig. 7.2 says that if the input is an event, then determining that it is part of a known plan would explain it. This is implemented in PAM by checking to see if there exists a prediction that such an event would be encountered. This is an example of the function of the predictive component of Fig. 7.1. STEP 2 of Fig. 7.2 is taken when no pre-existing plan explains the event, and a plan must be hypothesized. This is an example of the function of the bottom-up component of Fig. 7.1. STEP 3 of Fig. 7.2 is implemented by checking predictions, and thus is implemented by the predictive component, just as STEP 1 is.

In general, finding a connection between an input or an inference and something already in the story representation is done predictively; inferring an explanation not already present in the representation is done through the bottom-up mechanism.

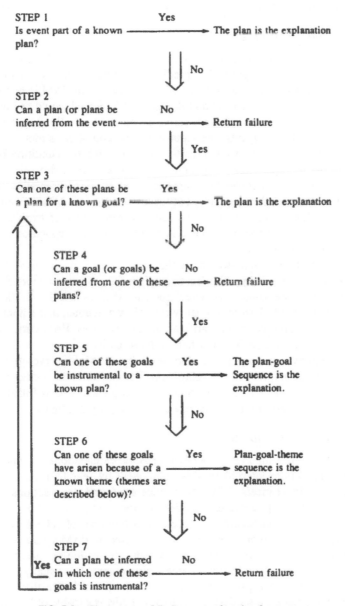

STEP 1
Is event part of a known ——————— Yes ——————► The plan is the explanation
plan?
                                    No

STEP 2
Can a plan (or plans be   No
inferred from the event ——————————————► Return failure
                                    Yes

STEP 3
Can one of these plans be   Yes
a plan for a known goal? ══════════════► The plan is the explanation
                                    No

STEP 4
Can a goal (or goals) be   No
inferred from one of these ————————► Return failure
plans?
                                    Yes

STEP 5
Can one of these goals   Yes   The plan-goal
be instrumental to a ———————————►   Sequence is the
known plan?   explanation.
                                    No

STEP 6
Can one of these goals   Yes   Plan-goal-theme
have arisen because of a —————————► sequence is the
known theme (themes are   explanation.
described below)?
                                    No

STEP 7
Yes Can a plan be inferred   No
     in which one of these ——————————► Return failure
     goals is instrumental?

FIG. 7.2. The process of finding an explanation for an event.

Description of Components

The following are brief descriptions of the components that make up Fig. 7.1:

Predictive Component

The predictive component of PAM is the first mechanism that tries to explain each new input to the program. The predictive component has access to a number of predictions made previously by PAM. A prediction in PAM is really just the condition part of a condition-action rule that PAM guessed would be important in understanding new inputs. The predictive component serially checks the condition of each such rule against the input until one condition is met.

If a prediction is confirmed, then the rule to which the condition belongs is passed to the incorporation component. The action part of this rule should tell that component how to connect the input to the existing representation. Actually, PAM may have cycled through this sequence several times before finally finding a prediction that has been met. In the process, a sequence of explanatory rules has been found. This entire sequence is passed to the incorporation component when a prediction is finally met.

If no prediction is satisfied, then the input is passed on to the bottom-up component, which will hypothesize an explanation. If two or more predictions are true at the same time, this would indicate that there exist multiple explanations for the input. That is, the story itself is ambiguous, and a human reader would probably have to ask for clarification in these cases. PAM currently cannot ask for clarification, and does not handle these cases.

The predictive component is also used by PAM to serve several other functions that are not related to explanation. For example, the predictive component determines whether an input means that a goal has been fulfilled. These details are described in the technical view of the program below.

Bottom-Up Component

The bottom-up component generates plausible explanations for inputs. Plausible explanations are inferred by this component by searching for rules whose conditions the input meets. When such rules are found, their actions are taken. Each action infers a possible explanation for the input.

The bottom-up component has access to a large set of rules that constitute PAM's long-term memory, and that are the crux of PAM's knowledge about intentions. These rules are indexed, using a discrimination net, to minimize the time required to find the rules that match a given input. It is usually the case that only a few rules are applicable to a given input, and hence that only a few plausible explanations are inferred. However, PAM is capable of handling situations in which any number of rules may come into play.

When the bottom-up component uses the action of a rule to make an inference, it does so in such a way that the actual representation for the story that has been built up previously is not modified. Any particular rule used at this point may eventually turn out to be a blind alley, and the inferences it makes will not ultimately be a part of the explanation for the input. Thus the bottom-up component makes inferences in "test-mode", in which the inference is made without adding it to the representation or causing any side-effects that cannot easily be undone.

If the bottom-up phase is successful, the inferred explanations it creates are passed back to the predictive component. The predictive component will treat each of these inferences just as if it were an input. That is, it will try to find a prediction that is met by one of these inferences. If it does so, the component will stop and enter the incorporation phase; if it does not, it will pass the inference back to the bottom-up component to hypothesize an explanation for that inference.

If the bottom-up phase cannot find any rules corresponding to an input, then PAM will fail to understand the input. This situation corresponds to when a human reader cannot find a reason for a particular event.

The bottom-up component also does the bookkeeping needed to keep track of which rule is used to make each inference, and the order in which rules are used to hypothesize explanations. When a sequence of rules is found that relates an input to a prediction through a chain of inferences, the incorporation component can then add the inferences to the story representation.

Incorporation Component

When a prediction is confirmed by an input, or by an inference made from the input, the input and the inferences must be integrated into the story representation built up so far. This is the function of the incorporation component. The incorporation component takes as input a sequence of rules. These are the rules used by the bottom-up component to make a series of inferences, the last of which met some prediction. The prediction itself is the condition part of some rule and that rule is also passed to the incorporation phase.

The incorporation phase takes these rules and uses them once again to make inferences. This time, however, the inferences are added into the actual story representation. The creation of these inferences sometimes causes a side-effect that may change the story representation.

After it has used all these rules to add inferences to the story representation, the incorporation component must remove the prediction that connected the chain of inferences to the story representation. In addition, there may be a number of other predictions that were in competition with the one that was met, and these too must be removed. For example, PAM might have several predictions at once, each predicting that the same character will pursue a different plan. When one of these predictions is confirmed, all the others must be removed, since the right plan is now known and the unused predictions are thus all invalid.

In addition to removing predictions, the incorporation component is responsible for making predictions in the first place. Associated with a rule in PAM is a set of other rules that may be useful. These rules are tested during the incorporation phase. Those whose conditions are found to be true are used immediately; this generally adds another assertion to the representation. Those whose conditions are not yet true are predictions about future events. These become the predictions that the predictive component will use to explain subsequent inputs.

An Example

This section contains a non-technical description of how PAM uses the understanding algorithm sketched above to understand the following story:

a) John wanted Bill's bicycle.
b) He walked over to Bill
c) and asked him if he would give it to him.
d) Bill refused.
e) Then John told Bill he would give him five dollars for it,
f) but Bill would not agree.
g) John told Bill he would break his arm if he didn't let him have it.
h) Bill let John have the bicycle.

Inputs to PAM are in the form of Conceptual Dependencies (CDs), as produced by Riesbeck's conceptual analysis program (Riesbeck, 1975). Thus the first line above would be parsed as:

```
((CON ((ACTOR (BICYCLE REL ((ACTOR (BICYCLE)
                                    IS (*POSS* PART (BILL)))))
          IS (*POSS* PART (JOHN))))
     IS (*GOAL* PART (JOHN))))
```

This CD encodes the information that John has the goal of possessing a bicycle that is currently owned by Bill.

PAM now tries to find an explanation for the input. Since this is the first sentence of the story and no previous goals or plans have yet been seen, the predictive component fails, and the input is passed to the bottom-up component to hypothesize an explanation. The input is a statement of a goal, and goals can be explained either by instrumentality or by themes. Thus PAM must see if it knows of any themes that can give rise to this particular goal, or of any plans for which this goal would be a subgoal. The goal of possessing any object can arise from the theme of liking that object. Also, possessing an object with a standard function can be instrumental to using that object. PAM therefore infers two plausible explanations for this sentence. One is that John wants to have Bill's bicycle simply because he likes it, and the other is that John wants Bill's bicycle because he wants to ride it.

To arrive at these explanations, the bottom-up component searches for rules that are applicable to this input, and finds the following:

(1) If a person wants to possess an object, then he may have the attitude of liking that object.

(2) If a person wants to possess an object that has a function, then he may want to use that object to perform its function.

The bottom-up component then uses these rules to produce inferences. Rule (1) generates the inference that John may be fond of the bicycle. Rule (2) produces the inference that John may want to ride the bicycle.

Having accessed the rules whose conditions are met by the input CD, and having made the inferences indicated by the actions of these rules, PAM is left with two alternative explanations for the sentence. These are passed back to the predictive component. At the beginning of the understanding process, PAM has no way of determining which of these explanations is the correct one. However, since it has determined several plausible explanations, it need not continue inferring. Instead, we would like PAM merely to record both plausible inferences in the story representation for the time being. This is accomplished by inserting a prediction at the start of story understanding that looks for situations with several plausible explanations. Several such predictions are necessary to get the story understanding process "off the ground".

Having found inferences that confirm a prediction, PAM enters the incorporation phase. The rules which were used to make these inferences are now used to add them to the story representation.

The incorporation phase also makes the prediction that John may try some plan to achieve his goal of getting Bill's bike, and that he may also try to achieve some goal instrumental to such a plan. These are rather standard predictions that are made when new goals become known to PAM. These predictions will be used by the predictive component of the program to find the connection between future inputs and John's known goal.

The understander now reads line (b), converts it into CD, and passes it to PAM; which tries to find an explanation for the CD. The predictive component fails here—it is currently looking only for plans for, or immediate subgoals of, John's goal of getting Bill's bicycle. That is, walking over to someone is a plan for changing one's location, not for gaining possession of an object. Thus PAM must pass control to the bottom-up component.

Once again, this component tries to access those rules in memory whose conditions are satisfied by the input. In this case, the following rule is found:

If

an actor does a PTRANS whose instrument is the actor moving a bodypart,

then

that actor is using the plan of moving under his own power.

That is, one way of changing one's location is through the use of one's own body. Since this is indicated by the instrument in the CD representation, John must be using this plan. Thus PAM infers that John's action is an instance of the plan of changing one's location under one's own power.

This inference is passed back to the predictive component. It again fails, since no explicit prediction exists stating that John will execute such a plan. The inference is now passed back to the bottom-up component to try to infer an explanation for it.

According to the theory of explanation, a goal is needed to which this plan can be connected. PAM therefore tries to infer the goal behind John's plan. By accessing and applying rules as above, PAM infers that John wanted to be near Bill. This inference is then passed back to the predictive component.

This time, the prediction that John will have a goal instrumental to his change of possession goal is confirmed. That is, PAM has stored along with each goal a list of goals that are often instrumental to the plans for that goal. One such goal stored as instrumental to change of possession is change of location. Thus a prediction is confirmed and an explanation found. The rules used to find this explanation are now passed to the incorporation component.

This component uses the rules once more to make their respective inferences, but this time the representation of the story is changed. Added to the representation are the inferences that John had the goal of being near Bill, that he achieved this goal by moving himself under his own power, and that this goal is instrumental to some yet unknown plan to get Bill's bicycle. The prediction used to connect these inferences with the story representation is also removed at this point.

Now line (c)—"and asked him if he would give it to him."—is read, converted to CD, and passed to the predictive component. This component fails to explain the input. Line (c) is an action, and the only prediction available expects to see a *plan* for a goal. Thus the input is passed to the bottom-up component for consideration. This component finds a rule whose condition matches this input and whose action infers that the input is an instance of the plan of asking someone for something. This inference is passed back to the predictive component.

Now the prediction that PAM would encounter a plan for John's goal is met. Stored in the reader's memory along with each goal is a list of the plans normally associated with that goal. The prediction looking for a plan for John's goal checks the list associated with the goal of getting something from someone, and finds that this list includes asking. Thus this plan must be the unknown plan John intended to use when he walked over to Bill.

The rule used to infer this plan, as well as the prediction that connects this plan to the story presentation, are passed to the incorporation component. These rules are used to modify the representation, and the prediction used to explain the input is removed. In addition, several new predictions are added. These predictions come from rules associated with the rule that inferred the ask plan. Essentially, they predict the various ways a person asked might respond to the ask plan, e.g., agreeing or refusing. The action parts of the rules making these predictions are capable of changing the story representation to show whether the plan has failed or succeeded, respectively.

After the incorporation phase, the story representation looks like Fig. 7.3.

Predictions, as they are used by PAM, are really predictions about the likelihood that some knowledge will be useful for understanding a story. They are not necessarily predictions about future events. For example, suppose John asks Bill a question. One way Bill might respond is by answering the question. When I say this response is predicted by the asking event, I mean that a prediction is made that the following knowledge will be useful: "If Bill tells John what John was trying to find out, then Bill told this to John in response to John's question." This is not a prediction that Bill will answer the question, or that he is even likely to answer it. Rather, it is a prediction that knowledge about responding will be useful for understanding subsequent sentences of the story. This sense of prediction is similar to that used by Kuno and Oettinger (1962) and Riesbeck (1975).

Predictions may be thought of as demon-like routines (see Charniak, 1972, and Selfridge, 1959) that examine subsequent inputs and inferences. The particular form of prediction used in PAM is modelled after the *requests* used in Riesbeck's conceptual analysis program (see Riesbeck, 1975). A request is a kind of rule, in that it has a condition part and an action part. In addition, requests can suggest additional requests that may be useful for subsequent processing. The condition part of a request serves as a prediction, the action describes how to connect the input to the story representation, and the suggested requests become new predictions.

For example, after line (c), Bill's subsequent behavior is likely to be in response to John's question. If he gives John the bicycle, a reader should infer

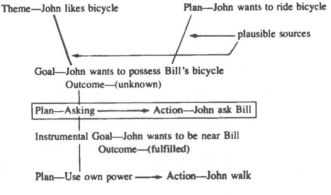

FIG. 7.3.   The story representation after line (c).

that it was because John asked him for it. If he refuses, then the reader should assume he is refusing to do what John asked. However, before the reader sees line (d), the reader cannot know what Bill's reaction is going to be. Therefore, PAM sets up two predictions, one for each possible outcome. When line (d) is encountered, the prediction looking for a denial of the request is confirmed, and an explanation of Bill's action is created.

The top-down nature of prediction is useful here because it enabled PAM to interpret line (d) as a refusal of John's request. The actual sentence, however, does not mention what Bill was refusing, so it would have been difficult to make this inference in a strictly bottom-up system, i.e., one that made all its inferences directly from the input.

Predictions are also used to find explanations for the other sentences in the story. For example, when John's plan fails in (d), a new prediction is added which looks for a new plan to achieve the same goal. When line (e) is read, it is inferred to be an instance of the plan of bargaining. Since this plan can be used for John's goal, the new prediction is fulfilled, and the event is explained. Predictions are then set up which are similar to those made after line (c), looking for the different possible outcomes. Line (f) confirms the prediction that Bill might decline the deal. The confirmation of this prediction causes another prediction to be set up looking for yet another plan.

Line (g) confirms this prediction because the bottom-up inference process infers that this is an instance of the plan of threatening, also a way to get something from someone. Predictions are set up again which look for possible outcomes. One of the predictions set up by the plan of threatening is that if the person threatened does the action requested of him, then he does it to prevent the threat from happening. Thus when line (h) is read, it is this prediction that is confirmed. The prediction explains line (h) by building the interpretation that Bill

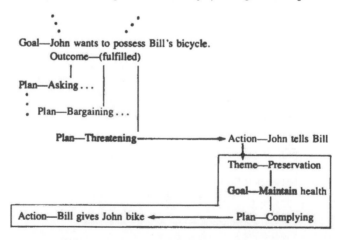

FIG. 7.4. The story representation after line (h).

must have wanted to maintain his health, and therefore complied with John's demand. The representation of the story now includes this (Fig. 7.4).

Here John's plan induced a conflict with Bill's previous desire, so Bill chose to comply with John's request by giving John the bicycle. This fulfilled John's original goal of having Bill's bicycle, and the goal is marked as such in the representation.

Computer Example

This section consists of an annotated PAM run on the above story.

> [PHOTO: Recording initiated Thu 30-Mar-78 4:29PM]
>
> @RUN PAM
>
> *(UNDERSTAND CD6)
>
> THE STORY IS
>
> JOHN WANTED BILL'S BICYCLE.
> HE WENT OVER TO BILL
>   AND ASKED HIM IF HE WOULD GIVE IT TO HIM.
> BILL REFUSED.
> JOHN TOLD BILL HE WOULD GIVE HIM FIVE DOLLARS FOR IT,
>   BUT BILL WOULD NOT AGREE.
> THEN JOHN TOLD BILL HE WOULD BREAK HIS ARM
>   IF HE DIDN'T LET HIM HAVE IT.
> BILL GAVE HIM THE BICYCLE.

Computer Output	Annotation
PROCESSING ...	
NEXT INPUT IS: (JOHN WANTED BILL'S BICYCLE)	

CONCEPTUALIZATION IS:
 ((CON
  ((ACTOR PHYS0 IS
  (*POSS* PART HUM0))
  TIME (FORM11))
  IS (*GOAL* PART HUM0))
  TIME (FORM12))
	PHYS0 is a token (representation for an individual entity) created by PAM for the bicycle. HUM0 is a token for John, and HUM1 a token for Bill. The time forms contain information about time predications in an internal format. For example, FORM12 states that the entire event occurred in the past, and FORM11 states that John's having the bicycle may exist in the future.

(continued)

Computer Output	Annotation
NOT A PREDICTED INPUT BEGIN SEARCH FOR EXPLANATION	Since no prediction is available to explain the input, PAM uses its bottom-up mechanism to find an applicable rule.
TESTING EXPLANATION OFFERED BY DCONT-EPISODE-REQ	This is the name of the rule found (recall that rules in PAM are called requests). DCONT denotes a "change of control" goal.
EXPLANATION IS GOAL: (*DCONT* PLANNER HUM0 OBJECT PHYSQ OWNER HUM1 RECIPIENT HUM0) NO PREDICTION CONFIRMED ASSUMING EXPLANATION CONTINUING SEARCH	The rule found states that John has the goal of taking possession of the bicycle. Now an explanation for this goal is sought.
TESTING EXPLANATION OFFERED BY USE-VEHICLE-REQ FONDNESS-REQ	PAM finds that the goal could have come from liking the object or wanting to use it to get someplace.
EXPLANATION IS PREDICTED PLAN: *PB-USE-VEHICLE*	This is the name of a plan for changing one's location,
EXPLANATION IS PREDICTED THEME: *FONDNESS*	and this is a theme that represents liking something.
EXPLANATION CONFIRMS PREDICTION INIT-REQ FOUND EXPLANATION SEQUENCE: DCONT-EPISODE-REQ → USE-VEHICLE-REQ	INIT-REQ is a prediction made at the start of a story that looks for a goal with plausible but uncertain sources. This rule is a way of letting PAM know when to stop processing the initial sentence of a story. The rules used to find the explanation are now used to actually connect the input to the representation.
*** ADDING TO STORY REPRESENTATION:	
LOADING PREDICTION DCONT-ATTEMPT-REQ	This predictions looks for a plan for John's goal to appear in the story.
GOAL: (*DCONT* PLANNER HUM0 OBJECT PHYS0 OWNER HUM1 RECIPIENT HUM0) NEXT INPUT IS: (HE WENT OVER TO BILL) CONCEPTUALIZATION IS: ((ACTOR HUM2 <=> (*PTRANS*) OBJECT HUM2 TO (*PROX* PART HUM1) INST (NIL)) TIME (FORM17))	

(continued)

Computer Output	*Annotation*
NOT A PREDICTED INPUT	Again, PAM goes bottom-up to find an explanation. PAM finds a rule that it uses to infer that John wanted to be near Bill to do some plan to get his bicycle. The rest of the processing of this sentence has been deleted from the story trace for the sake of brevity.
BEGIN SEARCH FOR EXPLANATION	
TESTING EXPLANATION OFFERED BY WALK-GOAL-EPISODE-REQ	

EXPLANATION IS GOAL:
(*DPROX* PLANNER HUM2 OBJECT HUM2
 LOCATION (*PROX* PART HUM1))
 PLAN: (*PB-WALK* PLANNER HUM2
LOCATION (*PROX* PART HUM1))

      .
      .
      .

NEXT INPUT IS:
 (AND ASKED HIM IF HE WOULD GIVE IT
 TO HIM)

CONCEPTUALIZATION IS:
((ACTOR HUM3 <=> (*MTRANS*)
 MOBJECT
 ((CON
   ((ACTOR HUM4 <=> (*ATRANS*)
    OBJECT PHYS0 to HUM3)
   TIME (FORM33))
  LEADTO
  ((ACTOR HUM3
    TOWARD (*JOY* VAL (NIL)))
   INC (2.) TIME (FORM34))))
 TO (*CP* PART HUM4))
 TIME (FORM35))

NOT A PREDICTED INPUT

BEGIN SEARCH FOR EXPLANATION

TESTING EXPLANATION OFFERED BY ASK-REQ	PAM finds a rule interpreting the input as part of the plan of asking.

EXPLANATION IS
 PLAN: (*PB-ASK* PLANNER HUM3
PERSUADEE HUM4 REQUEST
((ACTOR HUM4 <=> (*ATRANS*) OBJECT
 PHYS0 TO HUM3) TIME (TIMK5)))

EXPLANATION CONFIRMS PREDICTION DCONT-ATTEMPT-REQ	The prediction set up after reading the first sentence recognizes this as a plan for the goal of getting the bicycle, so the input is explained.
FOUND EXPLANATION SEQUENCE: ASK-REQ	

(continued)

Computer Output	Annotation

*** ADDING TO STORY REPRESENTATION:

INFERRED
 PLAN: (*PB-ASK* PLANNER HUM0
PERSUADEE HUM1 REQUEST
((ACTOR HUM1 <=> (*ATRANS*) OBJECT
 PHYS0 TO HUM0) TIME (TIMK5)))

LOADING PREDICTION   Predictions are loaded for the possible responses
COMPLIANCE-GOAL-REQ   to John's plan.

LOADING PREDICTION
REFUSAL-GOAL-REQ

NEXT INPUT IS:
 (BILL REFUSED)

CONCEPTUALIZATION IS:
((ACTOR HUM1 <=> (*MTRANS*)
 MOBJECT
 ((ACTOR HUM1 <=> (*DO*))
 MODE (FORM45) TIME (FORM46))
 TO (*CP* PART HUM5))
 TIME (FORM47))

NOT A PREDICTED INPUT

BEGIN SEARCH FOR EXPLANATION

TESTING EXPLANATION OFFERED BY   PAM infers that Bill was trying to tell John
TELL-REQ   something,

EXPLANATION IS:
PLAN: (*PB-TELL* PLANNER HUM1
TELLEE HUM0 FACT
((ACTOR HUM1 <=> (*ATRANS*)
OBJECT PHYS0 TO HUM0)
MODE (FORM52) TIME (TIMK5)))

NO PREDICTION CONFIRMED

ASSUMING EXPLANATION
CONTINUING SEARCH

TESTING EXPLANATION OFFERED BY
INFORM-DECISION-REQ

EXPLANATION IS GOAL: and that his goal was to inform John of the
(*DKNOW* PLANNER HUM1   decision he had reached.
RECIPIENT HUM0 FACT
 ((ACTOR HUM1 <=> (*ATRANS*)
  OBJECT PHYS0 TO HUM0)
  MODE FORM52) TIME (TIMK5)))

(continued)

Computer Output	Annotation

PLAN: (*PB-TELL* PLANNER
HUM1 TELLEE HUM0 FACT
  ((ACTOR HUM1 <=> (*ATRANS*)
    OBJECT PHYS0 TO HUM0)
  MODE (FORM52) TIME (TIMK5)))

EXPLANATION CONFIRMS PREDICTION
REFUSAL-GOAL-REQ

FOUND EXPLANATION SEQUENCE:

TELL-REQ → INFORM-DECISION-REQ

*** ADDING TO STORY REPRESENTATION:

INFERRED
 PLAN: (*PB-TELL* PLANNER HUM1
 TELLEE HUM0 FACT
 ((ACTOR HUM1 <=> (*ATRANS*) OBJECT
 PHYS0 TO HUM0) MODE (FORM52)
 TIME (TIMK5)))

  GOAL: (*DKNOW* PLANNER HUM1
 RECIPIENT HUM0 FACT
 ((ACTOR HUM1 <=> (*ATRANS*) OBJECT
 PHYS0 TO HUM0) MODE (FORM52)
 TIME (TIMK5)))

INPUT CONFIRMS PREDICTION
REFUSAL-GOAL-REQ

INFERRED GOAL: (*PCONT* PLANNER
HUM1 OWNER HUM1 OBJECT PHYS0)

INFERRED
 PLAN: (*PB-REFUSE* PLANNER HUM1
 RECIPIENT HUM0 FACT
 ((ACTOR HUM1 <=> (*ATRANS*) OBJECT
 PHYS0 TO HUM0) MODE (FORM52)
 TIME (TIMK5)))

NEXT INPUT IS:
  (JOHN TOLD BILL HE WOULD GIVE HIM
  FIVE DOLLARS FOR IT)

CONCEPTUALIZATION IS:
((ACTOR HUM0 <=> (*MTRANS*)
  MOBJECT
  ((CON
    ((ACTOR HUM6 <=> (*ATRANS*)
      OBJECT PHYS0 TO HUM0)
    TIME (FORM66))

Annotation column:

This inference confirms the prediction that Bill might refuse the request, so an explanation for the input has been found.

The prediction that interpreted the input also adds to the representation that Bill wanted to keep the bicycle, and that he did so by refusing John's request.

John tries bargaining. This sentence and the next are processed almost identically to the last two, so their processing will be skipped over here.

(continued)

Computer Output	Annotation

```
  LEADTO
  ((ACTOR HUM0 <=> (*ATRANS*)
    OBJECT MONEY1 TO HUM6)
    TIME (FORM67))))
 TO (*CP* PART HUM6))
 TIME (FORM68))
                    .
                    .
                    .


NEXT INPUT IS:
((ACTOR HUM0 <=> (*MTRANS*)
 MOBJECT
 ((CON
  ((ACTOR HUM1 <=> (*ATRANS*)
    OBJECT PHYS0 TO HUM1)
    MODE (FORM99) TIME (FORM100))
   LEADTO
   ((CON
    ((ACTOR HUM0 <=> (*DO*))
    TIME (FORM101))
   LEADTO
   ((ACTOR PART0
     TOWARD (*PSTATE* VAL (NIL)))
     INC (-5.) TIME (FORM102))))))
 TO (*CP* PART HUM1))
 TIME (FORM103))
```

NOT A PREDICTED INPUT

BEGIN SEARCH FOR EXPLANATION

TESTING EXPLANATION OFFERED BY THREATEN-REQ	PAM identifies this action as a threat,

```
EXPLANATION IS:
 PLAN: (*PB-THREATEN* PLANNER HUM0
REQUEST
((ACTOR HUM1 <=> (*ATRANS*)
 OBJECT PHYS0 TO HUM1)
 MODE (FORM110) TIME (TIMK15))
PERSUADEE HUM1 THREAT
((CON
 ((ACTOR HUM0 <=> (*DO*))
  TIME (TIMK16))
 LEADTO
 ((ACTOR PART0 TOWARD
  (*PSTATE* VAL (NIL)))
  INC (-5.) TIME (TIMK17)))))
```

(continued)

Computer Output	Annotation

EXPLANATION CONFIRMS PREDICTION
DCONT-ATTEMPT-REQ

which is identified as another plan to get the bicycle.

FOUND EXPLANATION SEQUENCE:

THREATEN-REQ

*** ADDING TO STORY REPRESENTATION:

INFERRED
 PLAN: (*PB-THREATEN* PLANNER HUM0
REQUEST
((ACTOR HUM1 <=> (*ATRANS*)
 OBJECT PHYS0 TO HUM1)
 MODE (FORM113) TIME (TIMK15))
PERSUADEE HUM1 THREAT
(((CON
 ((ACTOR HUM0 <=> (*DO*))
  TIME (TIMK16))
 LEADTO
 ((ACTOR PART0 TOWARD
  (*PSTATE* VAL (NIL)))
  INC (−5.) TIME (TIMK17)))))

LOADING PREDICTION THR-COMPLY-REQ
THR-COMPLY-REQ

Predictions are loaded for possible responses.

LOADING PREDICTION EVADE-THREAT-REQ

LOADING PREDICTION
RESULT-IN-DCONT-REQ

NEXT INPUT IS:
 (BILL GAVE HIM THE BICYCLE)

CONCEPTUALIZATION IS:
((ACTOR HUM1 <=> (*ATRANS*) OBJECT
 PHYS0 TO HUM8) TIME (FORM115))

INPUT CONFIRMS PREDICTION
RESULT-IN-DCONT-REQ
 OUTCOME OF GOAL: (*DCONT* PLANNER
HUM0 OBJECT PHYS0 OWNER HUM1
RECIPIENT HUM0) IS (*SUCCEED*)

PAM recognized that John's goal has been fulfilled, but it still must find an explanation for Bill's action.

NOT A PREDICTED INPUT

BEGIN SEARCH FOR EXPLANATION

TESTING EXPLANATION OFFERED BY
GIVE-REQ

(continued)

Computer Output	Annotation

EXPLANATION IS
  PLAN: (*PB-GIVE* PLANNER HUM1
RECIPIENT HUM0 OBJECT PHYS0)

NO PREDICTION CONFIRMED

ASSUMING EXPLANATION
CONTINUING SEARCH

TESTING EXPLANATION OFFERED BY
GIVE-GOAL-REQ
    PAM infers that Bill must have wanted John to have the bicycle, and tries to explain this goal.

EXPLANATION IS GOAL:
(*DCONT* PLANNER HUM1 OBJECT PHYS0
 OWNER (NIL) RECIPIENT HUM0)
 PLAN: (*PB-GIVE* PLANNER HUM1
RECIPIENT HUM0 OBJECT PHYS0)

EXPLANATION CONFIRMS PREDICTION
THR-COMPLY-REQ
    The prediction stating that Bill might give in to John is confirmed by this goal.

FOUND EXPLANATION SEQUENCE:

GIVE-REQ → GIVE-GOAL-REQ

*** ADDING TO STORY REPRESENTATION:

 INFERRED GOAL: (*DCONT* PLANNER
HUM1 OBJECT PHYS0 OWNER (NIL)
RECIPIENT HUM0)

 OUTCOME OF GOAL: (*DCONT* PLANNER
HUM1 OBJECT PHYS0 OWNER (NIL)
RECIPIENT HUM0) IS (*SUCCEED*)

INFERRED GOAL: (*PHEALTH*
PLANNER HUM1 RECIPIENT HUM1)
    PAM adds to the representation that Bill wanted to preserve his health, and that this goal conflicted with his goal of keeping the bicycle.

INFERRING CONFLICT WITH GOAL:
(*PCONT* PLANNER HUM1 OWNER HUM1
OBJECT PHYS0)

FINISHED UNDERSTANDING PHASE

```
***********************************************************
*                                                         *
*     Some question-answering and paraphrasing follow to demon-  *
*     strate the level of understanding achieved.         *
*                                                         *
***********************************************************
```

*(DOQA)

QUESTION: Q1
    Why did John walk over to Bill?
    Because he wanted to get his bicycle.

QUESTION: Q2

> Why did Bill give his bicycle to John?
> Because he didn't want to get hurt.

QUESTION: Q3

> What were the consequences of John's walking over to Bill?
> This enabled him to ask him to give him Bill's bicycle.

QUESTION: Q4

> What were the consequences of John's asking Bill to give him Bill's bicycle?
> Bill told him that Bill wouldn't give him Bill's bicycle.

```
***************************************************************
*                                                             *
*        Expressing the story from different points of view....   *
*                                                             *
***************************************************************
```

*(TELL)

WHO SHOULD TELL THE STORY? *JOHN

> I wanted to get Bill's bicycle. So I walked over to him, and I asked him to hand it over. He told me that he wouldn't hand it over. So I asked him to sell it to me for five dollars. Then he told me that he wouldn't hand over his bicycle. I told him that if he didn't hand it over then I would break his arm. He handed over his bicycle.

WHO SHOULD TELL THE STORY? *BILL

> John came over. He asked me to give him my bicycle. I wanted to keep the bicycle, so I told him that I wouldn't give it to him. Then he offered to buy it for five bucks. I wanted to keep the bicycle, so I told him that I wouldn't give it to him. He told me that if I didn't give it to him then he would break my arm. I didn't want to get hurt. So I gave him my bicycle.

[PHOTO: Recording terminated Thu 30-Mar-78 4:34PM]

A TECHNICAL DESCRIPTION OF PAM

Introduction

The components of PAM interact heavily. The predictive component and bottom-up component pass conceptualizations back and forth to one another; the rules that these components find useful are passed to the incorporation component to be added to the representation; the incorporation component removes predictions and adds new ones, thus influencing the way in which the predictive component will act in the future.

Due to their heavy interaction, it is difficult to describe the details of any one module without describing the details of the others. Instead, it is more instructive to discuss what is central to all these mechanisms and their interactions, namely, the nature of the rules they use and how these are manipulated. This section provides a simplistic description of PAM's processing in order to display the structure of the rules it uses and describe how this structure is used by the various components of the program. The following sections describe the processing in more detail.

Consider the following simple story:

(1) John was hungry. He ate at a restaurant.

The representation PAM produces for this example should include the following elements. The story has a theme, John's being hungry, which generates John's goal of satisfying his hunger. To achieve this goal, John chose the plan of doing the restaurant script. Then John executed this plan by eating at a restaurant.

PAM reads the first sentence, which has the following representation in Conceptual Dependency:

((ACTOR HUM0 IS (*HUNGER* VAL (−3)))))

This sentence actually falls outside the scope of the explanation algorithm defined above. The sentence is a state, not an action, plan, or goal, and we have not specified what to do with states. PAM does not try to explain states. Instead, PAM determines if the state may give rise to a goal, and if it does, PAM will infer that goal. While this is not an explanatory inference, it is an inference that PAM makes by using the same mechanisms and rule structures, and thus serves just as well as an illustration.

First, PAM's predictive component checks to see if it has predicted the input. Since it has not, control is passed to the bottom-up component. PAM uses this component to determine if there are any rules whose conditions are met by this input, and finds that it has such a rule. Rules in PAM are stored as LISP atoms with conditions, etc., kept as properties of those atoms. For example, the rule found might be called HUNGER-RULE, and has the following condition:

HUNGER-RULE
    Condition: CD matches "Person is hungry"

Each condition predicate is a function of one argument, usually a CD form.

Applying this predicate to the input conceptualization returns true, so PAM now proceeds to evaluate the action of this rule. The action of HUNGER-RULE is written as follows:

HUNGER-RULE
    Action: ADD GOAL: S-HUNGER PLANNER ()
                       SOURCE: THEME = HUNGER-DRIVE
                       PLAN: ()

This action builds a structure called a goal episode, and contains three roles: a goal, a goal source, and a plan. The GOAL role is filled with a representation denoting the goal Satisfy-hunger, the SOURCE with the theme of having the hunger drive, and the PLAN role is left empty.

An empty role in a representation is called a *gap* (Riesbeck, 1975). A gap is a piece of representation that could be filled by subsequent sentences. The gap for a plan role in the structure built by HUNGER-RULE means that goals usually give rise to plans, and that although the plan to be used for this goal is not known, it may become apparent later on in the story.

Thus a gap is a place in a story representation that the understander knows must exist because of the nature of the knowledge being applied. That is, PAM knows that goals have sources that generate them, and plans that effect them. This knowledge is expressed by structures that contain places for these items even if the particular items themselves are not known.

After the bottom-up component builds this structure, the structure is passed back to the predictive component, which checks once again to see if a prediction has been confirmed. It is necessary to have some very general predictions around at the start of story understanding for the purpose of getting things off the ground. One such prediction is implemented by an active request whose condition looks for a structure that has a theme in it. This condition is met by the structure built by HUNGER-RULE, thus terminating PAM's inference cycle. HUNGER-RULE and this request are then passed to the incorporation phase.

In the incorporation phase, the action of HUNGER-RULE is again evaluated, but this time its structure is added to the story representation. We will discuss exactly how this is done below. However, in addition to building structures, PAM must also make predictions about how gaps in these structures may be filled. For example, a prediction about the gap for the plan in the structure built by HUNGER-RULE is that it will be filled by a structure denoting a plan for satisfying hunger. To use this prediction to fill the gap, it is necessary to state the prediction in the form of a rule: If a plan for satisfying hunger is encountered, then this plan is a plan for John's Satisfy-hunger goal.

Thus we want to set up a prediction that is looking at the input for an appropriate plan, and if such a plan is spotted, place the plan into the PLAN gap already present in the story representation. This is accomplished in the incorporation phase as follows: Stored along with every rule in PAM is a list of other rules. These rules are used to make predictions about how to fill a gap in the representation created by the original rule. Since these rules suggest how to fill gaps, they are termed *suggestions*. The idea of attaching suggestions to rules is due to

Riesbeck (1975), who used this idea in his conceptual analysis program. He called these rules that contain suggestions *requests*, and I use this terminology here.

Each suggestion specifies the gap in the story representation it is intended to fill, and where it will look to find the filler. For example, the HUNGER-RULE request has the following suggestion:

    HUNGER-RULE
        Suggestions: Set TARGET = PLAN
                       To FOCUS = !INPUT!
                       Using SUITABLE-PLAN-RULE

The TARGET field specifies the role of the structure built by HUNGER-RULE that the suggestion is trying to fill, in this case the PLAN gap. The FOCUS field denotes the place where the request is to look to find the plan. This suggestion specifies that the focus is the special gap !INPUT!, which is the place in PAM where new CD forms that are parsed or inferred are put.

Lastly, the name of the request to be used is given. In this example, the request is called SUITABLE-PLAN-RULE. So this suggestion says that the request SUITABLE-PLAN-RULE should be used to try to fill the target PLAN gap in the structure that HUNGER-RULE builds, and it should do so by examining its focus, the special gap !INPUT!, where new conceptualizations are placed. SUITABLE-PLAN-RULE is a request whose condition will be true if its focus contains a structure denoting a plan for a particular goal. Its action is simply to return this plan structure.

When PAM processes a story, it creates *nodes* for the gaps in the CD forms. Thus notes are created for the empty PLAN and PLANNER roles when HUNGER-RULE is executed. PAM uses requests by making copies of them, replacing the symbolic names like !INPUT! and !FOCUS! with the names of the internal nodes of the CD structures it is currently working with. An instance of a request that is attached to a story representation in this manner is called an *active request*.

By separating out the focus and target fields of a request from the condition and action fields, requests can be stored in memory without specifying where the structures they build should go, or where they should look to see if their conditions have been met. Several active instances of the same request may exist simultaneously, each focused and targeted on different locations.

Active requests serve to implement predictions about what will fill a gap, and where the filler might come from. PAM checks to see if a prediction has been confirmed whenever a gap that has a request focused on it is changed. A request is not looked at except when the gap it is focused on changes, which helps reduce the amount of work PAM has to do at any one time.

With respect to the processing of the request HUNGER-RULE, there are a number of points which the preceding discussion ignored. For example, the action of HUNGER-RULE was given as:

Action: ADD GOAL: S-HUNGER PLANNER ()
                SOURCE: THEME = HUNGER-DRIVE
                PLAN: ()

Note that the PLANNER role of the Satisfy-hunger goal is empty in the structure built by this action, but it should be filled with JOHN. PAM uses suggestions for this purpose as well. That is, there is a second suggestion made by HUNGER-RULE:

Suggestions: Set TARGET = PLANNER of GOAL
                    To FOCUS = ACTOR
                    Using FOCUS-REQ

The target of the suggestion is the PLANNER role of the GOAL form in the structure HUNGER-RULE builds. The focus is the ACTOR role of the input conceptualization. FOCUS-REQ is a request that simply moves its focus into its target if the focus is not empty. Thus this suggestion activates a request that will move JOHN from the ACTOR role filler from the input conceptualization into the gap for the PLANNER in the structure built by HUNGER-RULE. Since the focus of this request is already filled, the condition of the request is true immediately, and the request will fill the gap as soon as it is activated. This technique of using a request to specify the details of the structure built by another request is used widely throughout PAM.

The next sentence of the story has the following Conceptual Dependency representation:

((<=> ($RESTAURANT CUSTOMER HUM0 RESTAURANT ORG0)))

That is, John played the role of the customer in doing the restaurant script at some restaurant.

PAM places this conceptualization in the input gap and enters the predictive component. As always, this component examines the requests which are focused upon this gap. The request SUITABLE-PLAN-RULE does *not* have its condition met by this input, because the input is stated in the form of an action, not a plan. Thus PAM must go into bottom-up mode and find the rules applicable to this sentence.

In this case PAM finds a rule called DO-RESTAURANT-PLAN-RULE whose condition is met by the input. Once again, the question of how this rule is found is deferred until later. DO-RESTAURANT-PLAN-RULE has the following structure:

DO-RESTAURANT-PLAN-RULE

Condition: CD matches "Person do restaurant script"

Action: ADD PLANBOX: DO-$RESTAURANT-PLAN
                    PLANNER ()
                    RESTAURANT ()
           ACTIONS: ()
           SUBEPISODES: ()

Suggestions: Set TARGET = PLANNER of PLANBOX
              To FOCUS = CUSTOMER of script
              Using FOCUS-REQ

              Set TARGET = RESTAURANT of PLANBOX
              To FOCUS = RESTAURANT of script
              Using FOCUS-REQ

              Set TARGET = ACTIONS
              To FOCUS = !FOCUS!
              Using FOCUS-REQ

The action of this rule builds a structure denoting a plan. This structure has the following components: a planbox, a list of actions, and a list of sub-episodes. The planbox here is simply doing the restaurant script. Its planner and the restaurant used are filled in by the first two suggestions. The ACTIONS role is used to specify the actual events to which the plan gave rise. In this example, this is filled with the third request which moves the input into this gap. The SUBEPISODES gap is used to store episodes whose goals were instrumental to the use of this plan. This slot is left empty in this story.

Having built the structure specified by request DO-RESTAURANT-PLAN-RULE, PAM places this structure into !INPUT! and re-enters that predictive component. This component checks to see if any requests focused on this gap predict the structure. This time, the condition of the active copy of the suggestion from the HUNGER-RULE is met. This condition, SUITABLE-PLAN-PREDICATE, examines a list of plans associated with a goal to determine if the input is a plan for that goal. Since DO-$RESTAURANT-PLAN is contained in the list of plans for the goal S-HUNGER, the predicate returns true. PAM then evaluates the action of the HUNGER-RULE suggestion, which fills the PLAN gap in the structure that HUNGER-RULE built. Since a prediction has been satisfied, and the structures built from each input have been joined together, an explanation for the input has been found.

PAM now passes the rule it has found and the prediction that confirmed it to the incorporation component. This component fires off the action of the rule, and then the action of the active request, which changes the actual story representation. The suggestions are then taken, i.e., made into active requests. In this case, these requests all just add details to the current structure rather than make predictions about future events.

Figure 7.5 shows a schematic story representation, and the representation produced by PAM. The numbers in the representations indicate correspondences between the two. For the sake of clarity, the nodes present in the actual PAM representation have been replaced by their values.

In sum, the process of understanding this story is as follows: PAM reads in a conceptualization representing a sentence of a story, and places it in the input gap; then PAM tests the conditions of the requests focused on this gap to see if any of them predicted the input. In the sample story no such request was found, so PAM had to search for rules that might be applicable to the input.

PAM then found the request HUNGER-RULE whose condition was met by the input. HUNGER-RULE built a structure denoting an episode with the goal, theme and plan. The plan part of this structure was left empty, constituting a gap,

Theme—Hunger ^{1}

GOAL—Satisfy-hunger ^{2}

Plan—Do-restaurant-script $\xrightarrow{3}$ Action 4
(John eat)

Actual story representation, shown by replacing nodes with their values

This part built by HUNGER-RULE

((GOAL (S-HUNGER PLANNER HUM0) ^{2}

SOURCE (THEME VAL (HUNGER-DRIVE)) ^{1}

PLAN   ((PLANBOX (DO-$RESTAURANT-PLAN
                    PLANNER HUM0 RESTAURANT ORG0) ^{3}

ACTIONS ((((<=> ($RESTAURANT
                    CUSTOMER HUM0 4
                    RESTAURANT ORG0))))

SUBEPISODES (NIL)))))

This part built by SUITABLE-PLAN-RULE

FIG. 7.5. Schematic story representation.

but HUNGER-RULE made a suggestion as to how this gap may be filled. This suggestion consisted of attaching a copy of the request SUITABLE-PLAN-RULE to this gap, and focusing the request on the input gap.

Next the structure built by HUNGER-RULE was placed in the input gap to see if it met any expectations. An active request was found that was looking for an episode containing a theme. Since this request predicted this structure, PAM stopped processing and went on to the next sentence.

The next sentence was likewise not predicted by PAM. PAM had to search for rules applicable to the sentence, and found the rule DO-RESTAURANT-PLAN-RULE. This rule built a plan structure that was then placed in the input gap. The version of SUITABLE-PLAN-RULE activated by the previous sentence predicted such a plan, and inserted it in the plan gap in the story representation. This input had now led to an inference predicted by PAM, and thus processing could stop.

The understanding process in terms of rule manipulation is shown in Fig. 7.6.

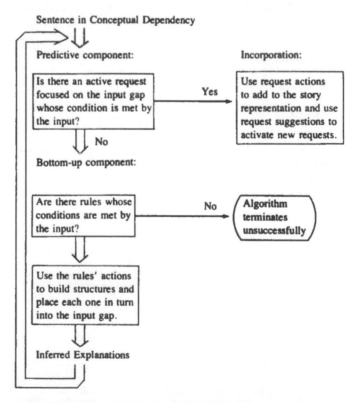

FIG. 7.6.   PAM's processing algorithm in terms of rule manipulation.

Request Chains

As was discussed previously, when a request is activated it is attached to a gap PAM is trying to fill, and focused on a gap to which its condition is to be applied. Most of the requests shown above were focused on the special gap where PAM placed input, but this need not be the case. For example, some of the requests used in suggestions were used simply to move a piece of representation from the focus into the structure built by the request making the suggestion, and were therefore focused on a filler of a role within the input conceptualization.

In addition, requests are often set up in such a way that the focus of one request is the target of another. Whenever a gap is filled, PAM checks to see if any requests are focused on that gap, and tests the conditions of those that are. If one of these conditions is met, PAM builds the structure specified by the action of the request, and uses it to fill the request's target. Since this is a gap that has just been filled, PAM checks to see if it has any requests focused on it, and reiterate the cycle with these requests. In principle, the firing of one request can trigger a chain reaction of pending requests, each of which is focused on another's target.

This feature of chaining together requests is useful in a number of places. For example, one feature needed by PAM is the ability to determine if a goal has been fulfilled, and if a plan used in the service of a goal has succeeded. It is convenient to implement this ability by having a role in each plan structure that describes whether or not the plan worked. This role is called the OUTCOME, and may be filled with either a structure denoting success or one denoting failure. Thus a plan structure actually has the following format:

    ((PLANBOX (...) ACTIONS (...)
     SUBEPISODES (...) OUTCOME (...)))

All requests that build plan structures make a suggestion targeted at this gap that can identify the success of that particular plan. These requests are all focused on the input gap, and test for a particular condition that marks the success of their particular plan.

In addition, each goal episode built also has an OUTCOME role. This role can be filled with a structure denoting fulfillment, abandonment, or failure. Thus goal episode structures appear as follows:

    (((GOAL (...) SOURCE (...) PLAN (...) OUTCOME (...)))

Another suggestion is used to activate the request PLAN-SUCCESS-RULE. PLAN-SUCCESS-RULE is targeted at the outcome gap of the goal episode and focused on the outcome gap of the plan structure. This request has the following simple form:

PLAN-SUCCESS-RULE
Condition: Successful plan
Action: ADD Goal fulfilled

That is, the condition of PLAN-SUCCESS-RULE holds if the focus is filled with a structure representing the success of a plan. The action of the request builds a structure denoting the fulfillment of a goal.

Request Types

The reader may have noticed that requests that determine plan outcomes are not explanatory requests. That is, a request that determines that an event implies that a plan has succeeded does not in itself explain why that event occurred. For example, if John threatened to harm Bill if he didn't give him some money, then Bill's giving John the money indicates that this plan has succeeded. However, noticing that the plan has succeeded does not constitute an explanation for why Bill gave John the money; such an explanation requires inferring the goal behind Bill's action. This is done by using a rule separate from the rule that determines that John's plan has succeeded.

The problem here is that the rule that determines a plan's outcome is a prediction. PAM is supposed to stop processing an input when a prediction is confirmed, but this prediction confirmation might stop the processing before an explanation is inferred. That is, if the explanation for the sentence requires a bottom-up inference, and the rule detecting plan success is triggered directly from the input, then PAM will stop processing before an explanation for the input has been found.

To prevent this situation from occurring, PAM flags those requests that provide explanations as being WHY requests. For example, a request that determines the outcome of a plan would not be marked as a WHY request. On the other hand, a request that inferred that the goal behind Bill's giving John the money was to preserve his life would be marked as a WHY request. Thus in processing the sentence "Bill gave John the money" after hearing that John threatened Bill, the request looking for plan success will be triggered first. Since this is not a WHY request, PAM continues to process this sentence and eventually find an explanation for Bill's action that is predicted by some WHY request.

Thus an input can trigger any number of non-WHY requests without stopping the inference cycle. Once a WHY request goes off, however, the explanation cycle will terminate and PAM will go on to the next sentence. This distinction provides a way of doing non-explanation functions in PAM without interfering with the basic flow of control in the explanation cycle.

Another problem that arises with requests involves communication between a request and the suggestions it makes. For example, SUITABLE-PLAN-RULE, a request for determining if an input could be a plan for a goal, was given earlier as follows:

    SUITABLE-PLAN-RULE
        Condition: SUITABLE-PLAN-PREDICATE
        Action: !FOCUS!

The problem is that SUITABLE-PLAN-PREDICATE needs some way to refer to the goal for which it is trying to find a suitable plan. That is, this request is targeted at a gap in a structure that contains a goal, but has no way to reference the goal in that structure when it is trying to determine if its condition has been met.

To solve this problem, PAM marks requests that build certain important structures as being FOUNDERs. The name of the last FOUNDER built in the course of activating requests is kept around and can be referenced by all those requests activated by the FOUNDER, or by the suggestions of a FOUNDER, and so on.

FOUNDERs are almost always goal episodes. A request activated by a request that builds a goal episode can activate another request, and as long as a new FOUNDER request is not activated, the new requests can all use !PARENT! to refer back to the FOUNDing request. In addition, the use of !PARENT! within a request that is a FOUNDER will reference the structure built by the last FOUNDing request. Thus a request that is loaded through several levels of suggestions can still reference a structure built by a request many levels before.

Removing Requests

Up until now we have been concerned mostly with the activation and use of requests. Another important part of PAM is its ability to remove requests. Removing requests is important for two reasons. First, a request that has outlived its usefulness may find its condition met by chance later on in the story, and go off unexpectedly, filling some gap with an inappropriate value. Second, even if there is no chance that the request will go off, the program may still waste time checking the request's condition whenever the gap on which it is focused is filled.

Removing a request means that the request name is taken out of the list of requests under the "Focused-requests" property of the gap focused upon. The request will then no longer be tested when that gap is filled. PAM removes requests under the following circumstances:

1. Any request that has fired off (i.e., its condition has been confirmed, its action taken and its suggestions activated) is removed.

2. If a request fills a gap, then all the requests targeted at that gap are removed.
3. If a request fills a gap that will not be filled again, then all the requests focused on that gap are removed after they are tested.

Requests targeted at a gap are removed when the gap is filled because there is no longer anything left for them to do. The requests were targeted at the gap in the first place in order to fill it, and now that it has been filled, they serve no useful purpose. For example, upon encountering a planbox like ASK or BARGAIN that requires a response from someone, PAM sets up one request predicting compliance, and another predicting denial. Both requests are targeted at a gap for the RESPONSE role of the plan. If one of the requests is confirmed and the RESPONSE gap filled, then both requests are removed. Thus this technique provides a way of removing requests whose purpose no longer exists even if the request was not used.

To find the requests targeted at a gap, PAM maintains a list of such requests under a property of each gap. When a gap is filled, then PAM goes through this list of targeted requests and removes each one in turn.

Requests focused on a gap are removed when the gap is filled since these gaps will not change again. This is true of all the gaps in PAM, with the exception of the input gap. This gap is filled many times throughout a story, and it would be undesirable to remove predictions that might be applicable to future sentences whenever the gap were filled. When a gap other than the input gap is filled, however, it is filled for good. All the requests focused on it have been tested, and those requests that did not fire will never be tested again. These requests can be removed for convenience since they no longer serve any function.

Suggestions, chains of requests, and request removal are all means of organizing rules so that the appropriate rule is activated at the right time, without having many unnecessary rules around also. One additional mechanism used for this purpose involves attaching requests to target gaps. PAM has a number of rules that suggest attaching requests to target gaps without checking to see if the gap is in fact filled. This corresponds to a situation in which PAM has a number of heuristics for filling a gap but does not know which one is applicable in the present case. Thus one request may have already filled a gap using some heuristic, and later on another request may try to fill the gap again using another heuristic. This situation is desirable because in a very similar situation the first request may be unable to fill the gap, thus making PAM dependent on the second request to do the job.

If a suggestion is made to attach a request to a target gap, but that gap is already filled, PAM simply refuses to heed the suggestion. Thus suggestions are in fact just that—ideas about where to find a filler that PAM may choose to ignore under some circumstances. If a request has already filled the gap, the suggestion is ignored; if the gap is empty, PAM will activate the suggestion to try

When a gap changes:

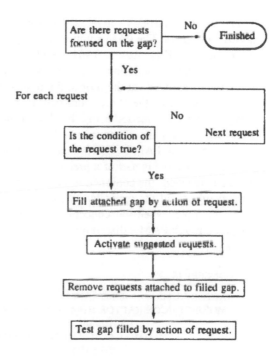

FIG. 7.7.   Request testing and activation sequence.

to fill it. In this manner, a number of heuristics for gap filling may be scattered throughout a set of rules without concern for overlap—an attempt to do something already done by a previous heuristic is harmless.

Thus PAM engages in request access, request activation, request testing and request removal. The flow of control in this process is summarized in Fig. 7.7.

The Bottom-Up Mechanism

If PAM has no active requests that predict an input, it must try to find rules whose condition is met by the input. For example, suppose PAM sees an event of the form

John told Bill he would give him five dollars if he gave him his bicycle.

PAM needs to find a rule that will interpret this sentence as an instance of bargaining. If no active request can interpret the sentence, PAM must locate an inactive request that can. That is, PAM must find a rule whose condition is met by this sentence, and whose action will be to build a structure denoting a BARGAIN-OBJECT planbox. Then the predictive component can be used again to see if there is any gap in the story representation to which this plan may be attached.

The primary difficulty here is that we need to find such a rule amidst a haystack of others. The PAM solution to this problem uses a discrimination net to index requests (Feigenbaum, 1961). PAM's discrimination net is a binary tree with predicates at each non-terminal node. The net is applied to an input as follows: The predicate at the root of the tree is applied to the input, and depending on the outcome, the "true" sub-tree or the "false" sub-tree will be chosen. This procedure is reiterated using the chosen sub-tree until a leaf (terminal node) is reached. This node is then returned.

The leaves of PAM's discrimination net are the names of requests. Each predicate in the tree is part of a predicate of some request, so that when a leaf of the tree is reached, the conjunction of predicates tested on the way is equivalent to the condition of the requests at that leaf.

For example, when the conceptualization underlying the sentence above is dropped through PAM's discrimination net, the following series of predicates is evaluated:

```
CONCEPT IS

((ACTOR HUM0 <=> (*MTRANS*)
    MOBJECT ((CON ((ACTOR HUM1 <=> (*ATRANS*) OBJECT PHYS0
                    TO HUM0))
            LEADTO ((ACTOR HUM0 <=> (*ATRANS*) OBJECT MONEY0
                    TO HUM1))
        ))
    TO (*CP* PART HUM1)
))
```

PREDICATE TRACE:

(HAS (MODE) *NEG*)	FALSE
(HAS (MODE) *CAN*)	FALSE
(EQU (<=>) NIL)	FALSE
(EQU (<=>) *ATRANS*)	FALSE
(EQU (<=>) *MTRANS*)	TRUE
(SAMETOK (MOBJECT IS PART) (ACTOR))	FALSE
(EQU (MOBJECT IS) *GOAL*)	FALSE
(EQU (MOBJECT CON <=>) NIL)	FALSE
(SAMETOK (MOBJECT CON ACTOR) (TO ACTOR))	TRUE
(HAS (MOBJECT CON MODE) *NEG*)	FALSE
(SAMETOK (MOBJECT CAUSAL ACTOR) (ACTOR))	TRUE
(EQU (MOBJECT CAUSAL <=>) NIL)	FALSE
(EQU (MOBJECT CAUSAL <=>) *ATRANS*)	TRUE

REQUEST CLUSTER : BARGAIN-OBJECT-CLUSTER

Each predicate tests a piece of the conceptual structure specified by a path. For example, the path (MOBJECT CON ACTOR) says to look first at the conceptualization in the MOBJECT slot of the main conceptualization, then to look in its CON slot, and finally, to look in the ACTOR slot of that conceptualization. This slot is filled with the token HUM1, which points to a representation for Bill.

The predicates in the above example first ask if the conceptualization is negative, and then if it is potential, both of which are false. It then asks if it is an action, and when this is confirmed, what kind of action. Finding that it is an MTRANS, the program then asks if it is an internal MTRANS (remembering would be an instance of such an event). Since it is not, various other MTRANS possibilities are tried, until it is established that the object of the MTRANS is a causal, that the actor in the first part of the causal is the same as the person to whom the MTRANS is directed, and finally, that what he does will cause the speaker to give him something. At this point a leaf of the tree is reached. This leaf is called BARGAIN-OBJECT-CLUSTER, and it contains a list of one request—a request whose action will build a BARGAIN-OBJECT planbox.

As described above, when a bottom up request is used to build a structure, that structure is placed in the input gap, and the requests focused on the gap are examined. If a request predicts the structure, PAM can stop. Otherwise the cycle is reiterated. For example, suppose that no request predicted the BARGAIN-OBJECT structure just described. In this case, this structure would be thrown back into the discrimination net, which would return requests that would explain the bargaining. One such request might build a structure denoting a change of possession goal. If no active request predicted this structure, it too would be thrown back down the net. This time, a request would be returned that stated that this goal was instrumental to a plan to use the bicycle. If a request existed that predicted a plan for changing one's location, its condition would now be met and the explanation cycle could cease.

Testing

When PAM finds a request in bottom-up fashion, it must go through a test phase before it can actually use the request. PAM will occasionally retrieve more than one rule when using the discrimination net, and each rule may offer a different interpretation of the input. Eventually a decision is made as to which rule to use because the structure produced by one rule will be predicted by some request, but that produced by another will not. Since the suggestions specified by some of these rules may change the story representation in various ways, it is desirable to find the correct rules to use before the actions the rules dictate are actually taken.

To test a rule, PAM activates the requests it finds via the discrimination net by focusing them on the input gap and targeting them on a dummy gap. That is, PAM builds a copy of the request just as it does when it obeys a suggestion. Then PAM performs the normal evaluation of the action and suggestions of this rule, with the following exceptions: PAM does not activate suggestions that would change the story representation outside of the structure built by a request. Thus no global changes are made. Also, the requests activated by these suggestions are kept separate from the requests already activated.

When PAM finds a sequence of rules that can explain the input, it first removes any requests activated in the test phase that are still present. Then it activates each rule that it used in the explanation sequence, making the target of one rule the focus of the next, and so on. Eventually a chain of requests is activated starting at the input gap and ending with some prediction already in the story representation. The input gap is then tested again in the normal manner. Since a request just activated is now focused on the input gap and has a condition met by the input, a request chain is fired off. This time, all the suggestions made by the requests are heeded, and the actual story representation is altered.

Pronouns

PAM finds the correct reference for all the pronouns used in the stories it can process. PAM makes these references without any special reference heuristics. Instead, these references are resolved as a by-product of the other processes PAM must perform anyway to understand the story.

As PAM processes a story, it evaluates many predicates, including those in its discrimination net, and those in the conditions of requests it may test. Often these predicates ask to compare a piece of input or inferred conceptualization to a piece of story representation. Whenever the structures being compared are picture producers (PPs), PAM does the comparison via a special routine. This routine states that the items being compared are the same if the new one *could be* the old one. That is, if the routine is matching the representation for "John" against the representation for "he", it will decide that they are the same since "he" could be "John". This routine then puts the pair on an association list for future reference. When the sentence being processed is eventually understood, PAM goes through the structures built up and replaces each item on the pronoun association list with its referent.

For example, consider the following story:

> John wanted some money. He got a gun and walked into a liquor store. He told the owner he wanted some money.

After reading these sentences, PAM has made a prediction that if the owner gives John the money, he will do so in response to John's threat. Suppose the next sentence were "He gave him the money." The condition of the request predicting compliance must check to see if the actor of this conceptualization is the owner, and the recipient John. Since the condition uses the special comparison routine, it will compare the representation for the first "he" in the sentence with that for the owner, and the second with that for John. These both match, and the condition is found to hold. Thus references to the first "he" will be replaced by references to the owner, and references to the second by references to John. This scheme is similar to that used by Charniak (1972) and Cullingford (1978).

Summary

A snapshot of PAM as it is processing a story shows a representation filled with gaps, and requests attached to these gaps waiting for events to trigger them. When a new input occurs, PAM tests the requests awaiting input, and if one of them has a condition that is true, it adds it to the story representation. The request may also make suggestions that other requests be activated.

If no request has its condition made true by the input, PAM drops the input down a discrimination net to find new requests that can explain it. If one is found, its action is taken, and the explanation it builds is placed in the input gap. The requests waiting for input have their conditions tested again. The cycle continues until a request waiting for input finally sees its prediction confirmed, or until PAM can no longer infer explanations from the input.

8 Micro PAM

INTRODUCTION

McPAM is a small, simple program that captures the essential flavor of PAM's explanation algorithm. McPAM is written for clarity, not for generality or efficiency.

McPAM differs from PAM in a number of important ways. Most importantly, McPAM has been designed to separate out as much as possible knowledge about planning from knowledge about explanation. That is, the rules in McPAM's memory are simple declarative patterns. They encode facts about which plans are applicable to which goals, etc., without specifying how these facts should be used in story understanding. In contrast, PAM's rules are much more procedural in nature—they specify what predictions to make, and how to fill in a story representation.

In McPAM, knowledge about how to use rules to understand a story is built into the control structure. For example, in PAM, predictions arise from requests that are triggered to explain inputs. These requests explicitly predict future inputs. In McPAM, the control structure keeps lists of known goals, plans, and themes. An input or inference is considered to have been predicted if it relates to an item on one of these lists.

For example, if a plan is input to or inferred by McPAM, McPAM will check its list of known goals to see if the plan is applicable to any of them. If so, the plan has been predicted by this goal, and therefore has been explained. Each time a new plan, goal or theme is added to the story representation, the appropriate list is updated.

Storing McPAM's rules about intentionality this way is an improvement over PAM. In PAM, every prediction has to be made explicitly by some request, so there is no way for PAM to take advantage of similar cases. For example, each request that builds a goal in PAM must predict that a suitable plan for that goal will be seen. The suggestion to predict this is stored with every such request. In McPAM, such predictions are made automatically and are not repeated in each rule.

More importantly, because the rules in McPAM are declarative, they may be used a number of different ways. For example, a rule that links a particular plan to a certain type of goal is used both by the bottom-up mechanism to infer that goal given the plan, and by the predictive mechanism to explain an inferred plan given the known goal. In PAM, these two functions require separate requests because the procedural requirements are different.

McPAM has a number of drawbacks, however. Its automatic predictive mechanism is concise and clean, but it is also very restrictive. The predictive mechanism in PAM can be used to predict almost anything. For example, it is easy to add a request to PAM such that the occurrence of a threat leads to a prediction that says if the person threatened does what is asked of him, then he did this because he chose to comply with the threat. However, McPAM cannot easily make this prediction without changing the prediction types built into the control structure.

A possible solution to this problem is to have a prediction mechanism that is also rule-based, but which uses rules separate from those used to encode knowledge about intentions. These rules could specify which predictions to make in a given situation. This design would contain a flexible prediction mechanism yet preserve the declarative nature of the system's knowledge about planning.

Another disadvantage of McPAM is that none of its rules are indexed. The entire list of rules must be searched sequentially to find an applicable one. Adding an indexing scheme, such as a discrimination net, would speed up the processing.

McPAM also has no facility for handling the more sophisticated goal relationships discussed in the previous chapter. PAM can handle these because its requests are free to make the appropriate predictions for different situations. Once again, McPAM is limited by its simple predictive mechanism.

When there is more than one plausible explanation that can be inferred from an input, PAM infers all of them, and the predictive mechanism eventually selects one and discards the others. For simplicity in McPAM, one of the inferences is made, and if it proves unprofitable, McPAM backs up and tries another possibility. Thus McPAM uses a depth-first search where PAM uses a breadth-first one.

SAMPLE OUTPUT

The following is a log of the McPAM program, applied to the CD forms for
"Willa was hungry. She grabbed the Michelin guide. She got in her car."

[PH: Initiation. 8-Jan-80 2:52PM]

. . .

(PROCESS-STORY WILLA-STORY)

Trying to explain
    (IS (ACTOR (PERSON (NAME (WILLA)))) (STATE (HUNGER (VAL (5.)))))

Does not confirm prediction

No usable inferences from
    (IS (ACTOR (PERSON (NAME (WILLA)))) (STATE (HUNGER (VAL (5.)))))

No inference chain found—adding
    (IS (ACTOR (PERSON (NAME (WILLA)))) (STATE (HUNGER (VAL (5.)))))
—theme

Trying to explain
    (GRASP (ACTOR (PERSON (NAME (WILLA))))
            (OBJECT (BOOK (TYPE (RESTAURANT-GUIDE)))))

Does not confirm prediction

Possible explanation assuming
    (TAKE-PLAN (PLANNER (PERSON (NAME (WILLA))))
            (OBJECT (BOOK (TYPE (RESTAURANT-GUIDE)))))

Does not confirm prediction

Possible explanation assuming
    (GOAL (PLANNER (PERSON (NAME (WILLA))))
            (OBJECTIVE (POSS (ACTOR (PERSON (NAME (WILLA))))
                    (OBJECT (BOOK (TYPE (RESTAURANT-GUIDE)))))))

Does not confirm prediction

Possible explanation assuming
    (READ-PLAN (PLANNER (PERSON (NAME (WILLA))))
            (OBJECT (BOOK (TYPE (RESTAURANT-GUIDE)))))

Does not confirm prediction

Possible explanation assuming
    (GOAL (PLANNER (PERSON (NAME (WILLA))))
            (OBJECTIVE (ENJOYMENT (ACTOR (PERSON (NAME (WILLA)))))))

Does not confirm prediction

No usable inferences from
    (GOAL (PLANNER (PERSON (NAME (WILLA))))
            (OBJECTIVE (ENJOYMENT (ACTOR (PERSON (NAME (WILLA)))))))

Possible explanation assuming
    (GOAL (PLANNER (PERSON (NAME (WILLA))))
        (OBJECTIVE (KNOW (ACTOR (PERSON (NAME (WILLA))))
            (FACT (IS (ACTOR RESTAURANT) (PROX NIL))))))

Does not confirm prediction

Possible explanation assuming
    (GOAL (PLANNER (PERSON (NAME (WILLA))))
        (OBJECTIVE (PROX (ACTOR (PERSON (NAME (WILLA))))
            (LOCATION RESTAURANT))))

Does not confirm prediction

Possible explanation assuming
    (DO-$RESTAURANT-PLAN
    (PLANNER (PERSON (NAME (WILLA))))
    (RESTAURANT RESTAURANT))

Does not confirm prediction

Possible explanation assuming
    (GOAL (PLANNER (PERSON (NAME (WILLA))))
        (OBJECTIVE (IS (ACTOR (PERSON (NAME (WILLA))))
            (STATE (HUNGER (VAL (0.))))))))

Confirms prediction from
    (IS (ACTOR (PERSON (NAME (WILLA)))) (STATE (HUNGER (VAL (5.)))))

Adding inference chain to data base
    (GRASP (ACTOR (PERSON (NAME (WILLA))))
        (OBJECT (BOOK (TYPE (RESTAURANT-GUIDE)))))

    (TAKE-PLAN (PLANNER (PERSON (NAME (WILLA))))
        (OBJECT (BOOK (TYPE (RESTAURANT-GUIDE)))))

    (GOAL (PLANNER (PERSON (NAME (WILLA))))
        (OBJECTIVE (POSS (ACTOR (PERSON (NAME (WILLA))))
            (OBJECT
                (BOOK (TYPE (RESTAURANT-GUIDE)))))))

    (READ-PLAN (PLANNER (PERSON (NAME (WILLA))))
        (OBJECT (BOOK (TYPE (RESTAURANT-GUIDE)))))

    (GOAL (PLANNER (PERSON (NAME (WILLA))))
        (OBJECTIVE (KNOW (ACTOR (PERSON (NAME (WILLA))))
            (FACT (IS (ACTOR RESTAURANT) (PROX NIL))))))

    (GOAL (PLANNER (PERSON (NAME (WILLA))))
        (OBJECTIVE (PROX (ACTOR (PERSON (NAME (WILLA))))
            (LOCATION RESTAURANT))))

    (DO-$RESTAURANT-PLAN
    (PLANNER (PERSON (NAME (WILLA))))
    (RESTAURANT RESTAURANT))

```
(GOAL (PLANNER (PERSON (NAME (WILLA))))
      (OBJECTIVE (IS (ACTOR (PERSON (NAME (WILLA))))
                     (STATE (HUNGER (VAL (0.)))))))
```

Trying to explain
```
(PTRANS (ACTOR (PERSON (NAME (WILLA))))
        (OBJECT (PERSON (NAME (WILLA))))
        (TO (CAR)))
```

Does not confirm prediction

Possible explanation assuming
```
(WALK-PLAN (PLANNER (PERSON (NAME (WILLA)))) (LOCATION (CAR)))
```

Does not confirm prediction

Possible explanation assuming
```
(GOAL (PLANNER (PERSON (NAME (WILLA))))
      (OBJECTIVE (PROX (ACTOR (PERSON (NAME (WILLA))))
                       (LOCATION (CAR)))))
```

Does not confirm prediction

Possible explanation assuming
```
(USE-VEHICLE-PLAN (PLANNER (PERSON (NAME (WILLA)))) (OBJECT (CAR)))
```

Confirms prediction from
```
(GOAL (PLANNER (PERSON (NAME (WILLA))))
      (OBJECTIVE (PROX (ACTOR (PERSON (NAME (WILLA))))
                       (LOCATION RESTAURANT))))
```

Adding inference chain to data base
```
(PTRANS (ACTOR (PERSON (NAME (WILLA))))
        (OBJECT (PERSON (NAME (WILLA))))
        (TO (CAR)))

(WALK-PLAN (PLANNER (PERSON (NAME (WILLA)))) (LOCATION (CAR)))

(GOAL (PLANNER (PERSON (NAME (WILLA))))
      (OBJECTIVE (PROX (ACTOR (PERSON (NAME (WILLA))))
                       (LOCATION (CAR)))))

(USE-VEHICLE-PLAN (PLANNER (PERSON (NAME (WILLA)))) (OBJECT (CAR)))
```

[PH: Termination. 8-Jan-80 2:53PM. PS:<RIESBECK>EIGHT.LOG.5]

FLOW CHARTS

The flow charts in Figs. 8.1 and 8.2 show the two central functions in McPAM:
JUSTIFY and PREDICTED. The flow chart for JUSTIFY includes the flow of
control for its two subparts: TRY-INFERENCE and TRY-RULES.

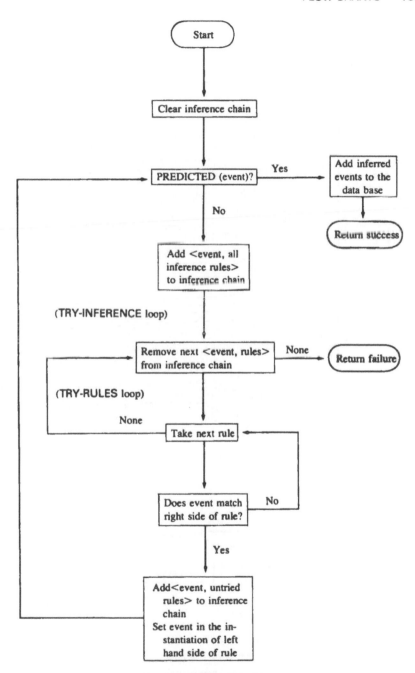

FIG. 8.1.   JUSTIFY(event).

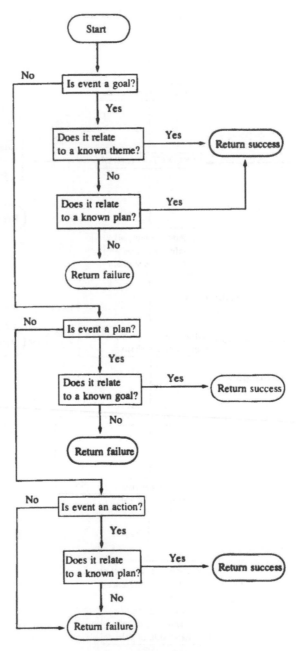

FIG. 8.2.   PREDICT(event).

THE PROGRAM

```
-  **********************************************************************
-                          MICRO PAM PROGRAM
-  **********************************************************************
```

```
-PROCESS-STORY takes the entire story and feeds it one
-line at a time to the PROCESS-CD routine.
```

```
(DE PROCESS-STORY (STORY)
 (CLEAR-GLOBALS)
 (FOR (CD IN STORY) (DO (PROCESS-CD CD)
```

```
-PROCESS-CD handles one CD of the story at a time. Each CD is sent
-to JUSTIFY to be explained.
```

```
(DE PROCESS-CD (CD) (JUSTIFY CD)
```

```
-JUSTIFY tries to find some explanation for its input CD. First it
-tries to see if this input was predicted. If it has not been, then
-it tries to make a bottom-up explanatory inference from the input,
-and then JUSTIFY the inferred explanation. This loop forms a chain
-of CDs: CD → CD1 → CD2 → CD3...
-If a CD is finally inferred that matches a prediction, then the
-CDs in the chain can be added to the data-base.
- NOTE: since the chain has the most recent CDs first, it is reversed
- before the CDs are added to the data base.
```

```
-TRY-INFERENCE will back up to previous CDs in the chain and try
-different inference rules if the newest CD triggers no inferences.
```

```
(DE JUSTIFY (INPUT)
 (MSG T "Trying to explain")
 (SPRINT INPUT 4)
 (MSG T)
 (LOOP (INITIAL *CHAIN* NIL CD INPUT)
       (UNTIL (PREDICTED CD))
       (DO (MSG T "Does not confirm prediction" T)
           (PUSH (LIST CD *INFERENCE-RULES*) *CHAIN*))
       (WHILE (SETQ CD (TRY-INFERENCE)))
       (RESULT (COND (CD
                   (MSG T "Adding inference chain to data base")
                   (FOR (CD-INF IN (REVERSE *CHAIN*))
                       (DO (UPDATE-DB (CAR CD-INF))))
                   (UPDATE-DB CD))
                   (T (MSG T "No inference chain found—adding")
                   (UPDATE-DB INPUT)
```

```
-PREDICTED checks to see if CD can be directly related to a known
-theme, goal or plan via some rule in the data-base.
-*KNOWN-THEMES* is a list of all themes encountered or inferred
-   in a story.
-*KNOWN-GOALS* is a list of all goals.
-*KNOWN-PLANS* is a list of all plans.
```

¯¯*PLANSFOR* is a list of the rules that relate goals to possible
¯ plans.
¯¯*SUBFOR* is a list of the rules relating plans to the subgoals they
¯ may generate.
¯¯*INSTOF* is a list of the rules relating plans to their
¯ instantiated forms.
¯¯*INIT-RULES* is a list of rules relating themes to the goals they
¯ initiate.

```
(DE PREDICTED (CD)
 (COND
   (((ISA 'GOAL CD)
    (OR (RELATE CD *KNOWN-THEMES* *INIT-RULES*)
        (RELATE CD *KNOWN-PLANS* *SUBFOR*)))
   (((ISA 'PLAN CD) (RELATE CD *KNOWN-GOALS* *PLANSFOR*))
   (((ISA 'ACTION CD) (RELATE CD *KNOWN-PLANS* *INSTOF*]
```

¯RELATE tries to relate an input to some item in ITEM-LIST using
¯some rule in RULE-LIST. The embedded FOR-EXISTS loops are
¯equivalent to saying "there exists an item such that there exists a
¯rule such that the input is related to the item by the rule."

```
(DE RELATE (CD ITEM-LIST RULE-LIST)
 (LET (BD NIL)
  (FOR (ITEM IN ITEM-LIST)
    (EXISTS
     (FOR (RULE IN RULE-LIST)
        (EXISTS (COND ((AND (SETQ BD (MATCH-SIDE (RHS RULE) CD NIL))
                            (MATCH-SIDE (LHS RULE) ITEM BD))
                     (MSG T "Confirms prediction from")
                     (SPRINT ITEM 4)
                     (MSG T)
                     T]
```

¯TRY-INFERENCE tries to make an inference from the chain, which is
¯a list of pairs of the form (CD rules). The first pair is removed
¯and an inference from the CD with the rules is tried. If it
¯succeeds, the new CD is returned (and TRY-RULES puts an updated
¯(CD rules) pair at the front of the chain). If this fails, then
¯the next (CD rules) from the chain is taken. If the chain runs
¯out, then all possible inferences have been tried and failed.

```
(DE TRY-INFERENCE ()
 (LOOP (INITIAL CD-INF NIL CD NIL)
      (WHILE *CHAIN*)
      (DO (SETQ CD-INF (POP *CHAIN*))
          (COND ((NULL (SETQ CD (TRY-RULES (CAR CD-INF)
                                           (CADR CD-INF))))
                (MSG T "No usable inferences from")
                (SPRINT (CAR CD-INF) 4)
                (MSG T))))
      (UNTIL CD)
```

```
(RESULT (COND (CD (MSG T "Possible explanation assuming")
                  (SPRINT CD 4)
                  (MSG T)
                  CD]
```

‾TRY-RULES matches CD against the result pattern of each rule until
‾one fits, in which case: 1) the CD and the remaining untried rules
‾are put on *CHAIN*; 2) the CD inferred from the rule is returned.
‾If no rules match, NIL is returned.

```
(DE TRY-RULES (CD RULES)
 (LOOP (INITIAL RULE NIL BD NIL)
       (WHILE RULES)
       (DO (SETQ RULE (POP RULES)))
       (UNTIL (SETQ BD (MATCH-SIDE (RHS RULE) CD NIL)))
       (RESULT
        (COND (BD
                   (PUSH (LIST CD RULES) *CHAIN*)
                   (INSTANTIATE (CAR (LHS RULE)) BD]
```

‾UPDATE-DB adds a CD to the data base. It also maintains separate
‾data-bases of themes, goals, and plans.

```
(DE UPDATE-DB (CD)
 (MSG T) (SPRINT CD 4) (MSG T)
 (ADD-CD CD)
 (COND ((ISA 'IS CD)
        (MSG "—theme" T)
        (PUSH CD *KNOWN-THEMES*))
       ((ISA 'GOAL CD)
        (PUSH CD *KNOWN-GOALS*))
       ((ISA 'PLAN CD)
        (PUSH CD *KNOWN-PLANS*]
```

‾*DATA-BASE* is simply a list of the statements we wish remembered.
‾New items are added to the end of the list.

```
(DE ADD-CD (CD)
 (SETQ *DATA-BASE* (CONS-END *DATA-BASE* CD))
 CD]
```

‾MATCH-SIDE is used to match a side of a rule to an input.
‾A side matches only if the pattern matches and the semantic
‾constraint expression evaluates to true. The expression may
‾refer to variables bound by the pattern match.

‾*CURRENT-BD* is a binding list of variables within a rule. It is
‾referred to by *VAR*. Outside of MATCH-SIDE it's NIL.

```
(DE MATCH-SIDE (SIDE CONST BD)
 (LET (*CURRENT-BD* (MATCH (PATTERN:SIDE SIDE) CONST BD))
  (AND *CURRENT-BD*
       (EVAL (CONSTRAINT:SIDE SIDE))
       *CURRENT-BD*]
```

"(ISA 'y x) test if x is a y. For example, (ISA 'BOOK ?Z) checks
"to see if either Z = BOOK or (BOOK ...) or (... (TYPE BOOK) ...)
"or the header of Z has the property ISA with value BOOK.

```
(DE ISA (TYPE CD)
 (COND ((NUMBERP CD) NIL)
        ((ATOM CD) (ISA-CHECK TYPE CD))
        (T (OR (ISA-CHECK TYPE (HEADER:CD CD))
              (LET (X (FILLER:ROLE 'TYPE CD))
                (COND (X (ISA-CHECK TYPE (HEADER:CD X]
```

"ISA-CHECK is a subfunction of ISA that applies only to atoms.

```
(DE ISA-CHECK (TYPE X) (OR (EQUAL TYPE X) (EQUAL TYPE (GET X 'ISA]
```

"POS-VAL (CD) returns T if CD is a positive number.

```
(DE POS-VAL (CD)
 (COND ((CONSP CD) (SETQ CD (CAR CD))))
 (AND (NUMBERP CD) (NOT (MINUSP CD)) (NOT (EQUAL CD 0]
```

"PLANFOR adds rules about possible plans for goals
" to the inference-rule data base.

```
(DF PLANFOR (RULE)
 (PUSH RULE *PLANSFOR*)
 (PUSH RULE *INFERENCE-RULES*]
```

"INSTANTIATION adds rules about possible instances of a plan
"to the inference-rule data base.

```
(DF INSTANTIATION (RULE)
 (PUSH RULE *INSTOF*)
 (PUSH RULE *INFERENCE-RULES*]
```

"SUBGOAL adds rules about the preconditions of a plan
"to the inference-rule data base.

```
(DF SUBGOAL (RULE)
 (PUSH RULE *SUBFOR*)
 (PUSH RULE *INFERENCE-RULES*]
```

"INITIATE adds rules that relate themes to goals.

```
(DF INITIATE (RULE)
 (PUSH RULE *INIT-RULES*)
 (PUSH RULE *INFERENCE-RULES*]
```

"CLEAR-GLOBALS clears the global for the data base.

```
(DE CLEAR-GLOBALS()
 (SETQ *KNOWN-THEMES* NIL)
 (SETQ *KNOWN-GOALS* NIL)
 (SETQ *KNOWN-PLANS* NIL)
 (SETQ *DATA-BASE* NIL)
 (SETQ *CURRENT-BD* NIL]
```

¯(*VAR* X) is the form produced by ?X. Normally it is just used as
¯a flag for variables in patterns, recognized by the predicate
¯IS-VAR. However, the predicate expressions appearing in the left
¯and right hand sides of rules have forms like (ISA 'CAR ?X) which
¯is the same as (ISA 'CAR (*VAR* X)). By defining *VAR* to be
¯a function that returns the binding of X—using the binding list
¯*CURRENT-BD* which is set when sides of rules are matched—we can
¯pass to the function ISA what X refers to.

(DF *VAR* (L) (FILLER:ROLE (CAR L) *CURRENT-BD*]

```
¯  *******************************************************************
¯                          DATA STRUCTURES
¯  *******************************************************************
```

¯A story is a list of CDs. A CD is either a primitive atom
¯(e.g., STORE) or a predicate (PTRANS, PERSON, etc.) plus
¯zero or more (role filler) arguments.
¯An example of a 3-line story is:

(SETQ WILLA-STORY
        '(¯Willa was hungry.
          (IS (ACTOR (PERSON (NAME (WILLA))))
              (STATE (HUNGER (VAL (5)))))
          ¯She picked up the Michelin guide
          (GRASP (ACTOR (PERSON (NAME (WILLA))))
                 (OBJECT (BOOK (TYPE (RESTAURANT-GUIDE)))))
          ¯She got into her car
          (PTRANS (ACTOR (PERSON (NAME (WILLA))))
                  (OBJECT (PERSON (NAME (WILLA)))) (TO (CAR]

¯Rules have the form (<left hand side> <right hand side>).
¯LHS gets the left hand side of a rule, RHS gets the right hand side.

(DE LHS (RULE) (CAR RULE]
(DE RHS (RULE) (CADR RULE]

¯Each side of a rule has the form (<pattern> <expression>). If
¯the expression is left off, it is T (= true) by default.

(DE PATTERN:SIDE (SIDE) (CAR SIDE]
(DE CONSTRAINT:SIDE (SIDE)
 (COND ((CDR SIDE) (CADR SIDE)) (T T]

```
¯  *******************************************************************
¯                              RULES
¯  *******************************************************************
```

¯Rules in McPAM are of the following general form:

¯   ((pattern pred) (pattern pred))

¯Both the right and left hand sides of a rule consist of a pattern
¯followed by an optional predicate. The predicate is used by the
¯pattern matcher MATCH-SIDE to restrict the types of objects that
¯might match a variable in a pattern.

There are four kinds of rules in McPAM:
- Instantiation rules, which relate events to plans they may be part of;
- Planfor rules, which relate plans to goals to which they may be applicable;
- Subgoal rules, which relate goals to plans to which they may be instrumental;
- Initiate rules, which relate themes to goals they may give rise to.

Initialize a few lists to NIL. They will be filled in later on.

```
(SETQ *PLANSFOR* NIL)
(SETQ *SUBFOR* NIL)
(SETQ *INSTOF* NIL)
(SETQ *INIT-RULES* NIL)
(SETQ *INFERENCE-RULES* NIL)

(CLEAR-GLOBALS)
```

Define some ISA links.

```
(DEFPROP PTRANS                        ACTION   ISA)
(DEFPROP GRASP                         ACTION   ISA)
(DEFPROP TAKE-PLAN                     PLAN     ISA)
(DEFPROP READ-PLAN                     PLAN     ISA)
(DEFPROP DO-$RESTRAURANT-PLAN          PLAN     ISA)
(DEFPROP WALK-PLAN                     PLAN     ISA)
(DEFPROP USE-VEHICLE-PLAN              PLAN     ISA)
(DEFPROP TAKE-PLAN                     PLAN     ISA)
```

The following rules are those needed by McPAM to understand the
Michelin Guide story

```
(INSTANTIATION
((TAKE-PLAN (PLANNER ?X) (OBJECT ?Y)))
((GRASP (ACTOR ?X) (OBJECT ?Y]

(INSTANTIATION
((WALK-PLAN (PLANNER ?X) (LOCATION ?Y)))
((PTRANS (ACTOR ?X) (OBJECT ?X) (TO ?Y]

(PLANFOR
((GOAL (PLANNER ?X) (OBJECTIVE (POSS (ACTOR ?X) (OBJECT ?Y)))))
((TAKE-PLAN (PLANNER ?X) (OBJECT ?Y]

(PLANFOR
((GOAL (PLANNER ?X)
       (OBJECTIVE (KNOW (ACTOR ?X)
                               (FACT (IS (ACTOR RESTAURANT) (PROX ?Z))) ))))
((READ-PLAN (PLANNER ?X) (OBJECT ?W)) (ISA 'RESTAURANT-GUIDE ?W]

(PLANFOR
((GOAL (PLANNER ?X) (OBJECTIVE (ENJOYMENT (ACTOR ?X)))))
((READ-PLAN (PLANNER ?X) (OBJECT ?W)) (ISA 'BOOK ?W]
```

```
(PLANFOR
 ((GOAL (PLANNER ?X)
        (OBJECTIVE (IS (ACTOR ?X) (STATE (HUNGER (VAL (0))))))))
 ((DO-$RESTAURANT-PLAN (PLANNER ?X) (RESTAURANT ?Y]

(PLANFOR
 ((GOAL (PLANNER ?X) (OBJECTIVE (PROX (ACTOR ?X) (LOCATION ?Y)))))
 ((WALK-PLAN (PLANNER ?X) (LOCATION ?Y]

(PLANFOR
 ((GOAL (PLANNER ?X) (OBJECTIVE (PROX (ACTOR ?X) (LOCATION ?Y)))))
 ((USE-VEHICLE-PLAN (PLANNER ?X]

(SUBGOAL
 ((READ-PLAN (PLANNER ?X) (OBJECT ?Y)))
 ((GOAL (PLANNER ?X)
        (OBJECTIVE (POSS (ACTOR ?X) (OBJECT ?Y)))) (ISA 'BOOK ?Y]

(SUBGOAL
 ((GOAL (PLANNER ?X) (OBJECTIVE (PROX (ACTOR ?X) (LOCATION ?Y)))) )
 ((GOAL (PLANNER ?X)
        (OBJECTIVE (KNOW (ACTOR ?X) (FACT (IS (ACTOR ?Y) (PROX ?Z]

(SUBGOAL
 ((DO-$RESTAURANT-PLAN (PLANNER ?X) (RESTAURANT ?Y)))
 ((GOAL (PLANNER ?X)
        (OBJECTIVE (PROX (ACTOR ?X) (LOCATION ?Y))))
  (ISA 'RESTAURANT ?Y]

(SUBGOAL
 ((USE-VEHICLE-PLAN (PLANNER ?X) (OBJECT ?Y)))
 ((GOAL (PLANNER ?X)
        (OBJECTIVE (PROX (ACTOR ?X) (LOCATION ?Y)))) (ISA 'CAR ?Y]

(INITIATE
 ((IS (ACTOR ?X) (STATE (HUNGER (VAL ?N)))) (POS-VAL ?N))
 ((GOAL (PLANNER ?X)
        (OBJECTIVE (IS (ACTOR ?X) (STATE (HUNGER (VAL (0)
```

EXERCISES

1. Add the inference rules needed to process this story: "John wanted Bill's bike. He asked Bill to sell it to him for $10. Bill gave him the bike." The CD forms for this story are:

```
(SETQ ASK-STORY

 "John wanted Bill's bike.

     (GOAL (PLANNER (PERSON (NAME (JOHN))))
           (OBJECTIVE
               (POSS (ACTOR (PERSON (NAME (JOHN))))
                     (OBJECT (BIKE
                             (OWNER (PERSON (NAME (BILL)))))))))
```

He asked Bill to sell it to him for $10.

```
(MTRANS (ACTOR (PERSON (NAME (JOHN))))
        (TO (PERSON (NAME (BILL))))
        (MOBJECT
            (SELL-PLAN
                (OWNER (PERSON (NAME (BILL))))
                (BUYER (PERSON (NAME (JOHN))))
                (OBJECT (BIKE
                            (OWNER (PERSON (NAME (BILL))))))
                (PRICE (MONEY (AMOUNT ($10)))))))
```

Bill gave him the bike.

```
(ATRANS (ACTOR (PERSON (NAME (BILL))))
        (OBJECT (BIKE (OWNER (PERSON (NAME (BILL))))))
        (TO (PERSON (NAME (JOHN)
```

You will have to add the following:

1. a rule to relate the goal of wanting something owned by another person to the PLANFOR of asking the owner to sell it to you.
2. two rules relating this plan to two SUBGOALs, namely the buyer's goal of saying that he would like to buy the object, and the seller's goal that the buyer should end up possessing the object.
3. a rule relating the goal of wanting another person to have an object with a PLANFOR achieving it by giving it to them.
4. a rule indicating that the INSTANTIATION of a "give" plan is an ATRANS.
5. a rule relating the goal of wanting another person to know something with the PLANFOR achieving it by telling them.
6. a rule indicating that the INSTANTIATION of a "tell" plan is an MTRANS.

Model your rules after the ones for WILLA-STORY. Remember to specify the ISA property for any new plans or actions you use.

2. a. Try running McPAM on the following story, which differs from WILLA-STORY only in that the first sentence gives the goal ("be not hungry") instead of the theme ("be hungry").

```
(SETQ WILLA-STORY2
    '(
```

Willa wanted to be not hungry

```
(GOAL (ACTOR (PERSON (NAME (WILLA))))
      (OBJECTIVE (IS (ACTOR (PERSON (NAME (WILLA))))
                     (STATE (HUNGER (VAL (0)))))))
```

She picked up the Michelin guide

```
(GRASP (ACTOR (PERSON (NAME (WILLA))))
       (OBJECT (BOOK (TYPE (RESTAURANT-GUIDE)))))
```

She got into her car

```
(PTRANS (ACTOR (PERSON (NAME (WILLA))))
        (OBJECT (PERSON (NAME (WILLA)))) (TO (CAR)
```

b. In doing WILLA-STORY2, McPAM infers the theme of being hungry from the goal of not being hungry. But since this theme does not match any prediction, it is thrown away. Fix this problem by changing PRE-DICTED in McPAM to say that a theme is always predicted. Thus if a theme can be inferred from an action, that theme constitutes an adequate explanation for the action. Re-run WILLA-STORY and WILLA-STORY2.

c. Now add the following reasonable inference rule, which relates the goal of enjoyment to the theme of being happy:

```
(INITIATE
 ((IS (ACTOR ?X) (STATE (HAPPINESS (VAL ?N)))) (POS-VAL ?N))
 ((GOAL (PLANNER ?X) (OBJECTIVE (ENJOYMENT (ACTOR ?X))
```

Run the modified version of McPAM from (b) on WILLA-STORY. Why doesn't it work any more?

d. The modified McPAM now says that when Willa picked up the book, she did it because of the HAPPY theme. If "Willa picked up a book" were the first line of a story, then this would be right. But after "Willa was hungry" it's not. This indicates that McPAM shouldn't always accept thematic explanations just because they exist. Modify McPAM so that it won't automatically accept a thematic explanation if another theme for the character has already been encountered.

3. This exercise involves adding the inference rules needed to get McPAM to work on the following, somewhat complex, story.

```
(SETQ LIQUOR-STORE-STORY

 '(¨John wanted money

 (GOAL (PLANNER (PERSON (NAME (JOHN))))
       (OBJECTIVE (POSS (ACTOR (PERSON (NAME (JOHN))))
                        (OBJECT (MONEY)))))

 ¨He got a gun
 (ATRANS (ACTOR (PERSON (NAME (JOHN))))
         (OBJECT (GUN))
         (TO (PERSON (NAME (JOHN)))))

 ¨He went to the liquor store
 (PTRANS (ACTOR (PERSON (NAME (JOHN))))
         (OBJECT (PERSON (NAME (JOHN))))
         (TO (LIQUOR-STORE)))

 ¨He told the owner he wanted some money
 (MTRANS (ACTOR (PERSON (NAME (JOHN))))
         (TO (PERSON (NAME (OWNER))))
         (MOBJECT (GOAL (PLANNER (PERSON (NAME (JOHN))))
                        (OBJECTIVE
                         (POSS (ACTOR (PERSON (NAME (JOHN))))
                               (OBJECT (MONEY)))))))
```

```
¯The owner gave him the money
(ATRANS (ACTOR (PERSON (NAME (OWNER))))
        (OBJECT (MONEY))
        (TO (PERSON (NAME (JOHN)))))

¯John left
(PTRANS (ACTOR (PERSON (NAME (JOHN))))
        (OBJECT (PERSON (NAME (JOHN))))
        (TO (HIDEOUT))
        (FROM (LIQUOR-STORE))
```

Do the story one sentence at a time. Do not try to get everything to work at once. The rules you add should involve the relation between **ATRANS** and possession, between possession of a weapon and plans for getting money, between plans for getting money and being at a suitable place, between plans for getting money and carrying out a threat, between **MTRANS** and someone knowing something, and so forth.

4. In this version of McPAM, when you want to give several subgoals to a plan, you have to write separate rules for each subgoal, repeating the plan each time. A better way would be to allow a rule to have more than one pattern-expression pair in the right hand side, and each would specify one subgoal of the plan on the left hand side. Modify McPAM to do this by modifying **RHS**, **RELATE** and **TRY-RULES** to handle more than one pair.

9 TALE-SPIN

James Meehan

INTRODUCTION

Overview of TALE-SPIN

TALE-SPIN (Meehan, 1976) is a program that writes simple stories. It is easily distinguished from any of the "mechanical" devices one can use for writing stories, such as filling in slots in a canned frame. The goal behind the writing of TALE-SPIN was to find out what kinds of knowledge were needed in story generation. The writing of TALE-SPIN embodied the traditional AI cycle of research. Step 1 was to define a theory. Step 2 was to write a program modeling that theory and to add it to the existing system. Step 3 was to run the system and to observe where the model was incorrect or inadequate, thereby identifying the need for some more theory.

Of course, there were theories or parts of theories that never made it past step 1. Some of these, such as a more complete goal calculus, were beyond the range of any current theories. Others, like the addition of personal pronouns to the output, would have enhanced the quality of the output but were not central to the problem of generating the events of a story.

The program, simply described, simulates a small world of characters who are motivated to act by having problems to solve. When an event occurs, it is expressed in English, thus forming the text of the story. Central to the simulation, therefore, are the techniques for solving problems. These were derived from Schank and Abelson's D-goals (Schank and Abelson, 1977), which described common knowledge that we use when we comprehend a narrative involving plan-based behavior. I used the same ideas to simulate such behavior.

197

The adaptation of the original theory was not without its differences, even at the level of plans. The plan for communication, DKNOW, in their theory encompasses a variety of communication tasks. In TALE-SPIN, there is a clear distinction between transmitting and acquiring information, and they are described by independent procedures.

I also merged the problem-solving knowledge with information about social relationships and personal characteristics, principally as preconditions to acts of persuasion. The "scales" I used derived from some of the work of Myron Wish (1975), which was extended to describe the more specific requirements of the stories the program was writing.

The second largest part of TALE-SPIN, after the problem-solving component, is the English-language generator. Originally, I used a version of Goldman's BABEL (Goldman, 1975), but the match was not ideal, and in the standard but unfortunate tradition of AI, I wrote my own from scratch. Gradually, it relied more and more on the memory (chronological record), so that it would say "Joe Bear returned to his cave" instead of "Joe Bear went to the cave," and it knew when to say "Irving Bird wasn't hungry any more" as opposed to the simpler "Irving Bird wasn't hungry."

The inference mechanism began with the simple, "context-free" consequences that are part of the definition of the primitive acts of Conceptual Dependency. These were extended to include three new areas: the social-state knowledge mentioned above; the effects of "noticing" whenever anyone moved from one place to another (unfortunately but unavoidably, a large source of simple inferences); and "reactions", or the inferences from MLOC, nearly equal in number to all the inferences from the rest of the system.

Of the many domains that might have been investigated, the representation of physical space seemed difficult to postpone, and the resulting theory and implementation of "maps" and "blueprints" most closely resemble Minsky's definition of frames. This information was used when new characters and new settings were generated; e.g., if something is a house, then it has a front door, and may have an upstairs bedroom, and so on. Since the characters in TALE-SPIN are talking animals and humans, the world blueprint describes meadows and valleys and the like. They are created on demand (when a journey takes place).

Finally, TALE-SPIN reflects a theory of stories that is easy to state: stories are both coherent and interesting, and they span a number of levels. To explain that statement, let me first describe the overall control for the simulator.

When an event occurs, it is "asserted", which means that it is recorded and all its consequences are computed and likewise asserted. One kind of event is called a goal statement, such as "John wants to visit Mary." When a goal statement is asserted, the corresponding problem-solving procedure is called, i.e., one for the goal of transportation (DPROX), one for the goal of communication (DKNOW), and so on. These procedures invoke subgoals and eventually produce new events, which are then asserted, continuing the cycle. The simulation begins by establishing a "setting" and a cast of characters. One of the characters is given a problem to solve. In the course of solving that problem, the character may interact with other characters. If one character persuades another to do something, then the second character goes about solving problems. The simulator keeps track of all the characters.

This is the model of coherence—the behavior of the characters should be rational—and it provides the test for the theories of problem solving. But beyond that, stories must be interesting. In TALE-SPIN, an interesting story sets up a particular problem and a focal problem domain called the domain of interest. The story is "about" solving that problem. The details of the solution should pertain to the domain of interest, and the problem should not be too easily solved. The level of the domain of interest is what distinguishes a simple adventure story from a work such as Conrad's *Heart of Darkness*. Left to its own devices, as it were, the simulator will create a low-level story about characters driven by very basic needs such as hunger, and the similarity between these stories and actual folk tales has been noted (de Beaugrande and Colby, 1979). But in order to tell a higher-level story, the simulator requires that some of the setting be established ahead of time, particularly relationships between characters so that their predicted behavior corresponds to the needs of the story. In this way, TALE-SPIN is able to generate stories with a "point", such as the simpler of the Aesop fables.

Examples

Here is an example of a TALE-SPIN story. After an initial dialogue with the user, establishing the characters and the physical setting, the story begins when each of the characters is made thirsty. The story required no information about the social relationships, because all characters are motivated to rescue anyone in danger of death.

Most of the "resultant" inferences have been omitted from the output for brevity. Paragraphs have been added here to indicate separate stories that use the same set of characters and locations.

ONCE UPON A TIME GEORGE ANT LIVED NEAR A PATCH OF GROUND. THERE WAS A NEST IN AN ASH TREE. WILMA BIRD LIVED IN THE NEST. THERE WAS SOME WATER IN A RIVER. WILMA KNEW THAT THE WATER WAS IN THE RIVER. GEORGE KNEW THAT THE WATER WAS IN THE RIVER. ONE DAY WILMA WAS VERY THIRSTY. WILMA WANTED TO GET NEAR SOME WATER. WILMA FLEW FROM HER NEST ACROSS A MEADOW THROUGH A VALLEY TO THE RIVER. WILMA DRANK THE WATER. WILMA WAS NOT THIRSTY ANY MORE.

GEORGE WAS VERY THIRSTY. GEORGE WANTED TO GET NEAR SOME WATER. GEORGE WALKED FROM HIS PATCH OF GROUND ACROSS THE MEADOW THROUGH THE VALLEY TO A

RIVER BANK. GEORGE FELL INTO THE WATER. GEORGE
WANTED TO GET NEAR THE VALLEY. GEORGE COULDN'T GET
NEAR THE VALLEY. GEORGE WANTED TO GET NEAR THE
MEADOW. GEORGE COULDN'T GET NEAR THE MEADOW.
WILMA WANTED GEORGE TO GET NEAR THE MEADOW. WILMA
WANTED TO GET NEAR GEORGE. WILMA GRABBED GEORGE
WITH HER CLAW. WILMA TOOK GEORGE FROM THE RIVER
THROUGH THE VALLEY TO THE MEADOW. GEORGE WAS DE-
VOTED TO WILMA. GEORGE OWED EVERYTHING TO WILMA.
WILMA LET GO OF GEORGE. GEORGE FELL TO THE MEADOW.
THE END.

The two relationship states at the end are "demon" inferences—George
would have reacted that way to anyone who pulled him out of the water.

Here's an example showing "verbose mode" where every inference is
printed. The relationships between the characters were established by a dialogue
with the user, which has been omitted.

ONCE UPON A TIME JOHN BEAR LIVED IN A CAVE. JOHN
KNEW THAT JOHN WAS IN HIS CAVE. THERE WAS A BEEHIVE IN
A MAPLE TREE. TOM BEE KNEW THAT THE BEEHIVE WAS IN
THE MAPLE TREE. TOM WAS IN HIS BEEHIVE. TOM KNEW THAT
TOM WAS IN HIS BEEHIVE. THERE WAS SOME HONEY IN TOM'S
BEEHIVE. TOM KNEW THAT THE HONEY WAS IN TOM'S BEE-
HIVE. TOM HAD THE HONEY. TOM KNEW THAT TOM HAD THE
HONEY. THERE WAS A NEST IN A CHERRY TREE. ARTHUR BIRD
KNEW THAT THE NEST WAS IN THE CHERRY TREE. ARTHUR
WAS IN HIS NEST. ARTHUR KNEW THAT ARTHUR WAS IN HIS
NEST. ARTHUR KNEW THAT JOHN WAS IN HIS CAVE. JOHN
KNEW THAT ARTHUR WAS IN HIS NEST. JOHN KNEW THAT
TOME WAS IN HIS BEEHIVE. THERE WERE SOME BOYSENBER-
RIES NEAR A BUSH. THERE WAS A LILY FLOWER IN A
FLOWERBED. ARTHUR KNEW THAT THE BOYSENBERRIES WERE
NEAR THE BUSH. JOHN KNEW THAT THE LILY FLOWER WAS IN
THE FLOWERBED.

ONE DAY JOHN WAS VERY HUNGRY. JOHN WANTED TO
GET SOME HONEY. JOHN WANTED TO FIND OUT WHERE THERE
WAS SOME HONEY. JOHN LIKED ARTHUR. JOHN WANTED AR-
THUR TO TELL JOHN WHERE THERE WAS SOME HONEY. JOHN
WAS HONEST WITH ARTHUR. JOHN WASN'T COMPETITIVE
WITH ARTHUR. JOHN THOUGHT THAT ARTHUR LIKED HIM.
JOHN THOUGHT THAT ARTHUR WAS HONEST WITH HIM. JOHN
WANTED TO ASK ARTHUR WHETHER ARTHUR WOULD TELL

JOHN WHERE THERE WAS SOME HONEY. JOHN WANTED TO GET
NEAR ARTHUR. JOHN WALKED FROM A CAVE EXIT THROUGH A
PASS THROUGH A VALLEY THROUGH A MEADOW TO THE
GROUND BY THE CHERRY TREE. JOHN WAS NEAR THE GROUND
BY THE CHERRY TREE. JOHN KNEW THAT JOHN WAS NEAR THE
GROUND BY THE CHERRY TREE. JOHN KNEW THAT ARTHUR
WAS IN HIS NEST. ARTHUR KNEW THAT JOHN WAS NEAR THE
GROUND BY THE CHERRY TREE. JOHN ASKED ARTHUR WHETHER
ARTHUR WOULD TELL JOHN WHERE THERE WAS SOME HONEY.
ARTHUR DIDN'T HAVE MUCH INFLUENCE OVER JOHN. ARTHUR
REMEMBERED THAT ARTHUR LOVED JOHN. ARTHUR WAS
HONEST WITH JOHN.

At this point, Arthur has decided to tell John where some honey is. This is just
the first third of the story. The rest tells how John Bear goes to Tom Bee's hive to
get some honey and he refuses. The point to be made by this is that TALE-SPIN
is not putting words together to make a story. It has a very complex model of a
small multi-actor world, and the sentences that are finally printed show just a tiny
fraction of what the program really knows.

Summary of Program Behavior

The program can currently create eight different kinds of characters that are
directly coded, and forty-six kinds of physical locations (e.g., meadows,
bridges) that are data-driven (constructed from abstract descriptions). There are
explicit problem-solving procedures for transportation (DPROX), acquisition of
objects (DCONT), acquisition of information (DKNOW), transfer of information (TELL), persuasion (PERSUADE), bargaining (BARGAIN), and asking
favors (ASK). The standard set of CD primitives was extended to include the acts
PLAN and *WANT*, and thirteen "social" states were used (e.g., honesty,
affection). There are forty-one inference procedures.

The generator uses a vocabulary consisting of fifty verbs in addition to the
nouns for every object and several adjectives (or adjectival phrases) for every
state in the system (e.g., for the "energy" scale, the generator can choose from:
wiped out, exhausted, tired, rested, lively, energetic, hyper). It uses past, present, and future tenses, negations, contractions, infinitive phrases ("Joe asked
Irving *to tell him* . . ."), interrogatives (who, what, where), conditionals
(whether), modals (can, might, would), and "mass" nouns (e.g., "some"
honey, not "a" honey).

In addition to the domains already described, TALE-SPIN includes a symbolic arithmetic package, where all numerical concepts are represented as points
in a directed graph, so that partial-order comparisons can be made without
assigning numerical values. This is used, for example, in representing the time at

which an event occurs; we need to compare the relative times of two events to generate the proper tense in the English output.

One of the enduring points in TALE-SPIN's favor is that it provides, conceptually, a wealth of "small" topics to be invented or extended. That is, if you wish to improve the stories by improving the representation of physical space, making travel-distance a planning precondition, for instance, it's not difficult to find out where to add that code. The generator's vocabulary and range of grammatical constructions are easily extended. "Large" topics, of course, like redesigning the top-level control, are not easy.

The major drawback to TALE-SPIN is its size, not surprisingly. When it ran at Yale under Stanford LISP 1.6 (Quam, 1969), in 1976, it required 75K (PDP-10 words) to load, and an additional 25K would make the response reasonable. Today, TALE-SPIN is entirely compiled and runs at UCI under UCI LISP (Meehan, 1979) requiring about 90K to load. Part of that increase is due to the additional facilities in UCI LISP, but most of it comes simply from the extended capabilities of the system. Both versions of TALE-SPIN were written in MLISP (Smith, 1970), an ALGOL-like language that is converted by a pre-processor into LISP code for execution.

The system is not particularly robust. Some errors are detected by the program itself, which prints a message and waits for a response. Some of these are ignorable. When the generator cannot produce a translation, its "error message" is "Uh . . . Uh . . . mumble", a phrase borrowed from Goldman's BABEL. (In fact, TALE-SPIN's generator is called MUMBLE.) But other messages, unfortunately, are meaningless to anyone but me. Errors in the internal syntax of CD expressions, for example, or contradictions in the time-net (A is before B and B is before A), still occur. In long stories, one can encounter the familiar resource limitations. My favorite error message occurred in the middle of generating a sentence: JOE BEAR KNOWS THAT FREE STG EXHAUSTED.

Issues

TALE-SPIN has three main theoretical concerns:

1. *Plans and goals*. The program shows a new side to the Schank-Abelson theory of intentionality, the principal exposition for which has always been in the comprehension, rather than the generation, of text. The theory, for example, doesn't specify the rules for acquisition or rejection of new plans and goals (sometimes referred to as the goal calculus), nor is much said about the connection between certain social relationships and various problem-solving techniques—issues that I was forced to face in building the system.
2. *The nature of stories*. TALE-SPIN explores the connection between storytelling and problem solving by defining a story's impetus in terms of

characters who are in pursuit of various goals. Even starting with such low-level goals as hunger and thirst, it takes very little to produce a story involving trust, affection, good intentions, and the lack of same. Stories are certainly *more* than problem-solving narratives, but they may not be less.

3. *Simulation as a form of cognition.* At first, I thought that the difficulties in managing a simulation were primarily issues of programming (how to imitate parallelism, for example). But once I had the characters doing simulations themselves as a technique for planning ahead, I began to believe in simulation as a form of memory, in which case the rules for controlling it become far more significant, and programming tricks must be abandoned.

Much remains to be done in these three areas. The goal calculus has yet to be worked out, and every time the theory of goals changes (usually by expansion), the old calculus requires a major overhaul. For example, how many "background" goals do you have? How are they organized? Without answers to such questions, reasonable-sounding calculus heuristics like "Compare a new goal to the background goals to decide whether to pursue it" are too vague.

Good stories are coherent and interesting on many levels of meaning—the more, the better. This may be the hardest of the three areas to develop, because it presumes that we know how to represent meaning on many levels, and in particular, that the lower levels are simpler. The difficulty I see is that those lower levels require either a great engine to do all the busy-work of computing the obvious consequences of, say, every physical action, or some very smart processor that ignores all those details that *we* know to be unnecessary. If only we knew *how* we know they're unnecessary!

An immediate problem with using simulation as a form of memory is knowing how *not* to get bogged down with the details that will arise during the actual execution of a plan, and how to make intelligent guesses in the face of incomplete information.

OVERVIEW OF TALE-SPIN

An Example of the Program in Question

We will begin our discussion of the inner workings of TALE-SPIN with a look at what the program does in an interactive session with it.

The upper-case text is from the program. The comments (in lower-case) describe how the program proceeds. We begin with a dialogue to establish the characters.

```
*(START)

********** WELCOME TO TALE-SPIN **********

CHOOSE ANY OF THE FOLLOWING CHARACTERS FOR THE STORY:

1: BEAR     2:BEE      3: BOY          4: GIRL     5: FOX
6: CROW     7 ANT      8: CANARY
*1 2
```

By answering with 1 and 2, we ask the program to make up a bear and a bee. Their names and sexes (except for 3 and 4) are chosen at random. When characters are created, some local setting is included: their homes, and some objects likely to be found there. Initially, all characters start out at home. The narrative is told in past tense.

> ONCE UPON A TIME SAM BEAR LIVED IN A CAVE. SAM KNEW THAT SAM WAS IN HIS CAVE.

All characters are made aware of their initial locations.

> THERE WAS A BEEHIVE IN AN APPLE TREE. BETTY BEE KNEW THAT THE BEEHIVE WAS IN THE APPLE TREE. BETTY WAS IN HER BEEHIVE. BETTY KNEW THAT BETTY WAS IN HER BEEHIVE. THERE WAS SOME HONEY IN BETTY'S BEEHIVE. BETTY KNEW THAT THE HONEY WAS IN BETTY'S BEEHIVE. BETTY HAD THE HONEY. BETTY KNEW THAT BETTY HAD THE HONEY.

The model for bees is that they live in beehives and "own" honey. The model for beehives specifies that they are found in trees, so the creator adds all of these items to the simulated world.

The sentences beginning "Betty knew that..." are included to show that the program is storing that information, to be used in solving problems and making inferences.

> —DECIDE: DOES BETTY BEE KNOW WHERE SAM BEAR IS?   *NO
> —DECIDE: DOES SAM BEAR KNOW WHERE BETTY BEE IS?   *YES
> SAM KNEW THAT BETTY WAS IN HER BEEHIVE.
> SAM KNEW THAT BETTY HAD THE HONEY.

We get to decide whether the characters know about each other.

> —DECIDE: DO YOU WANT ANY OF THESE IN THE STORY?
> (BREADCRUMBS CHEESE BASEBALL)   *NO

These are props that can be included and given to the characters, but in this case we decided not to use any of them.

—DECIDE: DO YOU WANT ANY OF THESE IN THE STORY?
(BERRIES FLOWER WATER WORM)   *YES
WHICH ONES?
1: BERRIES   2: FLOWER   3: WATER   4: WORM
*2
THERE WAS A ROSE FLOWER IN A FLOWERBED.
WHO KNOWS ABOUT THE ROSE FLOWER?
1: BETTY BEE   2: SAM BEAR
*2
SAM KNEW THAT THE ROSE FLOWER WAS IN THE FLOWERBED.

These props can be created, too, but they don't belong to any of the characters. Instead, we get to decide who knows where they are.

THIS IS A STORY ABOUT...
1: BETTY BEE   2: SAM BEAR
†2
HIS PROBLEM IS THAT HE IS...
1: HUNGRY   2: TIRED   3: THIRSTY   4: HORNY
*1

The last thing we need in the initial setting is a "main character" and a problem for that character to begin working on. The choice of initial problems is the set of S-goals (cyclic goals of satisfaction).

ONE DAY SAM WAS VERY HUNGRY.

From this point on, after we assert that Sam is hungry, the control is out of our hands. The simulator takes over, computing consequences and invoking the planning procedures. The procedure now running is S-HUNGER, and it calls DCONT so that Sam will get some food. The list of foods bears eat is stored, and honey is chosen at random.

SAM WANTED TO GET SOME HONEY.

DCONT calls DKNOW to have Sam find out where there's some honey. DKNOW first checks to see whether Sam already knows where some honey is. The pattern matcher matches the non-specific honey he's looking for with the particular honey that Betty owns, since Sam knows about that. Had he not known already, DKNOW would have started its own procedures for finding out information (e.g., ask a friend).

HOW HONEST WAS SAM?   *NOT AT ALL
SAM WAS DISHONEST.
HOW VAIN DID SAM THINK THAT BETTY WAS?   *NOT AT ALL
SAM THOUGHT THAT BETTY WAS HUMBLE.

DCONT's first technique is to ask whether the honey is free for the taking. It does that by searching the memory to see whether Sam thinks that anyone owns the honey. Of course, Betty does, so the honey isn't free, and that technique won't work.

The second technique is simply to persuade the owner to hand over the honey, but before we do that, we consider whether a trick might work here. The particular trick works only if the person who wants the honey is dishonest and the owner is vain, and it involves flattery. The memory doesn't say anything about those characteristics of Sam and Betty, so the system asks us directly. The question is written out by the English generator. The answer is matched against a list of canned phrases such as LOTS, NOT MUCH, SOMEWHAT, and so on. In any case, the first condition was met, but not the second, so we give up the idea of that trick and consider simple persuasion.

```
SAM WANTED BETTY TO GIVE SAM THE HONEY.
HOW DECEITFUL DID SAM FEEL TOWARDS BETTY?    *VERY
SAM WAS INCLINED TO LIE TO BETTY.
```

The "persuade package" contains four techniques for getting someone to do something for you. You can ask, you can give them a good reason, you can bargain, or you can threaten. If it is your intent to deceive that person, however, you won't ask or bargain. The search for a good reason will be described in detail later; it was not successful here.

```
HOW MUCH DID SAM LIKE BETTY?    *LOTS
SAM LOVED BETTY.
SAM DECIDED THAT BETTY WOULDN'T GIVE SAM THE HONEY.
```

The fourth planbox (threaten) won't work if you like the person, and that's the last option, so this whole attempt to persuade Betty to give Sam the honey fails. But the "persuade package" was only one of the ways DCONT knows about. The next planbox in DCONT is theft—if you want something, steal it. Before we can use this option, of course, we need to know whether Sam is honest. His dishonesty was established earlier, so we don't need to ask the question again. The plan for theft is very simple: get the owner away from the object, and take it.

```
SAM WANTED BETTY TO FLY AWAY FROM HER BEEHIVE.
```

The procedure now active is D-NEG-PROX, where the goal is not to get Betty *to* some particular place, but rather to get her *away* from her beehive. There are two techniques in D-NEG-PROX. The first is to persuade Betty to go by herself. The second is to use DPROX to get Betty to some nearby area, using any applicable technique known to DPROX, including simply pulling her out. We start with the persuasion.

The first persuasion technique is a simple request, but it's blocked by the fact that Sam intends to deceive Betty. The second technique is to find a good reason for Betty to leave. The task is to find some goal of Betty's that would be aided by having her leave the beehive; that is, we want to find a causal chain that links leaving the hive to achieving one of her goals. The search is done breadth-first and starts by considering the goals Betty can always be assumed to have. The two goals that bees have in TALE-SPIN are hunger and rest, and bees "eat" flowers.

The inference mechanism is most often used to compute consequences, but it can also compute preconditions, or "backwards" inferences. The precondition for resting (more precisely, for achieving a state of rest) is sleeping, which is described by means of a script. The precondition for that script is being located at your home. The precondition for that is that someone bring you home (possibly you yourself). The preconditions for that are knowing where your home is, and its being located near you, and so on, backing up the causal chains. Every time we get a new precondition, we try to match it against the desired event, which in this case is Betty leaving the beehive. Nothing in the chain leading to resting matches, at least not up to a preset length. However, going backwards from "Betty is not hungry," we compute "Betty eats some food," "Betty has some food," "X (unspecified actor) gives Betty the food," "X is near the food," and "Y (unspecified) moves X to the food." This finally matches "Betty leaves the beehive" (more precisely, Betty moves Betty from the beehive to anywhere except the beehive), since we can extend this (as in unification) to "Betty moves Betty from the beehive to the flower."

But this is not enough. Sam has to trick Betty into doing that. We continue searching back up causal chains until we find a precondition that Sam can fulfill. Before Betty can go to the flower, she must know where a flower is. In order for that to happen, someone must tell her where a flower is. This, finally, is the precondition Sam can fulfill. (If Sam thought that Betty already knew where a flower was, this strategy would be rejected, and other alternatives would be tried.)

SAM DECIDED THAT IF SAM TELLS BETTY WHERE THERE WAS A FLOWER THEN BETTY MIGHT NOT BE NEAR HER BEEHIVE.

This example shows how the inference mechanism that the simulator uses can be used by the characters to do their own planning. In this case, the characters are computing "backward" inferences (preconditions); in the case of considering a request, the characters use the "forward" inferences (consequences) to help them decide whether to comply with the request.

There's no guarantee that the plan will work. Some plans depend on particular social relationships, and even though Bill Fox may think Henry Crow is vain, Henry may not be, in which case Bill's plan could fail.

SAM WANTED TO TELL BETTY WHERE THERE WAS A FLOWER.

In order for this trick to work, Sam has to talk to Betty. The TELL procedure is now active.

SAM WANTED TO GET NEAR BETTY.

The first planbox in TELL is to go directly to Betty. If that failed, Sam would try using a messenger.

SAM WALKED FROM A CAVE EXIT THROUGH A PASS THROUGH THE VALLEY TO THE GROUND BY THE APPLE TREE.
SAM WAS NEAR THE GROUND BY THE APPLE TREE.
SAM KNEW THAT SAM WAS NEAR THE GROUND BY THE APPLE TREE.
BETTY KNEW THAT SAM WAS NEAR THE GROUND BY THE APPLE TREE.

The module in charge of physical layouts has created all the intervening landscape, and Sam successfully arrives at Betty's tree, a fact of which both are made aware.

SAM TOLD BETTY THAT THE ROSE FLOWER WAS IN THE FLOWERBED.
BETTY KNEW THAT SAM TOLD BETTY THAT THE ROSE FLOWER WAS IN THE FLOWERBED.

This is all he has to do. If the trick works, the rest will happen automatically.

HOW DECEITFUL DID BETTY THINK THAT SAM FELT TOWARD HER?
*NOT AT ALL
BETTY THOUGHT THAT SAM WAS HONEST WITH HER.
BETTY KNEW THAT SAM KNEW THAT THE ROSE FLOWER WAS IN THE FLOWER-BED.

If Betty thinks Sam is being honest with her, then she'll believe that *he* believes what he just told her.

HOW MUCH DID BETTY TRUST SAM?   *LOTS
BETTY TRUSTED SAM COMPLETELY.
BETTY KNEW THAT THE ROSE FLOWER WAS IN THE FLOWERBED.

In order for Betty to *accept* what Sam said as being true, she must also trust him. While it may seem at first that we're being overly cautious, this actually allows us to have characters *fail* in their attempts to deceive one another, which makes for more interesting stories than those in which everyone always believes everyone else.

HOW HUNGRY WAS BETTY?   *VERY
BETTY WAS FAMISHED.

When Betty finds out where some food is (remember that bees eat flowers here), a possible consequence (reaction) is that she will go eat it. But we haven't established yet whether Betty is hungry, so TALE-SPIN asks. Had we said no, Sam's plan would have failed. Since we reply that she is, S-HUNGER is reactivated, this time with Betty Bee as the hungry character. Again, we call DCONT and then DPROX.

```
BETTY WANTED TO GET A FLOWER.
BETTY WANTED TO GET NEAR THE ROSE FLOWER.
```

The unspecific flower has been resolved to the particular rose, whose location she knows (thus bypassing DKNOW).

```
BETTY FLEW FROM HER BEEHIVE THROUGH A VALLEY THROUGH A VALLEY TO
THE ROSE FLOWER.
BETTY WAS NEAR THE ROSE FLOWER.
BETTY KNEW THAT BETTY WAS NEAR THE ROSE FLOWER.
```

The latter two sentences are consequences of her journey.

```
BETTY TOOK THE ROSE FLOWER.
BETTY HAD THE ROSE FLOWER.
BETTY KNEW THAT BETTY TOOK THE ROSE FLOWER.
BETTY KNEW THAT BETTY HAD THE ROSE FLOWER.
```

DCONT, called by S-HUNGER, has now succeeded. S-HUNGER specifies that the next thing to do is to eat the flower.

```
BETTY ATE THE ROSE FLOWER.
THE ROSE FLOWER WAS GONE.
BETTY WAS NOT HUNGRY.
BETTY THOUGHT THAT THE ROSE FLOWER WAS GONE.
```

A consequence of eating something is that it is destroyed. At this point, Betty has no more goals to pursue, so this part of the story is done. Still pending, of course, are the actions Sam has in mind.

```
SAM TOOK THE HONEY.
SAM HAD THE HONEY.
SAM KNEW THAT SAM TOOK THE HONEY.
SAM KNEW THAT SAM HAD THE HONEY.
SAM ATE THE HONEY.
THE HONEY WAS GONE.
SAM WAS NOT HUNGRY.
SAM THOUGHT THAT THE HONEY WAS GONE.
THE END.
```

In similar fashion, he takes the honey and eats it. He has no more goals to pursue, and since his was the top-level goal, the story ends.

MODULES

Problem Solving Procedures

To produce the above story, it was necessary to give TALE-SPIN detailed knowledge of how to achieve goals by planning. The examples in this section describe the implementation of the planning methods that the characters in the stories use. Some of the preconditions for particular techniques involve the social relationships between characters (e.g., affection, trust) or personality traits (e.g., kindness). These are all represented as scales from -10 to $+10$. For example, if X likes Y, this is represented as (affection > 0).

REQUEST (X, Y, Z)
X has asked Y to do Z

If Y dislikes X or distrusts X or dominates X, then Y will refuse.

If Y likes X a lot or is indebted to X, then Y will agree.

If there are "positive" consequences, that is, if some consequence includes increased happiness ($+$joy) or is a precondition to some constant goal, then Y will agree.

If there are "negative" consequences, then Y will refuse.

If Y is kind, then Y will agree. Otherwise, Y will refuse.

PROMISE (X, A, Y, B)
Y has offered to do B if X will do A

If X is inclined to deceive Y, then X will *say* yes but will actually plan on insulting Y when X learns that Y has done B. (The deferred plan is implemented with a demon.)

If X likes Y, then X will say yes and will plan on doing A. Otherwise, X will refuse.

BARGAIN (X, Y, ACT)
X wants to bargain with Y to do ACT

X considers the goals that Y can be assumed to have all the time (the cyclic S-goals). For those goals that require physical objects (e.g., food for S-HUNGER), X asks Y whether Y would do ACT if X brought Y one such object. (If X thinks Y already has that object, or if the acquisition of the object is already on X's goal-stack, then that plan is abandoned.) After asking the question (via TELL), the procedure checks whether X now knows that Y would not agree to the bargain—that piece of information would be generated by the inference mechanism when Y reacts to the question, so the answer could be known when TELL returns. If Y agrees to the deal, then X tries to get the object. If unsuccessful, X abandons the idea. Otherwise, X gives Y the object. Again, as soon as that happens, Y reacts one way or the other (either carrying out his part of the bargain or not), so the bargaining is judged a success if the ACT occurs.

DCONT (X, Y)

X wants to acquire Y

As in all the goal procedures, we check to see whether X already has Y—in which case the D-goal succeeds—or whether X was currently in the process of acquiring Y—in which case the goal fails. If X doesn't know where Y is (or who owns Y), then DKNOW is called to find out. If that fails, so does DCONT.

The first "planbox" (technique) is to ask whether Y is owned by someone. If not, the X goes directly to Y (calling DPROX); if X can't get there, DCONT fails. Once X is there, we test again whether X knows who owns Y. This is required in case the idea that no one owned Y was mistaken—there are stories where characters lie to each other about such matters. If all is well, then X attempts to take Y (DO-ATRANS), and DCONT succeeds if the attempt succeeds.

The second technique is for X to persuade the owner to give Y to X. However, if X is dishonest and if X can get to the owner (DPROX), then X will try to trick the owner by figuring out (via "backward" inferences) what act the owner could do that would cause Y to be near X, and then figuring out (via "reason" inferences) what X could do to motivate the owner to do that act. One example of this is flattery in "The Fox and the Crow" fable: the crow is holding a piece of cheese that the fox wants, and the fox thinks that the crow is vain, so he praises the crow's singing and requests a song, knowing that if the crow begins to sing, he'll drop the cheese. In another example, one bear challenges another (who's holding some honey) to a race. The second bear puts down the honey and takes off, so the first bear takes the honey and runs, in the opposite direction. The flattery plan required that the fox think that the crow was vain, and in order for it to work, the crow did, in fact, have to be vain. Those two ideas are independent—the fox could have been wrong, in which case, the plan would have failed. Similarly, the challenge required a competitive attitude between the two characters.

If the trick option is not used, or if it fails, then X tries simple persuasion. If that doesn't work, then X considers outright theft if he's dishonest.

X tries to get the owner away from Y (D-NEG-PROX), and then X goes and tries to take Y (DO-ATRANS).

DKNOW (X, Q)
X wants to find out the answer to question Q

X tries to persuade a friend, whose location he already knows, to tell him the answer to Q. Barring that, he asks the friend to tell him where he might find his other friends, and then he asks them about Q. Finally, X tries to persuade his friends to find out the answer to Q themselves, and then tell him.

(There is not yet a check on who these friends are, and it is easy to get stuck here. A recent, actual example: "SUE WANTED TO ASK PEGGY WHETHER PEGGY WOULD ASK BETTY WHETHER BETTY WOULD ASK PEGGY WHETHER PEGGY WOULD ASK BETTY WHETHER BETTY WOULD ASK PEGGY WHETHER PEGGY WOULD ASK BETTY WHETHER BETTY WOULD ASK PEGGY WHETHER PEGGY WOULD TELL SUE WHERE THERE WAS SOME CHEESE IF SUE GAVE PEGGY SOME HONEY IF SUE GAVE BETTY SOME HONEY IF SUE GAVE PEGGY SOME HONEY IF SUE GAVE BETTY SOME HONEY IF SUE GAVE PEGGY SOME HONEY IF SUE GAVE BETTY SOME HONEY IF SUE GAVE PEGGY SOME HONEY." The answer, incidentally, was no.)

TELL (X, A, Y)
X wants to communicate A to Y

A is a "fact", not a question, so TELL is simpler than DKNOW. X tries to tell Y directly (calling DPROX). If that fails, X tries to persuade any one of his friends to carry the message.

DPROX (X, Y, Z)
X wants Y to be at location Z

The first technique is for X to try to move Y directly to Z. (This requires that Y be movable.) When Joe Bear wants to visit Irving Bird, we call DPROX

DPROX(Joe Bear, Joe Bear, Irving Bird)

which says that Joe Bear wants to change Joe Bear's location to Irving Bird. Here X=Y (i.e., Joe Bear wants to move himself). If X is not the same as Y, then first we must call DPROX (X, X, Y) and X picks up Y (DO-GRASP). X has to find out where Z is (via DKNOW), and there has to be a route from X to Z (DLINK). Then X actually goes to Z (DO-PTRANS). Once there, X lets go of Y (unless X=Y), and the plan succeeds. However,

X may not really have gotten there. That is, X may have been misinformed (during the DKNOW) as to Z's actual location, deliberately or otherwise. In this case, if X can remember who misled him, his relationship with that person deteriorates (trust and affection drop to −6, and suspicion of deceit rises to +6), and the plan fails.

If X couldn't even get to Y, then he tries to persuade Y to transport himself to Z. Next, he tries to persuade some friend to take Y to Z. Finally, he tries to persuade a friend to bring Z to Y. The obvious preconditions are checked (e.g., trees are immovable, rocks are movable but cannot move themselves, and neither trees nor rocks can be persuaded to do anything).

PERSUADE (X, Y, Z)
X wants to persuade Y to do Z

The first technique is for X simply to ask Y, but this is not used if X wants to deceive Y, feels competitive with Y, dislikes Y (affection, or if X thinks that Y dislikes him, or is trying to deceive him. Assuming that all works, X simply asks the question (via TELL). Y will respond one way or the other before we "return" from TELL, so PERSUADE simply checks to see whether Y did Z. If so, then PERSUADE succeeds.

The second method is for X to figure out a good reason why Y should do Z. If Z is a precondition to one of Y's goals, then X will try to help Y do Z by meeting some of Z's preconditions. Y may or may not get the hint.

The third method is to bargain, which requires only that X not be trying to deceive Y.

The fourth method is for X to threaten Y with bodily harm. This tactic won't be used if X likes Y, if X is dominated by Y, or if X doesn't feel at all competitive with Y. Nor will it be used if Y is taller or heavier than X. (Every character is given a height and weight at the time of creation.) X communicates the threat (via TELL). Y will respond one way or the other upon hearing the threat. If Y does not acquiesce and X really dislikes Y, then X carries out the threat and slugs Y.

S-HUNGER (X)
X is hungry

The plan here is very simple: X should obtain some food (DCONT) and eat it (DO-INGEST). If X already knows where some food is, he will try that first. Otherwise, we randomly pick any one of the kinds of food that he eats as the desired meal.

S-THIRST (X)
X is thirsty

The plan here is for X to get near some water (DPROX) and drink it.

S-SEX (X)
X wants sex

X tries to persuade a friend to "fool around" (the generator's phrase).

S-REST (X)
X is tired

X simply does a DPROX to his bed (or home) and goes to sleep.

Inferences

Although it may not be obvious at first glance, it is necessary for TALE-SPIN to be able to make inferences. It needs to do so in order to correctly assess the effects of the events that it generates. TALE-SPIN uses four types of inferences for each of the CD primitives. Type-1 inferences specify the previous states or acts, in a strict causal sense. These are the "backwards inferences" that the characters themselves use in planning. The type-1 inferences from "Joe gave the berries to Jack" (ATRANS) are that Joe had the berries (CONT) and that the berries were near Joe (LOC).

Type-2 inferences are the consequences, and they constitute the majority of all the inferences. The simulation is essentially driven by type-2 inferences. The largest subclass of these inferences specifies who becomes aware of the consequences (MLOC), and these are called *reaction* inferences. When characters are threatened or praised or insulted, for example, their motivation to respond comes from the reaction inferences.

Type-3 inferences apply only to the states, and they specify the acts for which the states are preconditions, according to the planboxes.

Type-4 inferences apply only to the acts, and they specify what other acts might follow.

These inference-procedures depend on the current state of memory. For instance, Joe Bear's reaction to seeing honey depends on how hungry he is at the time. Apart from that, the range of inferences is the same. However, there is a separate class of *demon-inferences* that are not constant. While the consequences are immediately true, the demon-inferences are used to represent things that may become true at some point in the future. For example, if Irving promises (in good faith) to tell Joe where some honey is after Joe brings him a worm, then a demon-inference for Irving upon receiving the worm is to keep his promise and tell Joe where some honey is, which is obviously not one of the normal consequences of getting a worm.

Relationships

When a plan has a precondition concerning the relationship between characters ("How much does Joe like Maggie?") or the personality of a single character

("How kind is Irving?"), the program checks the memory. If no answer is found, the program asks the user. It does this on the assumption that there is an answer, but it just hasn't been established yet. This treatment is quite different from the other preconditions ("Does Joe know where any honey is?") where failing to find the answer in memory is equivalent to answering no.

The question is represented in CD and simply passed to the English generator. The program will accept a number of predefined responses that eventually correspond to an integer. For example, when the program asks "How much does Joe think that Maggie likes Henry?" the responses VERY, LOTS, or A LOT will produce an "affection" value of 7. The responses A LITTLE or SOMEWHAT will produce a value of 3. The responses NOT VERY MUCH, NOT VERY, or NOT MUCH will produce a 0. The responses NONE or NOT AT ALL will produce a -3.

It's a trivial matter to extend the possible responses, to use different integers for the input, or to change the numbers in the preconditions themselves. The above numbers are simply rough guidelines.

Memory

The term "memory" in TALE-SPIN refers to the chronology of facts, which are grouped according to who believes the facts. The "true" facts are simply those believed by the simulator, and these include such things as details of the physical world. The characters have their own beliefs. There are no "true" beliefs about relationships: in TALE-SPIN, the statement "John likes Henry" means "John believes that he likes Henry." It would make no sense in TALE-SPIN to say that "It is true that John likes Henry" *and* that "John thinks that he dislikes Henry."

When facts are "asserted", they are added to memory. When that happens, the state of memory is checked for consistency. Contradicted and superseded facts are removed. Memory is stored in !TRUEFACTS, contradicted facts are saved in !OLDFACTS, and superseded facts are simply deleted.

Contradictions are mutually exclusive states. If Joe Bear is in his cave, that fact will be in !TRUEFACTS. If he goes to visit Irving Bird, his new location is the tree where Irving lives. Thus, "Joe is at the maple tree" contradicts "Joe is at his cave.' The contradicted statement is saved so that, for example, if Joe goes to the cave later on, the generator will be able to say "Joe *returned* to his cave" instead of "Joe went to his cave."

Superceded facts are those that are more clearly specified. If Joe is talking to Irving, the CD representation of the statement "Joe is at the maple tree" is stored in !TRUEFACTS as one of Irving's beliefs. If Joe walks away, the statement "Joe is not at the maple tree" is added to Irving's beliefs, and the former statement is moved to !OLDFACTS since it is now contradicted. But suppose Irving later finds out through a third party that Joe is near the river. The statement "Joe is near the river" supersedes but does not contradict "Joe is not near the maple tree," so that belief is simply deleted.

The Creator and the Travel Agent

When characters are introduced, a program called the "creator" constructs a physical setting for that character. The particular items in the setting are specified by abstract descriptions of the simulated world, called *blueprints*. The created versions of these are called *maps;* they are used to represent all physical locations in TALE-SPIN.

Routes through this world are computed by a program called the "travel agent". The maps are all part of a hierarchy. The central idea is that an individual map is of fixed size and resolution, and you ascend the hierarchy to find maps covering a larger overall range but less detail, and descend to do the opposite. When the travel agent is asked to find a route from point A to point B, it "zooms out" (ascends the hierarchy) until it finds a map that encompasses, at some depth, both A and B. It figures the route from A's "terminal" (the point in this high-level map that contains A) to B's "terminal." Then it zooms back in on the map "below" A's terminal and computes the route from A to that terminal, using the same procedure, and does the same for B. The result is a series of low-level trip segments.

If no such route exists, the travel agent calls the creator to construct the necessary pieces, according to the blueprints. When there is more than one possible solution, the creator asks the user questions such as "Do you want a new mountain?"

Symbolic Arithmetic

TALE-SPIN had to be able to handle relationships between numerical quantities. For example, the problem solver had to know if A happened before or after B, as did the generator when choosing tenses. Some plans asked questions like "Is Joe Bear taller than Jack Bear?" We wanted to be able to do this without having to specify exact times for things, or exact heights, or whatever. It was the comparative relationships that were important.

The program, called XARITH, represents these relationships (which in mathematics are considered to be "partially ordered") with a directed graph. It processes assertions and queries, and it can detect contradictions (A is before B, and B is before A) and redundant information (A is before B, B is before C, and A is before C). When numerical information is known, it uses a total ordering. It can deduce that two points in the graph are actually the same. In TALE-SPIN, it is used primarily to follow transitivity chains, so that it can answer whether A is before B without having seen that explicit assertion. It has not yet been used to represent the duration of events (the difference between the "starting" and "ending" times) nor second-order information (the difference between durations, as in "It took less time to fly from New Orleans to New York than it did to get from JFK airport to Manhattan by bus").

The English Generator

The generator works on single CD expressions. It first determines whether the expression represents an act, a state, a state-change, or a causal link. It chooses which verb to use depending on the particular CD expression involved (e.g., for MTRANS, it uses ask, offer, deny, refuse, agree, and tell) and on the memory (e.g., for ATRANS, give vs. give back). Embedded sentences can have infinities ("Joe wanted Irving to tell him . . .") and can omit the subject of infinitives ("Joe wanted to ask Irving . . .").

The subject and verb are processed by a single function, relying on the fact that in English, the effects of negation, mood, tense, etc., can be local to the subject-verb pair. For example, in the sentence "Joe sees Irving," the direct object ("Irving") follows the subject-verb pair, not only in this form but also in these: Joe saw, Joe will see, Did Joe see, Will Joe see, Can Joe see, Was Joe able to see, Joe doesn't see, Wouldn't Joe be able to see, Joe might be able to see, etc.

The social states use a variety of phrases depending on the degree of the relationship (e.g., for AFFECTION: hate, dislike, like, love, be devoted to). Finally, there is a post-processor that uses first names of characters, articles (a, an, the, any, some), and punctuation (period or question mark).

Mis-spun Tales

One of the best ways to see why all the above components are necessary to a story generator is to see how *we* learned that they were necessary. It is not always obvious how a computer program will actually function while it is still in the planning stages. Important parts of a program are often left out because there was no way to know that they would be needed.

TALE-SPIN, in its early stages, frequently told rather strange stories. These "mistakes" caused many re-definitions in the original program. Since this process of "mistakes" followed by new theory is characteristic of AI programs in general it is worthwhile to look at these "mistakes" and consider what had to be done to fix them. (The output of the original stories has been simplified for ease of reading.)

****** 1 ******

One day Joe Bear was hungry. He asked his friend Irving Bird where some honey was. Irving told him there was a beehive in the oak tree. Joe threatened to hit Irving if he didn't tell him where some honey was.

Joe has not understood that Irving really has answered his question, albeit indirectly. Lesson: answers to questions can take more than one form. You've got to know about beehives in order to understand that the answer is acceptable.

*** 2 ***

One day Joe Bear was hungry. He asked his friend Irving Bird where some honey was. Irving told him there was a beehive in the oak tree. Joe walked to the oak tree. He ate the beehive.

Increasing the range of acceptable answers is not enough. You have to know what the answers really mean.

*** 3 ***

In the early days of TALE-SPIN, all the action focused on a single character. Other characters could respond only in very limited ways, as in answering direct questions, for example. There was no concept of one character "noticing" what another character had done. Hence the following story, which was an attempt to produce "The Ant and the Dove", one of the Aesop fables:

Henry Ant was thirsty. He walked over to the river bank where his good friend Bill Bird was sitting. Henry slipped and fell in the river. He was unable to call for help. He drowned.

That *wasn't* supposed to happen. Falling into the river was deliberately introduced to cause the central "problem" of the story. Had Henry been able to call to Bill for help, Bill would have saved him, but I had just added the rule that being in water prevents speech, which seemed reasonable. Since Bill was not asked a direct question, he didn't notice his friend drowning in the river. "Noticing" is now an inference from change of location, so Bill sees Henry in the river, deduces that Henry's in danger, and rescues him.

*** 4 ***

Here are some rules that were in TALE-SPIN when the next horror occurred. If A moves B to location C, we can infer not only that B is in location C, but that A is also. If you're in a river, you want to get out, because you'll drown if you don't. If you have legs you might be able to swim out. With wings, you might be able to fly away. With friends, you can ask for help. These sound reasonable. However, when I presented "X fell" as "gravity moved X," I got this story:

Henry Ant was thirsty. He walked over to the river bank where his good friend Bill Bird was sitting. Henry slipped and fell in the river. Gravity drowned.

Poor gravity had neither legs, wings, nor friends. Now "X fell" is represented with PROPEL, not PTRANS, that is, as "the force gravity applied to X," and the inference from PROPEL are not the same as for PTRANS.

*** 5 ***

The inclusion of awareness meant that I couldn't set up the stories that way I used to.

> Once upon a time there was a dishonest fox and a vain crow. One day the crow was sitting in his tree, holding a piece of cheese in his mouth. He noticed that he was holding the piece of cheese. He became hungry, and swallowed the cheese. The fox walked over to the crow. The end.

That was supposed to have been "The Fox and the Crow", of course. The fox was going to trick the crow out of the cheese, but when he got there, there was no cheese. I fixed this by adding the assertion that the crow had eaten recently, so that even when he noticed the cheese, he didn't become hungry.

*** 6 ***

Before there was much concern in the program about goals, I got this story:

> Joe Bear was hungry. He asked Irving Bird where some honey was. Irving refused to tell him, so Joe offered to bring him a worm if he'd tell him where some honey was. Irving agreed. But Joe didn't know where any worms were, so he asked Irving, who refused to say. So Joe offered to bring him a worm if he'd tell him where a worm was. Irving agreed. But Joe didn't know where any worms were, so he asked Irving, who refused to say. So Joe offered to bring him a worm if he'd tell him where a worm was ...

Lesson: don't give a character a goal if he or she already has it. Try something else. If there isn't anything else, then that goal can't be achieved.

*** 7 ***

Here are some more rules. If you're hungry and you see some food, you'll want to eat it. If you're trying to get some food and you fail, you get sick. If you want some object, try bargaining with the object's owner. Innocuous, right?

> One day Henry Crow sat in his tree, holding a piece of cheese in his mouth, when up came Bill Fox. Bill saw the cheese and was hungry. [Bill has just been given the goal of satisfying hunger.] He said, "Henry, I like your singing very much. Won't you please sing for me?" Henry, flattered by this compliment, began to sing. The cheese fell to the ground. Bill Fox saw the cheese on the ground and was very hungry. [Satisfying hunger is about to be added to Bill's goals again.] He became ill. [Because satisfying hunger was already a goal of Bill's, it can't be added again. Hence, Bill fails to satisfy

his hunger, so he gets sick.] Henry Crow saw the cheese on the ground, and he became hungry, but he knew that he owned the cheese. He felt pretty honest with himself, so he decided not to trick himself into giving up the cheese. He wasn't trying to deceive himself, either, nor did he feel competitive with himself, but he remembered that he was also in a position of dominance over himself, so he refused to give himself the cheese. He couldn't think of a good reason why he should give himself the cheese [if he did that, he'd lose the cheese], so he offered to bring himself a worm if he'd give himself the cheese. That sounded okay, but he didn't know where any worms were. So he said to himself, "Henry, do you know where any worms are?" But of course, he didn't, so he . . . [And so on.]

The program eventually ran aground for other reasons. I was surprised it got as far as it did. I fixed it by adding the rule that dropping the cheese results in loss of ownership.

TECHNICAL VIEW OF TALE-SPIN

The Top Level of TALE-SPIN

In this section, I would like to explain in more detail how TALE-SPIN runs—what its basic execution cycle is.

There is an initial dialogue with the user, specifying the characters and some details of setting, but the cycle doesn't really begin until the user specifies that the main character has a problem. Once that fact is asserted, the top-level cycle takes over automatically.

It is possible, in fact, to start the cycle even during the initial dialogue. If you create a bear and some berries and tell the bear where the berries are, TALE-SPIN will ask how hungry the bear is. That is due to the fact that the inference part of the cycle wants to know whether the bear is now going to use the information about the berries—an automatic trigger.

When an event is *asserted*, we do one of two things. If it is a CD expression for "John thinks that John has X as a goal", then we save "John has X as a goal" on a list (PLAN-LIST). Otherwise, we simply add the event to the memory. If it is of the form "John thinks Y", then it is stored with the things John "knows". Otherwise it's stored as a "true" fact (known to the storyteller). Notice that "John thinks that Mary has Z as a goal" does *not* go onto the PLAN-LIST, but it is stored in memory.

Next, we compute all the consequences of the asserted event, which will also be a list of CD expressions. If there are any, then we repeat the whole process on them, adding them either to the PLAN-LIST or to memory. Finally, when there are no more consequences, we send each of the plans on the list to the problem solver. That is, each item on that list is the statement that some character has some goal, so we now call the appropriate problem-solver for the goal. If the goal is to reduce hunger, we call S-HUNGER. If the goal is acquisition of some object, we call DCONT. If the goal is not a state but a direct *act*, such as MTRANSing some piece of information, then we call a routine (DO-IT) that simulates the actual events.

DO-IT

For all but a few of the acts, DO-IT simply asserts the event, but for others there are *runtime preconditions* to take care of. These are *not* part of the planning process, but rather take care of details, including obstacles that represent the difference between what the characters *imagine* is going to happen, and what actually *does* happen.

Part of the bookkeeping detail for DO-MTRANS and DO-PTRANS is calling the creator and the travel agent. If Irving Bird has decided to tell Joe Bear where some honey is and we haven't already created some honey that he knows about, we do so now. If Irving is being honest, then this is exactly like the "real" creation in the initial dialogue. But if Irving is lying, then we've got to be trickier. *Some* of the material gets created, but other material is only hypothetically created. For instance, Irving might tell Joe that there's some honey in such-and-such an oak tree. If he's lying, then there will be an oak tree, but it won't have a beehive in it, and if Joe goes there, he'll find that out and realize that he's been tricked.

DO-PTRANS has some bookeeping to do, too. When Joe Bear goes to visit Irving Bird who lives in a nest in a maple tree, we want to be sure that Joe doesn't wind up in the nest, but rather stays on the ground near the maple tree.

Consequences

The most important part of the cycle is the generation of consequences. Some of the consequences are constant, or context-free, but many depend on the state of memory, what specific facts people know, and what attitudes they have about themselves and others.

There are two principal advantages to the data-driven consequence cycle. First, the more information you put into the inferences, the more will happen "automatically" so that you can make the planning procedures less explicit. This makes good methodological sense as well, since all the planning procedures have equal access to the inference mechanism, and you're more likely to spot conceptual errors. That is, you may have added inference X for situation Y, but the system may surprise you, pleasantly or otherwise, by making inference X in situation Z.

The second advantage is that when the characters *themselves* are planning, they use the same inference mechanism that the simulator does. That is, when Joe Bear is trying to figure out whether to do something, such as complying with a request, he considers the consequences, as computed by the inference mechanism from his point of view. They may differ from what would actually occur, since his knowledge, especially of interpersonal relationships, need not be consistent with the truth. For example, he may surmise that Maggie Bee is quite friendly and will gladly offer him some honey, so in his *hypothetical simulation* he achieves his goal, thus suggesting that that particular plan is a good one. When he actually confronts Maggie Bee, in the *real simulation*, she may dislike him intensely and refuse to give him anything. In this view, then, hypothetical simulation is a major component of the process of planning.

The disadvantages of the consequence-cycle are the potential for proliferation of facts, especially irrelevant facts, and the tendency for the characters to spend all their time second-guessing each other, endlessly. The first problem is a familiar plague in AI systems. If you need a particular inference once, then you get it all the time, needed or not. One alternative is to "enable" the inference ahead of time, and "disable" it afterwards, which is outright cheating. Another popular approach is somehow to "structure" the information so that the context determines which inferences should be made. Unfortunately, TALE-SPIN's contexts are not yet that structured. A third tactic is to have an intelligent garbage collector, also known as a forgetting mechanism, to solve what is essentially a "system" problem, not a theoretical problem, at least not at the level of simulation.

The second-guess syndrome is actually a special case of the inference explosion. The theoretical weakness in planning by simulating is that you need to control the level of detail. When you're actually doing something, everything actually happens. When you're merely thinking about doing something, you cannot imagine all the details. Fortunately, TALE-SPIN doesn't get stuck here since the information that a character has is both incomplete and imperfect, so the inferences do die out. Also, as noted above, the inference cycle does *not* pursue the consequences of "John thinks that Mary has X as a goal." If it did, and went on to compute that "John thinks that Mary has Y as a goal" where Y is one of the subgoals of X, we'd quickly get into the game of representing "John thinks that Mary thinks that Bill thinks that John thinks that . . ." and all the associated problems, theoretical and practical.

Example

In the story given earlier where George Ant falls in the river and Wilma Bird rescues him, the entire rescue scene is part of one call to the inference mechanism. It begins when we assert that George fell into the water. An inference from that is that George is in the water. Two inferences from that are that George knows that he's in the water and that Wilma does, too. She's sitting nearby, and a change of location produces such an inference for every nearby character. An inference from knowing that someone is in some water is knowing that the person might die. (Exceptions could be made for fish, etc.) An inference from knowing that some event might cause death is having the goal to avoid or undo that event. (Both George and Wilma infer these things.) The "inference" from having a goal is acting on that goal, i.e., calling the problem solver. In this case, D-NEG-PROX is called: George wants to get out of the river. D-NEG-PROX calls DPROX on nearby areas, and so now "George wants to get near the meadow," which is the creator's name for one of the river banks. George knows where the river bank is (a precondition in DPROX), but when DO-PTRANS is called, one of the runtime obstacles prevents him from leaving: very small creatures cannot PTRANS themselves through rivers. George's DPROX goal thus fails, and so does his D-NEG-PROX. Fortunately, Wilma has the same goal, so D-NEG-PROX is called again. This time, it's Wilma who wants George out of the river. D-NEG-PROX calls DPROX, getting George to the river bank. Wilma knows where George is, and DO-PTRANS succeeds since she is flying. DPROX continues by having her grab George, bringing him to the river bank, and letting him go. The inference from letting something go (un-GRASP) is that they land on whatever is below them (creator/travel agent used again here), so George falls to the meadow. Of course, George was aware of everything that happened to him (more knowledge-state inferences), and when he knew he was in danger, a demon inference was established so that if he were to be rescued, his relationship to his rescuer would change (affection + 10, in-debtedness + 10); hence, "George was devoted to Wilma. George owed every-thing to Wilma."

All of this happened in one call to the assertion mechanism, when we said that George had fallen into the water.

Data Structures and Control Structures

DKNOW, DPROX, etc., are directly coded as procedures. The advantage of this approach is that it makes it easier to handle the flow of control from one planbox to the next and to keep track of the binding of variables. Another typical approach, made popular by MICRO-PLANNER and its like, is to define such procedures as "data" and to program a separate interpreter for them, the advan-tage being that one could now "read" the plan instead of only being able to execute it. I chose not to use this approach for several reasons. First of all, it suggests that reading a plan is the same as carrying out a plan—that you have access to the same information, which isn't true. Second, the planning informa-tion that the characters do need is simpler and can be encoded in other ways. Third, the interpreter requires a lot of bookkeeping code for binding variables and matching patterns, which didn't seem worth the effort for the simulator, which is naturally oriented towards execution. Finally, many of the same effects can be achieved by the "hypothetical simulation" discussed earlier. That is, the purpose of reading a plan is to be able to predict in advance what will be needed, what is likely to occur, etc. By having the characters call the planning procedures directly, using "hypothetical" memory (initially the same as current memory), and "observing" what happens, the same effect is possible. While there is still a serious issue about the level of detail in a hypothetical versus actual execution of plans, the simulation idea has some appeal on psychological grounds.

Memory

In the original implementation of TALE-SPIN, the memory, which contains what each character knows and what the storyteller knows, was a list of CD expressions indexed by the person who "knows" the represented events, sub-indexed under the role-fillers, and further sub-indexed under the role-names. This was an attempt to model a theory of memory where all the things John knew specifically about Mary would be grouped together, as opposed to simply grouping together all the things that John knew about anything. In practice, however, TALE-SPIN never used that feature, i.e., nothing in the system depended on the particular grouping of events in memory. In the current implementation, the sub-indices have simply been removed, and while the pattern matcher does a little more work now looking for answers to questions like "Where does John think Mary is?", the substantially reduced overhead for the structure itself more than compensates.

The Inference Mechanism

Each of the CD acts and states has a corresponding set of inference functions (types 1–4). The inference generator uses the top-level act (e.g., PTRANS), state (e.g., MLOC), or connective (e.g., CANCAUSE), and calls the appropriate procedure.

Each procedure constructs a list of CD expressions that are the inferences. For example, the consequences (type-2 inferences) from an ATRANS event are specified as follows:

> The TO filler now has the OBJECT filler.
> The FROM filler no longer has the OBJECT filler.
> The TO filler knows that the ATRANS occurred.
> Everyone else at the same location as the ACTOR filler
>   knows that the ATRANS occurred.

Suppose the event were "John gave Mary a book." That is represented as

```
((ACTOR (JOHN) <=> (ATRANS) OBJECT (BOOK)
         FROM (JOHN) TO (MARY)))
```

Then the ATRANS type-2 inference procedure returns the list of inferences: John no longer has the book, Mary has the book, John knows that the ATRANS occurred, Mary knows that the ATRANS occurred. If this event really happened (as opposed to being part of someone's advance planning), then each inference is asserted, the consequences of each inference is computed and asserted, and so on.

The "reaction inferences" are simply invoked by the procedure that computes the consequences for MLOC, in the same fashion as the top level of the inference generator.

The Generator

Like the inference mechanism, the English generator takes a CD expression and calls the procedure associated with the main act, state, or connective. The generator's principal function is to produce the correct order of the words and the correct form of the verb. For each of fifty verbs, it knows the conjugation for singular and plural in the past, present, and future tenses. Those are pre-computed. It constructs at runtime the negations, interrogatives, and so on, which requires only a small amount of information about auxiliaries such as "do" and "will".

The function TN produces the subject-verb pair. TN takes two parameters, the infinitive from of the verb and the subject. The only reason the subject is used is that it may have to be embedded, as in "Did John go . . . ?" The other pieces of information are the tense and the "mode-list". The mode-list is part of the CD expression, i.e., it is a necessary part of the meaning. The tense of the top-level sentence is arbitrary. Narratives are customarily told in the simple past tense. But given the tense of the top-level sentence, the tense to be used for the embedded expression is computed by calling the timekeeper, e.g., "John thinks that Mary was in New York" versus "John thinks that Mary will be in New York." Possible elements of the mode-list are: *NEG* if the concept is a negation; *MAYBE*, which would be added, for instance, when one character can only guess the likely response of another, as in "Joe thought that Irving might tell him where some honey was"; *CAN* to indicate ability; and *?* to indicate a question.

For example, suppose the subject is MARY, the infinitive (as determined by the PTRANS generator procedure) is WALK, and the mode-list is (*NEG* *?* *CAN*), and the tense is future. The procedure first tests for the presence of *CAN* in the mode-list. Given that, and the future tense, the infinitive gets "BE ABLE TO" concatenated to it, and we know that we will need an auxiliary, in this case, DO. The verb we use is either the auxiliary (if we have decided we need one) or the infinitive, so in this case, it's DO, and we look up its future-tense form. For DO, that's stored as WILL. Next, we look up the negative form of that since *NEG* is in the mode-list; that's stored as WON'T. Next, we write out the "verb" and then the subject, since *?* is present, and finally, if we used an auxiliary, we type out the infinitive, thus producing WON'T MARY BE ABLE TO WALK. When the sentence is finished, another function will add the question mark.

Suppose the subject is MARY, the infinitive is WALK, but the mode-list is (*MAYBE*), and the tense is present. If *MAYBE* is in the mode-list, we use the auxiliary MIGHT as the "verb", the present-tense form of which is MIGHT. We write the subject, then the verb, and finally the infinitive, producing MARY MIGHT WALK.

There's nothing particularly sacred about this procedure. I determined the order of the tests simply by working with conjugations for a while, and this pattern emerged. It is sufficient for all the constructions that TALE-SPIN can produce. It won't produce examples such as "It was John who went to New York", because there's nothing in the CD representation to indicate that kind of emphasis.

Nouns are far simpler. The creator puts the English names and first names on the property lists of the system names for each character it creates, e.g., the system name for Joe Bear is *JOEBEAR*. His English name is the list (JOE BEAR), and his first name is stored as JOE. For physical objects, the creator puts only English names on the property lists. The generator uses this information after the order of the words in the output sentence has already been determined. It goes through the list of words, inserting articles (a, an, the, any, some) and punctuation. The generator has already included possessives. That is, if it was producing *NEST*3, it checks to see whether anyone owns that object. If so, it inserts "IRVING'S", for example. When stating the location of some object, it will use "THERE" plus the appropriate form of the verb *to be*.

The generator calls the memory to decide between such things as "go" and "return", "take" and "take back", "isn't hungry" and "isn't hungry any more".

Looking Back on the Implementation

The diversity of TALE-SPIN's components is both its pride and its curse. That is, it's nice to see dynamically created mountains, correct English tenses and modals, theft and lying, automatic inferences, competition and indebtedness, pattern matchers, plans and goals, directed graphs, and so on, in the same system, but keeping track of it all isn't easy. Changing it in any major way is a very risky business, because the system is highly interconnected. To ask the user whether John likes Mary, we need the generator. To be able to say "the maple tree', the generator needs information from the creator. The creator needs to know where birds live. DPROX needs to know the difference between Irving Bird, his nest, the tree containing that nest, and the ground around the tree. BARGAIN needs access to the reaction-inferences. As part of a theory of human knowledge, such integration is highly desirable. As a characteristic of a 90K LISP program, such integration complicates the programming tasks. As a feature of a cognitive model, it runs the risk of spreading the knowledge too thin.

10 Micro TALE-SPIN

INTRODUCTION

The micro versions of the storyteller (TALE-SPIN) and the English generator (MUMBLE) have the same basic cycle of assertions and inferences as the full system, but the details have been greatly simplified.

Most of the planning procedures have been retained, but they use simpler techniques, connected by ANDs and ORs ("do this AND this OR else do that AND that"). In particular, the characters cannot plan ahead by hypothetical simulation. Scales, such as hunger and affection, have been replaced by a simple yes or no, represented as MODE (POS) and MODE (NEG).

The top level of the inference mechanism is the same, but only type-2 inferences (consequences) appear here, and simpler versions of them, at that. No social states, for example, are ever inferred in the micro system, so no matter how often Joe slugs Irving, Irving's feelings toward Joe remain stalwartly the same. The only S-goals used here are S-HUNGER and S-THIRST.

Most of the social states have been preserved, though the restrictions on the social preconditions have been loosened, making it somewhat easier for a "successful" story to happen. The creator and the travel agent have been dispensed with altogether. The initial world description is explicitly declared by the function INIT-WORLD, which is called by the top-level function (SPIN).

A generator has been included so the story can be followed. Even in its crude form, it's a much better alternative to tracing certain key functions than decoding CD forms written in LISP. Micro-MUMBLE uses about twenty-five verbs and prefaces all physical objects with the article "the". Names for characters and objects come straight from the internal identifier, so Joe Bear always comes out

227

as "JOE", never "THE BEAR" or "HE", and the cave always comes out as "THE CAVE", never "IT" or "THERE". While the default tense can be changed so that the story can be told in either the past or present tense, there is no other provision for changes, such as generating passives or the like.

The syntax of modes is more complex in McSPIN than in the other micro programs. McSPIN needs to be able to represent whether a CD is true or false (POS or NEG), a question or not (QUES), and terminating or not (TF, for Transition Final). Since several modes could apply at once (e.g., a question about the negation of a termination of an action), the filler of the MODE role in McSPIN is a list of these atoms. Thus a negative mode is represented with the filler (NEG), not just NEG.

SAMPLE OUTPUT

Here are sample runs of McSPIN, showing both successful and unsuccessful attempts by both characters to satisfy goals. NOTE: computer output is in **upper case**; comments are in lower case.

[PH: Initiation. 28–Jan–80 4:02PM]

. . .

*(SPIN)

ONCE UPON A TIME . . .
　　　JOE WAS NEAR THE CAVE.
　　　JOE KNEW THAT JOE WAS NEAR THE CAVE.
　　　IRVING WAS NEAR THE OAK-TREE.
　　　IRVING KNEW THAT IRVING WAS NEAR THE OAK-TREE.
　　　JOE KNEW THAT IRVING WAS NEAR THE OAK-TREE.
　　　THE WATER WAS NEAR THE RIVER.
　　　JOE KNEW THAT THE WATER WAS NEAR THE RIVER.
　　　THE HONEY WAS NEAR THE ELM-TREE.
　　　IRVING KNEW THAT THE HONEY WAS NEAR THE ELM-TREE.
　　　THE WORM WAS NEAR THE GROUND.
　　　JOE KNEW THAT THE WORM WAS NEAR THE GROUND.
　　　IRVING KNEW THAT JOE WAS NEAR THE CAVE.
　　　THE FISH WAS NEAR THE RIVER.
　　　IRVING KNEW THAT THE FISH WAS NEAR THE RIVER.

McSPIN first prints out, in English, the facts pre-stored in its data base. In this story and all the ones that follow, the same core data base was used. Next McSPIN asks who the story should be about and what the problem (S-goal) should be.

CHOOSE A CHARACTER FROM THIS LIST (JOE IRVING)
*IRVING

CHOOSE A PROBLEM FROM THIS LIST (HUNGRY THIRSTY)
*THIRSTY

ONE DAY,
    IRVING WAS THIRSTY.
    IRVING WANTED NOT TO BE THIRSTY.
    IRVING WANTED TO BE NEAR THE WATER.
    IRVING WANTED TO KNOW WHERE THE WATER WAS.
    IRVING THOUGHT THAT JOE LIKED IRVING. [Y/N]? N

Irving's goal is to DPROX to some water, which means he has the subgoal of
DKNOWing where the water is. He knows where Joe is, so if Joe is a friend,
then Irving can ask him where some water is. We respond that Joe is not a friend.

IRVING THOUGHT THAT JOE DOMINATED IRVING. [Y/N]?N

If Joe is not a friend, asking won't work, but if Irving thinks he's a match for Joe,
then he can force Joe to tell him. McSPIN asks if Irving thinks Joe can beat him
up and we say no, so Joe is still the person Irving will go to, but for a different
reason.

    IRVING WANTED JOE TO TELL IRVING WHERE THE WATER WAS.
    IRVING THOUGHT THAT JOE DECEIVED IRVING. [Y/N]? Y

Will Irving believe Joe when he answers? We say no.

    IRVING WANTED JOE TO THINK THAT IF JOE WOULD NOT TELL IRVING WHERE
    THE WATER WAS THEN IRVING WOULD STRIKE JOE.
    IRVING WANTED TO BE NEAR JOE.
    IRVING WENT TO THE CAVE.
    IRVING WAS NEAR THE CAVE.
    IRVING TOLD JOE THAT IF JOE WOULD NOT TELL IRVING WHERE THE WATER
    WAS THEN IRVING WOULD STRIKE JOE.
    JOE THOUGHT THAT IRVING DECEIVED JOE. [Y/N]? N

Irving has just threatened Joe. It doesn't matter whether Joe believes him, but
McSPIN wants to know one way or the other, so we say yes.

    IRVING STRUCK JOE.
    JOE WAS NOT ALIVE.
    IRVING THOUGHT THAT JOE WOULD NOT TELL IRVING WHERE THE WATER WAS.
    IRVING THOUGHT THAT IRVING DID NOT KNOW WHERE THE WATER WAS.
    IRVING THOUGHT THAT IRVING WAS NOT NEAR THE WATER.
    IRVING KNEW THAT IRVING WAS THIRSTY.

    THE END.

In this simple world, hitting someone is fatal. Irving's plan fails because a dead person can't tell you anything. Since no one else is around, Irving goes thirsty.

This same story could have been told without the questions from McSPIN by calling SPIN-DEMO with the variable STORY1:

```
STORY1 =
(IRVING THIRSTY
        (IRVING '(LIKE (ACTOR JOE) (TO IRVING) (MODE (NEG))))
        (IRVING '(DOMINATE (ACTOR JOE) (TO IRVING) (MODE (NEG))))
        (IRVING '(DECEIVE (ACTOR JOE) (TO IRVING) (MODE (POS))))
        (IRVING '(LIKE (ACTOR IRVING) (TO JOE) (MODE (NEG))))
        (JOE '(DECEIVE (ACTOR IRVING) (TO JOE) (MODE (NEG)))))
```

Another story variable we have set is STORY2:

```
STORY2 =
(JOE HUNGRY
        (JOE '(LIKE (ACTOR IRVING) (TO JOE) (MODE (NEG))))
        (JOE '(DOMINATE (ACTOR IRVING) (TO JOE) (MODE (POS)))))

*(SPIN-DEMO STORY2)

ONCE UPON A TIME...
```

```
        JOE WAS NEAR THE CAVE.
        JOE KNEW THAT JOE WAS NEAR THE CAVE.
        IRVING WAS NEAR THE OAK-TREE.
        IRVING KNEW THAT IRVING WAS NEAR THE OAK-TREE.
        JOE KNEW THAT IRVING WAS NEAR THE OAK-TREE.
        THE WATER WAS NEAR THE RIVER.
        JOE KNEW THAT THE WATER WAS NEAR THE RIVER.
        THE HONEY WAS NEAR THE ELM-TREE.
        IRVING KNEW THAT THE HONEY WAS NEAR THE ELM-TREE.
        THE WORM WAS NEAR THE GROUND.
        JOE KNEW THAT THE WORM WAS NEAR THE GROUND.
        IRVING KNEW THAT JOE WAS NEAR THE CAVE.
        THE FISH WAS NEAR THE RIVER.
        IRVING KNEW THAT THE FISH WAS NEAR THE RIVER.
        JOE THOUGHT THAT IRVING DID NOT LIKE JOE.
        JOE THOUGHT THAT IRVING DOMINATED JOE.
```

These are the same facts as before, except for the last two that come from STORY2. STORY2 also says that the story will be about Joe's being hungry.

```
ONE DAY,
        JOE WAS HUNGRY.
        JOE WANTED NOT TO BE HUNGRY.
        JOE WANTED TO HAVE THE HONEY.
        JOE WANTED TO KNOW WHERE THE HONEY WAS.
        JOE THOUGHT THAT JOE DID NOT KNOW WHERE THE HONEY WAS.
        JOE THOUGHT THAT JOE DID NOT HAVE THE HONEY.
```

JOE WANTED TO HAVE THE BERRIES.
JOE WANTED TO KNOW WHERE THE BERRIES WERE.
JOE THOUGHT THAT JOE DID NOT KNOW WHERE THE BERRIES WERE.
JOE THOUGHT THAT JOE DID NOT HAVE THE BERRIES.
JOE WANTED TO HAVE THE FISH.
JOE WANTED TO KNOW WHERE THE FISH WAS.
JOE THOUGHT THAT JOE DID NOT KNOW WHERE THE FISH WAS.
JOE THOUGHT THAT JOE DID NOT HAVE THE FISH.
JOE KNEW THAT JOE WAS HUNGRY.

THE END.

Here we have a case of total plan failure. Joe eats honey, berries, and fish, but since he doesn't know where any of them are, he would have to ask Irving. But Joe thinks that Irving doesn't like him and is stronger than him, so Joe can neither ask nor force Irving to tell him where any of the foods are. Hence Joe goes hungry.

STORY3 = (JOE THIRSTY)

STORY3 just says that the story will be about Joe's being thirsty. In this and the last example, I have omitted the initial data base printout.

*(SPIN-DEMO STORY3)

ONE DAY,
     JOE WAS THIRSTY.
     JOE WANTED NOT TO BE THIRSTY.
     JOE WANTED TO BE NEAR THE WATER.
     JOE WENT TO THE RIVER.
     JOE WAS NEAR THE RIVER.
     JOE DRANK THE WATER.
     JOE WAS NOT THIRSTY.

THE END.

Here we have a simple case of plan success, without the need for another agent. Joe is thirsty, he knows where water is, so he goes and gets it.

```
STORY4 =
(JOE HUNGRY
     (WORLD '(HUNGRY (ACTOR IRVING) (MODE (POS))))
     (JOE '(LIKE (ACTOR IRVING) (TO JOE) (MODE (POS))))
     (JOE '(DECEIVE (ACTOR IRVING) (TO JOE) (MODE (NEG))))
     (JOE '(LIKE (ACTOR JOE) (TO IRVING) (MODE (POS))))
     (IRVING '(LIKE (ACTOR IRVING) (TO JOE) (MODE (POS))))
     (IRVING '(DOMINATE (ACTOR IRVING) (TO JOE) (MODE (POS))))
     (IRVING '(DECEIVE (ACTOR IRVING) (TO JOE) (MODE (NEG)))))
```

STORY4 says that the story is about Joe's being hungry (so is Irving, but he's not the main character). Furthermore, they like each other and believe each other. Irving also thinks he's stronger than Joe.

```
*(SPIN-DEMO STORY4)

ONE DAY,
    JOE WAS HUNGRY.
    JOE WANTED NOT TO BE HUNGRY.
    JOE WANTED TO HAVE THE HONEY.
    JOE WANTED TO KNOW WHERE THE HONEY WAS.
    JOE WANTED IRVING TO TELL JOE WHERE THE HONEY WAS.
    JOE WANTED IRVING TO THINK THAT IRVING TOLD JOE WHERE THE
    HONEY WAS.
```

Joe is going to ask Irving. A natural side-effect will be that Irving will know that he's answered, but the English generation of that fact looks peculiar.

```
        JOE WANTED TO BE NEAR IRVING.
        JOE WENT TO THE OAK-TREE.
        JOE WAS NEAR THE OAK-TREE.
        JOE ASKED IRVING WHETHER IRVING WOULD TELL JOE WHERE THE
        HONEY WAS.
        IRVING PLANNED TO TELL JOE THAT IRVING WOULD NOT TELL JOE
        WHERE THE HONEY WAS.
        IRVING TOLD JOE THAT IRVING WOULD NOT TELL JOE WHERE THE HONEY
        WAS.
```

Irving turns the request down, so Joe tries bargaining.

```
        JOE DECIDED THAT IF JOE WOULD GIVE IRVING THE WORM THEN IRVING
        MIGHT TELL JOE WHERE THE HONEY WAS.
        JOE WANTED IRVING TO THINK THAT IRVING WOULD TELL JOE WHERE
        THE HONEY WAS IF JOE GAVE IRVING THE WORM.
        JOE WANTED TO BE NEAR IRVING.
```

Note that Joe's goal of being near Irving is already satisfied, so nothing is done.

```
        JOE ASKED IRVING WHETHER IRVING WOULD TELL JOE WHERE THE
        HONEY WAS IF JOE GAVE IRVING THE WORM.
        IRVING DECIDED THAT IF JOE WOULD GIVE IRVING THE WORM THEN
        IRVING WOULD TELL JOE WHERE THE HONEY WAS.
        IRVING TOLD JOE THAT IF JOE WOULD GIVE IRVING THE WORM THEN
        IRVING WOULD TELL JOE WHERE THE HONEY WAS.
```

Irving agrees to the bargain, so now Joe has the subgoal of getting the worm. This he already knows how to do.

JOE WANTED TO HAVE THE WORM.
JOE WANTED TO BE NEAR THE WORM.
JOE WENT TO THE GROUND.
JOE WAS NEAR THE GROUND.
JOE TOOK THE WORM.
JOE HAD THE WORM.
THE WORM WAS NEAR JOE.
JOE WANTED TO BE NEAR IRVING.
JOE WENT TO THE OAK-TREE.
JOE WAS NEAR THE OAK-TREE.
JOE GAVE IRVING THE WORM.
IRVING HAD THE WORM.
THE WORM WAS NEAR IRVING.
JOE DID NOT HAVE THE WORM.
IRVING TOLD JOE THAT THE HONEY WAS NEAR THE
ELM TREE.

Irving is honest and keeps his half of the bargain. He's also hungry so he eats the worm.

IRVING WANTED NOT TO BE HUNGRY.
IRVING ATE THE WORM.
IRVING WAS NOT HUNGRY.
JOE WANTED TO BE NEAR THE HONEY.
JOE WENT TO THE ELM-TREE.
JOE WAS NEAR THE ELM-TREE.
JOE TOOK THE HONEY.
JOE HAD THE HONEY.
THE HONEY WAS NEAR JOE.
JOE ATE THE HONEY.
JOE WAS NOT HUNGRY.

THE END.

Once Joe has the necessary knowledge, he can finish the DCONT of honey plan and everybody's happy.

[PH: Termination. 28–Jan–80 4:05PM. PS: <RIESBECK>TEN.LOG.26]

FLOW CHARTS

The flow charts in Figs. 10.1 and 10.2 show the two central functions in McSPIN: ASSERT and GOAL-EVAL.

FIG. 10.1.   ASSERT(fact).

THE PROGRAM

```
- *******************************************************************
-                 MICRO TALE-SPIN PROGRAM
- *******************************************************************

-SPIN asks for the character and problem, then tells the story.
-Note that all it really does is call ASSERT with the main
-character's problem—everything else follows from reactions to
-that.

(DE SPIN ()
 (LET (MAIN-CHARACTER NIL PROBLEM NIL)
 (MSG T "ONCE UPON A TIME..." T)
 (INIT-WORLD)
 (SETQ MAIN-CHARACTER (PICK-ONE 'CHARACTER *PERSONAE*))
 (SETQ PROBLEM (PICK-ONE 'PROBLEM *GOALS*))
 (MSG T T "ONE DAY,")
```

```
(ASSERT (MLOC 'WORLD (STATE MAIN-CHARACTER PROBLEM 'POS)))
(MSG T T "THE END." T]
```

SPIN-DEMO lets you predefine more facts for a story. STORY should
be a list of the form (character problem fact fact...) where
-   character is either JOE or IRVING,
-   problem is either HUNGER or THIRST, and
-   facts have the form (character 'CD-form). The character field
-       says who knows this fact.

```
(DE SPIN-DEMO (STORY)
 (LET (MAIN-CHARACTER (CAR STORY)
       PROBLEM (CADR STORY)
       *INIT-FACTS* (APPEND *INIT-FACTS* (CDDR STORY)))
  (MSG T "ONCE UPON A TIME..." T)
  (INIT-WORLD)
  (MSG T T "ONE DAY,")
  (ASSERT (MLOC 'WORLD (STATE MAIN-CHARACTER PROBLEM 'POS)))
  (MSG T T "THE END." T]
```

PICK-ONE is used to get the character and problem from the terminal.

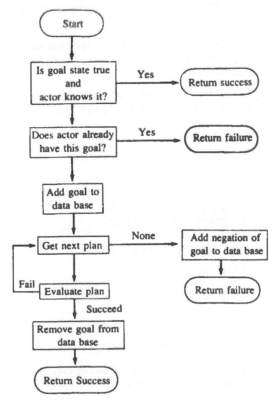

FIG. 10.2.   GOAL-EVAL (Actor, Goal, Plans).

```
(DE PICK-ONE (NAME L)
 (LOOP (INITIAL A NIL)
       (DO (MSG T "CHOOSE A " NAME " FROM THIS LIST " L T)
           (SETQ A (READ)))
       (UNTIL (MEMBER A L))
       (DO (MSG T "TRY AGAIN."))
       (RESULT A]
```

¨GOAL evaluator: executes each plan until one works and the goal
¨can be removed, or until none do and the character fails to get the
¨goal. If the goal is already true (and the actor knows that), then
¨return success immediately. If the actor already has the goal,
¨then he's in a loop and has failed. Otherwise, set up the goal and
¨go.

```
(DE GOAL-EVAL (ACTOR GOAL PLANS)
 (COND ((KNOWS ACTOR GOAL) T)
       ((HAS-GOAL-OF ACTOR GOAL) NIL)
       (T (GETS-NEW-GOAL-OF ACTOR GOAL)
          (COND ((FOR (PLAN IN PLANS) (EXISTS (EVAL PLAN)))
                 (FORGETS-GOAL-OF ACTOR GOAL)
                 T)
                (T (NOWKNOWS ACTOR (NEGATE (FUTURE GOAL)) T)
                   NIL]
```

¨GEN-PLANS replicates the same plan with different objects—
¨e.g., trying to get any one of several different foods with
¨the same bargaining plan.

```
(DE GEN-PLANS (VAR POSSIBLES PLAN-FORM)
 (FOR (X IN POSSIBLES) (SAVE (SUBST (LIST 'QUOTE X) VAR PLAN-FORM]
```

¨Two S-goals—thirst and hunger:

¨To satisfy thirst, go to some water and drink it.

```
(DE STHIRST (ACTOR)
 (GOAL-EVAL ACTOR (STATE ACTOR 'THIRSTY 'NEG)
  '((AND (DPROX ACTOR ACTOR 'WATER)
         (DOIT (INGEST ACTOR 'WATER]
```

¨To satisfy hunger, get some food and eat it.

```
(DE SHUNGER (ACTOR)
 (GOAL-EVAL ACTOR (STATE ACTOR 'HUNGRY 'NEG)
  (GEN-PLANS 'FOOD (GET-ISA 'FOOD ACTOR)
   '(AND (DCONT ACTOR FOOD)
         (DOIT (INGEST ACTOR FOOD]
```

¨Three D-goals—DCONT, DKNOW, DPROX:

¨To get an object: if you know someone has it, persuade them to
¨give it to you; otherwise try to find out where the object is, go
¨there and take it.

```
(DE DCONT (ACTOR OBJECT)
 (LET (OWNER (KNOWS-OWNER ACTOR OBJECT))
  (GOAL-EVAL ACTOR (HAS ACTOR OBJECT)
   (COND (OWNER '((PERSUADE ACTOR OWNER
                            (ATRANS OWNER OBJECT ACTOR OWNER)
                            GOAL)))
         (T '((AND (DKNOW ACTOR (WHERE-IS OBJECT))
                   (DPROX ACTOR ACTOR OBJECT)
                   (DOIT (ATRANS ACTOR OBJECT ACTOR NIL)
```

¯To find out something: find a friend to tell you.

```
(DE DKNOW (ACTOR INFO)
 (GOAL-EVAL ACTOR (MLOC ACTOR INFO)
  (GEN-PLANS 'AGENT (REMOVE ACTOR *PERSONAE*)
     '(AND (KNOWS-LOC ACTOR AGENT)
           (OR (IS-FRIEND-OF AGENT ACTOR)
               (NOT (RELATE ACTOR AGENT ACTOR 'DOMINATE)))
           (PERSUADE ACTOR AGENT (MTRANS AGENT INFO ACTOR AGENT)
                     GOAL)
```

¯To move an object (including yourself) to where some other
¯person or object is: get the first object (if not yourself), then
¯find out where the second object is and go there with the first
¯object. If this doesn't work, try persuading the object to go
¯there itself.

```
(DE DPROX (ACTOR OBJECT NEW-OBJECT)
 (GOAL-EVAL ACTOR (IS-AT OBJECT NEW-OBJECT)
  (APPEND
     '((AND (OR (EQUAL ACTOR OBJECT) (DPROX ACTOR ACTOR OBJECT))
            (DKNOW ACTOR (WHERE-IS NEW-OBJECT))
            (OR (EQUAL ACTOR OBJECT) (DOIT (GRASP ACTOR OBJECT)))
            (OR (IS-PROX ACTOR (LOC-NAME-OF NEW-OBJECT))
                (DOIT (PTRANS ACTOR OBJECT
                              (KNOWS-LOC ACTOR NEW-OBJECT)
                              (KNOWS-LOC ACTOR ACTOR))))
            (OR (EQUAL ACTOR OBJECT) (DOIT (UNGRASP ACTOR OBJECT))))
       (AND (NOT (EQUAL ACTOR OBJECT))
            (MEMBER OBJECT *PERSONAE*)
            (PERSUADE ACTOR OBJECT
                      (PTRANS OBJECT OBJECT NEW-OBJECT
                              (LOC-NAME-OF OBJECT))
                      GOAL)
```

¯Subgoals and plans—PERSUADE, ASK, BARGAIN, THREATEN, and TELL:

¯You can persuade someone to do something by either asking them,
¯giving them food or threatening them.

```
(DE PERSUADE (ACTOR AGENT ACTION RESULT)
 (GOAL-EVAL ACTOR ACTION
  (APPEND (LIST ASK-PLAN)
          (GEN-PLANS 'FOOD (GET-ISA 'FOOD AGENT) BARGAIN-PLAN)
          (LIST THREAT-PLAN)
```

¯The success of asking something depends on whether the other person
¯is honest and likes you.

```
(SETQ ASK-PLAN
       '(AND (NOT (RELATE ACTOR AGENT ACTOR 'DECEIVE))
             (RELATE ACTOR ACTOR AGENT 'LIKE)
             (TELL ACTOR AGENT (QUESTION ACTION))
             (IS-TRUE RESULT]
```

¯The success of bargaining with someone by giving them food depends
¯on whether the other person is honest, you don't already have the
¯goal of getting the food you're going to bargain with, and you can
¯get the food to the other person.

```
(SETQ BARGAIN-PLAN
       '(LET (ATRANS-FOOD (ATRANS ACTOR FOOD AGENT ACTOR))
          (AND (NOT (RELATE ACTOR AGENT ACTOR 'DECEIVE))
               (NOT (KNOWS ACTOR (HAS AGENT FOOD)))
               (NOT (HAS-GOAL-OF ACTOR (HAS ACTOR FOOD)))
               (DOIT (MBUILD ACTOR
                             (CAUSE ATRANS-FOOD (MAYBE ACTION))))
               (TELL ACTOR AGENT
                     (QUESTION (CAUSE ATRANS-FOOD (FUTURE ACTION))))
               (DCONT ACTOR FOOD)
               (DPROX ACTOR ACTOR AGENT)
               (DOIT ATRANS-FOOD)
               (IS-TRUE ACTION]
```

¯The success of threatening depends on whether you dominate the other
¯person.

```
(SETQ THREAT-PLAN
       '(AND (NOT (RELATE ACTOR AGENT ACTOR 'DOMINATE))
             (TELL ACTOR AGENT
                   (CAUSE (NEGATE ACTION)
                          (FUTURE (PROPEL ACTOR 'HAND AGENT))))
             (OR (IS-TRUE ACTION)
                 (AND (DOIT (PROPEL ACTOR 'HAND AGENT))
                      (IS-TRUE ACTION]
```

¯To tell someone something, go there and say it.

```
(DE TELL (ACTOR AGENT INFO)
(GOAL-EVAL ACTOR (MLOC AGENT INFO)
 '((AND (DPROX ACTOR ACTOR AGENT)
        (DOIT (MTRANS ACTOR INFO AGENT ACTOR]
```

¯——————— The simulator ———————

¯The $ readmacro makes accessing CD roles easier to write.
¯ $(role list) produces (CDPATH '(role list) *CD*), where *CD* is
¯   always set to the event being worked on.

```
(DRM /$ (LAMBDA () (LIST 'CDPATH (LIST 'QUOTE (READ)) '*CD*]
```

ˉDOIT adds a CD and its consequences to the data base, by calling
ˉASSERT. MTRANSes with ?UNSPECs have to be filled out, as in "Irving
ˉtold Joe WHERE the honey was"—the WHERE being represented in the
ˉCD with an ?UNSPEC form.

```
(DE DOIT (*CD*)
 (COND ((AND (EQUAL (HEADER:CD *CD*) 'MTRANS)
             (KNOWS $(ACTOR) $(OBJECT)))
        (SETQ *CD* (SETROLE 'OBJECT
                            (KNOWS $(ACTOR) $(OBJECT))
                            *CD*))))
 (ASSERT *CD*)
 *CD*]
```

ˉASSERT is one of the central control functions. It starts with
ˉone fact, infers the consequences, infers the consequences of the
ˉconsequences, etc. Besides the simple results put in *CONSEQS*
ˉ(e.g., PTRANS changes LOCs), new states may lead to response actions
ˉ(put in *ACTIONS*) or new plans (put in *PLANS*). The plans are
ˉdone after all the consequences are inferred.

```
(DE ASSERT (X)
 (LET (*ACTIONS* NIL *PLANS* NIL)
  (LOOP (INITIAL L (LIST X) *CONSEQS* NIL)
        (DO (SETQ *CONSEQS* NIL)
            (FOR (I IN L)
                 (DO (NOWKNOWS 'WORLD I NIL)
                     (CONSEQS I))))
        (WHILE (SETQ L *CONSEQS*)))
  (FOR (CD IN *ACTIONS*)
       (DO (DOIT (SETROLE 'TIME *DEFAULT-TENSE* CD))))
  (FOR (X IN *PLANS*) (DO (EVAL X]
```

ˉEach act and state is associated with a function for calculating
ˉthe consequences.

```
(DE CONSEQS (*CD*)
 (SELECTQ (HEADER:CD *CD*)
          (ATRANS (ATRANS-CONSEQS))
          (GRASP (GRASP-CONSEQS))
          (INGEST (INGEST-CONSEQS))
          (LOC (LOC-CONSEQS))
          (MBUILD (MBUILD-CONSEQS))
          (MLOC (MLOC-CONSEQS))
          (MTRANS (MTRANS-CONSEQS))
          (PLAN (PLAN-CONSEQS))
          (PROPEL (PROPEL-CONSEQS))
          (PTRANS (PTRANS-CONSEQS))
       NIL]
```

ˉADD-CONSEQ add (and return) a CD to the list of consequences.

```
(DE ADD-CONSEQ (X) (SETQ *CONSEQS* (CONS-END *CONSEQS* X)) X]
```

```
¨Consequences of an ATRANS: everyone in the area notices it and the
¨resulting change of possession, the object changes location, and the
¨FROM filler knows he no longer has it.

(DE ATRANS-CONSEQS ()
 (NOTICE $(ACTOR) *CD*)
 (NOTICE $(ACTOR) (ADD-CONSEQ (HAS $(TO) $(OBJECT))))
 (ADD-CONSEQ (IS-AT $(OBJECT) $(TO)))
 (COND ($(FROM)
         (NOTICE $(ACTOR) (ADD-CONSEQ (NEGATE (HAS $(FROM) $(OBJECT)]
```

```
¨Consequences of a GRASP: everyone knows that the actor either has or
¨(in the case of a TF (transition final or the end of an action)
¨of the GRASP) doesn't have the object.

(DE GRASP-CONSEQS ()
 (NOTICE $(ACTOR)
         (ADD-CONSEQ
          (COND ((IN-MODE 'TF) (NEGATE (HAS $(ACTOR) $(OBJECT))))
                (T (HAS $(ACTOR) $(OBJECT]
```

```
¨Consequences of an INGEST: everyone knows that the actor is no longer
¨hungry or thirsty.

(DE INGEST-CONSEQS ()
 (NOTICE $(ACTOR)
         (ADD-CONSEQ
          (STATE $(ACTOR) (COND ((EQUAL $(OBJECT) 'WATER) 'THIRSTY)
                                (T 'HUNGRY))
          'NEG]
```

```
¨Consequences of a LOC change: everyone knows it.

(DE LOC-CONSEQS () (NOTICE $(ACTOR) *CD*]
```

```
¨Consequences of an MBUILD: if the object is a causal then a demon is
¨set up for the actor that will be triggered by the antecedent.

(DE MBUILD-CONSEQS ()
 (COND ((EQUAL $(ACTOR) $(OBJECT CONSEQ ACTOR))
         (PUTPROP $(ACTOR)
                  (CONS (CONS $(OBJECT ANTE) $(OBJECT CONSEQ))
                        (GET $(ACTOR) 'DEMONS))
                  'DEMONS)
         NIL]
```

```
¨Consequences of an MLOC change: check the demons to see if the
¨learned fact affects the learner. Also check the reaction list
¨for general responses to learning such facts.

(DE MLOC-CONSEQS ()
 (DEMON-CHECK $(VAL PART) $(CON))
 (COND ((NOT (MEMBER 'NEG $(CON MODE)))
         (SELECTQ (HEADER:CD $(CON))
                  (LOC (LOC-REACT))
                  (MLOC (MLOC-REACT))
```

```
        (HUNGRY (HUNGER-REACT))
        (THIRSTY (THIRST-REACT))
        NIL]
```

~ Stored under each character is a list of "demons". A demon is
~ a CD pattern plus an action. Whenever the character learns
~ something this list is checked to see if there is a response to make.
~ Demons are set up by things like the MBUILD in a BARGAIN-PLAN.

```
(DE DEMON-CHECK (WHO EVENT)
 (PUTPROP WHO
          (FOR (I IN (GET WHO 'DEMONS))
               (WHEN (NOT (COND ((MATCH (CAR I) EVENT NIL)
                                 (PUSH (CDR I) *ACTIONS*)))))
               (SAVE I))
          'DEMONS]
```

~ Consequences of an MTRANS: If there is a QUES in the CD MTRANSed,
~ and if it is a causal, then it is a bargaining promise; otherwise
~ it is a request (assuming the actors in the sub-CD are in the right
~ places). If there is no QUES in the CD MTRANSed, then the hearer
~ knows about the MTRANS, and if he believes the speaker, then he
~ believes what the speaker believes.

```
(DE MTRANS-CONSEQS ()
 (LET (ACTOR $(ACTOR) OBJECT $(OBJECT) HEARER $(TO PART))
  (COND ((MEMBER 'QUES $(OBJECT MODE))
         (COND ((AND (EQUAL (HEADER:CD OBJECT) 'CAUSE)
                     (EQUAL ACTOR $(OBJECT ANTE ACTOR))
                     (EQUAL HEARER $(OBJECT CONSEQ ACTOR)))
                (PROMISE-CONSEQS HEARER $(OBJECT CONSEQ)
                                 ACTOR $(OBJECT ANTE)))
               ((EQUAL $(OBJECT ACTOR) HEARER)
                (REQUEST-CONSEQS ACTOR HEARER
                                 (FUTURE (UN-QUESTION OBJECT))))))
        ((NOT (EQUAL ACTOR HEARER))
         (ADD-CONSEQ (MLOC HEARER *CD*))
         (COND ((NOT (RELATE HEARER ACTION HEARER 'DECEIVE))
                (ADD-CONSEQ (MLOC HEARER (MLOC ACTOR OBJECT]
```

~ Consequences of Y asking X to promise to do XDO if Y does YDO:
~ If X deceives Y, then after YDO, X will call Y stupid, but says
~ that he will do XDO in return for YDO;
~ else if X likes Y, then X will do XDO after YDO and says so.
~ Otherwise X says no.

```
(DE PROMISE-CONSEQS (X XDO Y YDO)
 (LET (A (CAUSE YDO (AFFIRM XDO)))
  (COND ((RELATE X X Y 'DECEIVE)
         (ADD-CONSEQ (MBUILD X
                             (CAUSE YDO
                                    (FUTURE (MTRANS X
                                                    (STATE Y 'SMART 'NEG)
                                                    Y X)))))
```

```
                        (ADD-CONSEQ (MTRANS X A Y X)))
                       ((RELATE X X Y 'LIKE)
                        (ADD-CONSEQ (MBUILD X A))
                        (ADD-CONSEQ (MTRANS X A Y X)))
                       (T (ADD-CONSEQ (MTRANS X (NEGATE A) Y X]
```

¯ Consequences of X asking Y to do Z:
¯ If Y doesn't like X or dominates X, then Y will say no; otherwise
¯ Y will do Z.

```
(DE REQUEST-CONSEQS (X Y Z)
 (ADD-CONSEQ
  (COND ((OR (NOT (RELATE Y Y X 'LIKE))
             (RELATE Y Y X 'DOMINATE))
         (PLAN Y (FUTURE (MTRANS Y (NEGATE Z) X Y))))
        (T (PLAN Y Z]
```

¯ Consequences of a PLAN: If the actor of the PLAN act is the actor of
¯ the object of the plan, then add the object to the list of actions.

```
(DE PLAN-CONSEQS ()
 (COND ((EQUAL $(ACTOR) $(OBJECT ACTOR))
        (PUSH $(OBJECT) *ACTIONS*)
        NIL]
```

¯ Consequences of a PROPEL: the object struck dies.

```
(DE PROPEL-CONSEQS ()
 (COND ((MEMBER $(TO) *PERSONAE*)
        (ADD-CONSEQ (STATE $(TO) 'HEALTH 'NEG]
```

¯ Consequences of a PTRANS: location change, for both actor and
¯ object.

```
(DE PTRANS-CONSEQS ()
 (ADD-CONSEQ (IS-AT $(OBJECT) $(TO)))
 (COND ((NOT (EQUAL $(ACTOR) $(OBJECT)))
        (ADD-CONSEQ (IS-AT $(ACTOR) $(TO]
```

¯ Reactions to learning of a location change: if it's food or water,
¯ check to see if learner is hungry or thirsty.

```
(DE LOC-REACT ()
 (AND (OR (MEMBER $(CON ACTOR) (GET-ISA 'FOOD $(VAL PART)))
          (EQUAL $(CON ACTOR) 'WATER))
      (SGOAL-CHECK $(VAL PART)
                         (COND ((EQUAL $(CON ACTOR) 'WATER) 'THIRSTY)
                               (T 'HUNGRY]
```

¯ If a character is hungry or thirsty, add the appropriate S-goal to
¯ the list of plans.

```
(DE SGOAL-CHECK (ACTOR SCALE)
 (AND (IN-STATE ACTOR SCALE)
      (PUSH (LIST (COND ((EQUAL SCALE 'THIRSTY) 'STHIRST)
                        (T 'SHUNGER))
                  (LIST 'QUOTE ACTOR))
            *PLANS*]
```

```
~ Reactions to learning that someone has learned something:
~ if it's someone else, and it's about himself or you believe he
~ doesn't deceive you, then you believe it too.

(DE MLOC-REACT ()
 (AND (NOT (EQUAL $(VAL PART) $(CON VAL PART)))
      (OR (EQUAL $(CON CON ACTOR) $(CON VAL PART))
          (NOT (RELATE $(VAL PART) $(CON VAL PART) $(VAL PART)
                       'DECEIVE)))
      (ADD-CONSEQ (MLOC $(VAL PART) $(CON CON]

~ Reactions to learning that you're hungry: add S-goal to list of
~ plans.

(DE HUNGER-REACT ()
 (PUSH (LIST 'SHUNGER (LIST 'QUOTE $(CON ACTOR))) *PLANS*]

~ Reactions to learning that you're thirsty: add S-goal to list of
~ plans.

(DE THIRST-REACT ()
 (PUSH (LIST 'STHIRST (LIST 'QUOTE $(CON ACTOR))) *PLANS*]

~ NOTICE says that everyone in the same location as WHO knows
~ about CD.

(DE NOTICE (WHO CD)
 (LET (WHERE (LOC-NAME-OF WHO))
  (FOR (I IN *PERSONAE*)
     (WHEN (EQUAL (LOC I) WHERE))
     (DO (ADD-CONSEQ (MLOC I CD]

~ ─────────── MEMORY functions & pattern matcher ───────────
~ ADDFACT adds a CD to KNOWER's knowledge set. Also If WORLD
~ learns a character has died, then the character is removed from the
~ global list of characters.
~ The CD is added to the front of the fact list, so that MEMQUERY
~ will get the most recent CD that matches its query pattern. Older
~ contradicted facts are still on the list but are not seen.

(DE ADDFACT (KNOWER CD)
 (PUTPROP KNOWER (CONS CD (GET KNOWER 'FACTS)) 'FACTS)

~ Now check for deceased people.

(COND ((AND (EQUAL KNOWER 'WORLD)
            (EQUAL (HEADER:CD CD) 'HEALTH)
            (MEMBER 'NEG (CDPATH '(MODE) CD)))
      (SETQ *PERSONAE* (REMOVE (CDPATH '(ACTOR) CD) *PERSONAE*))))
 NIL]

~ IS-STATE returns non-NIL if CD is one of the state forms.

(DE IS-STATE (CD)
 (MEMBER (HEADER:CD CD)
         '(LOC MLOC CONT LIKE DECEIVE DOMINATE
           HUNGRY THIRSTY HEALTH SMART]
```

¨ NOWKNOWS adds WHAT to the data base for WHO. It also prints in
¨ English this new fact. If WHO = WORLD (a true fact) and WHAT is
¨ an MLOC, then save the content of the MLOC under the person who
¨ learned it. If SAY-FLAG is T, then MLOCs are always generated in
¨ English; otherwise only facts (WHO = WORLD) are generated. This
¨ reduces the volume of output.

```
(DE NOWKNOWS (WHO WHAT SAY-FLAG)
 (COND ((AND (EQUAL WHO 'WORLD) (EQUAL (HEADER:CD WHAT) 'MLOC))
        (SETQ WHO (CDPATH '(VAL PART) WHAT))
        (SETQ WHAT (CDPATH '(CON) WHAT))))
 (COND ((OR SAY-FLAG (EQUAL WHO 'WORLD))
        (SAY (MLOC WHO WHAT))))
 (ADDFACT WHO WHAT]
```

¨ KNOWS(KNOWER,FACT) returns FACT if FACT is in data base for KNOWER:
¨ —if FACT = KNOWS(KNOWER,SUBFACT), assume everyone knows what they
¨   know and look up SUBFACT,
¨ —if FACT has a ?UNSPEC, then return the filler that replaces the
¨   ?UNSPEC in the data base.

```
(DE KNOWS (KNOWER FACT)
 (COND ((AND (EQUAL (HEADER:CD FACT) 'MLOC)
             (EQUAL (CDPATH '(VAL PART) FACT) KNOWER))
        (SETQ FACT (CDPATH '(CON) FACT))))
 (MEMQUERY KNOWER FACT]
```

```
(DE KNOWS-LOC (KNOWER OBJECT)
 (CDPATH '(VAL) (KNOWS KNOWER (WHERE-IS OBJECT]
```

```
(DE KNOWS-OWNER (KNOWER OBJECT)
 (CDPATH '(VAL) (KNOWS KNOWER (WHO-HAS OBJECT]
```

```
(DE KNOWS-IF (KNOWER CD)
 (CDPATH '(MODE) (KNOWS KNOWER (SETROLE 'MODE '?UNSPEC CD]
```

¨ MEMQUERY finds the first item in KNOWER's data base that matches
¨ FACT.

```
(DE MEMQUERY (KNOWER PAT)
 (PAT-MEMBER PAT (GET KNOWER 'FACTS]
```

¨ PAT-MEMBER finds the first item in CD-LIST that matches PAT and
¨ returns CD-LIST from that item on.

```
(DE PAT-MEMBER (PAT CD-LIST)
 (LET (CDS (FOR (CD IN CD-LIST) (EXISTS (MATCH PAT CD NIL))))
      (AND CDS (CAR CDS]
```

¨ Returns non-NIL if ACTOR has GOAL.

```
(DE HAS-GOAL-OF (ACTOR PAT)
 (PAT-MEMBER PAT (GET ACTOR 'GOALS]
```

¨ Adds goal to data base.

```
(DE GETS-NEW-GOAL-OF (ACTOR GOAL)
 (PUTPROP ACTOR (CONS GOAL (GET ACTOR 'GOALS)) 'GOALS)
 (SAY (WANTS ACTOR GOAL]
```

¨ Removes goal from data base.

```
(DE FORGETS-GOAL-OF (ACTOR GOAL)
 (PUTPROP ACTOR
          (REMOVE (HAS-GOAL-OF ACTOR GOAL) (GET ACTOR 'GOALS))
          'GOALS]
```

¨ Returns non-NIL if X is in a state, e.g., HUNGRY.

```
(DE IN-STATE (X ST)
 (FIND-OUT 'WORLD (STATE X ST 'POS]
```

¨ Returns non-NIL if X believes that Y relates to Z in a certain way.
¨ Usually either Y or Z is X.

```
(DE RELATE (X Y Z REL)
 (FIND-OUT X (RELATION Y Z REL 'POS]
```

¨ Looks up CD in the data base for WHO. If there, return non-NIL if
¨ the CD is not a negative fact. If not there, ask the user at the
¨ terminal and save the result. Note that the generator is used to
¨ ask the questions.

```
(DE FIND-OUT (WHO CD)
 (LET (MODE (KNOWS-IF WHO CD))
  (COND (MODE (MEMBER 'POS MODE))
        (T (SAY (MLOC WHO CD))
           (MSG " [Y/N]? ")
           (LET (ANSWER (EQUAL (READ) 'Y))
            (ADDFACT WHO (SETROLE 'MODE
                                  (LIST (COND (ANSWER 'POS) (T 'NEG)))
                                  CD))
           ANSWER]
```

¨ True if Y thinks X is a friend of his.

```
(DE IS-FRIEND-OF (X Y)
 (AND (NOT (EQUAL X Y)) (RELATE Y X Y 'LIKE]
```

¨ Returns location of X.

```
(DE LOC (X) (KNOWS-LOC 'WORLD X]
```

¨ True if X and Y are in the same place.

```
(DE IS-PROX (X Y) (EQUAL (LOC-NAME-OF X) (LOC-NAME-OF Y]
```

¨ A CD is true if it's an MLOC and the content is in the person's
¨ data base, or it's in the data base for 'WORLD.

```
(DE IS-TRUE (CD)
 (COND ((EQUAL (HEADER:CD CD) 'MLOC)
        (KNOWS (CDPATH '(VAL PART) CD) (CDPATH '(CON) CD)))
       (T (KNOWS 'WORLD CD]
```

```
˜ LOC-NAME-OF returns the real location of X. This may involve going
˜ up several levels—e.g., when Joe takes a worm, it's location is
˜ stored as JOE, but it's real location is the location JOE is at.

(DE LOC-NAME-OF (X)
 (LOOP (INITIAL A NIL L (LIST X))
       (WHILE (SETQ A (LOC X)))
       (UNTIL (MEMBER A L))
       (DO (PUSH (SETQ X A) L))
       (RESULT X]

˜ GET-ISA is like GET but checks IS-A node for X if X has no Y
˜ property.

(DE GET-ISA (X Y) (OR (GET Y X) (GET (GET Y 'IS-A) X]

˜————————— Functions to build CD forms —————————

˜————————— ACTS —————————

(DE ATRANS (ACTOR OBJECT TO FROM)
 (LIST 'ATRANS (LIST 'ACTOR ACTOR)
               (LIST 'OBJECT OBJECT)
               (LIST 'TO TO)
               (LIST 'FROM FROM]

(DE CAUSE (X Y)
 (LIST 'CAUSE (LIST 'ANTE X)
              (LIST 'CONSEQ Y]

(DE GRASP (ACTOR OBJECT)
 (LIST 'GRASP
       (LIST 'ACTOR ACTOR)
       (LIST 'OBJECT OBJECT]

(DE UN-GRASP (ACTOR OBJECT)
 (TF (GRASP ACTOR OBJECT]

(DE INGEST (ACTOR OBJECT)
 (LIST 'INGEST (LIST 'ACTOR ACTOR)
               (LIST 'OBJECT OBJECT]

(DE MBUILD (ACTOR OBJECT)
 (LIST 'MBUILD
       (LIST 'ACTOR ACTOR)
       (LIST 'OBJECT OBJECT]

(DE MTRANS (ACTOR OBJECT TO FROM)
 (LIST 'MTRANS (LIST 'ACTOR ACTOR)
               (LIST 'OBJECT OBJECT)
               (LIST 'TO (LIST 'CP (LIST 'PART TO)))
               (LIST 'FROM FROM]

(DE PLAN (ACTOR OBJECT)
 (LIST 'PLAN (LIST 'ACTOR ACTOR)
             (LIST 'OBJECT OBJECT]
```

```
(DE PROPEL (ACTOR OBJECT TO)
 (LIST 'PROPEL (LIST 'ACTOR ACTOR)
             (LIST 'OBJECT OBJECT)
             (LIST 'TO TO]

(DE PTRANS (ACTOR OBJECT TO FROM)
 (LIST 'PTRANS (LIST 'ACTOR ACTOR)
             (LIST 'OBJECT OBJECT)
             (LIST 'TO TO)
             (LIST 'FROM FROM]

(DE WANTS (ACTOR GOAL)
 (LIST 'WANT (LIST 'ACTOR ACTOR)
             (LIST 'OBJECT GOAL]
```

` ─────── STATES ───────`

```
(DE HAS (ACTOR OBJECT)
 (LIST 'CONT (LIST 'ACTOR OBJECT) (LIST 'VAL ACTOR]

(DE IS-AT (ACTOR LOK)
 (LIST 'LOC (LIST 'ACTOR ACTOR) (LIST 'VAL LOK]

(DE MLOC (ACTOR CON)
 (LIST 'MLOC (LIST 'CON CON) (LIST 'VAL (LIST 'CP (LIST 'PART ACTOR]

(DE STATE (ACTOR ST MODE)
 (LIST ST (LIST 'ACTOR ACTOR) (LIST 'MODE (LIST MODE]

(DE RELATION (ACTOR OBJECT REL MODE)
 (LIST REL (LIST 'ACTOR ACTOR) (LIST 'TO OBJECT)
           (LIST 'MODE (LIST MODE]

(DE WHERE-IS (X) (LIST 'LOC (LIST 'ACTOR X) (LIST 'VAL '?UNSPEC]

(DE WHO-HAS (X) (LIST 'CONT (LIST 'ACTOR X) (LIST 'VAL '?UNSPEC]
```

` ─────── MODE FUNCTIONS ───────`

```
(DE MODE (CD) (CDPATH '(MODE) CD]
```

` AFFIRM/NEGATE set the MODE of a CD to true/false.`

```
(DE AFFIRM (CD)
 (COND ((MEMBER 'POS (MODE CD)) CD)
       (T (SETROLE 'MODE (CONS 'POS (REMOVE 'NEG (MODE CD))) CD]

(DE NEGATE (CD)
 (COND ((MEMBER 'NEG (MODE CD)) (AFFIRM CD))
       (T (SETROLE 'MODE (CONS 'NEG (REMOVE 'POS (MODE CD))) CD]
```

` MAYBE makes a CD hypothetical—doesn't matter if it's true or`
` false.`

```
(DE MAYBE (CD)
 (COND ((MEMBER 'MAYBE (MODE CD)) CD)
       (T (SETROLE 'MODE (CONS 'MAYBE (MODE CD)) CD]
```

˜ QUESTION/UNQUESTION make a CD a question/non-question—doesn't
˜ matter if it's true or false.

```
(DE QUESTION (CD)
 (COND ((MEMBER 'QUES (MODE CD)) CD)
          (T (SETROLE 'MODE (CONS 'QUES (MODE CD)) CD]

(DE UN-QUESTION (CD)
 (SETROLE 'MODE (REMOVE 'QUES (MODE CD)) CD]
```

˜ TF adds "transition final" to a CD—doesn't matter if it's true or
˜ false.

```
(DE TF (CD)
 (COND ((MEMBER 'TF (MODE CD)) CD)
          (T (SETROLE 'MODE (CONS 'TF (MODE CD)) CD]
```

˜ FUTURE sets a CD to a future time.

```
(DE FUTURE (CD) (SETROLE 'TIME 'FUTURE CD]
```

˜ ——————— PATH ———————

˜ CDPATH finds the filler at the end of the role list in CD.

˜ For example,
˜ if CD =
˜   (MTRANS (ACTOR JOE)
˜   (OBJECT (PTRANS (ACTOR JOE) (OBJECT WORM) (TO IRVING)
˜   (FROM JOE))))

˜ then
˜   (CDPATH '(ACTOR) CD) returns JOE
˜   (CDPATH '(OBJECT) CD) returns
˜   (PTRANS (ACTOR JOE) (OBJECT WORM) (TO IRVING) (FROM JOE))
˜   (CDPATH '(OBJECT OBJECT) CD) returns WORM.

˜ If a role doesn't exist in a CD form, then CDPATH returns NIL.

```
(DE CDPATH (ROLELIST CD)
 (FOR (ROLE IN ROLELIST)
    (DO (SETQ CD (FILLER:ROLE ROLE CD))))
 CD]
```

˜ INIT-WORLD sets up a bunch of facts such as Joe is a bear, birds
˜ eat worms, and so on. The variable *INIT-FACTS* contains location
˜ and relationship facts, along with which character knows them.

```
(DE INIT-WORLD ()
 (PUTPROP 'JOE 'BEAR 'IS-A)
 (PUTPROP 'JOE 'CAVE 'HOME)
 (PUTPROP 'IRVING 'BIRD 'IS-A)
 (PUTPROP 'IRVING 'TREE 'HOME)
 (PUTPROP 'BEAR '(HONEY BERRIES FISH) 'FOOD)
 (PUTPROP 'BIRD '(WORM) 'FOOD)
 (SETQ *PERSONAE* '(JOE IRVING))
 (SETQ *GOALS* '(HUNGRY THIRSTY))
```

```
(SETQ *ALL-LOCATIONS* '(CAVE OAK-TREE ELM-TREE GROUND RIVER))
(SETQ (ALL-OBJECTS*
       (APPEND *ALL-LOCATIONS* '(HONEY BERRIES FISH WORM WATER)))
(FOR (X IN (CONS 'WORLD *PERSONAE*))
   (DO (PUTPROP X NIL 'FACTS)
        (PUTPROP X NIL 'GOALS)
        (PUTPROP X NIL 'DEMONS)))
(FOR (X IN *INIT-FACTS*)
   (DO (NOWKNOWS (CAR X) (EVAL (CADR X)) T]
```

˜ This is the initial data base. It can be extended before running
˜ a story.

```
(SETQ *INIT-FACTS*
      '((WORLD (IS-AT 'JOE 'CAVE))
        (JOE (IS-AT 'JOE 'CAVE))
        (WORLD (IS-AT 'IRVING 'OAK-TREE))
        (IRVING (IS-AT 'IRVING 'OAK-TREE))
        (JOE (IS-AT 'IRVING 'OAK-TREE))
        (WORLD (IS-AT 'WATER 'RIVER))
        (JOE (IS-AT 'WATER 'RIVER))
        (WORLD (IS-AT 'HONEY 'ELM-TREE))
        (IRVING (IS-AT 'HONEY 'ELM-TREE))
        (WORLD (IS-AT 'WORM 'GROUND))
        (JOE (IS-AT 'WORM 'GROUND))
        (IRVING (IS-AT 'JOE 'CAVE))
        (WORLD (IS-AT 'FISH 'RIVER))
        (IRVING (IS-AT 'FISH 'RIVER]
```

˜ ***
˜   MICRO-MUMBLE
˜ ***

˜ Micro English generator:

˜ SAY prints a CD as an English sentence. If CD is an MLOC of the
˜ WORLD, then only the fact itself is said, otherwise the whole MLOC
˜ is used. The original CD is returned. SAY1 is called with the
˜ infinitive flag off and the say-subject flag on.

```
(DE SAY (CD)
(COND ((MATCH '(MLOC (VAL (CP (PART WORLD)))) CD NIL)
       (SETQ CD (CDPATH '(CON) CD))))
(MSG T)
(SAY1 CD (OR (CDPATH '(TIME) CD) *DEFAULT-TENSE*) NIL T)
(MSG ".")
CD]
```

˜ SAY1 prints *CD* according to the program under the head predicate.
˜ If no program is there, the CD is printed with <>s around it.

˜ These generation programs are lists of expressions to be evaluated.
˜ Attached to primitive acts, they are normally concerned with
˜ generating subject-verb-object clauses. Since some of the acts,

~ such as MTRANS, WANT and PLAN, take subclauses, the generator has to
~ be recursive, so that the ATRANS program that generates the clause
~ "JOE GAVE IRVING THE WORM" can also generate the subclause in "JOE
~ PLANNED TO GIVE IRVING THE WORM." This means that the programs have
~ to know when to say or not say the subject, when to use the
~ infinitive form, and what tense to use.
~   *SUBJ* = true means print the subject
~   *INF* =   true means use the infinitive form
~   *TENSE* is set to either PAST, PRESENT, FUTURE, or COND (for
~   conditional, i.e., hypothetical)

```
(DE SAY1 (*CD* *TENSE* *INF* *SUBJ*)
 (LET (SAY-PROG (GET (HEADER:CD *CD*) 'SAY-PROG))
  (COND (SAY-PROG (FOR (X IN SAY-PROG) (DO (EVAL X))))
        (T (MSG " <" *CD* "> "]
```

~ SUBCLAUSE recursively calls SAY1 with the subconcept at the
~ endpoint of ROLELIST. WORD, if non-NIL, starts the subclause,
~ unless RELATIVE-PRONOUN has a better idea. Tense is calculated by
~ SUB-TENSE.

```
(DE SUBCLAUSE (WORD ROLELIST TENSE)
 (AND WORD (MSG " " (OR (RELATIVE-PRONOUN ROLELIST) WORD)))
 (LET (SUBCD (CDPATH ROLELIST *CD*))
  (SAY1 SUBCD (SUB-TENSE TENSE SUBCD) NIL T]
```

~ SUB-TENSE is given a tense and a CD and picks the tense to use.
~ The given tense is used, except with states (i.e., don't
~ say "he told him where the honey would be" even though conceptually
~ that's right), and with past statements about the future (i.e., say
~ "he said he would" rather than "he said he will").

```
(DE SUB-TENSE (TENSE SUBCD)
 (COND ((IS-STATE SUBCD) *DEFAULT-TENSE*)
       ((AND (EQUAL TENSE 'PAST)
             (EQUAL (CDPATH '(TIME) SUBCD) 'FUTURE))
        'COND)
       (T TENSE]
```

~ RELATIVE-PRONOUN returns the word to start the subclause for the
~ CD at the end of the CD role path.

```
(DE RELATIVE-PRONOUN (ROLELIST)
 (LET (CD (CDPATH ROLELIST *CD*))
  (COND ((AND (EQUAL (HEADER:CD CD) 'LOC)
              (EQUAL (CDPATH '(VAL) CD) '?UNSPEC))
         'WHERE)
        ((EQUAL (NEXT-SUBJECT) '?UNSPEC) 'WHO)
        (T NIL]
```

~ NEXT-SUBJECT returns the subject of a subconcept, which is normally
~ the ACTOR slot, except for CONT (where it's in the VAL slot) and
~ MLOC (where it's in the PART slot of the VAL slot).

```
(DE NEXT-SUBJECT ()
 (LET (CD  $(OBJECT))
  (CDPATH (SELECTQ (HEADER:CD CD)
                    (CONT '(VAL))
                    (MLOC '(VAL PART))
                '(ACTOR))
          CD]
```

¨ INFCLAUSE calls recursively calls SAY1 with the subconcept at the
¨ endpoint of ROLELIST. An infinitive is printed, and the subject
¨ is suppressed.

```
(DE INFCLAUSE (ROLELIST SUBJ-FLAG TENSE)
 (SAY1 (CDPATH ROLELIST *CD*) TENSE T SUBJ-FLAG]
```

¨ (DSP CD-pred expl exp2 . . .) stores a SAY1 program for the predicate.

```
(DF DSP (L)
 (PUTPROP (CAR L) (CDR L) 'SAY-PROG)
 (CAR L]
```

¨ ATRANS may go to either TAKE (if ACTOR = TO) or GIVE.

```
(DSP ATRANS
 (COND ((EQUAL $(ACTOR) $(TO))
        (SAY-SUBJ-VERB '(ACTOR) 'TAKE)
        (SAY-FILLER '(OBJECT))
        (SAY-PREP 'FROM '(FROM)))
       (T (SAY-SUBJ-VERB '(ACTOR) 'GIVE)
          (SAY-FILLER '(TO))
          (SAY-FILLER '(OBJECT]
```

¨ MTRANS may go to either ASK-WHETHER or TELL-THAT.

```
(DSP MTRANS
 (COND ((MEMBER 'QUES $(OBJECT MODE))
        (SAY-SUBJ-VERB '(ACTOR) 'ASK)
        (SAY-FILLER '(TO PART))
        (SUBCLAUSE 'WHETHER '(OBJECT) 'COND))
       (T (SAY-SUBJ-VERB '(ACTOR) 'TELL)
          (SAY-FILLER '(TO PART))
          (SUBCLAUSE 'THAT '(OBJECT) $(TIME]
```

¨ PTRANS may go to either GO or MOVE.

```
(DSP PTRANS
 (COND ((EQUAL $(ACTOR) $(OBJECT))
        (SAY-SUBJ-VERB '(ACTOR) 'GO))
       (T (SAY-SUBJ-VERB '(ACTOR) 'MOVE) (SAY-FILLER '(OBJECT))))
 (SAY-PREP 'TO '(TO]
```

¨ MBUILD may go to either DECIDE-TO or DECIDE-THAT.

```
(DSP MBUILD
 (SAY-SUBJ-VERB '(ACTOR) 'DECIDE)
```

```
(COND ((EQUAL $(ACTOR) $(OBJECT ACTOR))
       (INFCLAUSE '(OBJECT) NIL 'FUTURE))
      (T (SUBCLAUSE 'THAT '(OBJECT) 'FUTURE]
```

 ̄ PROPEL goes to STRIKE.

```
(DSP PROPEL
 (SAY-SUBJ-VERB '(ACTOR) 'STRIKE) (SAY-FILLER '(TO]
```

 ̄ GRASP may go to either LET-GO-OF or GRAB.

```
(DSP GRASP
 (COND ((IN-MODE 'TF)
        (SAY-SUBJ-VERB '(ACTOR) 'LET)
        (MSG " GO OF"))
       (T (SAY-SUBJ-VERB '(ACTOR) 'GRAB)))
 (SAY-FILLER '(OBJECT]
```

 ̄ INGEST may go to either EAT or DRINK.

```
(DSP INGEST
 (SAY-SUBJ-VERB '(ACTOR)
     (COND ((EQUAL $(OBJECT) 'WATER) 'DRINK)
           (T 'EAT)))
 (SAY-FILLER '(OBJECT]
```

 ̄ PLAN goes to PLAN.

```
(DSP PLAN
 (SAY-SUBJ-VERB '(ACTOR) 'PLAN)
 (INFCLAUSE '(OBJECT) NIL 'FUTURE]
```

 ̄ WANT goes to WANT-TO—the second argument of INFCLAUSE is set to
 ̄ true if the subject of the subclause is different than the subject
 ̄ of the main clause.

```
(DSP WANT
 (SAY-SUBJ-VERB '(ACTOR) 'WANT)
 (INFCLAUSE '(OBJECT) (NOT (EQUAL $(ACTOR) (NEXT-SUBJECT)))
            'FUTURE]
```

 ̄ LOC goes to BE-NEAR.

```
(DSP LOC
 (SAY-SUBJ-VERB '(ACTOR) 'BE)
 (OR (EQUAL $(VAL) '?UNSPEC)
     (SAY-PREP 'NEAR '(VAL]
```

 ̄ CONT goes to HAVE.

```
(DSP CONT
 (SAY-SUBJ-VERB '(VAL) 'HAVE) (SAY-FILLER '(ACTOR]
```

 ̄ MLOC may go to either KNOW-THAT/WHETHER or THINK-THAT.

```
(DSP MLOC
 (SAY-SUBJ-VERB '(VAL PART)
     (COND ((OR (RELATIVE-PRONOUN '(CON))
                (IS-TRUE $(CON)))
            'KNOW)
           (T 'THINK)))
 (SUBCLAUSE 'THAT '(CON) *DEFAULT-TENSE*]
```

~ HEALTH goes to BE-ALIVE.

```
(DSP HEALTH
 (SAY-SUBJ-VERB '(ACTOR) 'BE)
 (MSG " ALIVE"]
```

~ SMART goes to BE-BRIGHT.

```
(DSP SMART
 (SAY-SUBJ-VERB '(ACTOR) 'BE)
 (MSG " BRIGHT"]
```

~ HUNGRY goes to BE-HUNGRY.

```
(DSP HUNGRY
 (SAY-SUBJ-VERB '(ACTOR) 'BE)
 (MSG " HUNGRY"]
```

~ THIRSTY goes to BE-THIRSTY.

```
(DSP THIRSTY
 (SAY-SUBJ-VERB '(ACTOR) 'BE)
 (MSG " THIRSTY"]
```

~ CAUSE may go to either X-IF-Y or If-X-THEN-Y.

```
(DSP CAUSE
 (LET (ANTE $(ANTE)
      CONSEQ $(CONSEQ))
  (COND ((IN-MODE 'QUES)
         (SUBCLAUSE NIL '(CONSEQ) 'FUTURE)
         (MSG " IF")
         (SUBCLAUSE NIL '(ANTE) (SELECTQ *TENSE*
                                         (FIGURE 'PRESENT)
                                         (COND *DEFAULT-TENSE*)
                                        *TENSE*)))
        (T (MSG " IF")
           (SUBCLAUSE NIL '(ANTE) 'FUTURE)
           (MSG " THEN")
           (SUBCLAUSE NIL '(CONSEQ) 'COND]
```

~ LIKE

```
(DSP LIKE
 (SAY-SUBJ-VERB '(ACTOR) 'LIKE)
 (SAY-FILLER '(TO]
```

~ DOMINATE

```
(DSP DOMINATE
 (SAY-SUBJ-VERB '(ACTOR) 'DOMINATE)
 (SAY-FILLER '(TO)

 ¯ DECEIVE

(DSP DECEIVE
 (SAY-SUBJ-VERB '(ACTOR) 'DECEIVE)
 (SAY-FILLER '(TO)
```

¯ SAY-FILLER prints the CD at the end of a CD role path.
¯ SAY-PP prints a CD (adds THE to objects).
¯ SAY-PREP prints a preposition plus a CD at the end of a role path,
¯ if any exists.

```
(DE SAY-FILLER (ROLELIST) (SAY-PP (CDPATH ROLELIST *CD*)

(DE SAY-PP (CD)
  (COND ((MEMBER CD *ALL-OBJECTS*) (MSG " THE")))
  (MSG " " CD)

(DE SAY-PREP (PREP ROLELIST)
 (LET (CD (CDPATH ROLELIST *CD*))
  (COND (CD (MSG " " PREP) (SAY-PP CD)
```

¯ IN-MODE tests whether X is in *CD*'s mode.

```
(DE IN-MODE (X) (MEMBER X $(MODE)
```

¯ SAY-NEG prints NOT if *CD* is negative.

```
(DE SAY-NEG () (COND ((IN-MODE 'NEG) (MSG " NOT")
```

¯ SAY-SUBJ-VERB prints the subject (unless suppressed by *SUBJ*=NIL,
¯ infinitives, or an ?UNSPEC as the subject) and verb, with auxiliary
¯ and tensing, if any. Note that future tense is treated as an
¯ auxiliary.

```
(DE SAY-SUBJ-VERB (ROLELIST INFINITIVE)
 (LET (SUBJECT (CDPATH ROLELIST *CD*))
  (COND (*INF*
         (COND (*SUBJ* (SAY-PP SUBJECT)))
         (SAY-NEG)
         (MSG " TO " INFINITIVE))
        (T
         (COND ((NOT (EQUAL SUBJECT '?UNSPEC)) (SAY-PP SUBJECT)))
         (LET (PLURAL (GET SUBJECT 'PLURAL)
               AUXILIARY
                   (COND ((IN-MODE 'MAYBE) 'MIGHT)
                         ((EQUAL *TENSE* 'FUTURE)
                          (COND ((EQUAL *DEFAULT-TENSE* 'PAST) 'WOULD)
                                (T 'WILL)))
                         ((EQUAL *TENSE* 'COND) 'WOULD)
                         ((AND (IN-MODE 'NEG)
                               (NOT (EQUAL INFINITIVE 'BE)))
                          'DO)))
```

```
                (COND (AUXILIARY
                          (SAY-TENSE AUXILIARY PLURAL)
                          (SAY-NEG)
                          (MSG " " INFINITIVE))
                      (T (SAY-TENSE INFINITIVE PLURAL)
                          (AND (EQUAL INFINITIVE 'BE) (SAY-NEG]
```

˜ SAY-TENSE prints a verb, with tense and number inflection.
˜ Conjugations of irregular verbs are stored under the PAST and PRESENT
˜ properties of the verb, in the format (singular plural) for each.
˜ For regular verbs, SAY-TENSE adds D, ED or S as appropriate.

```
(DE SAY-TENSE (INFINITIVE PLURAL)
 (LET (TENSE-FORMS (GET INFINITIVE *TENSE*))
  (MSG " ")
  (COND (TENSE-FORMS (MSG (COND (PLURAL (CADR TENSE-FORMS))
                                (T (CAR TENSE-FORMS)))))
        (T (MSG INFINITIVE)
           (SELECTQ *TENSE*
                (PAST (OR (EQUAL (LASTCHAR INFINITIVE) 'E) (MSG 'E))
                      (MSG 'D))
                (PRESENT (OR PLURAL (MSG 'S)))
                NIL]
```

˜ LASTCHAR returns the last character in X

```
(DE LASTCHAR (X) (CAR (LAST (EXPLODE X]
```

```
˜ *********************************************************************
˜                        GENERATOR DICTIONARY
˜ *********************************************************************
```

˜ Set the past and/or present tenses for irregular verbs.
˜ Each tense is of the form (Singular Plural)

```
(DEFPROP BE (WAS WERE) PAST)
(DEFPROP BE (IS ARE) PRESENT)
(DEFPROP DO (DID DID) PAST)
(DEFPROP DO (DOES DO) PRESENT)
(DEFPROP DRINK (DRANK DRANK) PAST)
(DEFPROP EAT (ATE ATE) PAST)
(DEFPROP GIVE (GAVE GAVE) PAST)
(DEFPROP GO (WENT WENT) PAST)
(DEFPROP GO (GOES GO) PRESENT)
(DEFPROP GRAB (GRABBED GRABBED) PAST)
(DEFPROP HAVE (HAD HAD) PAST)
(DEFPROP HAVE (HAS HAVE) PRESENT)
(DEFPROP KNOW (KNEW KNEW) PAST)
(DEFPROP LET (LET LET) PAST)
(DEFPROP MIGHT (MIGHT MIGHT) PAST)
(DEFPROP MIGHT (MIGHT MIGHT) PRESENT)
(DEFPROP PLAN (PLANNED PLANNED) PAST)
(DEFPROP STRIKE (STRUCK STRUCK) PAST)
```

```
(DEFPROP TAKE (TOOK TOOK) PAST)
(DEFPROP TELL (TOLD TOLD) PAST)
(DEFPROP THINK (THOUGHT THOUGHT) PAST)
```

``` - BERRIES is the only plural in the current set-up ```

```
(PUTPROP 'BERRIES T 'PLURAL)
```

```
- **************************************************************************
-              SPIN-DEMO VARIABLES FOR SAMPLE STORIES
- **************************************************************************
```

```
(SETQ STORY1
     '(IRVING THIRSTY
       (IRVING '(LIKE (ACTOR JOE) (TO IRVING) (MODE (NEG))))
       (IRVING '(DOMINATE (ACTOR JOE) (TO IRVING) (MODE (NEG))))
       (IRVING '(DECEIVE (ACTOR JOE) (TO IRVING) (MODE (POS))))
       (IRVING '(LIKE (ACTOR IRVING) (TO JOE) (MODE (NEG))))
       (JOE '(DECEIVE (ACTOR IRVING) (TO JOE) (MODE (NEG)))
```

```
(SETQ STORY2
     '(JOE HUNGRY
       (JOE '(LIKE (ACTOR IRVING) (TO JOE) (MODE (NEG))))
       (JOE '(DOMINATE (ACTOR IRVING) (TO JOE) (MODE (POS))
```

```
(SETQ STORY3 '(JOE THIRSTY)
```

```
(SETQ STORY4
     '(JOE HUNGRY
       (WORLD '(HUNGRY (ACTOR IRVING) (MODE (POS))))
       (JOE '(LIKE (ACTOR IRVING) (TO JOE) (MODE (POS))))
       (JOE '(DECEIVE (ACTOR IRVING) (TO JOE) (MODE (NEG))))
       (JOE '(LIKE ACTOR JOE) (TO IRVING) (MODE (POS))))
       (IRVING '(LIKE (ACTOR IRVING) (TO JOE) (MODE (POS))))
       (IRVING '(DOMINATE (ACTOR IRVING) (TO JOE) (MODE (POS))))
       (IRVING '(DECEIVE (ACTOR IRVING) (TO JOE) (MODE (NEG))
```

``` -Set the story telling in the past tense. ```

```
(SETQ *DEFAULT-TENSE* 'PAST)
```

EXERCISES

1. Make up a new story variable, **STORY5**, where Irving is the main character and he is thirsty. Furthermore, he thinks that he likes Joe, Joe likes
   him, Joe does not deceive him, and Joe dominates him. Also Joe is
   hungry, and thinks that he does not like Irving, and does deceive him. Run
   McSPIN on this story.
2. When McSPIN is run on **STORY5**, the story produced has Joe tricking
   Irving repeatedly. Each time Irving brings him some food, hoping Joe will

say where some water is, Joe accepts the food and says Irving is stupid. He clearly is, after the first time. We need to fix McSPIN so that it can infer new social relationships from events.

a. Change MTRANS-CONSEQS so that if someone calls someone else stupid, then the second person will no longer like the first person.

b. Change BARGAIN-PLAN so that if the ACTION sought is not carried out, then the ACTOR will believe that the AGENT deceives the ACTOR.
Since normally MLOC consequences are not generated in English, you should explicitly use SAY in both (a) and (b) so that the changes in relationships appear in the story output. Run McSPIN with STORY5 again. It should be shorter and Irving should change his mind about Joe when Joe reneges on the bargain.

3. The DCONT plan-box has only one thing to do if the object desired is already owned by someone: persuade them to give it to you. In the original TALE-SPIN program, a character could also trick the owner into leaving, and then take the object while the owner was gone. This exercise will add such a plan to McSPIN. Note that in order for the trick to work, there must be some way to persuade someone to leave even though you can't persuade them to give you something.

a. In PERSUADE, add MOVE-PLAN before ASK-PLAN. Define MOVE-PLAN to be a special case that says that if the desired ACTION is a PTRANS of the AGENT to some location, and the ACTOR doesn't like the AGENT, then the ACTOR should tell the AGENT that there is food for him at that location. Define a function NEW-FOOD so that (NEW-FOOD ACTOR AGENT) will return the name of some food for AGENT that ACTOR thinks AGENT doesn't already have. Use NEW-FOOD in MOVE-PLAN to create a reasonable lie for the ACTOR to tell. The last line of MOVE-PLAN should be (IS-TRUE RESULT). This will check to see if the lie succeeded.

b. In DCONT, in the case where an owner is known, change the PERSUADE expression to be

(OR (PERSUADE...) (LURE-AWAY ACTOR OWNER OBJECT)).

c. Define LURE-AWAY to be a conjunction of finding some new location to send the owner to, persuading the owner to go there, and taking the object when he goes. Define the function NEW-LOCATION so that (NEW-LOCATION OWNER) will return some location that OWNER is not at.

d. Make up a new story variable, STORY6, that says that Joe is hungry, knows that Irving has the honey, and thinks that Irving doesn't like him, deceives him, and dominates him. Also Irving is hungry, and thinks that Joe does not deceive him. Run McSPIN on STORY6. The output should be that Joe tricks Irving into going after the worm while Joe eats the honey.

e. Change STORY6 so that Irving thinks that Joe deceives him. The trick should not work now. Change STORY6 so that Irving is not hungry. Again, the trick should not work. Change STORY6 so Joe thinks that Irving already has the worm. This time Joe should not even try to trick him. Change STORY6 so that Joe likes Irving. Again, there should be no trick.

11 POLITICS

Jaime Carbonell

INTRODUCTION

The POLITICS system is a set of closely cooperating computer programs that simulate human ideological understanding of international political events. POLITICS assumes either a United States conservative ideology or a United States liberal ideology, and uses ideological beliefs to guide its understanding of and its responses to various types of international conflict situations. POLITICS' primary *raison d'etre* is to illustrate, test, and further develop a theory of subjective understanding. The domain of international politics is admirably suited to this task because of the diversity and richness of political beliefs.

A Historical Perspective

The idea of creating a computer system to simulate ideological understanding preceded the first inklings of a more comprehensive theory of subjective understanding. More than a decade ago, Abelson (1973) created his "Goldwater Machine", a first-generation computer simulation of Senator Barry Goldwater spewing ultra-conservative rhetoric in response to statements about international political issues. The program was successful most notably on two counts: in the modelling of some aspects of what Abelson termed "hot cognition", and in the creation of a simple, concise representation of an ideology as a "master script".

The Goldwater Machine suffered two interesting failings as well: its inability to deal with mundane reality and the lack of any common-sense planning facility. Both of these failings are illustrated in the following example. From the four propositions: "Communists do bad things to members of the free world",

"South American students threw eggs at Nixon", "Castro is a Communist", and "West Berlin is a free world city", the ideology machine concluded that Castro would throw eggs at West Berlin. A planning ability should focus on the purposes of actions and suggest them only if they are instrumental to achieving some goal, rather than suggest actions merely because they belong to the category of possible things that a given actor may do. Considerations of mundane reality ought to prevent the very notion of a chief of state throwing eggs at a city across the ocean from ever being conceived.

In the years that followed the development of the Goldwater Machine, Schank and Abelson developed their theory of knowledge structures representing mundane reality in human events (Schank and Abelson, 1977). POLITICS was originally conceived as an effort to reformulate the Goldwater Machine in light of the new theory of knowledge representation. In particular, Schank suggested the use and extension of scripts to encode stereotypical political events, with the idea that such a mechanism would constrain the new Goldwater Machine to consider only actions that accord with mundane reality. While scripts turned out to be a very effective mechanism of encoding knowledge of mundane, stereotypical behavior in the political world, as they had earlier proven useful in other domains, script theory left the more interesting problems of ideological simulation unsolved. Essentially, scripts did not address questions of when a political actor chooses a particular course of action, nor why any course of action should be chosen (or even considered as a viable plan). Moreover, scripts contributed nothing to the problem of understanding the radically different subjective interpretations of the same events by people with different belief systems.

Some Significant Developments

There was no general mechanism in the AI literature for encoding subjective knowledge. Hence, I needed to construct a means of representing and using the idiosyncratic knowledge contained in political ideologies, as well as develop a computational mechanism for applying this knowledge in the process of interpreting and formulating plans of action. In the process of investigating new knowledge structures and mechanisms, I set two basic requirements to measure their usefulness and to accord with intuitive notions of a psychologically plausible model of human subjective understanding. Briefly these criteria were:

1. The representation of political ideologies must contain all the information necessary for the reasoning mechanism to simulate widely differing ideological interpretations. None of the ideological differences must be hidden in the control structure. Hence, the simulation system should be able to model different ideological behavior merely with the substitution of a new ideology for its present beliefs.

2. A single unified model of common-sense reasoning in adverse situations was required. It was essential that this model be integrated, making use of whatever beliefs or information were at hand, and that the reasoning model be independent of the ideological beliefs. Reasoning should be influenced by ideological beliefs, but a system should be able to reason with or without ideological convictions. My premise is that all people are capable of exhibiting roughly the same reasoning processes, despite their political beliefs or factual knowledge. However, a single, unified reasoning process will come to different conclusions given different beliefs or different factual information.

Both criteria were successfully met in the development of the POLITICS system. *Goal trees* represent political ideologies, and *counterplanning strategies* encode high-level reasoning processes. These new knowledge structures will be discussed in detail, in addition to extensions of Schank and Abelson's scripts and other inference mechanisms.

A parallel concern in the development of the theory of *subjective understanding* was the implementation of the principle of *integrated reasoning*. This principle dictates that all knowledge can be brought to bear at each stage of the understanding process. The understanding process itself has no fixed algorithmic control structure. Rather, control depends on which knowledge source can add the most to fulfill the objectives of the understander at each step of the process. A similar idea was developed in HEARSAY-II (Reddy, 1976) for the purpose of bringing together different sources of knowledge in speech understanding tasks. The principle of integrated reasoning will be discussed at greater lengths in subsequent sections.

What POLITICS Can Do: An Example

Consider a political event interpreted by POLITICS, taken from a headline in the New Haven Register:

The US Congress is expected to approve the Panama Canal Treaty.

POLITICS interprets the headline first from the point of view of a conservative ideology, and later from a liberal ideology. The same system of computer programs can model any self-consistent ideology. The liberal and conservative ideologies are data structures encoding the significant motivations and evaluative beliefs that characterize each ideology. An evaluative belief tells the understander what course of action is more consistent with the ideological goals. The ideology is assimilated by POLITICS before interpreting an event. The story interpretations, illustrated by the respective question-answer dialogs, differ substantially in their evaluations of the headline and expectations of possible future events.

First, let us analyze the US-conservative interpretation of the Panama Canal story. POLITICS analyzes the headline and concludes that "approval of a treaty" by a legislative body (e.g., the US Congress) calls for the application of parliamentary procedures (encoded as the script *PARLIAMENT-PROC in POLITICS). More specifically, since the input event expresses the expectation of an outcome, the system concludes that the means of arriving at the outcome should be instantiated. The $PARLIAMENT-PROC script knows that the $VOTE scene is what normally produces a decision or outcome about an issue under consideration by a legislative body. The word "approve" when applied to an item under consideration by a voting body is considered to mean a positive outcome for the proposition under consideration.

POLITICS tries to infer the immediate result of the $VOTE on the state of the world, because the $VOTE script states that this is usually of importance. The inference generated is that everything in the Panama Canal Treaty will probably become fact. (The main provisions of the treaty are stored in POLITICS's memory.) The primary result of the treaty is the change in control of the Canal-zone (and therefore anything therein, such as the Canal itself) from the United States to Panama.

The initial phase of the headline interpretation appears below:

```
*(INTERPRET US-CONSERVATIVE)
INCORPORATING US-CONSERVATIVE IDEOLOGY GOAL TREES...
   GO: SOVIET-WORLDOM.
   G12: US-SAVEFREEWORLD.
   INITIALIZING PARSER ... DONE.

   INPUT STORY:   +THE US CONGRESS IS EXPECTED TO APPROVE THE
                   PANAMA CANAL TREATY.

PARSING ... COMPLETED.

INSTANTIATING SCRIPT: $PARLIAMENT-PROC
   EXPECTED TRACK:
      <=> (($VOTE VOTERS (#ORG NAME (CONGRESS) PARTOF (*US*))
              ISSUE (#TREATY NAME (PANAMA CANAL)
                             REF (TREATY03))
                      SIGNEES (*US* *PANAMA*))
           OUTCOME (*POS*) ))
```

US-conservative POLITICS takes the scriptal analysis and applies goal-directed inferences, using the goals and motivations of the US-conservative ideology. No new goals for the US are achieved as a result of the Panama Canal Treaty; in fact some active US goals suffer serious setbacks. One US goal is to be militarily as strong as possible. This goal suffers as a result of the abandonment of the Panama Canal, an important military outpost. The military strength goal is a subgoal of being stronger than the Communist nations (militarily, economically and politically), which is in turn a subgoal of Communist containment, the highest level US-conservative goal. Making the Communists aware of the new US weakness (i.e., the MTRANS inference listed below) violates the US military deterrent goal, which leads US-conservative POLITICS to believe that Russia may pursue its goal of expanding its military and political control over small nations.

The section of POLITICS protocol below illustrates the goal-directed inferences discussed above:

```
*CANAL-ZONE* FROM (*CONTROL* VAL (*US*))
             TOWARD (*CONTROL* VAL (*PANAMA*))

*US* GOAL VIOLATED:
*US* MILITARY STRENGTH DECREASED.

*US* GOAL VIOLATED:
ACTOR (#COUNTRY TYPE (*COMMUNIST*))
  <=> (*MTRANS*)
  MOBJ ((ACTOR (*US*) TOWARD (*STRENGTH* TYPE (*MILIT*))
                                      INC (-2)))
```

INTERPRETATION COMPLETED, READY TO ACCEPT QUESTIONS.

The question-answer (QA) dialog illustrates the necessity of the above inferences and scriptal knowledge for evaluating the situation in order to predict future events and to make suggestions for future actions by the United States. The first answer in the QA dialog below expresses a relative evaluation of the state of the world resulting from approval of the Panama Canal treaty compared to the present state of the world. The evaluation function considers only the changes in the state of the world brought to light in the preceding event interpretation process. The resulting negative evaluation is, of course, from the point of view of the United States. The second and third questions are answered directly from the goal-directed inferences generated in the understanding phase, namely the expected drop in US military strength and the ensuing activation of a Russian military/political expansion goal. The fourth answer reconstructs the reasoning chain which concludes that Russia may try to take over the Canal.

The question-answer dialog is presented below:

INTERPRETATION COMPLETED, READY TO ACCEPT QUESTIONS.

Q1: Should the US approve the treaty?
A1: NO, THE TREATY IS BAD FOR THE UNITED STATES.

Q2: Why is the treaty bad for the US?
A2: THE UNITED STATES WOULD LOSE THE CANAL TO PANAMA AND THE UNITED STATES WILL BE WEAKER.

Q3: What might happen if the United States loses the Canal?
A3: RUSSIA WILL TRY TO CONTROL THE CANAL.

Q4: Why would Russia try to take over the Canal?
A4: RUSSIA WANTS TO EXPAND ITS MILITARY CONTROL. THE PANAMA CANAL HAS HIGH MILITARY VALUE.

Q5: How might this happen?
A5: THE UNITED STATES MAY NOT BE ABLE TO STOP ANYONE TAKING OVER THE PANAMA CANAL. TORRIJOS IS A COMMUNIST. TORRIJOS WILL LET RUSSIA CONTROL PANAMA.

Q6: Why should the US worry about Russia taking over the Canal?
A6: BECAUSE RUSSIA WANTS TO CONTROL THE WORLD.

Q7: What should the US do to stop Russia from taking over the Canal?
A7: CONGRESS SHOULD VOTE AGAINST THE PANAMA CANAL TREATY.

The fifth question calls for some planning: How can Russia proceed in the pursuit of its newly activated goal? Since nothing to this effect was concluded in the event interpretation phase, the inference mechanism must be reinvoked with the objective of determining the most plausible Russian plan. There are various methods known to POLITICS whereby one country can achieve control of another country (or demographic region) such as invasion, causing revolution, economic dependence and direct influence achieved when the governments share a common ideology. The last alternative is chosen as Russia's probable choice because it involves the least cost. (Torrijos, hence Panama, is believed to have Communist tendencies by the US-conservative ideology.) The counterplanning module is called to evaluate the plausibility of the proposed Russian plan of action. (Counterplanning is the process that determines how an actor can thwart another actor's goals or plans.) Since the US removed its military and political control of the Canal-zone, the counterplanning module sees no effective way of preventing Russian actions in Panama. Hence, POLITICS is satisfied that the method is selected for a Russian takeover of the Panama Canal is indeed plausible.

"How" questions refer to instrumentality (Lehnert, 1978). The instruments of a plan are considered to be the preconditions that must be true in order for that plan to succeed. Therefore, the answer that is generated for the fifth question is a list of the preconditions for a Russian takeover: no effective opposition from the present party controlling the Canal, and no opposition from the party controlling the Canal in the future because of their perceived shared ideology. (The English generator is a little weak at expressing the causality present in the memory structures.)

The answer to the sixth question is obtained by examining Russia's goals in order to see what motivates Russia to expand its military control whenever possible.

The last two question-answer pairs reflect the counterplanning strategies that were applied to suggest the courses of action that the United States should choose in order to achieve its goals in light of the currently activated context. The conclusion is essentially that the only alternative available to the US is to reject the Panama Canal Treaty. This agrees with most of the recent statements voiced by conservatives around the nation.

The question-answering phase of POLITICS is based on Lehnert's (1978) question analysis process which determines precisely what a question is asking for. Once the desired information is specified, POLITICS searches the interpretation of the original event for the answer. If the search fails, further inference is tried, as illustrated in the hypothetical "what if" questions of the US-conservative QA dialog. The English text of each question is analyzed into Conceptual Dependency (CD) representation before the question-answering process is evoked. The analysis process is based on Riesbeck and Schank's (1976) description of an expectation-based parser, but the program is oriented towards the task of parsing into the memory structures used by the POLITICS system. Definite references to previously discussed objects and events are determined as part of the analysis process. The answers to the questions are translated from CD to English by a very simple English generator, which merely fills in the slots of a sentential template. Since neither the analyzer nor the generator are of central concern to the theory of subjective understanding, they will not be discussed at length here.

The liberal interpretation of the Panama Canal event proceeds in a similar way through the initial script-based interpretation of the event. The goal-directed inferences, however, find that the US action can indeed help to achieve some US goals. In the US-liberal ideology, the important United States goals include: reducing political tensions, avoiding conflicts and improving relations with all countries in general, and Latin American countries in the present context. POLITICS concludes that the Panama Canal treaty is an important step in achieving these goals; hence it arrives at a favorable evaluation of the proposed change in the state of the world brought about by approval of the Panama Canal treaty.

The counterplanning strategies are invoked to answer questions about what may happen if the US does not approve the treaties (i.e., keeps the Canal), and whether the Russians are likely to try to take over the Canal. The same counterplanning strategy of verifying a candidate plan for Russian control of Panama (hence the Canal) that was applied in the US-conservative ideology yields different results in the US-liberal ideology. Under the liberal ideology, Russia's goals of maintaining world peace and avoiding political and military conflicts are much more important than expansion of military or political control. Hence, since the Panama Canal Treaty has a section providing for US defense of the Canal, the counterplanning strategies conclude that if the Russians tried to take over Panama, they would come into conflict with the US. According to the US-liberal ideology, international conflict is less desirable for Russia than abandoning the goal of political/military control over Panama. Thus, the answers to the last two questions in the liberal interpretation differ greatly from the answers to the respective questions when posed to the conservative interpretation.

The US-liberal POLITICS interpretation and subsequent QA dialog for the Panama Canal headline is presented below:

```
*(INTERPRET US-LIBERAL)
INCORPORATING US-LIBERAL IDEOLOGY GOAL TREES ...
  GO: SOVIET-WORLDPEACE.
  G11: US-WORLDPEACE.
  INITIALIZING PARSER ... DONE.

  INPUT STORY:    +The US Congress is expected to approve the
                   Panama Canal treaty.

  PARSING ... COMPLETED.

INSTANTIATING SCRIPT: $PARLIAMENT-PROC
  EXPECTED TRACK:
    <=>  (($VOTE VOTERS (#ORG NAME (CONGRESS)
                  PARTOF (*US*))
              ISSUE (#TREATY NAME (PANAMA CANAL)
                       REF (TREATY03))
                     SIGNEES (*US* *PANAMA*))
           OUTCOME (*POS*) ))

*CANAL-ZONE* FROM (*CONTROL* VAL (*US*))
             TOWARD (*CONTROL* VAL (*PANAMA*))

($COLONIALISM CPOWER (*US*)
               COLONY (*CANAL-ZONE* PARTOF (*PANAMA*))
               (*PANAMA*))
ABORTED.   MAINCON NO LONGER MATCHES WORLD.

*US* GOAL ENABLED:
*US* AND *PANAMA* TO END CONFLICT.

*US* GOAL ENABLED:
(#COUNTRY  TYPE  (*THIRD-WORLD*)
PARTOF (*SOUTH-AMERICA*))
TO IMPROVE RELATIONS WITH *US*
```

INTERPRETATION COMPLETED, READY TO ACCEPT QUESTIONS.

Q1: Should the US approve the treaty?
A1: YES, THE PANAMA CANAL TREATY IS GOOD FOR THE UNITED STATES.

Q2: Why is the treaty good?
A2: THE PANAMA CANAL TREATY IMPROVES RELATIONS WITH LATIN AMERICAN COUNTRIES.

Q3: What happens if the US keeps the Canal?
A3: THIS WILL CAUSE DISCONTENT AND CONFLICT IN PANAMA AND LATIN AMERICA.

Q4: Why would this lead to conflict?
A4: THE CANAL ZONE IS A UNITED STATES COLONY. LATIN AMERICA DOES NOT LIKE COLONIALISM. THE UNITED STATES WOULD MAINTAIN COLONIALISM.

Q5: What if Russia tries to take over the Canal?
A5: RUSSIA DOES NOT WANT CONFLICT WITH THE US. RUSSIA WILL STAY OUT OF THE CANAL IF THE UNITED STATES DEFENDS IT. THE UNITED STATES DEFENDING THE CANAL IS PART OF THE TREATY.

The Panama Canal event is the most complicated type of scenario that the program can understand. POLITICS is limited in its domain of application to interpreting political events, but may of its mechanisms such as the counterplanning process are much more generally applicable.

Overall, POLITICS plus UCI-LISP and MLISP support functions requires almost a full address space of a DEC KL-10 computer (256K 36-bit words). On a dedicated TOPS-20/50 (i.e., with no competing time-sharing jobs on the system), POLITICS takes approximately 10 seconds to initialize an ideology, 30 seconds to interpret an event, and 10 seconds to answer a question. These times are much longer (by a factor of 5 to 20) when the system is servicing many users on a time-sharing basis.

Issues

The key issue in POLITICS is the question of what knowledge is necessary to enable subjective understanding. Here I list each knowledge source included in POLITICS, stating the processes that apply the information, the effectiveness of the knowledge encoding, the generality of the knowledge, and a rough measure of the amount of information implemented in the last version of the POLITICS system. The knowledge sources are listed in descending order according to the amount of effort it took to develop them and incorporate them into POLITICS.

Counterplanning Strategies

These encode very general, high-level knowledge of how to thwart one's adversaries and how to achieve one's goals in spite of intentional interference by adversaries. Such strategies are used by the planning/counterplanning process for both interpreting and formulating plans. The strategies, encoded as complex rules (about 30 lines of LISP code each), are effective for planning but not for introspection. (The program cannot query or alter the internal structure of a rule.) There are 40 such rules in the system, spanning most counterplanning situations.

Goal Trees

A goal tree is the general mechanism for encoding ideologies. They are static data structures open to inspection by all processes in the system. Each political ideology attributes a goal tree to every major political actor. The goal trees represent the ideological beliefs of the understander with respect to the intentions and underlying motives of every political actor. In its last implementation, POLITICS has two ideologies; each ideology has an average of 9 goal trees and each goal tree encodes approximately 12 goals.

Situational Scripts

Situational scripts encode detailed, domain-specific, episodic knowledge of stereotypical political situations. The scripts used by POLITICS are extensions of Schank and Abelson's scripts (1977); normative goals are associated with script roles and decision points. POLITICS has 13 scripts, covering only a modest fraction of all plausible political scenarios. Each script consists of about 3 pages of dense LISP code.

Context-Dependent Inference Rules.   These rules are triggered by the activation of one or more scripts. These are specific rules addressing mundane but nelessar12issues. There are approximately 10 such rules per script.

Context-Switching Rules.   These are the rules which activate or deactivate scripts. Their task is to identify the situation by contextual cues and the ideological beliefs of the actors involved. There are over 50 context-switching rules in POLITICS.

Dictionary Expectations.   These are rules used to analyze English sentences pertaining to political events. Each word may index from 1 to as many as 10 expectations. Some expectations are shared by different words. The dictionary size is approximately 200 words.

Utility Functions.   Utility functions take care of pattern matching, keeping track of a task agenda, updating and searching memory, script instantiation, question typing for question-answering dialogs, and low-level Conceptual Dependency inferences. These functions occupy 50K 36-bit words in memory.

There are many limitations to what POLITICS can do. Some of these are due to the limits of the underlying theory of subjective, integrated understanding. Other limitations arise from the fact that POLITICS is not a complete system, but rather an experimental vehicle for further research. Theoretical problems exist in POLITICS' understanding of complex conflict situations. These problems (discussed in Carbonell, 1979a) led to the development of the Basic Social Acts by Schank and Carbonell (1979) and the TRIAD system (Carbonell, 1979a).

All the POLITICS examples presented in this document, with the exception of the example below, are correctly processed event interpretations that illustrate various aspects of subjective interpretation and integrated understanding. POLITICS, like any other large AI program, sometimes makes mistakes in understanding new events.

Consider an example where POLITICS commits a serious error in judgment:

```
*(INTERPRET US-LIBERAL)
INPUT:   Russia massed troops on the Czech border.
           .
           .
           .
Q:   What should the US do about it?
A:   THE UNITED STATES SHOULD CONGRATULATE BREZHNEV.
```

Let us briefly discuss how POLITICS arrived at such an absurd answer. Because the liberal ideology opposes military conflicts, the counterplanning process tried to find a way to stop the pending invasion. Military means were rejected because they too can lead to armed conflict. Diplomatic means violate no US-liberal goals and are appropriate for the situation. However, a precondition to a US diplomatic initiative is blocked; the two countries involved must have good relations and this was not the case with the US and Russia. (The last story understood dealt with Russian spies being deported.) How can one country improve relations with another? Well, if the relations between the leaders are improved, it leads to better diplomatic relations on the whole. Demonstrating approval of someone's actions leads to improved relations. Therefore, congratulating Brezhnev was suggested as a means to achieve a precondition (subgoal) that would enable the US to apply diplomatic means to stop Russian military actions against Czechoslovakia.

There is no individual inference that leads to a logical flaw in the generation of an absurd response. The flaw lies in ignoring global considerations while pursuing local reasoning. POLITICS ignored the US goal of ending the Soviet-Czech conflict while independently pursuing its subgoal of improving US-Soviet relations. The reasoning process was not sufficiently integrated. The purpose of the counterplan should not have been ignored while considering plans to rectify the unfulfilled precondition. The method chosen to fulfill the precondition of improving diplomatic relations precluded the fulfillment of the primary purpose of negotiating with Russia to end the conflict. One cannot approve of X doing Y in order to be in a better position to ask X not to do Y. POLITICS needs a better understanding of the conflict situation and the resulting relations between the participants. This understanding must be used to guide the application of the counterplanning strategies to the conflict situation. It was not POLITICS' choice of the negotiation strategy that caused the problem; it was the way in which this strategy was applied to the particular conflict situation that was in error.

POLITICS makes, essentially, four kinds of errors typical to any AI system that implements a process model of a theory of understanding. We classify the errors into the following four categories:

1. TECHNICAL ERRORS   Errors in the implementation of the model
                           of understanding.
2. INCONSISTENCY   Parts of the process model embodied in the
                           computer programs are mutually inconsis-
                           tent.
3. INCOMPLETENESS   Some knowledge (fact, rule, or general
                           process) is not adequately specified in the
                           model.
4. LACK OF INTEGRATION   The component parts of the model are well
                           specified, but the manner in which these
                           components should interact has not been
                           specified.

The example above is an instance of errors 3 and 4 combined. The particular problem was rectified by making POLITICS always check that no preconditions to an active high-level goal are violated by the choice of a plan to fulfill instrumental goals. This is an important issue in the type of problem solving performed by POLITICS, which may not have been noticed before actually running the program. (Who would have foreseen it?) Therefore, building working programs is an integral part of formulating theories of human reasoning. Process models implemented as computer programs give theories a measure of completeness and internal consistency that they may not otherwise achieve.

OVERVIEW OF POLITICS

The Theory of Integrated Understanding

The POLITICS system is the result of an experiment in *integrated understanding* as well as a computer model of human ideological interpretation and decision making processes. Integrated understanding means that all the relevant knowledge contained in the system can be brought to bear at each stage of its processing. Indeed, there is no pre-determined order of knowledge application; rather, the control structure is dynamically influenced by the interaction between the subjective-belief component and incoming situational information. This is a marked contrast to more traditional AI systems, especially natural language understanding systems such as LUNAR (Woods et al., 1972), where the various modules are applied in a fixed linear sequence.

However, knowledge must be organized in some computationally meaningful way if it is to be selectively applied. Thus, POLITICS uses several sources of knowledge and goes through several phases of the understanding process. The former correspond to how the knowledge can be applied (e.g., episodic knowledge is used differently than knowledge of one's internal drives and motivations), and the latter is dynamically determined as a function of the knowledge state of the system in interpreting new situations.

POLITICS is essentially a rule-based system where sets of rules are activated or deactivated by changes in the situational context. Only active rules may be applied in the understanding process. Of course, some rules are *context-switching rules*, whose actions consist of detecting changes in the context and performing the appropriate activation or deactivation of other rules. Context-switching rules are always active.

Rectangles represent processes.
Ovals represent stored information.
Solid lines represent flow of control.
Dotted lines represent flow of information.

FIG. 11.1.   POLITICS: initial interpretation.

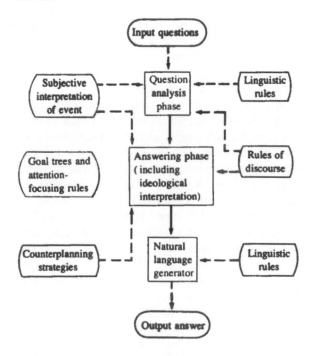

Rectangles represent processes.
Ovals represent stored information.
Solid lines represent flow of control.
Dotted lines represent flow of information.

FIG. 11.2.   POLITICS: question-answering.

The Internal Structure of POLITICS

Figure 11.1 shows the two primary phases in the POLITICS interpretation process, respectively labelled: *initial analysis phase* and *ideological interpretation phase*. Figure 11.2 shows the question-answering mode of POLITICS.

The initial analysis phase includes the natural language analysis, referent specification, situation characterization and hypothesis formation for possible goals pursued by the political actors. The ideological interpretation phase refines the situational context, confirms (or rules out) the hypothesized goals, identifies possible conflicts, and initiates the counterplanning process if the ideology and potential goal conflicts merit such considerations. Both phases use most of the knowledge sources. Reasoning on any one dimension is strongly influenced by conclusions drawn from other dimensions.

Note that question answering involves the same analysis of input that the understanding of the original story does. Questions are not just simple requests to print the content of memory. The intent of the questions must be understood and the most appropriate form of the answer must be chosen.

Script Application in POLITICS

POLITICS uses scripts (Schank and Abelson, 1977; Cullingford, 1978; and Carbonell, 1978) to encode much of its episodic world knowledge. Consider an illustration of a simplified version of a script used by POLITICS. The simplication consists only of translating the conceptual dependency structure into English, and eliminating second-order information such as the expected duration of each event and possible interference situations.

Much of the script-application machinery was adapted from the SAM system (Cullingford, 1978). However, POLITICS has access to much more information than SAM; in particular, POLITICS can take advantage of its knowledge of the goals of various actors. Therefore, in the spirit of integrated knowledge application, goals were associated with decision points in the manner described below.

As illustrated in Fig. 11.3, scripts may have more than one track. At each decision point between two parallel tracks, the script encodes which actor has to make the decision and what goals each alternative may fulfill. For instance, at the first decision point, the &INVADER must decide whether he wants military control of the &INVADEE (left branch) or just some measure of political control, causing him to prefer to avoid armed conflict (right branch). In interpreting an event, POLITICS predicts the appropriate track in the script by comparing its beliefs about the goals of the actor in question with the stored normative goal associated with the scriptal decision point. Thus, US-conservative POLITICS predicts the left branch of the first alternative when &ACTOR is the Soviet Union, whereas US-liberal POLITICS predicts the right branch under the same circumstances. In this manner, the script application algorithm is extended to use subjective beliefs of actors' goals to considerably reduce the number of plausible predictions. Hence, the ensuing search problem is significantly constrained.

Consider the following POLITICS run, as an illustration of the script application process for the $INVADE script in understanding a simple event. The items in brackets have been rephrased in English for legibility. The example below was chosen because a script is the dominant knowledge source used in the interpretation, as illustrated in the question-answer dialog.

(INTERPRET US-CONSERVATIVE)

INPUT TEXT: Russia massed troops on the Czech border.
PARSING ... COMPLETE

INFERENCE: (*FORCES* PARTOF (*RUSSIA*))
INSTANTIATING SCRIPT: $INVADE

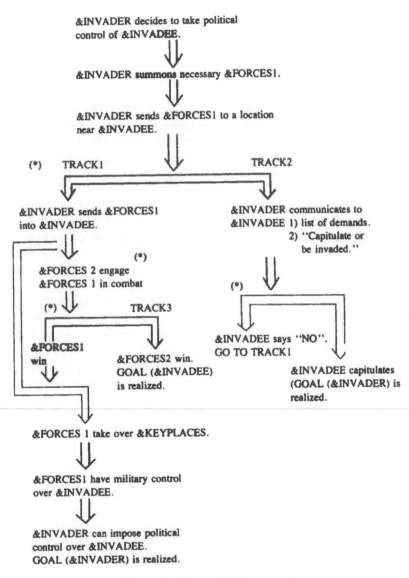

FIG. 11.3.   Uninstantiated invade script.

INSTANTIATED SCRIPT ROLES:
&INVADER ← *RUSSIA*
&INVADEE ← *CZECHOSLOVAKIA*
&FORCES1 ← (*FORCES* PARTOF (*RUSSIA*))
&FORCES2   <uninstantiated>
&KEYPLACES <uninstantiated>

INSTANTIATED GOALS:
    GOAL OF RUSSIA: <Take political control of
                                Czechoslovakia.>
          SUBGOAL: <Take military control of
                                key places in Czechoslovakia.>
    GOAL OF CZECHOSLOVAKIA: <Prevent Russia from
                                taking political control.>
          SUBGOAL: <Prevent Russian forces from taking
                                military control of key places.>

INTERPRETATION COMPLETED, READY TO ACCEPT QUESTIONS.

Q1: Why did Russia do this?
A1: BECAUSE RUSSIA THOUGHT THAT IT COULD TAKE POLIT-
ICAL CONTROL OF CZECHOSLOVAKIA BY SENDING
TROOPS.

Q2: What will Russia do next?
A2: RUSSIA MAY TELL ITS TROOPS TO START THE INVASION.

Q3: What else can Russia do?
A3: RUSSIA MAY WAIT FOR CZECHOSLOVAKIA TO GIVE IN TO
RUSSIAN DEMANDS.

Q4: What happens if Czechoslovakia does not give in?
A4: RUSSIA MAY DECIDE TO START THE INVASION.

Q5: What should the United States do?
A5: THE UNITED STATES SHOULD INTERVENE MILITARILY.

Q6: What else can the United States do?
A6: THE UNITED STATES CAN DO NOTHING, OR IT CAN INTER-
VENE DIPLOMATICALLY BY CONFERRING WITH RUSSIA
ABOUT CZECHOSLOVAKIA. THESE ALTERNATIVES ARE
BAD FOR THE UNITED STATES.

The first four questions and answers reflect POLITICS' knowledge of the
goals of Russia and Czechoslovakia as well as the information contained in
the $INVADE script. In answering question 2, POLITICS predicts one branch
of the script, but as question 3 indicates, when a prediction is specifically
contraindicated, alternative choices will be considered. The last two questions
illustrate the counterplanning strategies, discussed in a later section.

Situational Inference Rules

In addition to scripts, POLITICS encodes part of its situational knowledge in the
form of *SITUATION → ACTION* rules. There are two types of inference rules:

context dependent rules and *context switching* rules. I will discuss the need for each type of rule and give suitable examples.

Context-Dependent Rules

Context-dependent rules are associated with one or more scripts. They are activated only if these scripts are selected by the context-switching rules as appropriate for interpreting a given situation. At any time in POLITICS' processing, only active rules are tested.

Consider two instances of context-dependent rules, where the context is governmental funding:

> RULE-FUND#5
>   IF   the GOAL of the funding is of a MILITARY nature,
>   THEN expect a MILITARY agency to receive the AUTHORITY
>   to spend the money (i.e., CONTROL of the money).

> RULE-FUND#8
>   IF   &FUND-OBJ has a physical realization
>   AND &FUNDEE controls the creation of
>   objects of the same type as &FUND-OBJ,
>   THEN &FUND-CON = (&FUNDEE will build &FUND-OBJ).

Both of the above rules are useful in a governmental funding scenario, but totally inapplicable in other scenarios (such as military invasions and treaty negotiations). In addition, the second rule refers directly to $FUND (governmental funding) script roles. Clearly, it only makes sense to activate such rules if $FUND is applicable. This coupling between scripts and context dependent rules is central to the organization of POLITICS' episodic memory.

Context-Switching Rules

Context-dependent rules can only apply after the general context has been determined. This task is the function of the context-switching rules, which are always active. The test clause of a context-switching rule can test incoming episodic information, properties of the actors and objects either mentioned or inferred, ideological goals of political actors, and any scriptal information that may have been activated earlier. The action clause triggers a script for application and activates each of its associated context-dependent rules.

Deciding which scripts apply to a situation is a non-trivial task. The original SAM system had a relatively simple version of this problem to solve, because it considered only two or three possible (but internally very detailed) scripts. The FRUMP system (DeJong, 1979) can apply up to 50 (very sketchy) scripts, and script selection is perhaps its most difficult problem. The present implementation of POLITICS has 13 scripts—many more could be added to increase POLITICS' knowledge of political situations. However, unlike FRUMP or SAM, script application is not central to POLITICS' reasoning processes; it merely takes care of mundane but relevant details so that goal analysis and counterplanning can proceed. As such, POLITICS is often better able to decide which script to apply (via context-switching rules) because it can draw upon much more world knowledge, especially the goals of political actors.

The scripts in POLITICS are listed below:

$INVADE	—Military invasion
$FUND	—Governmental funding of a project
$DIPLOMATIC-INIT	—Initiate diplomatic action for a purpose
$ARMSRACE	—Simultaneous longterm buildup of military strength
$CONSTRUCT	—Building any large object for later use
$MILITARY-AID	—From one political entity to another
$ECONOMIC-AID	—From a political entity to any institution
$CONFRONTATION	—Military, diplomatic or economic standoff (crisis situation)
$PARLIAMENT-PROC	—Legislative governmental action on a given issue
$VOTE	—Legislative approval/disapproval
$ARMSALE	—Like $MILITARY-AID, but repayment is in currency instead of political influence
$NEGOTIATE	—Coming to agreement by mutual compromise
$ESPIONAGE	—Any form of obtaining information from a political entity without its consent

Consider once again the POLITICS example from the last section. The input stated: "Russia massed troops on the Czech border." Why did POLITICS assume this was an instance of a probable $INVADE? Why not $MILITARY-AID? If the input had said: "The US massed troops on the West German border", would this be an invasion or a NATO maneuver (an instance of military aid to western Europe)? POLITICS makes its decision according to both situational cues (these rule out $VOTE and $PARLIAMENTARY-PROC, for instance) and its beliefs about the goals of the parties involved. In its US-conservative mode, POLITICS assumes that Russia wants to expand its political control over other countries above all else. This can be accomplished by an invasion (of the reform-oriented Dubcek government in Czechoslovakia), not by aiding the maverick regime. However, the US, under the US-conservative ideology, has the very important goal of Communist containment. This can be accomplished by aiding allies who are fighting Communism, not by provoking military conflict among non-Communists. Thus POLITICS selects $MILITARY-AID as the appropriate script for the second scenario. The context-switching rules below are used to make this decision.

Let X be a small country, and Y be a large country.

CONTEXT-RULE#13
  IF   Y moves armed forces near to or inside of X
      AND X is involved in a military conflict and needs
              assistance
      AND having X win the conflict helps Y achieve
              one of its goals,
  THEN   Y will have the goal of militarily aiding X.

CONTEXT-RULE#14
  IF   Y moves armed forces near to or inside of X
      AND having X militarily stronger does not help
              Y achieve one of its goals
      AND expanding its political control is a
              high level goal for Y,
  THEN   Y has the goal of a military takeover of X.

A script is activated if its normative goal matches a goal of one of the central participants mentioned in the event and, in addition, if the input event matches one of the key scriptal events. A *key event* is either an event in the initial sequence of the script or the main event of one of the later sequences (called the *main concept of a scene* in Schank and Abelson, 1977, and Cullingford, 1978). Thus, in the Czechoslovakia example, $INVADE is chosen because context-rule 14 asserts that Russia has the goal of military takeover (the normative goal of $INVADE), and because troop movements towards a target country is an event in the initial scene of $INVADE.

Goal Trees: An Encoding of Subjective Beliefs

POLITICS is essentially a subjective understander; it models a political ideology by using its beliefs to focus and color its understanding process. Political ideologies in POLITICS are represented by sets of goal trees. Each goal tree encodes the motivations of a political actor as perceived by the ideology in question. For instance, under the US-conservative ideology, the Soviet goal tree contains "world domination", "leadership of Communist world", "strong military", etc. The US goal tree, under the same ideology, contains "Communist containment", "preservation of free enterprise" and "strong military". Similarly, other countries of groups of countries have their own goals as perceived by the political ideology. In essence, a political ideology consists only of information about the motives of political actors: what their long range goals are and what means they are willing to use.

The ideologically-perceived goals of political actors are represented as trees because it is often important to know which goals are instrumental to others, which goals are subjectively more important to each political actor, and which goals may be inconsistent with others. These relations are encoded in the links between the nodes of the tree. (Each goal is a node in a goal tree.) The root node of each tree is the most important goal for that political actor. We allow subgoals to be instrumental to more than one higher level goal, so mathematically speaking, our goal trees are really directed acyclic graphs. Similarly, relative-importance relationships may exist between many different goals in the graph.

Goal trees specify what goals are active for each actor. Previous sections showed that goals help determine which context is relevant, as applied by the context-switching rules. Further, the active goals of an actor help predict his decisions at branching points in scripts. What we need to define now is the actual process for putting the information contained in goal trees to use. That is, given an actor with an ideologically attributed goal tree, and a (partial) description of a situation, which goal(s) in the actor's goal tree will guide his future behavior? We have a small set of rules that perform the goal selection, given a goal tree. Before we analyze these rules let us consider an example. Figure 11.4 is part of the US goal tree under the US-conservative ideology. A relative-importance (RI) link means that the goal at the head of the arrow is believed to be more important to the actor than the goal at the tail of the arrow. Instrumentality is similarly encoded by "subgoal-links".

GOAL1:   The US should have strong, loyal and fully supplied armed forces.

GOAL2:   The US should give military aid to countries who oppose Communism.

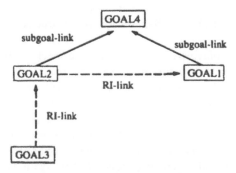

FIG. 11.4.   Relative importance and subgoal links.

GOAL3:   The US should try to preserve human rights and lives throughout the world.

GOAL4:   Communist containment = preservation of the free world.

Suppose a US conservative, who attributes the above goal tree to the United States, was posed the question: "Should the United States send aid to the dictator of Buthan, who is struggling against Communist guerrillas?" Three of the above goals are potentially active (goals 2, 3, and 4). We expect a conservative to answer "Yes, definitely" because both of the goals that would be helped are of greater importance than the goal that would be hindered (aiding a dictatorship may hinder human rights). However, if the question were "Should we send the new F-15 fighters that our own airforce needs to Buthan?" the answer may be negative, because goal 1 (which is more important than goal 2) would be violated.

Counterplanning

The counterplanning process is encoded as a set of heuristic strategies applicable to general conflict situations, and a control-flow algorithm that determines when to apply the various classes of counterplanning strategies.

There are two general types of conflict situations where an actor may apply the counterplanning process. The first situation is characterized by an actor (X) trying to thwart another actor (Y) from achieving his goal G(Y). X may prevent Y from achieving G(Y) by directly making the goal state impossible to achieve, or by repeatedly blocking Y's plans to fulfill G(Y). We call this process *obstructive counterplanning*. The second type of counterplanning scenario is essentially the reverse of the first type: An actor X is trying to achieve his goal G(X) in spite of potential attempts by Y to nullify the goal state G(X) or block X's plans for pursuing G(X). This process, called *constructive counterplanning*, differs from obstructive counterplanning only in terms of the subjective perspective of the counterplanner. The perspective shift causes the counterplanner to apply different strategies at different times, as the application of strategies is goal driven. Figure 11.5 is a control-flow diagram for the obstructive counterplanning process.

To illustrate the obstructive counterplanning mechanism, consider a simple example. Prison guard X wants to prevent prisoner Y from escaping. Hence, G(Y) is the state "Y is free outside the prison". We enter Figure 11.5 at the top. Does the guard know the prisoner's escape plan? Let us assume that he does not. His next step is to determine what, if any, plan the prisoner may have formulated. This plan determination may itself involve some planning: Should the guard ask the prisoner? Should he threaten him? (See Schank and Abelson, 1977, for a discussion of social planning units). Let us again assume that the guard fails. At this point we enter the third box in Figure 11.5. The guard can ask himself, "What would I do if I were trying to escape?" If he finds a reasonable

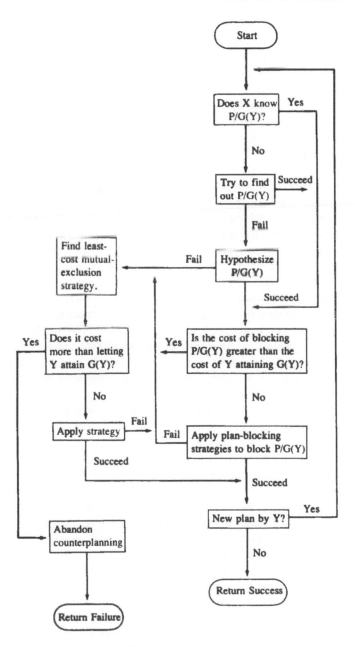

Actor X attempts to block actor Y from achieving G(Y) with plan P/G(Y).

FIG. 11.5.   Obstructive counterplanning.

plan, he may hypothesize that this is the prisoner's plan and he can then apply obstructive counterplanning strategies to block that plan. For instance, the guard may find that stealing the key is a reasonable plan, in which case he can apply the violate-necessary-precondition strategies (discussed later) to conclude that he should keep the keys away from the prisoner.

If no plan presents itself, the only option open to the guard is to take general precautions (i.e., apply mutual exclusion strategies) such as pointing a gun at the prisoner and informing him that either he remains put, or he will be dead. Thus escaping and staying alive become mutually-exclusive states in the prisoner's mind.

There are exit conditions in the counterplanning algorithm. For instance, if the prisoner's plan is to blow up the prison (and he has the means to do so), the guard may decide that the risk of being blown up is more costly than his goal of thwarting the prisoner. Similarly, if he has to keep a gun trained on the prisoner for the length of the prison sentence, the guard may decide that this is more costly than letting the prisoner escape. Cost measures in counterplanning are briefly discussed in (Carbonell, 1979b).

Figure 11.6 is the control-flow for constructive counterplanning. Let us consider the same situation from the point of view of the prisoner. We enter the first box in Fig. 11.6: Is the prisoner's escape goal directly blocked by the guard? If this is the case, the only recourse open to the prisoner is obstructive counterplanning against the guard's actions. For instance, if the guard has a gun trained on his head, the prisoner must address this problem before formulating any specific escape plan.

If his goal is not directly blocked by a mutual-exclusion state, the prisoner can then address the problem of escaping. If he is able to formulate a workable plan and the guard does not counterplan, the prisoner succeeds. Otherwise, he must address the guard's obstructive counterplanning. First, the prisoner can analyze the reasons for the guard's counterplanning. For instance, if the reason is that the guard needs his job to make money, the prisoner may try bribing the guard (a mutual-benefit strategy, in effect forming a temporary alliance with the guard). If he discovers a more important goal that the guard pursues and he is able to threaten this goal, the guard may be diverted from his counterplanning efforts. For instance, the prisoner may convince the guard (truthfully or not) that he is about to blow up the prison and thereby induce the guard to pursue his higher-level goal of staying alive by fleeing.

Finally, the prisoner may pursue a different set of counterplanning strategies. These strategies depend upon his analysis of the method used by the guard to counterplan against him. For instance, the guard may be blocking a precondition (e.g., keeping the keys away from the prisoner), or limiting an essential resource such as time, materials, or outside assistance. There are heuristic strategies for attempting to overcome each type of blocking action. Constructive counterplanning also has exit conditions based on the relative cost of abandoning or continuing the effort.

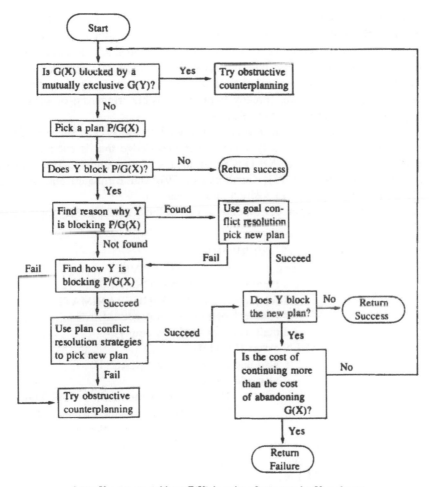

Actor X wants to achieve G(X) in spite of attempts by Y to thwart
his plans or directly nullify his goal G(X).

FIG. 11.6.   Counterplanning process-constructive phase.

A DETAILED VIEW OF POLITICS

Dictionary Expectations

The first knowledge source used in POLITICS is its dictionary. Since the initial
language-analysis phase was patterned after Riesbeck's ELI system (Riesbeck
and Schank, 1976 and Riesbeck, 1975), our word definitions bear a close resem-
blance to the ELI dictionary entries. The primary difference is that POLITICS'
dictionary entries contain domain-specific knowledge, making the language
analysis more robust, but also less general.

Each dictionary entry consists of a set of possible word senses for a given word. Each word is an expectation rule, whose condition side is a conjunction of syntactic, semantic and contextual tests. The right hand side is an assertion of the meaning of the word sense plus the activation of additional expectation rules. The functions of these rules range from connecting the meaning of the new word with conceptual structures already built, to possible triggering of scripts and hypotheses of what goals may be active.

Expectation-based language analysis is a well developed and successful technique. Here we illustrate only some of the knowledge that is encoded by the expectation rules used in POLITICS, by means of an example. The reader is referred to Riesbeck (1975), Gershman (1979), and Birnbaum and Selfridge (1979) for more detailed exposition and discussion.

The following diagram corresponds to part of the dictionary entry for the word "vote":

```
VOTE part-of-speech: (VERB NOUN)
     vote1: IF feature(focus) = LEGISLATIVE
               and type(object) = STATECHANGE
               and feature(recipient) = HIGHERANIMATE
               and feature(!context) = GOVERNMENT
               and main concept buffer is empty
            THEN assert (!AUTH)
                    also add request makereq(!AUTH)
                    also add request
                            IF nextword is member of (FOR TO)
                            THEN set object to the meaning of
                                    the next noun phrase
     vote2: IF feature(focus) = (#HUMAN number (1))
               and ...
            THEN ...
                    .
                    .
                    .
```

The word vote can have several meanings, each corresponding to a word sense (vote1, vote2, ...) in the dictionary entry. Vote1 refers to a resolution of a legislative body in a position of political power over its constituents (e.g., "Congress voted for national health insurance"). Other word senses include an individual expressing his preference at the polls (e.g., "John voted for Carter"). It is important to discriminate between these two possibilities because vote1 has, as a consequent, the following inference: The matter voted for becomes law by virtue of the vote. There is no similar inference for vote2. The social act !AUTH encodes the meaning of vote1 and similar social authorizations, decrees, etc., and also triggers the appropriate consequent inferences. (Schank and Carbonell, 1979, describe the social acts such as !AUTH in detail.)

The conjunction of tests in the "IF" clause determines the word sense. The actions in the "THEN" clause assert the word-sense meaning as well as add new requests (rules of the same form as the dictionary entry above). The process "makereq" analyzes a memory structure (e.g., the information keyed by !AUTH in our example) to generate further requests. For instance !AUTH expects to see the record of an authorization, such as a piece of legislation. This expectation would be able to disambiguate the word "bill" if it were to appear later in the sentence.

The expectation-based technique is flexible in the sense that information coming from different sources (e.g., word definitions, syntax, memory structures, scripts) can be encoded in the same manner, and hence applied uniformly without regard for its source.

Goal Analysis Rules

The goal analysis rules shown below are used to decide which goal in an actor's goal tree will determine his future behavior. The principle is simple: The most important goal in his goal tree that can be affected by the current situation is the one that he will pursue. Since goal trees are partial orderings, it is not always possible to determine that one of a set of goals is more important than the rest. In this case there may be more than one goal determining an actor's future behavior; POLITICS will assume that the actor is simultaneously pursuing all the goals of highest importance.

GOAL-RULE#1: If progress towards a goal can be achieved by a particular course of action, that course of action should be pursued.

GOAL-RULE#2: If a possible course of action violates a goal, it should be actively avoided.

GOAL-RULE#3: If a possible course of action has no relevance with respect to the goal tree, it should not be actively considered.

GOAL-RULE#4: If a course of action affects two goals, and no other rules determine which goal to focus on, the effect on the higher-importance goal determines whether the course of action should be pursued.

GOAL-RULE#5: Relative-importance links in a goal tree are transitive.

GOAL-RULE#6: Relative importance is transitive across subgoal links.

    CASE 1: If goal A is less important than a subgoal of goal B, then it follows that goal A is also less important than goal B.

    CASE 2: If goal A is less important than goal B, then each of the subgoals of goal A are also less important than goal B.

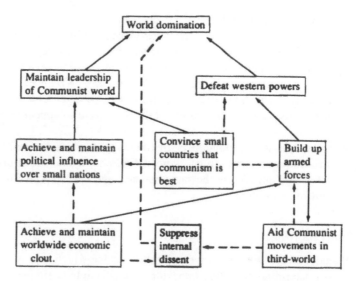

FIG. 11.7.   Soviet goal tree in US-conservative ideology.

To illustrate the goal trees in POLITICS and their application, consider the full US-conservative goal tree for the Soviet Union and the US-liberal tree for the United States as implemented in POLITICS. The conservative ideology is somewhat better developed, so its goal trees are a little more detailed here. In Figs. 11.7 and 11.8, solid lines indicate subgoal links, and dotted lines denote relative-importance links.

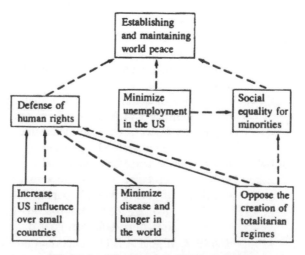

FIG. 11.8.   US goal tree in US-liberal ideology.

An Example of Goal Analysis

Now let us tie together the goal trees, goal activation rules, context-switching rules, and scriptal information with an annotated POLITICS run. The example below is a US-liberal interpretation of the Czechoslovakia event discussed earlier from a US-conservative viewpoint. The first thing POLITICS does is to incorporate the ideological goal trees. Then it interprets events and answers pertinent questions. The example below suppresses details of the language analysis and script application tasks, in order to highlight the goal-driven inferences.

```
****************************************************************
         Start of POLITICS interpretation and QA dialog.
****************************************************************
       PTYCON LOG FILE      2-Mar-78 12:15:36
    PTYCON> CONNECT (TO SUBJOB) 1
    [CONNECTED TO SUBJOB POL(1)]
```

Computer Run	Annotation
*(INTERPRET US-LIBERAL) INCORPORATING US-LIBERAL IDEOLOGY GOAL TREES...	
TOP GOAL: US-WORLDPEACE. INITIALIZING PARSER... DONE.	
INPUT STORY: +Russia massed troops on the Czech border.	
PARSING... COMPLETED. SPECIFICATION PHASE STARTED... . . . . INSTANTIATING $INVADE SCRIPT.	We skip over the parsing and initial script application phase of the POLITICS interpretation. What scripts require the concentration of a military force? POLITICS knows about military-aid, confrontations, and invasions. Military aid is rejected because Czechoslovakia does not have the goal of receiving aid. Confrontation is rejected because small countries (e.g., Czechoslovakia) do not pose a military threat to world powers (e.g., Russia). Context-switching rule#13 chooses $INVADE as the only candidate.
GOAL DETERMINATION PHASE STARTED...	
CZECHOSLOVAKIA GOAL G39 THREATENED	G39 = Maintain peace with neighboring countries.

Computer Run	Annotation
RUSSIA GOAL G29 THREATENED	G29 = Avoid armed conflicts, a subgoal of the Russian preservation of peace goal.
RUSSIA GOAL G27 ACTIVATED	G27 = Increase political influence over smaller nations.
INTERNAL CONFLICT (G103 G29) G103 REJECTED... TRY NEW TRACK OR NEW SCRIPT.	G103 = The goal of attaining military control of the invaded country. G103 is the default scriptal goal of $INVADE.

The Russian goal tree, according to the US-liberal ideology, has the goal of preserving peace (G29). However, this goal conflicts with the goal of military takeover (G103) which is associated with the INVADE script. Since any goal not in the goal tree of a country (i.e., the script-associated goal) is automatically ranked as less important than all the goals in the country goal tree POLITICS resolves the conflict by abandoning G103 and pursuing G29, the more important goal. (See GOAL-RULE#6.) Abandoning G103 means that either $INVADE was the wrong script to apply in the situation, or that $INVADE was correct but was applied for some purpose other than the default goal of taking military control of the invaded country.

Since POLITICS had previously rejected the two other possible scripts, it therefore checks whether there is an alternative purpose for applying $INVADE. This is found to be the case when the "threat" track of $INVADE is encountered. Since threats are used to exert political influence, and this matches a goal in the US-liberal goal tree for the Soviet Union, POLITICS has found a viable goal hypothesis.

We continue with the US-liberal interpretation of the event:

PREDICTED TRACK IN $INVADE
DEVIATES FROM DEFAULT PATH.

PREDICTION: ($THREAT1 IN
($INVADE & INVADEE
       CZECHOSLOVAKIA
    & INVADER *RUSSIA*))
&TRACK1 MAINCONS: CON23

    This track accords with the ideological Russian goals, therefore it is predicted by US-liberal POLITICS.

*(TXPN CON23 'EXPAND)
((CON ((ACTOR (*RUSSIA*)
    <=> (PB-THREATEN
          INSTR MILITARY)))
  INITIATE-REASON
    ((ACTOR (*CZECHOSLOVAKIA*)
     <=> (*DO*)))

    The "threat" track consists of a show of force for the purpose of achieving some measure of social control over the threatened country.

RESULT
    ((ACTOR (*RUSSIA*)
        IS (*SCONT* OBJECT
            (*CZECHOSLOVAKIA*)
            VAL (&BIGNUM))))))

POLITICS checks for the effects of the Russian action upon the ideological goals of the US.

POSSIBLE *US* GOAL
VIOLATION: G13

G13 is the US goal of increasing its influence over small nations.

POSSIBLE *US* GOAL
VIOLATION: G9

G9 is preserving human rights. (International military threats often violate this goal.)

SORTING GOALS: (G13 G9)
(*IMPREL* VAL (GREATER G9 G13))

This relation comes directly from the liberal tree for the US.

FOCUS OF COUNTERPLANNING: G9
COUNTERPLANNING STRATEGY CP6
INVOKED . . .

Here GOAL-RULE#5 determines the focus of cancelling Russian influence in Czechoslovakia.

PURSUING SUBGOAL G15
    OF MAINGOAL G9

G15 = decreasing influence of totalitarian regimes, a subgoal of preserving human rights.

MUTUAL EXCLUSION GOALS (G9 G27)
COUNTERPLANNING STRATEGY CP13
INVOKED . . .

US influence is considered a way of cancelling Russian influence by means of establishing a mutual exclusion goal conflict.

CP13 SUGGESTS
($DIPLOMATIC-INITIATIVE
    ACTOR: *US*
    RECIPI: *RUSSIA*
    FORUM: *UN*
    OBJECT: (*SCONT* OBJECT
                (*CZECHOSLOVAKIA*
                    VAL (0))
    MEANS: (*OPPOSITION* VAL G27))

How does the US block Russia's influence without violating higher level US goals? Counterplanning strategy CP13 suggests diplomatic intervention.

INFERENCE:
$DIPLOMATIC-INITIATIVE
SUGGESTED.

INTERPRETATION COMPLETED, READY TO ACCEPT QUESTIONS.

Q: Why did Russia do this?
A: BECAUSE RUSSIA WANTED TO INCREASE ITS POLITICAL
    INFLUENCE OVER CZECHOSLOVAKIA.

Q: What should the United States do?
A: THE UNITED STATES SHOULD DENOUNCE THE RUSSIAN
    ACTION IN THE UNITED NATIONS.

The US-liberal interpretation of the above event illustrates that not only is the recommended US policy different from that recommended by the US-conservative interpretation mentioned earlier, but the actual meaning of the Russian action is interpreted differently. The conservative ideology interpreted the Russian troop buildup as a pending invasion, based on the belief that Russians want to control small countries more than they want to avoid military conflict. The liberal interpreted the same action as a threat that would probably not be carried out. This is based on the relative-importance ranking of the goals in Russia's goal tree under the liberal ideology.

The Structure of the Counterplanning Strategies

Some of the most interesting inferences in POLITICS come not from the interpretation of why one actor did something, but rather from predictions about what will happen when two actors' goals come into conflict. Predicting what individual actors will do in a conflict situation is the job of the counterplanning module.

Our model of counterplanning is essentially a goal-directed rule-based system. Each strategy is a rule that tests the goal conflict state between the two actors, the goal trees of each actor, and the plan that each actor is pursuing. If the test of a rule is true, the action part of the rule suggests a counterplanning method that is likely to succeed. The action part of the rule may have additional conditions or refinements. The structure of a counterplanning strategy is illustrated below:

```
STRATEGY rule#k   title
      TRIGGER   test1 AND test2 AND . . . testn
           IF   testn+1 AND testn+2 AND . . .
         THEN   action1, action2, . . .
   REFINEMENT   subrule#k1, subrule#k2, . . .
```

The test part of each rule is divided into a "TRIGGER" clause and an additional "IF" clause. In order for a rule to apply, both clauses must be true in the counterplanning situation. The reason for our division of the test clause in such a manner is to reduce the time that the process model spends searching for an applicable strategy. All the trigger conditions are "inexpensive" tests; they can be applied directly to the situation without requiring further inference or complicated matching. These trigger conditions are compiled into a discrimination network. This organization allows the addition of new strategies without a corresponding linear increase in the search time required to test all the applicable counterplanning strategies.

Once the trigger conditions for a rule have been met, the additional "IF" tests are performed. These tests may be arbitrarily complex, perhaps requiring further inference and the invocation of other counterplanning strategies. However, the trigger conditions usually restrict the set of applicable counterplanning strategies to a small number in any given situation (typically three or four). Furthermore, counterplanning strategies reflect common-sense reasoning about how to deal with adverse situations. As such, each strategy is sufficiently general to apply across many reasonable types of human conflict. This means that the total number of counterplanning strategies is relatively small compared to the total number of rules and the information contained in the situation-specific scripts. We have found that approximately forty counterplanning strategies suffice to model the counterplanning actions in the situations and goal conflicts we have considered.

The action part of each strategy (preceded by "THEN") is a sequence of counterplanning methods to be applied in the current context by one of the actors. If a strategy is applied, the "refinement" field is checked as the sequence of actions is performed. The refinement contains one or more additional rules that usually provide further detail to the counterplanning situation. These rules are subrules to the counterplanning strategies because they are invoked only in the case that all the tests of the strategy are true, and, in addition, the test clause of each subrule is also true. Our strategies are much closer in structure to the rules found in expert systems such as MYCIN (Shortliffe, 1976) and PECOS (Barstow, 1979), than to those found in more constrained production systems such as the PSG system (Newell, 1973).

Diversionary Counterplanning Strategies

Let us now turn to some of the more specific counterplanning strategies applicable to a mutual-exclusion goal conflict. A frequently-encountered set of strategies operates on the principle of diverting the efforts of the opponent in the goal conflict away from direct pursuit of his goal. There are essentially three classes of such diversionary strategies, all of which rely on the fact that if an actor has to divert his efforts to other matters, he is less likely to succeed at his original task. We group the diversionary strategies into the three categories listed below:

DIVERSIONARY STRATEGIES.
1. Threaten opponent's higher-level goals.
2. Dissipation of effort: Threaten opponent's other goals.
3. Deception: Make opponent think other goals are threatened.

Let us look at one important diversionary strategy and its deceptive option. The process of convincing one's opponent that the actions of a counterplanning strategy have been carried out, without this being the case, is called the *deceptive option* of that strategy.

STRATEGY 1: THREATEN HIGHER-LEVEL GOAL
    TRIGGER Mutual-exclusion goal-conflict situation
         between G(Y) and G(X).
      IF X can find a goal G'(Y) to block, where
         G'(Y) is a goal of higher importance to
         Y than G(Y),
     THEN X should try to block G'(Y). X can expect
         Y to pursue G'(Y) and abandon G(Y).
  REFINEMENT X should choose G'(Y) such that:
         1) Y cannot pursue both G'(Y) and G(Y)
           simultaneously, or
         2) Y can accomplish G'(Y) only if the
           blocking action is abandoned.

Strategy 1 means that in a mutual-exclusion goal-conflict situation, one actor (X) may threaten a higher-level goal of the second actor (Y) in order to make Y divert his efforts to preserve that higher-level goal. Since an actor's attention, time, and material resources are limited, Y may not be able to protect his higher-level goal and pursue the goal that conflicts with X's goal simultaneously. Thus, X will be in a better position to win the conflict situation and achieve his own goal. The "refinement" part of the rule gives some advice to help X make his choice as to which of Y's higher-importance goals to threaten. X knows which goals Y may consider more important by examining Y's goal tree. (Our subjective-belief model assumes that the various actors know about each other's primary motivations.) X should threaten a goal that requires Y's full attention, time or material resources to protect. Alternatively, X can threaten an important goal that Y cannot protect. This gives X a bargaining position to tell Y that he will stop his threat only if Y abandons the (presumably less important) goal that conflicts with X's goal.

The deceptive version of strategy 1 is based on the same principle of diverting the attention and efforts of the opponent. However, the method used need not correlate with reality. As such, one should expect that a deceptive strategy is less likely to succeed.

STRATEGY 2: DECEPTION: FALSE THREAT
    Same as strategy 1 but either
      1) X only appears to threaten the higher
        level goal G'(Y), or
      2) X threatens to block G'(Y) but has
        falsely convinced Y that G'(Y) should
        be one of Y's high-level goals.

There are other diversionary strategies as well (listed in Carbonell, 1979a), all of which share a common principle: an actor cannot overtax his attention and resources by simultaneously pursuing multiple courses of action. Awareness of this simple principle as applied to other actors (as well as the counterplanner) guides our formulation of the diversionary counterplanning strategies. Each strategy is based on a different method of causing an actor to worry about more than one goal at a given time. There are various kinds of limitations on the different items that an actor can focus his attention on at one time. We classify the limitations to the simultaneous pursuit of multiple courses of action according to the following categories:

1. Limitations on available time.
2. Mental and physical limitations on the number of actions that can be performed simultaneously.
3. Limitations of material resources.
4. Limitations of ability.
5. Goal of avoiding certain consequences of one's actions.
6. Interactions between different courses of actions.

Counterplanning Against Blocked Preconditions

In order to successfully execute a plan, there are usually some preconditions that must hold true. Schank and Abelson (1977) classify preconditions into three categories: controllable, uncontrollable, and mediating. For instance, if John's plan is to ask Mary where the bank is located, the following preconditions must be met: 1) John must establish a communications link with Mary, such as telephoning her, or being in physical proximity; 2) Mary must know where the bank is located; and 3) Mary must be willing to convey this information to John.

The first precondition is a controllable precondition, because we assume that John can achieve it at will. The second is an uncontrollable precondition; John cannot bring this precondition about by any action on his part. The third precondition is a mediating precondition. Mediating means that the planner can try to bring this condition about, but its final outcome rests on the actions of another party. For instance, John can use persuasion strategies to convince Mary that she should tell him where the bank is, but there is no guarantee that John will succeed. In addition to persuasion, there are other methods that can be used to circumvent a blocked mediating precondition. These are listed in the following strategy. (Strategies for other types of violated preconditions are discussed in Carbonell, 1979a and 1979b. P/G(X) denotes the plan chosen by X to pursue his goal G(X).)

STRATEGY 3:   UNBLOCKING A MEDIATING PRECONDITION
          IF   Y is blocking a mediating precondition
               for P/G(X),

THEN   X should choose the least cost
alternative among:

1) Establish the goal G1(X) = Bring
   about the mediating precondition by
   some means independent of Y's actions.
   Suspend P/G(X) until G1(X) is achieved.
2) Choose a new plan P', such that P'/G(X)
   does not require this mediating
   precondition.
3) Set up the mutual-exclusion goal
   conflict G(X) = "Y is not blocking
   the mediating precondition to P/G(X)."
   Invoke the mutual-exclusion
   counterplanning strategies.

We will see how this strategy applies, in conjunction with four other counterplanning strategies, when we analyze the next POLITICS example. First, however, we must consider a crucial issue in the application of counterplanning strategies.

Predictive Versus Interpretive Reasoning

POLITICS does a better job at rationalizing (i.e., explaining why something happened) than at predicting exactly what will happen. Its hindsight is better than its foresight, but unfortunately it is not always applicable. This section discusses why this form of weak planning, called *interpretive reasoning*, is superior to *predictive reasoning*.

For the task of generating hypothetical scenarios, one can only use counterplanning strategies in a predictive manner. However, in story understanding tasks, the counterplanning strategies are used to interpret the actions of the actors. In such situations, it is better to apply the strategies in an interpretive manner. To see what we mean, consider the following event:

The United States supported Israel in the 1973 Middle-East war. Subsequently the Arabs imposed an oil embargo on the United States and its allies.

QUESTION: Why did the Arabs impose the oil embargo?

Strategy 1 (threaten higher-level goal) can be used in a predictive framework or in an interpretive manner. In understanding the above event, we need to pose and answer the question, "Why did the Arabs impose an oil embargo?" Using knowledge about the goals of the Arabs and the goal of the United States to help Israel, the understander can establish the goal conflict between the Arabs and the United States. The mutual-exclusion goal conflict is between the US goal of aiding Israel and the Arab goal of preventing US aid to Israel.

Having interpreted the situation thus far, an understander can proceed in two different manners. The first manner is to predict all the possible Arab counterplanning actions to make the US stop aiding Israel. If, in interpreting the rest of the event, the understander matches an action with one of the previously predicted counterplanning actions, the understander can then conclude that indeed the Arabs were counterplanning against the US and their counterplan was the predicted course of action. Such a process would require the understander to generate vast numbers of hypotheses and subsequently test each hypothesis as a possible explanation of the situation. There is no evidence to suggest that people generate all possible inference paths in a given interpretation in order to discard all but the one path that matches reality. It appears more plausible that people only pursue a small number of relevant inference paths. Therefore, generating all possible plans of action is not a reasonable psychological model of human thinking, nor does it lend itself to reasonable constraints on the computational time that the system may require in order to generate and test all possible alternative actions on the part of the Arabs.

A more reasonable alternative to the generate-and-test process is the following: Given the existence of the mutual-exclusion goal conflict, we can predict that the two actors may counterplan against each other. No further predictive inferences are generated at this point. The rest of the event should be interpreted in light of the expectation that the two actors may counterplan to resolve their goal conflict.

When the understander learns of the Arab oil embargo, he tries to see if this is a reasonable course of action to take as a counterplan against the US goal of aiding Israel. Counterplanning strategy 1 (refinement 2) matches the type of interaction between the Arab plan and the US goal. The Arabs are threatening a higher-level US preservation goal by cutting off oil supplies, and the US cannot do anything to directly remedy the situation. Now the Arabs can bargain to end the embargo in return for the end of US aid to Israel. Therefore, the understander can establish the Arab counterplanning actions by applying strategy 1 in an interpretive manner. The result of the Arab action is matched to the action part of the strategy. This match, suggested by our previous expectation that a counterplanning action was likely, allows the understander to infer that the Arabs were invoking counterplanning strategy 1. Therefore, we can say that the reason for the Arab action is specified by the test clause of the strategy. The general interpretive technique of predicting a general framework and subsequently instantiating its component parts has been successfully applied in other AI systems such as SAM (Cullingford, 1978) and HEARSAY-II (Hayes-Roth et al., 1978).

An Example of Counterplanning in Action

In most conflict events interpreted by POLITICS, many different counterplanning strategies may apply to the active goals, goal conflicts, and plan interferences. It is the interaction among the various strategies and their application to varied scenarios that makes POLITICS an interesting tool to test our hypotheses of subjectively-oriented reasoning. In order to illustrate the interaction among strategies, we will now consider how POLITICS interprets an event about the Angolan civil war. Strategy 3 (discussed earlier) interacts with four other counterplanning strategies in the course of understanding the event and suggesting appropriate US-conservative policy. First, we present the additional strategies (discussed in detail in Carbonell, 1979a):

STRATEGY 4:   EXTERNALLY IMPOSED CONFLICT
TRIGGER   Plan conflict between P/G(X) and P/G(Y).
IF   a plan conflict is caused by Z, an external agency,
THEN   X has the following alternatives:
1) Abandon P/G(X).
2) Bargain with Z to end the plan conflict.
3) Counterplan directly against P/G(Y), without the recourse of bargaining strategies.
4) Counterplan against the plan used by Z that imposed the plan conflict.
REFINEMENT   If G(X) and G(Y) match, then X should join forces with Y against Z on alternatives 2 and 4.

STRATEGY 5:   MULTI-GOAL STRATEGY
TRIGGER   Plan conflict between P/G(X) and P/G(Y).
IF   Y's plan can fulfill more than one high level goal,
THEN   X should:
1) Abandon any strategy whose purpose is to convince Y to change his plan or otherwise compromise, unless all other strategies fail.
2) Expect Y to concentrate more effort in the pursuit of P/G(Y) than normally expected.

STRATEGY 6: GOAL BLOCKAGE OPTION
   TRIGGER Plan conflict between P/G(X) and P/G(Y),
       where X cannot directly block P/G(Y).
     IF X cannot easily pursue a different
       P'/G(X),
   THEN X should counterplan to make Y abandon
       G(Y). (Thus, Y is left with no reason to
       pursue P/G(Y).)

STRATEGY 7: FOCUS ON MOST IMPORTANT GOAL FIRST
     IF Y is pursuing more than one goal that X
       wants to block,
   THEN X should rank these goals in terms of
       importance to Y, and block the most
       important G(Y) first. (Thus, X has the
       greatest leverage to apply to Y in a
       bargaining or in a confrontation
       situation.)

In the following example, we leave out processing details to concentrate attention on the discussion of how the five counterplanning rules cooperate.

*(INTERPRET US-CONSERVATIVE)

INPUT STORY: Cuba sent troops to aid the MPLA faction in Angola.

Q1: Why did Cuba send troops to Angola?
A1: BECAUSE RUSSIA PROBABLY TOLD CUBA TO SEND TROOPS, AND CUBA WANTS COUNTRIES TO BE COMMUNIST.

Q2: What should the US do about it?
A2: THE US SHOULD MAKE RUSSIA WITHDRAW THE CUBAN TROOPS.

In order to interpret this event, POLITICS used the military-aid script, information about the Angolan conflict, and the US goal trees. The following plan-interference scenario was inferred: The US should have been planning a military victory for UNITA, the non-Communist faction. (The US goal of UNITA's being in control of Angola was already in POLITICS's memory from the interpretation of a previous event.) Cuba's military aid plan blocks a mediating precondition for the US plan, namely that UNITA be stronger than the MPLA. Therefore, there is a plan-conflict situation between the US and Cuba. The mediating precondition triggers counterplanning strategy 3 as a possible explanation for future US actions. In establishing how Cuba's plan interacts with Cuba's goal trees, POLITICS discovers that Cuba could have been servicing two goals: the spread of Communism and acting as an agency to pursue Soviet goals. The latter goal is a subgoal for Cuba's getting Soviet aid, which is in turn a subgoal of all Cuban preservation goals. Cuba needs Soviet aid to survive. Having understood this much, POLITICS, working in an explanatory mode, is satisfied with its interpretation of the event. If there were more actions mentioned in the event, they would be interpreted in light of the expected counterplanning that would arise from the plan conflict.

Question 2 forces POLITICS to function in a predictive mode, that is, to generate a plausible counterplan from a United States perspective. Because the Cuban plan services multiple goals, strategy 5 constrains POLITICS from attempting to negotiate directly with Cuba, except as a last resort. Strategy 3 generates three possible counterplans: re-establish the mediating precondition (i.e., make UNITA stronger), choose a new plan to fulfill the US goal (i.e., put UNITA in control of Angola), or block the Cuban plan (i.e., recall the Cuban troops). The best alternatives in the counterplanning strategy are put first, as judged by previous experience. In its predictive mode, POLITICS processes each alternative until one course of action is found that fulfills the US goals. Making a country or a political faction stronger is the goal of the military-aid script.

POLITICS checks the preconditions of suggested plans of action. There are different types of preconditions that help to focus the counterplanning process, as discussed earlier. One mediating precondition for military aid on the part of the United States is Congressional approval. This precondition cannot be met, because there is a situational rule that says that Congress will veto any action which would involve the US in a foreign war. Therefore, this counterplanning alternative is abandoned; the next one (generating a new plan) also fails; and the third alternative is tried.

How does POLITICS counterplan to block Cuba's troop buildups? Strategy 5 states that since the Cuban plan is multi-purposed, Cuba is unlikely to compromise or negotiate. Strategy 6 is invoked since there were no applicable strategies to directly counterplan against Cuba's plan. Strategy 6 suggests direct counterplanning against Cuba's goals. This is refined by strategy 7 to be counterplanning against Cuba's most important goal. The Soviet-Agency goal is judged to be the more important one because it is a necessary subgoal to Cuba's highest level Preservation goals. Hence, POLITICS decides that the US should counterplan to block Cuba's goal of being a Soviet agency. Strategy 4 is triggered at this point (the Soviet Union is considered an external cause of the US-Cuban conflict) and POLITICS generates the application of strategy 4 as an answer to the second queston. That is, POLITICS suggests focusing the US counterplanning effort against the Soviet Union, in order to remove the most important cause of the Cuban troop buildup.

AN ANNOTATED EXAMPLE OF THE POLITICS SYSTEM

This section presents a detailed annotated run of the POLITICS system. The central motif is the cooperation of different knowledge sources brought together in an integrated understanding paradigm. Basically, the knowledge source that has sufficient data to perform its function is the one applied at each step of the processing.

Thus, the control flow is determined by the availability of data, not predetermined by the programmer. This method makes the most use of all available information at every step of the processing, rather than insisting on a rigid control structure independent of the system's knowledge state (e.g., deferring semantics until syntax is done, or deferring inference until an immediate meaning has been established by the semantics).

A Detailed US-Conservative Interpretation

POLITICS must incorporate an ideology before embarking on its event-interpretation process, which in turn must be completed before it can answer questions. POLITICS starts by reading into memory the US-conservative goal trees.

Each goal is either a preservation goal (P-goal) or an achievement goal (A-goal). P-goals are existing states of the world that must be maintained, and A-goals are desired changes to the present state of the world. If a P-goal is violated by an event, then that goal is replaced by an A-goal to re-achieve the violated state. The United States conservative goal of Communist containment and its subgoal of increased US military strength are encoded as follows:

```
[GOAL PART (*US*)
       GOALSTATE
            ((ACTOR (#POLITY GOVTYP (*COMMUNIST*))
                 IS (*PCONT* VAL (0))
            OBJECT (#GROUP NUMBER (*INDEF*)
                      MEMBER (#POLITY
                                 GOVTYP (*COMMUNIST*
                                         MODE
                                         (NEG))))))

       TOK G0
       GOALTYPE *PGOAL*
       SUPERGOALS (NIL)
       SUBGOALS (G1 G4 G5)
       GREATER-IMPORTANCE (NIL)
       LESSER-IMPORTANCE (G2 G3)]
```

```
[GOAL PART (*US*)
      GOALSTATE
        ((ACTOR    (*US*)
           TOWARD (*STRENGTH*
                     TYPE (*MILIT*)
                     INC (*POSVAL*)
                     VAL (*SPEC* GREATER
                                 (*STRENGTH* PART (*RUSSIA*)
                                             TYPE
                                             (*MILIT*))))))
      TOK G1
      GOALTYPE *AGOAL*
      SUPERGOALS (G0)
      SUBGOALS (G8 G9)
      GREATER-IMPORTANCE (NIL)
      LESSER-IMPORTANCE (G12 G19)]
```

Each goal in the ideology encodes the desired goal state or state transition and its relationships to other goals in the ideology. The first goal above is the US-conservative goal of Communist containment. We may read the goal state as follows: "The United States wants to keep all non-Communist countries free from Communist domination." Since Communist containment is the most important US goal, it is not a subgoal to other goals (i.e., it has no "supergoals"), and it has no greater-importance goals. There are, however, subgoals to Communist containment, such as military strength (goal G1). There are also less important goals in the US-conservative goal tree (goals G2 and G3). For instance, goal G2 is the preservation of free enterprise in the US.

The military strength goal state reads: "The United States should increase its military strength to be greater than Russian military strength." The relation between this goal and other goals in the US-conservative goal tree is defined by the subgoal, supergoal, greater-importance, and lesser-importance links.

The Initial Interpretation Phase

```
*****************************************************************

         Start of US-conservative POLITICS interpretation.

*****************************************************************

         PTYCON LOG FILE      1-Mar-78 2:44:20

PTYCON> CONNECT (TO SUBJOB) 1
[CONNECTED TO SUBJOB POL(1)]
```

Computer Processing	Annotation
*(INTERPRET US-CONSERVATIVE) INCORPORATING US-CONSERVATIVE IDEOLOGY GOAL TREES... INITIATING PARSER... DONE	Before processing any events, POLITICS incorporates the goal trees that encode a political ideology.

INPUT STORY:
  The United States Congress
  voted to fund the Trident
  submarine project.
 	
PARSING...
	The input event is typed in English to the
	POLITICS parser. Parsing in POLITICS is part
	of an integrated memory process. Inferences
	about voting and funding occur during the
	"parse".

...	After parsing "The United States Congress voted to fund..." the following inference occurs:

MEMORY ASSERTS $FUND
PRIMARY ACTION: ($FUND)
  INSTR ($PARLIAMENT-PROC)
  INSTR ($VOTE)
  EMBEDDED (*ATRANS*)
 	
...
	Voting, part of $PARLIAMENTARY-PROC, is
	not interesting since Congress always does it.
	$FUND however is interesting, involving an
	ATRANS of money.

((ACTOR (#ORG TYPE (*GOVT*)
          NAME (CONGRESS)
          PART (*US*)
          REF (DEF)
          TOK ORG0)
  <=> (*ATRANS*)
  OBJECT (*MONEY* AMOUNT
              (SUFF))
   TO (#ORG INVOLVING
      (#WEAPON
      TYPE (*SUBMARINE*)
      NAME (TRIDENT)
      REF (INDEF)
      TOK WEAPON0))
      TOK ORG1)
  FROM (*UNSPEC* REL ORG0)
  INSTR ($PARLIAMENT-PROC
        TRACK ($VOTE))
TIME ((AFTER NOW X))
MODE (*INTENTIONAL*))
TOK CON9)
	After parsing "... the Trident Submarine
	Project", POLITICS now has the fully
	instantiated event.
	
	The vote and parliamentary process scripts are
	instrumental to the funding event.

$FUND is the same script whose context-dependent rules we discussed in an earlier section. The representation of the main event in $FUND may be paraphrased as follows: An agency of the US government, called the Congress, has the intention of transferring money (from an unspecified source) to another agency which has something to do with weapons whose category is submarines and whose name is Trident. There is a note that the amount of money transferred is sufficient for its (as yet unspecified) purpose. This last fact comes from the dictionary definition of the word "fund". One should note that the word "fund" in the input event was not necessary to identify the $FUND script. The $FUND script was activated because the input event was an intentional transfer of money by a government agency. For example, the following two events are also recognized as instances of the $FUND script by POLITICS:

1. President Carter decided to allocate money for the jobs program.
2. The Senate budget provides for production of the cruise missile.

Since we are understanding the event as an instance of the $FUND script, we need to instantiate all the roles in the fund script. Instantiating these roles is essentially equivalent to answering the first four questions below. The fifth question is always asked in an ideological interpretation. As the following questions are answered by POLITICS, it uses the answers to integrate the event representation into its memory model.

1. What agency will receive the money?
2. What will the money be used for?
3. Where did the money come from?
   [already answered by the input]
4. What is the connection between the Trident submarines and the agency receiving the money?
5. What important implications (if any) does this action have on any high level US goal?

These questions are answered either from the input event or by context-dependent inference rules (also called "specification" rules when their purpose is to find a filler for a script role).

Ideological Interpretation Phase

We continue with the annotated POLITICS example, entering the ideological interpretation phase. (Phases in the understanding process are expository devices. We say that the initial phase terminates when goal analysis and counterplanning strategies have sufficient information to work on, and may therefore be applied. However, there is no actual change in POLITICS' processes.)

INFERENCE: $FUNDEE =
(#ARMEDFORCES PART (*US*)
                RANK (COMMAND)
                TOK AF0)

Trident submarines are weapons, therefore used by the military. Thus, &FUNDEE is probably a military agency.

...

INFERENCE: $FUND-CON =
((<=>
 ($CONSTRUCT
   ACTOR (#ARMEDFORCES
                PART (*US*)
                RANK (COMMAND)
                TOK AF0)
   ENABLEMENT (*MONEY*
                AMOUNT (SUFF))
   OBJECT (#WEAPON
                TYPE (*SUBMARINE*)
                NAME (TRIDENT)
                TOK WEAPON0)))
 MODE (*INTENTIONAL*)
 TIME ((AFTER NOW X)))

POLITICS Infers that funding the submarines is sufficient to enable them to be built

INTERMEDIATE RESULT INFERENCES.

((ACTOR (*US*) ISTOWARD
        (*POWER*
         TYPE (*MILITARY*)
         VAL (N)
         INC (POS))
 TOK CON13)

There are a small number of situational inferences that apply to the entire domain of international politics.

One such inference says that if a country builds or acquires weapons, it will be militarily stronger.

SEARCHING *US* GOAL TREE . . .

(GOAL G4 MATCHED)
G4 IS A SUBGOAL OF G0

((ACTOR (#POLITY
         TYPE (*COMMUNIST*)))
 TOWARD
 (*CONTROL*
   TYPE (OR (*POLITICAL*)
            (*MILITARY*)
            (*ECONOMIC*))
   OBJECT (#POLITY
            TYPE
            (*NONCOMMUNIST*))
   VAL (0)))

Increased military strength is found to be one of the goals in the US-conservative goal tree. It is a subgoal of Communist containment, the highest level US-conservative goal. Thus, POLITICS explains the US decision to build the Trident submarines in terms of the increase in military strength.

INTERPRETATION COMPLETED,
READY TO ACCEPT QUESTIONS.

Since no active goal conflicts were detected, POLITICS does not invoke counterplanning.

A goal directed inference process may be triggered from two sources of knowledge. The first source is contextual knowledge, encoded as scripts. For instance, in $FUND the FUNDER gives the money to the FUNDEE with the intention that the FUNDEE will fulfill the purpose that the FUNDER had in mind. This goal is usually well defined in terms of our full world knowledge, but it is poorly defined in terms of the linguistic realization of the Trident submarine event. The input event did not mention that the submarines would be built, nor did it mention why Congress may want the submarines. Building the submarines is a goal of the US armed forces, a fact that POLITICS inferred from knowledge about why projects are funded and submarines are built. This goal is instrumental to the ultimate purpose of the US Congress. That is, the scripts tell us *how* Congress intends to make the Trident submarines come into existence, not *why* Congress chose to do so. The goals that guide the actions of Congress are inferred from the ideological US goal tree. Thus, both contextual and ideological knowledge are necessary to model a person's interpretation of a political event.

The Question-Answering Phase

Questions are categorized into classes of question types (Lehnert, 1978) as part of the parsing process. The question types tell us the nature of the information sought. A discrimination network is used to test the question type and the body of the question in order to see where in memory to search for the answer (or, if it is not found in memory, what further inferences or counterplanning strategies to apply). Finally, the memory search is performed or the suggested inferences are applied. The first two questions in the question-answer dialog below are answered by searching the interpretation of the event. The third question requires counterplanning.

---

*What did the US Congress do
  this for?

PARSING...

  ...

SUGGESTED QTYP: GOAL-EVENT

APPLYING QSEARCH D-NET TO:

((ACTOR ORG0 <=> (*DO*))
  REL (*SPEC*)
  TOK CON15)

  ...

MATCHED CON15
EXTRACTING (*SELF*)
($FUND &FUNDER ORG0
    &FUNDEE AF0

Parsing and question classification proceed simultaneously. "What for" is matched as a split idiom that means a request for the purpose of a specified event.

POLITICS finds the Congressional funding event to be the main event, with Congress as the actor.

```
   &FUND-CON CON9
   &MONEY MONEY0
   TOK SCR2)
```

EXTRACTING (LAST)
CON13

CON13 is the purpose for the funding event.
CON13 is the US goal of increasing the military power of its armed forces.

THE ANSWER IS:
```
((ACTOR (*US*) ISTOWARD
        (*POWER*
            TYPE (*MILITARY*)
            VAL (N)
            INC (POS)))
 TOK CON13)
```

THE UNITED STATES CONGRESS
WANTS THE UNITED STATES ARMED
FORCES TO BE STRONGER.

The answer is generated in English by a template-based generator.

*Why should the US be stronger?

The next question involves a search for a goal.

PARSING . . .

```
((ACTOR (*US*) ISTOWARD
        (*POWER*
            TYPE (*MILITARY*)
            VAL (N)
            INC (POS)))
 TOK CON16)
```

CON16 MATCHES CON13
CON13 MATCHES G4

CON16, the meaning of the question, matches CON13, which was inferred during the understanding phase and identified with G4—the US military strength goal.

EXTRACTING (SUPERGOAL) OF G4
G0

```
((ACTOR (#POLITY
        TYPE (* COMMUNIST*))
    TOWARD
   (*CONTROL*
    TYPE (OR (*POLITICAL*)
             (*MILITARY*)
             (*ECONOMIC*))
    OBJECT (#POLITY
            TYPE
            (*NONCOMMUNIST*))
    VAL (0))))
```

The goal dominating military strength is Communist containment.

THE ANSWER IS:
```
 ((CON CON13 ENABLE G0))
```

THE UNITED STATES ARMED
FORCES SHOULD BE STRONG TO
STOP COMMUNIST EXPANSION.

*What should the US do if
 Russia also builds nuclear
 submarines?

 . . .

HYPOTHETICAL SCENARIO EXPECTED

((<=>
($CONSTRUCT
  ACTOR (*RUSSIA*)
  OBJECT (#WEAPON
          TYPE (*SUBMARINE*)
          TOK WEAPON1))
TIME ((AFTER NOW X))
TOK CON19)

INTERMEDIATE RESULT
INFERENCES.

((ACTOR (*RUSSIA*) ISTOWARD
         (*POWER*
              TYPE (*MILITARY*)
              VAL (N)
              INC (POS)))
TOK CON20)

TWO ACTORS WITH ACTIVE GOALS

SEARCHING GOAL CONFLICTS . . .

(MUTUAL-EXCLUSION
  ((*US* . G3)
   (*RUSSIA* . G35)))

  . . .

((<=>
($CONSTRUCT
  ACTOR (*US*)
  OBJECT (#WEAPON
          TYPE (*SUBMARINE*)
          NUMBER (*MANY*)
             TOK (WEAPON2)))
TIME ((AFTER NOW X))
MODE (*INTENTIONAL*)
TOK CON21)

  THE UNITED STATES SHOULD
  BUILD MORE SUBMARINES.

The third question is more interesting; the
answer is not to be found in the previous
interpretation of the event. Counterplanning is
required.

A query about an action followed by the word
"if" suggests that a hypothetical situation may
follow.

This represents the concept "Russia building
submarines" from the question.

The general inferences conclude that Russia will
be stronger.

POLITICS finds that the US goal of being
militarily stronger than Russia is mutually
exclusive with the Russian goal of being stronger
than the US.

The counterplanning concludes by extracting a
means of accomplishing the US military strength
goal: simply build submarines faster than the
Russians.

    The question-answering process not only queries memory structures built in
the event interpretation phase, but also may reactivate the inference process. We

saw the third question activating script application to understand Russia's building submarines and the counterplanning process to infer the ideological US response to the hypothetical Russian action.

Information about the goals of the actors is often used to advantage in the language analysis. In the third question the initial interpretation assumed that the submarines built by the Russians were for the same immediate purpose as the US Trident submarines, increasing military strength. (We humans make the same assumption. For example, it does not occur to us that the Russian submarines might be research or rescue vehicles.) Hence, the parser is able to interpret the question "What should the US do if Russia also builds submarines" as "What should the US response be to the Russian goal of increasing their military strength by building submarines," a much more concrete formulation of the task that the counterplanning strategies should address.

12 Micro POLITICS

INTRODUCTION

McPOL differs from POLITICS in a number of important ways. There is no parser for McPOL, although one can be added by using the McELI program (see Chapter 14). This is both an easy and worthwhile exercise. However the final result will be a two-module system, while the real POLITICS program stresses the unity of parsing and interpretation.

McPOL has only an abstract example of a goal hierarchy and inference rule system. In it, the United States wants to stop Russia from taking over the world, and its subgoals are simply that the United States be strong and Russia be weak. Russia's goal hierarchy is a mirror image of the one for the United States. The real POLITICS system has much more complex goal trees for both sides. Furthermore, POLITICS has a lot of knowledge about different political entities (it has to, in order to deal with real headlines). McPOL knows nothing more than that the United States and Russia are enemies.

McPOL does try to capture the three phases of understanding: bottom-up inference of the intent of an act, top-down integration of the intent with an actor's goal hierarchy, and, finally, the interaction of the act with other actors' goals. However, McPOL does all of this in a one-pass understanding of the input event. In POLITICS, much of the reasoning is triggered only when questions are asked. Thus McPOL predicts that submarine building by the United States strengthens the United States militarily, which conflicts with Russian goals. Furthermore, McPOL infers several things Russia could do to remove the conflict. POLITICS does not activate any of this inferencing until asked a hypothetical question about what might happen, or what should be done in the event of some new occurrence.

One final note should be made contrasting McPOL with McSAM and McPAM. While the syntax of the CD forms is the same for all three programs, McPOL uses an extended set of predicates. The example used has VOTE, FUND and BUILD, none of which are standard Conceptual Dependency acts. This is because understanding the political domain requires more complex knowledge structures dealing with power and authority relationships. These new predicates are like scripts in that they are chunks of knowledge which, in the real POLITICS system, are represented in turn by the basic CD primitives. For example, in the real POLITICS program, FUND is not only a predicate but is also understood to be an ATRANS of money to one agency by some other agency. In McPOL this underlying knowledge is omitted. The set of predicates appropriate to the political domain are discussed in more detail in Carbonell (1979a).

SAMPLE OUTPUT

The following is a log of the McPOL program, applied to the CD form for "The US voted to fund building submarines":

```
[PH: Initiation. 7-Feb-80 2:48PM]

. . .

(PROCESS-CD US-CD)

Input is
    (VOTE (ACTOR US)
        (OBJECT (FUND (ACTOR US)
                    (OBJECT  (BUILD  (ACTOR  US)
                                (OBJECT   SUBMARINES)))))


Inferred goal is
    (INCREASE (ACTOR US) (OBJECT MILITARY-STRENGTH) (MODE POS))

US had goal
    (INCREASE (ACTOR US) (OBJECT MILITARY-STRENGTH) (MODE POS))

    which is a subgoal of
    (CONTROL (ACTOR RUSSIA) (OBJECT WORLD) (MODE NEG))

Looking for conflicts from US having goal
    (INCREASE (ACTOR US) (OBJECT MILITARY-STRENGTH) (MODE POS))

Conflict found—RUSSIA has goal
    (INCREASE (ACTOR US) (OBJECT MILITARY-STRENGTH) (MODE NEG))

RUSSIA could resolve conflict by
    (CAUSE (ANTE (DO (ACTOR RUSSIA)))
            (CONSEQ (INCREASE (ACTOR US)
                        (OBJECT MILITARY-STRENGTH)
                        (MODE NEG))))
```

RUSSIA could resolve conflict by
    (INCREASE (ACTOR RUSSIA) (OBJECT MILITARY-STRENGTH)
    (MANNER FAST))

[PH: Termination. 7–Feb–80 2:49PM. PS:<RIESBECK>TWELVE.LOG.8]

FLOW CHARTS

The flow charts in Figs. 12.1 and 12.2 show the two central functions in McPOL: INTERPRET and SEARCH-GOAL-TREE. The flow chart for INTERPRET includes the flow of control for its three subparts: INFER-REASON, INTEGRATE, and COUNTER-PLAN.

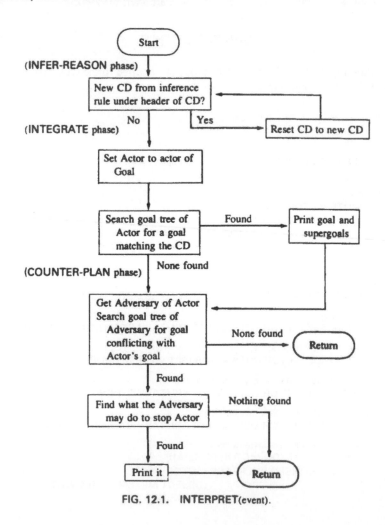

FIG. 12.1.   INTERPRET(event).

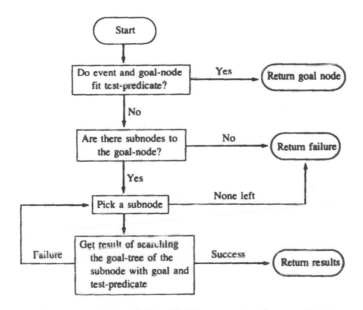

FIG. 12.2.   SEARCH-GOAL-TREE(event,goal-node,test-predicate).

THE PROGRAM

```
- **********************************************************************
-                      MICRO POLITICS PROGRAM
- **********************************************************************

(DE PROCESS-CD (CD)
 (MSG T "Input is")
 (SPRINT CD 4)
 (MSG T)
 (INTERPRET CD)
```

" INTERPRET is the main function. Given a CD, it first does
" bottom up inferences (e.g., "voting to do something implies doing
" it"), then it searches the actor's goal tree for a match to the
" last inferred item (e.g., "US increases strength" matches a subgoal
" of "US prevent Russian control of the world"), and finally it looks
" for conflicts and resolutions with the goals of the actor's
" adversary (e.g., "US increases strength conflicts with Russia's
" subgoal of US not increasing strength, which could be resolved if
" Russia stopped the US or if Russia increased its own strength
" faster").

```
(DE INTERPRET (CD)
 (LET (NEW-CD (INFER-REASON CD))
  (MSG T "Inferred goal is ")
  (SPRINT NEW-CD 4)
```

```
(MSG T)
(LET (ACTOR (FILLER:ROLE 'ACTOR NEW-CD))
 (COND ((CONSP ACTOR) (SETQ ACTOR (HEADER:CD ACTOR))))
 (COND ((NULL ACTOR) (MSG T "No actor found" T))
       (T (INTEGRATE ACTOR NEW-CD)
          (COUNTER-PLAN ACTOR NEW-CD]
```

¨ INFER-REASON does bottom-up inferences on a CD. The inference
¨ rules are stored under the various predicates (e.g., under VOTE,
¨ FUND, etc.). Each new CD inferred becomes the source of the next
¨ inference.

```
(DE INFER-REASON (CD)
 (LOOP (INITIAL NEW-CD NIL)
       (WHILE (SETQ NEW-CD (FIND-RULE CD)))
       (DO (SETQ CD NEW-CD))
       (RESULT CD]
```

¨ FIND-RULE finds the first rule that infers something from the CD.
¨ The rules are stored under the head predicate of the CD.

```
(DE FIND-RULE (CD)
 (LET (NEW-CD NIL)
  (FOR (RULE IN (RULES:HEADER (HEADER:CD CD)))
     (EXISTS (SETQ NEW-CD (APPLY-RULE CD RULE))))
  NEW-CD]
```

¨ APPLY-RULE matches the CD to the test pattern of the rule. If this
¨ works it instantiates the action pattern.

```
(DE APPLY-RULE (CD RULE)
 (LET (BINDINGS (COMPATIBLE (TEST:RULE RULE) CD))
  (COND (BINDINGS (INSTANTIATE (ACTION:RULE RULE) BINDINGS]
```

¨ INTEGRATE searches the actor's goal tree for a goal matching the
¨ CD. If one is found it prints a list of the super-goals.

```
(DE INTEGRATE (ACTOR CD)
 (LET (GOAL (GET ACTOR 'TOP-GOAL) MATCH-GOAL NIL)
  (COND ((NULL GOAL) (MSG T "No goals known for " ACTOR T))
        ((SETQ MATCH-GOAL (SEARCH-GOAL-TREE CD GOAL 'COMPATIBLE))
         (PRINT-SUPER-GOALS ACTOR MATCH-GOAL))
        (T (MSG T ACTOR " had no higher goals" T]
```

¨ PRINT-SUPER-GOALS prints the super-goals of GOAL.

```
(DE PRINT-SUPER-GOALS (ACTOR GOAL)
 (MSG T ACTOR " had goal")
 (LOOP (DO (SPRINT (GET GOAL 'FORM) 4) (MSG T))
       (WHILE (SETQ GOAL (GET GOAL 'SUPER-GOAL)))
       (DO (MSG T "   which is a subgoal of")))
 (MSG T]
```

¨ SEARCH-GOAL-TREE finds the first goal in the goal tree that
¨ satisfies the TESTFN. This does a depth-first left-to-right search
¨ of the tree.

```
(DE SEARCH-GOAL-TREE (CD GOAL TESTFN)
 (LET (FORM (GET GOAL 'FORM))
  (COND ((NULL FORM) NIL)
        ((APPLY TESTFN (LIST FORM CD)) GOAL)
        ((FOR (SUB-GOAL IN (GET GOAL 'SUB-GOALS))
            (EXISTS
              (SETQ GOAL (SEARCH-GOAL-TREE CD SUB-GOAL TESTFN))))
        GOAL]
```

¨ COUNTER-PLAN searches the goal tree of X's adversary for a goal
¨ that conflicts with GX. If one is found, then the methods Y might
¨ use against X's goal are looked for.

```
(DE COUNTER-PLAN (X GX)
 (MSG T "Looking for conflicts from " X " having goal")
 (SPRINT GX 4)
 (MSG T)
 (LET (Y (GET X 'ADVERSARY))
  (COND ((NULL Y) (MSG T "No adversary for " X))
        (T (LET (GY (FIND-CONFLICT Y GX))
           (COND (GY (MSG T "Conflict found—" Y " has goal")
                    (SPRINT GY 4)
                    (MSG T)
                    (FIND-COUNTER Y GX]
```

¨ FIND-CONFLICT searches Y's goal tree for a conflict with GX.

```
(DE FIND-CONFLICT (Y GX)
 (LET (GOAL (SEARCH-GOAL-TREE GX (GET Y 'TOP-GOAL) 'CONFLICT))
  (COND (GOAL (GET GOAL 'FORM]
```

¨ FIND-COUNTER prints all the conflict resolution rules that apply
¨ to Y's conflict with GX.

```
¨
(DE FIND-COUNTER (Y GX)
 (LET (CD NIL PAT (LIST 'CONFLICT (LIST 'ACTOR Y) (LIST 'GOAL GX)))
  (FOR (RULE IN *COUNTER-RULES*)
     (WHEN (SETQ CD (APPLY-RULE PAT RULE)))
     (DO (MSG T Y " could resolve conflict by ")
        (SPRINT CD 3)
        (MSG T]
```

¨ **
¨   DATA STRUCTURES AND ACCESS FUNCTIONS
¨ **

¨ These are the representations for "US votes funds to build
¨ submarines" and "Russia builds submarines."

```
(SETQ US-CD '(VOTE (ACTOR US)
                (OBJECT (FUND (ACTOR US)
                          (OBJECT (BUILD (ACTOR US)
                                     (OBJECT SUBMARINES]
```

```
(SETQ RUSSIA-CD '(BUILD (ACTOR RUSSIA) (OBJECT SUBMARINES)]
```

˜ All the inference rules are of the form
˜   (test-pattern action-pattern).
˜ When the test-pattern matches a CD, the action-pattern is
˜ instantiated (according to the bindings from the test match) and
˜ returned.

```
(DE TEST:RULE (RULE) (CAR RULE]
(DE ACTION:RULE (RULE) (CADR RULE]
```

˜ CD Predicates are atoms with a RULES property pointing to a list of
˜ inference rules. (ADD-RULES atom rule rule...) adds inference
˜ rules to a CD predicate and (RULES:HEADER atom) gets them.

```
(DF ADD-RULES (L)
 (PUTPROP (CAR L) (CDR L) 'RULES)
 (CAR L]
```

```
(DE RULES:HEADER (X) (AND X (GET X 'RULES]
```

˜ Here are the rules for voting, funding and building. The first two
˜ infer the object voted for or funded, i.e., "US voted to fund
˜ building submarines" means that 1) funding will occur, and
˜ 2) building will occur. BUILD infers that military strength is
˜ being increased.

```
(ADD-RULES VOTE ((VOTE (ACTOR ?X) (OBJECT ?Y)) ?Y]
(ADD-RULES FUND ((FUND (ACTOR ?X) (OBJECT ?Y)) ?Y]
(ADD-RULES BUILD ((BUILD (ACTOR ?X) (OBJECT ?Y))
                        (INCREASE (ACTOR ?X) (OBJECT MILITARY-STRENGTH)
                        (MODE POS]
```

˜ Define US and Russia to be mutual adversaries.

```
(DEFPROP US RUSSIA ADVERSARY)
(DEFPROP RUSSIA US ADVERSARY)
```

˜ *COUNTER-RULES* are called to find a way to stop a goal. The
˜ two here both try to achieve the same goal: that of the
˜ opponent getting stronger. One solution is to stop them and the
˜ other is to beat them to the punch. The form of a conflict
˜ rule is (test action) where the test has the form
˜ (CONFLICT (ACTOR...) (GOAL...)).

```
(SETQ *COUNTER-RULES*
      '(
        ((CONFLICT (ACTOR ?X)
                   (GOAL (INCREASE (ACTOR ?Y)
                                   (OBJECT MILITARY-STRENGTH)
                                   (MODE POS))))
         (CAUSE (ANTE (DO (ACTOR ?X)))
                (CONSEQ (INCREASE (ACTOR ?Y)
                                  (OBJECT MILITARY-STRENGTH)
                                  (MODE NEG)))))
```

```
((CONFLICT (ACTOR ?X)
          (GOAL (INCREASE (ACTOR ?Y)
                          (OBJECT MILITARY-STRENGTH)
                          (MODE POS))))
    (INCREASE (ACTOR ?X) (OBJECT MILITARY-STRENGTH)
              (MANNER FAST)))
))
```

```
¯ DEFINE-GOAL-TREE (and its subfunction MAKE-GOAL) allows us to define
¯ the goal tree for an actor by typing:
¯ (DEFINE-GOAL-TREE actor
¯   (top-goal CD-form
¯           (sub-goal CD-form (sub-goals...))
¯           (sub-goal CD-form (sub-goals...))
¯           ...))
```

```
¯ The top level goal is saved under the actor. Supergoal and subgoal
¯ links are saved with the goal names. The CDs are stored under the
¯ property FORM.
```

```
(DF DEFINE-GOAL-TREE (L)
(PUTPROP (CAR L)
         (MAKE-GOAL (CADR L) NIL)
         'TOP-GOAL)
(CAR L)
```

```
(DE MAKE-GOAL (L SUPER-GOAL)
(PUTPROP (CAR L) (CADR L) 'FORM)
(PUTPROP (CAR L) SUPER-GOAL 'SUPER-GOAL)
(PUTPROP (CAR L)
         (FOR (Y IN (CDDR L)) (SAVE (MAKE-GOAL Y (CAR L))))
         'SUB-GOALS)
(CAR L)
```

```
¯ We define the US goal tree to say that stopping Russia from
¯ controlling the world is on top, and the subgoals are the US
¯ getting stronger and Russia getting weaker.
```

```
(DEFINE-GOAL-TREE US
(US-G1 (CONTROL (ACTOR RUSSIA) (OBJECT WORLD) (MODE NEG))
       (US-G2 (INCREASE (ACTOR US) (OBJECT MILITARY-STRENGTH)
                        (MODE POS)))
       (US-G3 (INCREASE (ACTOR RUSSIA)
                        (OBJECT MILITARY-STRENGTH)
                        (MODE NEG)
```

```
¯ We define the Russian goal tree to say that controlling the world
¯ is on top, and the subgoals are Russia getting stronger and the US
¯ getting weaker.
```

```
(DEFINE-GOAL-TREE RUSSIA
(RUS-G1 (CONTROL (ACTOR RUSSIA) (OBJECT WORLD))
       (RUS-G2   (INCREASE   (ACTOR RUSSIA)
                             (OBJECT MILITARY-STRENGTH)
                             (MODE POS)))
```

```
(RUS-G3 (INCREASE (ACTOR US)
                 (OBJECT MILITARY-STRENGTH)
                 (MODE NEG]
```

˜ COMPATIBLE returns true if PAT matches CD.

(DE COMPATIBLE (PAT CD) (MATCH PAT CD NIL]

˜ CONFLICT returns true if PAT conflicts with CD. Defining conflict
˜ is an open problem. Here we make the MODE of PAT a variable and
˜ match PAT against CD. If they match but the MODE in CD is not
˜ equal to the MODE in PAT, then a conflict exists.

```
(DE CONFLICT (PAT CD)
 (LET (VAR-PAT (SETROLE 'MODE '?MODE PAT) BINDINGS NIL)
  (AND (SETQ BINDINGS (MATCH VAR-PAT CD NIL))
       (NOT (EQUAL (FILLER:ROLE 'MODE BINDINGS)
                   (FILLER:ROLE 'MODE PAT]
```

EXERCISES

1. When McPOL sees that the US is building submarines, it infers in the counterplanning phase that Russia may try to increase its own military strength. The original POLITICS program inferred more specifically that Russia might build submarines itself. However, McPOL can't do this because when it infers that building submarines increases military strength, it throws away the CD for building submarines.
   a. Change INFER-REASON so that all the CDs that are inferred, along with the original one, are saved in the list *INFERENCES*.
   b. Define a new function, MULTI-INFER, that takes a list of CD forms and a list of rules, and applies each rule to each CD form. Save each CD that leads to one or more inferences, plus the inferences, in a list of the form:

   ((CD inference inference...)
    (CD inference inference...)...)

   MULTI-INFER should return this list. If no inferences result from any CD, then MULTI-INFER should return NIL.
   c. Change FIND-COUNTER to use MULTI-INFER to find possible counter plans for the different CDs in *INFERENCES*. This will involve making a list of (CONFLICT...) forms from the list of CDs in *INFERENCES*, and also changing the output messages to specify what counter plans exist for each CD.
   d. Add a rule to *COUNTER-RULES* that says that a counter plan to an adversary's building something is to build it yourself.
2. Add the bottom-up inference rules necessary for McPOL to interpret "The US Congress is expected to approve the Panama Canal treaty," from the

US-conservative viewpoint. Rather than deal with what "expect" means and what the contents of the Panama Canal treaty are, assume the input CD is:

```
(VOTE (ACTOR US)
      (OBJECT (CONTROL (ACTOR US)
                       (OBJECT PANAMA-CANAL)
                       (MODE NEG)))
      (MODE MAYBE))
```

which represents "The US may vote to relinquish control of the Panama Canal." From this, McPOL should infer that the US will become weaker militarily, using a rule that says that giving up control leads to military weakness.

3. In Exercise (2), McPOL was given a CD that didn't fit the goal tree for the main actor, but it did nothing more than recognize this fact. Clearly more should be done. First, there should be a recognition of a goal conflict between what the US did and what the US should do. Second, there should be a recognition that the US has played into Russia's hands, so to speak. The POLITICS program, for example, using conservative ideology, inferred that Russia might try to take over the canal itself.

   a. Change INTEGRATE so that when no match is found in the actor's goal tree, INTEGRATE will look for a conflict instead. If a conflict is found, it should be printed, with a message saying that the actor has done something counterproductive. Finally INTEGRATE should call the function RESOLVE-CONFLICT with the actor and action as arguments.

   b. Define RESOLVE-CONFLICT to use MULTI-INFER and a list of conflict resolution rules called *CONFLICT-RULES* to generate and print actions that the actor should do instead of the one it is doing.

   c. Define the list *CONFLICT-RULES* to have at least a rule that says that if an actor may vote to do something, then something should be done to try to make the vote come out negative instead.

   d. Change COUNTER-PLAN so that if no conflict is found between an actor's action and the adversary's goal tree, then COUNTER-PLAN will look for a match. If one is found, then it should be printed, with a message saying that the adversary has been helped by the actor's action. Finally COUNTER-PLAN should call the function TAKE-ADVANTAGE, with the adversary and the action as arguments.

   e. Define TAKE-ADVANTAGE to use MULTI-INFER and the list of rules *ACHIEVE-RULES* to generate and print the actions that the adversary may do, now that one of his goals has been achieved for him.

   f. Define *ACHIEVE-RULES* to have at least a rule that says that if someone relinquishes control of an area, then the adversary should take over control of it.

13 Conceptual Analysis of Natural Language

Lawrence Birnbaum
Mallory Selfridge

INTRODUCTION

One of the crucial issues to be faced by any theory of natural language is the process of mapping natural language text into the memory structures that represent the meaning of that text. We call this process Conceptual Analysis. This chapter has two complementary goals. First, we hope to provide a clear introduction to conceptual analysis. Second, we will present the results of our own research concerning some of the unresolved problems in language analysis—of which there are many.

Research on conceptual analysis has been proceeding for several years now, starting with the work reported in Schank et al. (1970) and Riesbeck (1975). We have built on that work, concentrating on some important questions that we feel have not been sufficiently investigated:

1. What is the role of syntax in a semantics-oriented language analysis process?
2. How can we achieve a flexible balance of top-down and bottom-up processing?
3. How does short-term memory structure affect the analysis process?
4. What is the right vocabulary (formalism) for expressing the processing knowledge that the system has?
5. What are the criteria on the performance of a word-sense disambiguation process which we should strive to achieve?

Our work has provided some answers to the above questions, which have in turn enabled us to construct more flexible algorithms, capable of analyzing the kinds of complex noun groups and multiple-clause inputs found in most text.

318

Background

The goal of the conceptual analysis process is to map natural language input into a representation of its meaning. This goal differs from that assumed by most models of parsing, which hold that the purpose of the parsing mechanism is to perform a *syntactic* analysis of the input sentences. In other words, the goal of a conceptual analyzer is to derive the semantic and memory structures underlying an utterance, whereas the goal of a syntactic parser is to discover its (syntactic) structural description. Examples of syntactic parsers include: Thorne et al. (1968), Bobrow and Fraser (1969), Woods (1970), Winograd (1972), Kaplan (1975), and Marcus (1975, 1979). Other examples of semantics-oriented analyzers are those described by Wilks (1973, 1975a, and 1976), and by Burton (1976).

Early research in natural language processing assumed that a complete understanding system would require a syntactic analyzer as a front-end. We, on the other hand, do not believe that such prior syntactic analysis is necessary. This, of course, does *not* mean that we deny the existence of syntactic phenomena or of syntactic knowledge; rather we are arguing against the notion of a separate syntactic analysis phase.

Since the goal of conceptual analysis differs from the goal of syntactic parsing, it is understandable that the mechanisms which are employed differ as well. In particular, it is our goal that the conceptual analysis process use any and all available knowledge whenever helpful. Such knowledge may include syntactic knowledge, but is certainly not limited to that. It is a claim of our theory that non-linguistic knowledge is often crucial even at the earliest points in natural language processing.

Expectations

A language understander must connect concepts which are obtained from word meanings, and from inferences derived from word meanings, into a coherent representation of the input as a whole. Because of the possibilities of word-sense ambiguity or irrelevant inference, an understander must also be able to choose among alternative concepts. So, conceptual analysis consists mainly of connecting and disambiguating (i.e., choosing among) representational structures.

The processing knowledge which the system uses for this task is in the form of *expectations* (Schank et al., 1970; Riesbeck, 1975; and Riesbeck and Schank, 1976). When a person hears or reads words with certain meanings, he expects or predicts that words with certain other meanings may follow, or may have already been seen. People constantly predict what they are likely to see next, based on what they have read and understood so far and on what they know about language and the world. They use these expectations to disambiguate and connect incoming text.

Of course, expectations are used in syntactic analysis programs as well. The difference lies in the *origin* of the expectations. In syntactic analyzers, the expectations are derived from a grammar. In conceptual analyzers, the expectations are governed instead by the incomplete CD structures representing the meaning of the input.

To illustrate the use of expectations in understanding, suppose that the following simple sentence were the input to an expectation-based conceptual analysis system: "Fred ate an apple." Reading from left to right, the system first finds the word "Fred". The system understands this as a reference to some male human being named Fred, and stores the reference, represented as the token FRED, in some kind of short-term memory. The next word is "ate". This is understood as an instance of the concept of eating, which in Conceptual Dependency is represented by a CD frame something like this:

(INGEST ACTOR (NIL) OBJECT (NIL)).

Also, the meaning of "ate" supplies some expectations which give hints as to how to go about filling the empty slots of this frame. One of these expectations suggests that the ACTOR of the INGEST, an animate being, may have already been mentioned. So the analyzer checks short-term memory, finds FRED there, and fills the ACTOR slot of the INGEST:

(INGEST ACTOR (FRED) OBJECT (NIL)).

There remains an unfulfilled expectation, which suggests that some mention will be made of what it is that Fred ate, that it should be some edible thing (or at least a physical object), and that it should fill the OBJECT slot. Next, the word "an" is read. This creates an expectation that some instance of a concept should follow, with the instruction that if one is found, it should be marked as an indefinite reference. (This is information which can aid memory.) Finally, "apple" is read. It is understood as an instance of the concept APPLE, representing something which is known to be food. The expectation created when "an" was read is satisfied, so APPLE is marked as an object not previously seen, which we will represent as: (APPLE REF (INDEF)). The second expectation created when "ate" was read is also satisfied, so the OBJECT slot of the INGEST is filled by (APPLE REF (INDEF)). The system's current understanding of the input is represented as

(INGEST ACTOR (FRED) OBJECT (APPLE REF (INDEF))).

There are no more words to read, so the process halts.

The above example gives an idea of the conceptual analysis process. When a word is read, the conceptual structure representing the meaning of that word is added to short-term memory. In addition, expectations are created, which provide the processing knowledge necessary to connect up these conceptual structures into a representation of the input as a whole.

Evolution of Conceptual Analysis

The working hypothesis underlying conceptual analysis is that meaning is a crucial factor at the earliest stages in the language understanding process. Two observations led to this position originally. The first was the failure of syntax-oriented approaches to facilitate the construction of natural language processing systems, particularly in the early period of machine translation research. This failure seemed to indicate that a more meaning-based approach to language analysis was necessary.

The second observation was the rather common-sense one that it is easier to read a foreign language with which one has a passing acquaintance, than it is to speak or write it, especially if one knows something about the topic being discussed. This seemed to indicate that language analysis required less knowledge of syntax than generation, so that a meaning based approach to language analysis could be successful.

The subsequent development of Conceptual Dependency led to the recognition, in Schank et al. (1970), that the incomplete CD structures, used to represent the meaning of the input, generated expectations that could be used in language analysis. Riesbeck (1975) demonstrated the feasibility of such an approach in the MARGIE parser. He implemented the expectations by attaching small executable programs, called *requests*, to the words in the system's vocabulary. These requests were then used to connect the semantic representations of the words into a representation of the whole sentence.

The next parser written was Riesbeck's ELI (Riesbeck and Schank, 1976). ELI was an attempt to show how expectations could be used both to disambiguate words and to connect structures, by making the analyzer extremely top-down. In ELI, a conceptual structure was only accepted for processing if it satisfied a prior expectation. ELI's capabilities were expanded by the addition of Gershman's Noun Group Processor (NGP) program to handle complex noun groups and relative subclauses (Gershman, 1977 and 1979). The motivation for the work described here was the desire to make homogeneous the kinds of processing performed by ELI and by NGP.

Input/Output Examples

The following input/output examples are representative of our current conceptual analyzer's abilities. The program is called CA (Birnbaum and Selfridge, 1979):

```
*(CA '(MARY TOOK BILL AN APPLE.))

FINAL ANALYSIS: STM = (CON20)

CON20 =
(ATRANS ACTOR
        (PP PPCLASS (HUMAN) NAME (MARY) GENDER (FEMALE))
        OBJECT
```

```
(PP PPCLASS (FOOD) TYPE (APPLE) REF (INDEF))
FROM
(PP PPCLASS (HUMAN) NAME (MARY) GENDER (FEMALE))
TO
(PP PPCLASS (HUMAN) NAME (BILL) GENDER (MALE))
INST
(PTRANS ACTOR
        (PP PPCLASS (HUMAN) NAME (MARY) GENDER (FEMALE))
        OBJECT
        (PP PPCLASS (FOOD) TYPE (APPLE) REF (INDEF))
        FROM
        (NIL)
        TO
        (PP PPCLASS (HUMAN) NAME (BILL) GENDER (MALE))
        TIME
        (PAST))
TIME
(PAST))
```

The above CD representation means roughly the following: A female human named Mary ATRANSed a food, type apple, from herself to a male human named Bill. This was done by means of Mary's PTRANSing the apple to Bill. The above example demonstrates the ability of the analyzer to deal with certain kinds of ambiguity. In this particular case, the problem arises because "take" is a highly ambiguous word. For example, the system must also handle inputs like "Mary took the train to Boston", where the top-level conceptualization is a PTRANS, and "John took some aspirin", where the top-level conceptualization is an INGEST.

```
*(CA '(WHERE DID VANCE GO LAST WEEK?))

FINAL ANALYSIS: STM = (CON11)

CON11 =
(PTRANS ACTOR
        (PP PPCLASS (HUMAN) LASTNAME (VANCE) FIRSTNAME (NIL))
        OBJECT
        (PP PPCLASS (HUMAN LASTNAME (VANCE) FIRSTNAME (NIL))
        TO
        (LOC SPEC (*?*))
        FROM
        (NIL)
        TIME
        (TIME TYPE (WEEK) NUMBER (-1.))
        MODE
        (NIL))
```

The above is simply a typical example of the sorts of questions which the program is capable of analyzing. The CD representation means: A human with the last name Vance PTRANSed himself to some unknown place (the "*?*" indicates that this is the information the question is looking for) the week before the present one.

```
*(CA '(A SMALL PLANE STUFFED WITH 1500 POUNDS OF MARIJUANA CRASHED
        10 MILES SOUTH OF HERE YESTERDAY AS IT APPROACHED A LANDING
        STRIP KILLING THE PILOT.))

FINAL ANALYSIS: STM = (CON48 CON63)

CON48 =
(SAME-TIME-AS
      CON-A
      (PROPEL ACTOR
                  (PP CLASS (VEHICLE)
                        TYPE (AIRPLANE)
                        SIZE (SMALL)
                        REF (INDEF)
                        REL (PTRANS ACTOR
                                          (NIL)
                                          OBJECT
                                          (PP CLASS
                                              (PHYSOBJ)
                                              TYPE
                                              (MARIJUANA)
                                              AMOUNT
                                              (UNIT TYPE
                                                    (LB)
                                                    NUMBER
                                                    (NUM VAL (1500))))
                                          TO
                                          (INSIDE PART (PREVIOUS))
                                          FROM
                                          (NIL)
                                          TIME
                                          (PAST)))
                  OBJECT
                  (PP CLASS (PHYSOBJ) TYPE (GROUND))
                  PLACE
                  (LOC PROX (HERE)
                        DIR (SOUTH)
                        DIST (UNIT TYPE
                                    (MILE)
                                    NUMBER
                                    (NUM VAL (10))))
                  TIME
                  (TIME TYPE (DAY) NUMBER (-1.)))
      CON-B
      ($APPROACH VEH
                  (PP PPCLASS (NIL) REF (DEF))
                  FIELD
                  (LOC TYPE (LANDING-FIELD) REF (INDEF))))
```

```
CON63 =
(LEAD-TO ANTE
        (NIL)
        CONSE
        (HEALTH ACTOR
                (PP PPCLASS (HUMAN) TYPE (PILOT) REF (DEF))
                VAL
                (-10.)))
```

This example demonstrates the analyzer's ability to parse long inputs containing several clauses. The analysis consists of two CDs. The first, CON48, which is split into CON-A and CON-B, means roughly the following: CON-A says that a vehicle, type airplane, size small, into which someone had PTRANSed 1500 pounds of marijuana at some time in the past, hit (PROPELled) the ground at a location 10 miles south of the default variable HERE. CON-B says that at the same time some vehicle was engaged in the $APPROACH scene of the $AIRPLANE script. The second CD, CON63, means that something caused the death of a human playing the role of pilot in the $AIRPLANE script. The two CDs have not been connected, and references such as "here" in the location have not been specified, because the necessary information does not exist at the lexical level. Higher level processes, such as a script applier (Cullingford, 1978), discussed in Chapter 5, are needed to complete the representation.

The Issue of Flexibility

One of the major concerns in this work has been to increase the *flexibility* of the analysis process. In order to handle noun groups and the kinds of long, multiple-clause inputs found in most text, an analyzer must be capable of operating in both a top-down and bottom-up mode with equal facility. Within the framework of conceptual analysis, this means that the analyzer must be able to use expectations when they are available. But if no helpful expectations are available, the system must also be able to accept and save intermediate concepts and processing knowledge until such time as they can be used.

This point has two immediate corollaries for language processors. The first is that in order to save intermediate conceptual structures and processing knowledge when operating in a bottom-up fashion, an analyzer must have a sufficiently flexible short-term memory in which to hold them. In particular, noun groups and multiple-clause inputs often present cases in which several constituent conceptual structures must be saved until enough information is gathered to tie them together. Our analyzer uses a simple ordered list, and this has proven sufficient.

The second corollary has to do with the problem of word-sense disambiguation. A language processor cannot always decide among competing word senses (concepts and expectations) immediately upon reading an ambiguous word, because the necessary information may simply not be available yet. For example, consider the following pair of sentences:

John broke the pot.
John smoked the pot.

In the first sentence, "broke" creates an expectation for something which can be broken. This expectation can be used immediately upon reading the word "pot" to prefer the "container" sense and reject the "marijuana" sense. In the second sentence, "smoked" creates an expectation for something which can be burned and inhaled, and this expectation can be used immediately upon reading the word "pot" to choose the "marijuana" sense.

But now consider the passive forms of these sentences:

The pot was broken by John.
The pot was smoked by John.

Unlike the corresponding active cases, the word "pot" cannot be immediately disambiguated in the passive sentences because the semantic information necessary for choosing among the possible word senses does not appear until later in the input.

Some Conclusions

Probably the major theoretical hypothesis of conceptual analysis is the claim that a separate syntactic analysis phase is unnecessary in language understanding. Previous work has demonstrated the feasibility of this approach. We believe that our success in producing a significantly improved analysis process provides further evidence for this hypothesis.

The important issue for future work in language analysis is to gain a much better understanding of how higher level memory structures can be used in the analysis process (Schank et al., 1978). The importance of this question is apparent, we believe, particularly when addressing the problem of word-sense ambiguity. Very often, when a parser thinks that a word is ambiguous, it does so because it hasn't made use of, or possessed, the knowledge that should have been provided by higher memory structures. That is, it didn't really understand well enough what it had been reading. Of course, how well we can apply memory in the parsing process will depend on how well we understand memory. That remains the most difficult, but most crucial, question.

OVERVIEW OF THE ANALYZER

What mechanism can be used to implement expectations? Basing our work on Riesbeck (1975), we chose to implement expectations by using test-action pairs known as *requests*. If the test of a request is checked and found to be true, then the corresponding actions of the request are executed. Requests are thus a form of production (Newell, 1973).

Consider again the example used in the above section on expectations: "Fred ate an apple." We said that an expectation for an edible thing would be generated to fill the OBJECT slot of the INGEST structure built by "eat". Implemented as a request, this expectation would look something like this:

> TEST: Can a concept representing an edible object be found?
> ACTION: Put it in the OBJECT slot of the INGEST concept.

This request is *activated* when the word "ate" is read or heard. In the example, its test became true when the meaning of the word "apple" was understood. Its action specified that APPLE was to be taken as the OBJECT of the INGEST. (Usually, we will describe requests even more informally, as something like "If you can find an edible thing, then put it in the OBJECT slot.")

Using this approach, the conceptual analysis process can be most easily described as a special type of production system. Several questions then arise:

1. What kind of control structure is needed?
2. What kinds of tests and actions can requests perform?
3. Where are requests stored, and how are they accessed?

We will now give some preliminary answers to each of these questions in turn, by outlining a kind of "minimal" analyzer.

Control Structure and Data Structures

First of all, a conceptual analyzer needs some kind of working short-term memory (STM), a place to hold the conceptual structures being processed. Without a flexible STM, a conceptual analyzer would be unable to remember substructures which are to be integrated into the final representation of the input. Let us assume that this short-term memory is merely a list, called the *CONCEPT-LIST* or *C-LIST*. Whenever the processing knowledge of the system, in the form of requests, believes that some conceptual structure is relevant to representing the meaning of the input, that structure is added to the end of this list. This kind of flexibility in holding structures is essential if the parser is to function effectively in a bottom-up mode.

Second, a conceptual analyzer needs a data structure to hold the active requests. Without one, of course, the system would never be able to maintain any expectations. In our minimal analyzer, this is also a list, called the *REQUEST-LIST* or *R-LIST*. The system examines the requests on the R-LIST, and if the test of a request is true, its actions are executed. This process is called *request consideration*.

The control structure of a minimal conceptual analysis algorithm is straightforward:

1. Get the next lexical item (word or idiomatic phrase) from the input, reading from left to right. If none, the process terminates.
2. Load (activate) the requests associated with the new item into the R-LIST.
3. Consider the active requests in the R-LIST.
4. Loop back to step 1.

Requests

It is very important that the right vocabulary be devised to express the processing knowledge the system has. Given that we are using requests to embody that processing knowledge, this problem becomes one of choosing the right set of tests and actions that requests may perform.

There are two general classes of tests which requests may perform:

1. Test for the occurrence of a particular word or phrase.
2. Test for certain semantic or ordering properties of the conceptual structures on the C-LIST.

Requests with the first kind of test are called *lexical* requests, while those with the second kind are called *conceptual* requests (or usually, just requests).

A request may perform any of the following actions should its test become true:

1. Add a conceptual structure to the C-LIST.
2. Fill a slot in a conceptual structure with some other structure.
3. Activate other requests, i.e., add them to the R-LIST.
4. De-activate requests, including itself.

There are several variants of these basic actions which will be analyzed when they are discussed in turn in the section giving a detailed view of the program.

In practice, it seems convenient for requests to be more like the LISP "conditional" than traditional productions. That is, a request should consist of an ordered set of tests which control branching to mutually exclusive actions. This is particularly useful in allowing a request to notice when it is no longer appropriate and then to remove itself from active status. We can accomplish this by making one of the tests in the request look for clues that the request is no longer appropriate. Should that test become true, the associated action would simply have the request de-activate itself.

Requests are often simply organized under the particular words for which they are useful. That is, requests stored under words form a kind of dictionary. For example, the request created when reading "an" would simply be stored under the word "an", and activated for use whenever that word is read. This is one way of organizing requests so that only those relevant to the current situation are active in the system. Clearly, not all analysis expectations should be implemented as lexically indexed requests. For a discussion of "situationally indexed" expectations, see Gershman (1979).

An Example

Let us now examine in detail how the minimal conceptual analyzer we have described might work on another simple example, the statement "Fred gave Sally a book." (The step numbers refer back to the steps in the loop of the control structure sketched above.)

READ THE NEXT WORD (Step 1): In this case, the first word is "Fred".

ACTIVATE REQUESTS FROM THE DICTIONARY ENTRY (Step 2): There is only one in the entry for "Fred":

```
REQUEST—
      TEST:   T
      ACTIONS:   Add the structure (PP CLASS (HUMAN) NAME (FRED))
                 to the C-LIST
```

The symbol "T" in the test of this request is always true, so the action should always be performed. When activating this request, the system assigns it the name REQ0.

CONSIDER THE ACTIVE REQUESTS (Step 3): There is only one, REQ0, and it has a true test, so its action is performed. Now, C-LIST = CON1, where CON1 is the internal name generated for:

(PP CLASS (HUMAN) NAME (FRED)).

READ THE NEXT WORD (Step 1): "gave".

ACTIVATE REQUESTS FROM THE DICTIONARY ENTRY (Step 2): For the purpose of this example, there is just one request in the entry for "gave":

```
REQUEST —
      TEST:   T
      ACTIONS:   Add the structure
                 (ATRANS ACTOR (NIL) OBJECT (NIL)
                         TO (NIL) FROM (NIL)
                         TIME (PAST))
                 to the C-LIST
```

Activate the request
REQUEST—
  TEST: Can you find a human on the C-LIST
     preceding the ATRANS structure?
 ACTIONS: Put it in the ACTOR and FROM slots
     of the ATRANS

Activate the request
REQUEST—
  TEST: Can you find a human on the C-LIST
     following the ATRANS structure?
 ACTIONS: Put it in the TO slot of the ATRANS

Activate the request
REQUEST—
  TEST: Can you find a physical object on the
     C-LIST following the ATRANS structure?
 ACTIONS: Put it in the OBJECT slot of the ATRANS

When activating this request, the system assigns it the name REQ1.

CONSIDER THE ACTIVE REQUESTS (Step 3): There is only one, REQ1, and its test is true, so its actions are performed. First, it adds a new structure to the end of the C-LIST. So now C-LIST = (CON1 CON2), where CON2 is the internal name generated for the ATRANS structure which represents the meaning of "gave". Then, three new requests are activated, which strive to fill the gaps in the ATRANS structure. The first of these requests strives to fill the ACTOR slot of the ATRANS. When it is activated, the system assigns it the name REQ2. The next request strives to fill the TO slot of the ATRANS. When activated, it is assigned the name REQ3. The last new request, REQ4, strives to fill the OBJECT slot of the ATRANS.

 The system now considers these new requests, and REQ2 is found to have a true test. The action of REQ2 is executed, and so CON1, representing "Fred", is palced in the ACTOR slot of CON2 (the ATRANS) and removed from the C-LIST. The other two requests, REQ3 and REQ4, do not have true tests, so their actions are not executed. However, they do remain as active expectations on the R-LIST.

READ THE NEXT WORD (Step 1): "Sally".

ACTIVATE REQUESTS FROM THE DICTIONARY ENTRY (Step 2): There is a request in the entry for "Sally", which is almost exactly like the one for "Fred":

 REQUEST—
  TEST: T
 ACTIONS: Add the structure (PP CLASS (HUMAN) NAME (SALLY))
     to the C-LIST

When activating this request, the system assigns it the name REQ5.

CONSIDER THE ACTIVE REQUESTS (Step 3): REQ5 is found to have a true test, so its action is performed. Now C-LIST = (CON2 CON3), where CON3 is the structure representing "Sally". REQ3, which is still active, now also has a true test, and so CON3 is used to fill the TO slot (recipient) of CON2, the ATRANS structure. REQ4 still does not have a true test.

READ THE NEXT WORD (Step 1): "a".

ACTIVATE REQUESTS FROM THE DICTIONARY ENTRY (Step 2): There is only one request listed under "a":

> REQUEST—
>   TEST: Has a new structure been added to the
>   end of the C-LIST?
>   ACTIONS: Mark it as an indefinite reference

When activating this request, the system assigns it the name REQ6.

CONSIDER THE ACTIVE REQUESTS (Step 3): Neither REQ4 nor REQ6, the only active requests on the R-LIST, have true tests. So, nothing happens.

READ THE NEXT WORD (Step 1): "book".

ACTIVATE REQUESTS FROM THE DICTIONARY ENTRY (Step 2): There is only one request listed under "book":

> REQUEST—
>   TEST: T
>   ACTIONS: Add the structure
>   (PP CLASS (PHYSICAL-OBJECT) TYPE (BOOK))
>   to the C-LIST

When activating this request, the system assigns it the name REQ7.

CONSIDER THE ACTIVE REQUESTS (Step 3): REQ7 has a true test, so its action is performed: CON4 is added to the C-LIST, where CON4 is the structure which represents "book". REQ6 now has a true test, so CON4 is marked as an indefinite reference, like this:

> (PP CLASS (PHYSICAL-OBJECT) TYPE (BOOK) REF (INDEF)).

REQ4 also has a true test, so CON4 is used to fill the object slot of CON2, the ATRANS structure.

There are no more words in the input. The analysis halts, with the following final result representing the input:

(ATRANS ACTOR (PP CLASS (HUMAN) NAME (FRED))
         OBJECT (PP CLASS (PHYSICAL-OBJECT)
                   TYPE (BOOK) REF (INDEF))
         TO (PP CLASS (HUMAN) NAME (SALLY))
         FROM (PP CLASS (HUMAN) NAME (FRED))
         TIME (PAST))

THEORETICAL ISSUES

The Role of Syntax

Traditional notions of syntax include ideas like "part of speech" and "phrase marker" in discussing the structure of a sentence. What we would like to claim in this section is that these notions of syntax are inappropriate when attempting to describe and utilize syntactic knowledge in a language understanding process.

To begin with, what is the purpose of syntactic knowledge? Clearly, a major use of syntactic knowledge is to direct the combination of word meanings into utterance meaning when semantic information is not sufficient or is misleading. For example, in an utterance like "Put the magazine on the plate," it is syntactic knowledge that tells the understander which object is to be placed on top of which. From the point of view of its use in a conceptual analyzer, therefore:

> A large part of syntax is knowledge of how to combine word meanings based on their positions in the utterance.

How can this syntactic knowledge be characterized? We seek a specification which takes into account the fact that the point of syntax is its *use* in the understanding process. We have viewed the process of understanding as one of connecting representational structures, where a connection has been established between structures when one fills a slot in the other, or both fill a larger form. Thus syntactic knowledge is knowledge which specifies where in the utterance some word is to be found whose meaning can be connected (via slot-filling) with the meaning of another word. Of course, we must now specify the notion "position in an utterance".

Given that processing knowledge is encoded in requests, this problem reduces to the question of how positional information can be taken into account in the tests of requests. This may be done by having tests that check for:

1. Relative positions of input elements in short-term memory (the C-LIST).
2. The proper order for filling slots in structures.

These methods describe position in an utterance by use of relative positional information. Both are essentially ways of utilizing word order information. The first of these methods, using relative position in short-term memory, describes the position of a conceptual structure in direct relation to the other structures it might be connected with via slot-filling. For example, consider the following request from the example above:

REQUEST—
    TEST: Can you find a human on the C-LIST
                 preceding the ATRANS structure?
    ACTIONS: Put it in the ACTOR and FROM slots
                 of the ATRANS

The test of this request checks whether or not there is a conceptual object of a certain type (human) which has a certain position on the C-LIST relative to the ATRANS structure (precedes).

The second method, ordering of the slots to be filled, relates the position of a structure to other structures somewhat more indirectly. In particular, by constraining the order in which slots should be filled, we are relating the fillers of those slots *temporally*. For instance, a constraint that the ACTOR slot of a conceptualization be filled before the OBJECT slot reflects the fact that the ACTOR of that conceptualization should be seen before the OBJECT in an active construction.

Another important method relates the position of a conceptual structure to the position of a particular lexical item (i.e., a function word), rather than to another concept. Function words, including prepositions, post-positions, and affixes, are very important syntactic cues in conceptual language analysis.

The achievement of a flexible balance of top-down and bottom-up processing in our analyzer led to the discovery of an interesting side-effect, with implications for our notions of syntax. We found that it was not necessary for the analyzer to have any prior expectations at the start of a sentence, such as for an initial noun-group, or for a complete sentence. Most other parsers, whether syntax-based or semantics-based, do use such prior expectations at the start of a sentence.

However, if there is no prior expectation for a complete sentence, how can we explain the oddity of sentence (a) below, as opposed to sentence (b)?

(a) A plane stuffed with 1500 pounds of marijuana.
(b) A plane was stuffed with 1500 pounds of marijuana.

There is a real feeling of "incompleteness" in sentence (a) which would seem to argue that people *do* have prior expectations for complete sentences. However, consider how these two sentences would sound following this question:

(c) What crashed?

Following question (c), it is sentence (b) that sounds odd, while sentence (a) seems perfectly appropriate. Now, one could explain this phenomenon by saying that the expectations to be supplied at the beginning of a sentence can be varied, and that after question (c), a parser is no longer requiring a complete sentence. But of course, question (c) could equally well be followed by any of the following:

   (d) A plane carrying 1500 pounds of marijuana crashed.
   (e) Nothing crashed.
   (f) What are you talking about?
   (g) There wasn't any crash.
   (h) I didn't hear anything.

So obviously, a parser which depends on prior expectations cannot simply throw them out in the context of a question like (c). If it did, it would then be unable to handle inputs like (d) through (h). Further, these examples make clear that the presence or absence of prior syntactic expectations does not explain why (b) is odd in the context following (c). That can only be explained by reference to higher level processes, such as memory search and question answering. However, if we have such processes, then we can also explain why (a) is odd in a null context. Therefore, this phenomenon cannot be used as evidence against our contention that prior syntactic expectations, such as those for a complete sentence, are unnecessary.

We would claim, moreover, that the explanation for the symmetrical cases of (a) in a null context and (b) in the context of (c), ought to be the same. In other words, the explanation underlying this particular type of "gramaticality" judgment does not lie in a syntactic phenomenon at all. Rather, it is a phenomenon which should be explained by reference to such higher level processes as memory search and question answering.

Word-Sense Disambiguation

In conceptual analysis, word-sense ambiguity manifests itself when one word has two or more requests adding structures to the C-LIST. How can we insure that the structure representing the correct meaning "in context" can be chosen? What we describe in this section, of course, does not constitute anything like a complete answer to the problem of word-sense ambiguity. However, we do perhaps clarify what the possibilities are. Below we present a disambiguation algorithm based on the considerations presented here.

There are essentially two ways to handle word-sense disambiguation. Either the structures which represent alternate hypotheses check the context in order to decide whether they are appropriate, or the context checks the structures in some way, or both of these methods are used. In conceptual analysis terms, this means that there are two ways to accomplish the task of request selection in order to handle ambiguity. The first method is to have the tests of the requests check for clues as to whether or not the structure they would add to the C-LIST is appropriate. These tests could be at either a lexical level (i.e., checking for specific words or phrases), or at a conceptual level (i.e., checking other structures on the C-LIST). For example, to handle the difference between "John left the restaurant" (PTRANS) and "John left a tip" (ATRANS), the requests associated with the word "left" could check to see whether a location or an object is added to the C-LIST.

The second way to perform request selection is to have a function using the information in the context select the appropriate requests, based on the structures they build. The traditional method for doing this is to choose the structure which can be best connected with other structures the system has in its short-term memory. An early incarnation of this idea can be seen in the use of "selection restrictions" to rule out certain combinations of meanings (Katz and Fodor, 1963). In conceptual analysis, the most obvious application of this idea involves choosing that structure which can be used to fill gaps in other structures on the C-LIST, or that can use other structures on the C-LIST to fill its own gaps, or both. This is clearly not the only kind of "connectedness" or "coherence" which can cause us to favor one sense over another. In particular, the structures of the context which are used to check some potential structures need not be directly derived from the input, that is, should also include structures derived by inferential memory procedures.

Top-down selection of this sort would disambiguate "left" by choosing the ATRANS sense of "left" if "a tip" appeared, because ATRANS can use the structure associated with "tip" to fill its OBJECT slot. Similarly, it would choose the PTRANS sense of "left" if "the restaurant" appeared, because PTRANS can use the structure associated with "restaurant" to fill its FROM slot.

Neither of these two methods is new, of course. The MARGIE parser (Riesbeck, 1975) and ELI (Riesbeck and Schank, 1976) employed the first method, i.e., having requests test the context to determine their applicability, with some success (see also Small, 1978). Wilks' preference semantics scheme (Wilks, 1975a and 1976) includes probably the most highly developed mechanism for searching for connections (see also Hayes, 1977). ELI also employed a restricted form of this method.

Intelligent Error Correction

Recently, some attention has been focused on the idea of deterministic "wait and see" syntactic parsing, without backup (Marcus, 1975). Determinism is guaranteed by restricting the analysis process so that no structure which is built can later be discarded. This notion has been contrasted with the non-deterministic "guess and then backup" method typified by augmented transition network (ATN) parsers. While we are in complete agreement with the idea that it is undesirable to use blind backup as an integral part of the analysis process, we believe that Marcus' notions of determinism have ignored the possibilities of what might be called "intelligent error correction". For example, consider the following pair of sentences:

John gave Mary a book.
John gave Mary a kiss.

In the first sentence, "gave" should add the following structure to the C-LIST:

(ATRANS ACTOR (NIL) OBJECT (NIL) TO (POSSESSION-OF (NIL))
                    FROM (POSSESSION-OF (NIL)).

In the second sentence, "gave" is merely a dummy verb, and this structure is completely inappropriate. However, it turns out that there are two ways to handle this problem in a conceptual analyzer. The first approach in conceptual analysis is analogous to what Marcus calls "wait and see" syntactic analysis: don't build any top-level structure until either "book" or "kiss" is read. The second approach is "intelligent error correction". Using this method, the ATRANS structure is built in both cases, and the analyzer proceeds to fill the empty gaps with appropriate substructures. However, an additional request is activated which essentially says, "If you see another complete concept, i.e., action or state, rather than something that can fill the object slot of an ATRANS, then that is the actual top-level structure. Remove the ATRANS from the C-LIST, and fill the empty gaps in the new structure with the substructures which can be found in the ATRANS." Using either of these methods, the sub-structures which have been assembled along the way, such as the representations for "John" and for "Mary", are still available, and this after all is the key to avoiding back-up. Intelligent error correction would be the better approach in those cases where the initial hypothesis is usually correct (Gershman, 1979).

A DETAILED VIEW OF THE PROGRAM

This section provides further details about requests. We will describe the kinds of tests and actions that we found to be necessary to accomplish conceptual analysis, and discuss why they are necessary and the situations in which they are useful. We also provide further details about the control structure of a conceptual analyzer, and describe the motivations behind this structure.

Requests

Let us reiterate the actions which a request may perform:

1. Add a conceptual structure to the C-LIST.

2. Fill a gap in a conceptual structure with some other structure.
3. Activate other requests.
4. De-activate requests, including itself.

There is no restriction that a request perform only one of these actions. However, the convention that a request may add only one structure to the C-LIST is important for the purpose of designing word-sense disambiguation algorithms. Structures are always added to the end of the C-LIST.

Gap-Filling Requests

Conceptual structures are connected when one fills a gap in the other, or both fill a gap in some larger structure. Requests which fill gaps remove embedded conceptual objects from the C-LIST.

We characterize gap-filling requests in roughly two ways. Either the request knows which gap it's trying to fill and is looking for a filler, or it knows the filler and is looking for the proper gap. Requests of the first type are looking for some structure in order to embed it in another. We have already seen numerous examples of this type of gap-filling request in the previous examples. These requests may arise in two ways:

1. They may be activated by the request which built the conceptual structure containing the gap they strive to fill.
2. They may be brought in by function words (e.g., "to").

Gap-filling requests arising from function words are particularly important in that if a request activated by a function word seeks to fill some gap with a structure, it must be allowed to do so. If the gap is already filled by some other structure, the structure should be returned to the C-LIST. For example, consider the sentence "John gave Mary to the Sheik of X" (Wilks, 1975b). After reading "John gave Mary..." our conceptual analyzer would assume Mary to be the recipient of the giving action, and would build:

(ATRANS ACTOR (JOHN) OBJECT (NIL) TO (MARY) FROM (JOHN)).

However, "to the Sheik" clearly marks the Sheik as the recipient, and that explicit marking has high priority. Hence, the analyzer changes its representation to

(ATRANS ACTOR (JOHN) OBJECT (NIL) TO (SHEIK) FROM (JOHN)).

The concept MARY is returned to the C-LIST, and is then picked up as the OBJECT of the ATRANS.

The second type of gap-filling request has a filler and looks for some structure in which to embed it. These usually arise from words that appear in noun groups, particularly adjectives. For example, the word "red" has an associated request which looks for the representation of a physical object, in order to fill the COLOR slot of that object with the structure RED. This kind of gap-filling request also arises from words describing time and place settings. For example, in the sentence "Yesterday, Fred bought a car," the word "yesterday" has an associated request which looks for a concept, in order to fill the concept's TIME slot.

Once a gap in some structure is filled, all other requests which seek to fill it should be removed. That can be handled in two ways. The simplest is to have requests which seek to fill some particular gap test whether it has already been filled, and if so then remove themselves. This is how our current implementation operates. The other possibility is to use two-way pointers between gaps in conceptual structures and the requests which strive to fill them, and to place in the control structure a procedure which automatically removes unnecessary requests. Riesbeck's ELI uses this approach.

Activating Other Requests

Two major purposes motivate our use of requests to activate other requests. First, requests that add some conceptual structure to short-term memory will often activate requests which strive to fill gaps in that structure.

Second, requests can change the sense of some word in some local context (Riesbeck and Schank, 1976) by activating requests that test for specific input words, and adding requests to the dictionary entries of those words. Function words are an important instance of this notion of locally changing word sense, since in many cases they function only with respect to a particular construction.

Take the example of the word "of". The relationship it denotes depends on the construction in which it appears. One such construction includes examples such as "five yards of cloth" or "ten pounds of sugar". A good way to handle this construction is to have a request which is activated by the "unit" sense of words such as "yards" and "pounds". This request tests if the next word is "of". If it is, then the request activates another request which looks for the material to be modified by the unit, and when found attaches the description created by "five yards" or "ten pounds" to it.

In general, locally changing the sense of some word in this manner does not involve throwing out whatever requests are indexed directly under the word, but rather just augments them. In this way, if the newly activated requests should fail to be applicable, then all of the usual requests associated with the word are still available to continue processing. However, the specially added request needs to be guaranteed priority over the usual requests associated with the word.

De-activating Requests

The final request action is the ability to de-activate requests. One important use of this action is to have requests de-activate themselves under certain circumstances. In this way, a request which notices that it is no longer appropriate can remove itself before fouling up the analysis. For example, consider the request for locally extending the senses of the word "of", described in the last section. If the next word is *not* "of", then this request must de-activate itself. Otherwise, if "of" occurs later in the input, the request would change its meaning in a way which is no longer appropriate.

Another situation in which this action is useful occurs when there are several requests which represent competing hypotheses about the meaning of a word. The request which represents the correct meaning (however chosen) must de-activate the other requests.

Tests of Requests

The tests of requests examine either the actual words of the input text or the objects on the C-LIST. We have at this point distinguished two variants of the latter:

1. Searching for the occurrence of some structure on the C-LIST with the correct properties.
2. Testing whether or not certain gaps in some structure are filled.

Clearly the properties with which the first type of test is concerned will often be conceptual or semantic. For instance, one might write a test like "is there a PP on the C-LIST?" or "is there a PP on the C-LIST which is a higher animate?" We have seen these sorts of tests in the examples discussed previously. But, these tests may also have constraints on *where* in the C-LIST they should look, such as, for example, an instruction to look only on the end of the C-LIST, or to search only preceding or following some other object on that list. Such constraints are one way of utilizing the structural information derived from word order. In other words, these constraints, which can be expressed by predicates in the test, embody expectations related to sentence structure rather than content.

These expectations are necessary whenever there are several gaps in a representational structure which have the same semantic requirements. For example, both the ACTOR and the TO slots of an ATRANS can appropriately be filled by a "higher animate". Syntactic knowledge must then be used to decide which of several appropriate gaps a structure should fill.

Two predicates are useful in constraining where on the C-LIST to look: (1) a predicate which tests whether or not one structure *precedes* another on the C-LIST; and (2) a predicate which tests whether or not one structure *follows* another on the C-LIST. For example, the ATRANS sense of the word "give" activates the following request:

REQUEST—
      TEST: Can you find a human on the C-LIST
                   preceding the ATRANS structure?
    ACTIONS: Put it in the ACTOR and FROM slots
                   of the ATRANS

The other type of test for requests determines which of several empty gaps some candidate structure should fill on the basis of constraints on the order in which those gaps should be filled. These constraints are expressed by tests that check to see whether or not some gap is filled. For example, suppose we wanted to write a request to fill the TO slot of an ATRANS arising from the word "give". Because the same semantic constraints apply to the ACTOR and TO slots, we need a test to distinguish between them. Since, in an active sentence, the ACTOR will be seen *before* the recipient is seen, the following request will insure that the TO slot is not incorrectly filled with a structure that ought to fill the ACTOR slot:

REQUEST—
      TEST: Can you find a human on the C-LIST, and is
                   the ACTOR slot already filled?
    ACTIONS: Put it in the TO slot of the ATRANS.

Searching the C-LIST

An ordering problem arises in conceptual analysis when the test of a conceptual-level request is searching the C-LIST for some object with certain properties. If more than one item on the C-LIST satisfies the test, how can the system choose between them? Let's examine the following fragment: "The girl Fred saw in the park . . ." The request activated by reading "saw" activates another request that looks for an animate actor. But there are two possibilities: "the girl" and "Fred". In cases like this, we use a recency rule to select from among several possibilities. That is, when scanning the C-LIST looking for some object which satisfies certain predicates, the system should look at the more recently added objects first.

Organizing Requests: The Recency Rule

A large part of the theory of conceptual analysis is the problem of request organization, which is related to controlling how and when requests get considered. Similar control questions arise in all production systems. (For a good overview, see Davis and King, 1975.) The central problem is determining which control strategies are appropriate to which domains.

We have supposed, rather simplistically, that active requests are held in the R-LIST. Now consider the following example sentence: "Saul ate a big red apple." Our intuition is that the adjectives preceding the word "apple" modify the concept "APPLE" before the result is used to fill the INGEST frame added to the C-LIST by "ate". It appears that the requests activated by those adjectives are considered before the requests which were activated when the INGEST structure was added to the C-LIST. Examples like this, and others as well, have led us to adopt a rule of *request recency*. (Rules of this sort are common in production systems.) This rule states that requests are considered in the reverse order of their activation, from most recent to least. In addition to guaranteeing that the analysis proceeds according to our intuitions, this is a good heuristic principle, since newer requests represent newer, and so possibly better, information about what might be going on than older requests.

Let's look at another example: "Fred told John Bill hit Mary." When "told" is read, a request is activated which adds a conceptual structure to the C-LIST, roughly something like

(MTRANS ACTOR (NIL) MOBJECT (NIL) TO (NIL)).

In addition, requests are activated which try to fill the empty slots in this frame. One of these requests is looking for a concept to put in the MOBJECT slot. Then, when "hit" is read, a request is activated, which adds the conceptual structure

(PROPEL ACTOR (NIL) OBJECT (NIL))

to the C-LIST.

This request also activates some new requests that try to fill the empty slots in the PROPEL frame. Even though the system has already commenced scanning the list of active requests, these new requests are more recent. Thus, the requests which strive to fill gaps in the PROPEL frame are considered before the requests which strive to fill gaps in the MTRANS frame. "Bill" is used to fill the ACTOR slot of the PROPEL before the resulting structure is used to fill the MOBJECT slot of the MTRANS.

In many cases, more than one request is activated at the same time, and hence these requests have the same recency. Such a set is called a *request pool*. Thus, in order to implement the recency rule, our program uses an ordered list of request pools, each pool containing one or more requests.

The main import of the recency rule is that if a conceptual structure A is going to be used to fill a gap in some other structure B, then A is given a chance to fill its own gaps, before A is embedded in B. Thus, in the example "Fred told John Bill hit Mary", before the PROPEL structure is embedded in the MTRANS, "Bill" is used to fill the ACTOR slot of the PROPEL. In processing terms, this effect of the recency rule can be expressed as follows: if requests which assemble and modify lower level structures and requests which assemble these sub-structures into higher level structures are active at the same time, then the former have priority over the latter.

How are requests organized within pools? A certain amount of hierarchy is clearly necessary, since requests specifically added to change the sense of a word in some local context must be guaranteed priority.

In addition to this hierarchical organization, requests are organized within pools according to the actions they perform. For example, suppose that several requests in the same pool all add structures to the C-LIST, and suppose further that more than one of these has a true test. This is how word-sense ambiguity would manifest itself in a conceptual analyzer, and the problem is to select the correct request. The algorithm which controls request consideration must not only order the requests, it must sometimes choose among them, or make them all wait for more information.

Noun Groups

An analyzer implemented along the lines we have described up to now would have great difficulty processing noun groups with more than one noun correctly. The problem is that it is possible that a concept will incorrectly use some intermediate conceptual structure to fill a gap. For example, consider the sentence "George sat on the stairway handrail." The concept representing "sat" presumably has an empty slot for the object upon which the actor was sitting, and a request which tries to fill that slot (let us agree to call it the OBJECT slot). Since a stairway is a perfectly fine object to sit on, the algorithm as described up to this point would allow that request to fill its slot with "stairway", before the entire noun group had been analyzed. So, the problem is to somehow prevent any request trying to fill the OBJECT slot from firing prematurely, or correct the situation if that should happen. It is clear that when analyzing noun groups the control structure must consider requests in some manner different than so far described. Our problem is once again one of controlling request consideration.

To handle this, we use the following procedure for request consideration in noun groups: Consider only the requests associated with each incoming word, until the end of the noun group. That is, if the program is in a noun group, and a new word is input, then only the newly activated requests associated with that word are considered. Prior requests are not considered until the noun group is finished.

With this rule for processing requests during noun groups, the entire structure representing "stairway handrail" would be constructed *before* the request which strives to fill the OBJECT slot of the sitting action could be considered.

This rule for controlling request consideration has the additional effect of insuring that the head noun of the noun group is discovered before adjectives are attached. For example, consider how this algorithm would analyze the input "blue car seat". First the request associated with the word "blue" would be activated. Such a request would strive to fill the COLOR slot of some physical object to the right. Next, the request associated with the word "car" would add a structure to the C-LIST representing the concept of automobile. However, since the analyzer is in noun group mode, the prior expectation from "blue" would *not* be considered at this time. Finally, the word "seat" is read, and another structure is added to the C-LIST. Now, the structure representing "car seat" is built, and then the request associated with "blue" is considered. It would then ascribe the attribute of being colored blue to the seat, not to the car. Under certain circumstances, of course, this could be wrong, e.g., "red stairway railing" might refer to the railing of a red stairway, instead of the red railing of a stairway. We believe that a general solution to problems of this kind will depend on better understanding of the role of memory in parsing. However, the process described here does have the virtue of allowing noun groups to be completed before the resulting analysis is used in larger structures. For example, if the phrase "blue car seat" is embedded in the sentence "George sat on the blue car seat," then the analysis would determine that George sat on the seat, not on the car.

In order to use the process we sketched out above, an analyzer must first have requests organized by recency, and second, be able to determine when it should be in noun group mode and when it should be in normal mode. We have used, with slight modification, Gershman's (1977) heuristics for determining noun group boundaries. Some of these rules depend on conceptual, and some on syntactic, knowledge.

A Disambiguation Algorithm

Using requests to check the context in order to disambiguate themselves requires no special addition to the control structure of a conceptual analyzer, since the work is done by the requests. Using context to choose among competing requests, however, requires augmenting the mechanism which controls request consideration. We will make use of only those obvious connections between structures which arise when one can fill a gap in the other. The algorithm should be flexible, which means that if there is not enough evidence to make a selection, the system must be able to wait and try again later.

We will assume that requests are organized within pools according to their actions, and will concern ourselves with those requests which strive to add some structure to the C-LIST. The mechanism for controlling these requests within each pool must be applied any time the requests are considered. This mechanism works as follows:

1. Collect those requests which have true tests.
2. If more than one has a true test, then check the structures which these add to the C-LIST, to see if they can either fill a gap in some other structure

already on the C-LIST, or can use some other structures to fill one of their gaps.

At this point, three things can happen: either none of the requests succeed in this check for connections, only one succeeds, or several succeed. The first case is easy to handle:

    3a. If none of the requests succeed in the check for connections (step 2), then none should be allowed to fire (i.e., postpone making a decision).

The second case is also relatively easy, although complexities arise if the choice made turns out to be a bad one:

    3b. If only one of the requests succeeds in the check for connections (step 2), then perform the actions of the successful request and de-activate the rest.

The third case is quite difficult:

    3c. If neither of the above apply, then don't execute any of the requests. A more complex decision needs to be made.

This third case requires postponing a decision until one or the other structure is found to be the "best connected". In Wilks' system (1976), the "best connected" is the "most connected", and we use this measure as well. However, Wilks' analyzer performs this comparison only at what are essentially clause boundaries, and does not rule out any possibilities until then, whereas our system chooses the first structure to become more connected than any other. In this third case where several requests succeed in the check for connections, it seems plausible that those which do not could be de-activated immediately, thus reducing fairly quickly the set of viable alternatives.

    The use of some disambiguation process as outlined above places new requirements on the control structure of a conceptual analyzer. In particular, we have often depended on a fairly consistent correspondence between the order of input of some word, and the location in the C-LIST of any associated structure. But, since the requests which add structures to the C-LIST could be prevented from firing immediately by the disambiguation process, such a correspondence is no longer likely. The solution is to change the control and data structures a bit to guarantee the relationship between order of input and order on the C-LIST. The easiest way to do that is as follows: whenever a pool of requests is activated, a new empty node is to be added to the C-LIST. Should a request in that pool add some structure to the C-LIST, it should add it in the corresponding node, not at the end as previously described. Thus, the C-LIST consists of a list of such nodes, some with structures, and some empty. An empty node often has associated requests trying to add structures to the C-LIST in that position.

A DETAILED EXAMPLE

This section presents a detailed example of how the Conceptual Analyzer actually runs. The input we will use is: "A small plane stuffed with 1500 pounds of marijuana crashed 10 miles south of here." The dictionary entries exhibited, although not particularly general, do illustrate the variety of actions which the analyzer must perform. The example will trace the execution monitor, describing the states of the C-LIST and of the request pools as the sentence is analyzed. We assume that the C-LIST is NIL and there are no request pools at the start. (Note: The request names (REQ1,REQ2, etc.) are generated dynamically during the parse. We have added them to the sample definitions for the sake of clarity.)

GET THE NEXT ITEM: The first word of the sentence is "A". The program switches from normal to noun group mode. (The current mode is determined by using Gershman's (1977) heuristics for noun group boundaries.)

CONSIDER REQUESTS LOOKING FOR SPECIFIC WORDS: (There aren't any.)

LOAD THE REQUESTS FROM THE DICTIONARY ENTRY: The entry for "a" is:

```
(DEF A
  (REQUEST REQ1
      [TEST: "find a concept following 'a' "]
   [ACTIONS: "add (REF (INDEF)) to it"]])
```

The request is named REQ1 by the system and activated in POOL-1. This request adds the gap REF, and fills it with INDEF.

CONSIDER REQUESTS IN NOUN GROUP MODE: REQ1 is considered but does not fire.

GET THE NEXT ITEM: "small".

CONSIDER REQUESTS LOOKING FOR SPECIFIC WORDS: (There aren't any.)

LOAD THE REQUESTS FROM THE DICTIONARY ENTRY: The entry for "small" is:

```
(DEF SMALL
  (REQUEST REQ2
      [TEST: "find PP on C-LIST following 'small' "]
   [ACTIONS: "add (SIZE (SMALL)) to it"]])
```

The request is named REQ2 by the system and activated in POOL-2.

CONSIDER REQUESTS IN NOUN GROUP MODE: REQ2 is considered but does not fire.

GET THE NEXT ITEM: "plane".

CONSIDER REQUESTS LOOKING FOR SPECIFIC WORDS: (There aren't any.)

LOAD THE REQUESTS FROM THE DICTIONARY ENTRY: The entry for "plane" is:

```
(DEF PLANE
  (REQUEST REQ3
      [TEST: T]
   [ACTIONS:
      "add (PP CLASS (VEHICLE) TYPE (AIRPLANE)) to C-LIST"]]
```

Recall that all structures are added on the end of the C-LIST. The request is named REQ3 by the system and activated in POOL-3.

CONSIDER REQUESTS IN NOUN GROUP MODE: REQ3 is considered and fires. The result is that POOL-3 is now empty, and the C-LIST = (CON1) where CON1 = (PP CLASS (VEHICLE) TYPE (AIRPLANE)).

GET THE NEXT ITEM: "stuffed". The program switches from noun group to normal mode. Recall that normal mode requires the execution monitor to immediately consider all active requests. So, the monitor checks all of the request pools, from most recent to least. REQ2 and REQ1 both fire, and the end result is that all the request pools are empty, with CON1 = (PP CLASS (VEHICLE) TYPE (AIRPLANE) SIZE (SMALL) REF (INDEF)).

CONSIDER REQUESTS LOOKING FOR SPECIFIC WORDS: (There aren't any.)

LOAD THE REQUESTS FROM THE DICTIONARY ENTRY: The entry for "stuffed" is:

```
(DEF STUFFED
  (REQUEST REQ4
      [TEST: T]
   [ACTIONS:

      "Set STR0 to (PTRANS ACTOR (NIL)
                          OBJECT (NIL)
                          TO (INSIDE PART (NIL)))
      Add STR0 to C-LIST"
```

```
''activate
 (REQUEST REQ5
      [TEST: ''the next word is WITH'']
    [ACTIONS:
     ''activate in the next pool, marked high priority:
      (REQUEST REQ6
            [TEST: ''find PP on C-LIST and (TO PART) slot of
                      STR0 is filled'']
       [ACTIONS: ''put it in the OBJECT slot of STR0''])
      (REQUEST REQ7
            [TEST: ''find PP on C-LIST, preceding STR0'']
       [ACTIONS: ''add (REL (STR0)) to it and
                      put it in (TO PART) slot of STR0'']]]
```

The local variable STR0 (which is replaced by a system-unique symbol) is set to the PTRANS when the request is executed. STR0 is used to save the structure for other requests to reference. The request is named REQ4 by the system and activated in POOL-4.

CONSIDER REQUESTS IN NORMAL MODE: REQ4 is triggered, so now C-LIST = (CON1 CON2), where CON2 is the PTRANS. Another request is activated as REQ5, which is put in the special pool looking for particular words.

GET THE NEXT ITEM: ''with''.

CONSIDER REQUESTS LOOKING FOR SPECIFIC WORDS: REQ5 is triggered. Because of the nature of the action of REQ5, the execution monitor proceeds, noting it must add two new requests, REQ6 and REQ7, to the next request pool.

LOAD THE REQUESTS UNDER THE DICTIONARY ENTRY: In this instance, it doesn't really matter what the requests listed under ''with'' are, since the requests added by REQ5 are the proper sense of the word in this local context. Hence, when POOL-5 is built, REQ6 and REQ7 are added to it. They have a higher priority than the standard requests listed under ''with'' in the dictionary.

CONSIDER REQUESTS IN NORMAL MODE: REQ7, which builds the REL structure, is triggered, and so now C-LIST = (CON1), where CON1 =

```
(PP CLASS (VEHICLE)
    TYPE (AIRPLANE)
    SIZE (SMALL)
    REL (PTRANS ACTOR (NIL)
               OBJECT (NIL)
               TO (INSIDE PART (CON1))))
```

The only remaining active request is REQ6, which strives to fill the OBJECT slot of the PTRANS.

GET THE NEXT ITEM: "1500". The execution monitor changes to noun group mode.

CONSIDER REQUESTS LOOKING FOR SPECIFIC WORDS: (There aren't any.)

LOAD THE REQUESTS FROM THE DICTIONARY ENTRY: The program recognizes that "1500" is a number, and for the sake of convenience generates a corresponding literal atom *1500*, with a definition like this:

```
(DEF *1500*
 (REQUEST REQ8
    [TEST: T]
    [ACTIONS: "add (NUM VAL (1500)) to C-LIST"]]
```

This is named REQ8 by the system, and activated in POOL-6.

CONSIDER REQUESTS IN NOUN GROUP MODE: REQ8 is triggered, and the C-LIST = (CON1 CON3) where CON3 = (NUM VAL (1500)).

GET THE NEXT ITEM: "pounds".

CONSIDER REQUESTS LOOKING FOR SPECIFIC WORDS: (There aren't any.)

LOAD THE REQUESTS FROM THE DICTIONARY ENTRY: the entry for "pound" is:

```
(DEF POUND
 (REQUEST REQ9
    [TEST: T]
   [ACTIONS:

    "Set STR0 to (UNIT TYPE (LB)
                      NUMBER (NIL))
     Add STR0 to C-LIST"

    "activate
     (REQUEST REQ10
         [TEST: "find a number preceding STR0
                 on the C-LIST"]
       [ACTIONS: "put it in the NUMBER slot of STR0"])
     (REQUEST REQ11
         [TEST: "next word is OF"]
```

[ACTIONS:
    "activate in the next pool, marked high priority:
        (REQUEST REQ12
                [TEST: "if you find a PP on C-LIST following STR0"]
        [ACTIONS: "add (AMOUNT STR0) to it"]]]

This is named REQ9 and activated in POOL-7 by the system.

CONSIDER REQUESTS IN NOUN GROUP MODE: REQ9 is triggered, so that
the C-LIST = (CON1 CON3 CON4) where CON4 is the representation for
"pounds". Also, the request looking for a number is activated as REQ10 in
POOL-8, which should be considered in noun group mode. The other request is
activated in the pool for requests testing for particular words as REQ11. REQ10
triggers, and C-LIST = (CON1 CON4), where CON4 = (UNIT TYPE (LB)
NUMBER (NUM VAL (1500))).

GET THE NEXT ITEM: "of".

CONSIDER REQUESTS LOOKING FOR SPECIFIC WORDS: REQ11 is
triggered, and because of the nature of its action, the execution monitor proceeds, noting it must add a new request, REQ12, to the next request pool.

LOAD THE REQUESTS FROM THE DICTIONARY ENTRY: Again, since the
sense of this word is locally changed, it doesn't matter what they re. However,
POOL-9 is built, and REQ12 is activated in it.

CONSIDER REQUESTS IN NOUN GROUP MODE: REQ12 is considered, but
fails to fire.

GET THE NEXT ITEM: "marijuana".

CONSIDER REQUESTS LOOKING FOR SPECIFIC WORDS: (There aren't
any.)

LOAD THE REQUESTS FROM THE DICTIONARY ENTRY: the entry for
"marijuana" is:

    (DEF MARIJUANA
    (REQUEST REQ13
        [TEST: T]
        [ACTIONS: "add (PP CLASS (PHYSOBJ) TYPE (MARIJUANA)) to C-LIST"]]

This is named REQ13 by the system and activated in POOL-10.

CONSIDER REQUESTS IN NOUN GROUP MODE: REQ13 is triggered, so
now C-LIST = (CON1 CON4 CON5), where CON5 is the representation for
"marijuana".

GET THE NEXT ITEM: "crashed". The execution monitor switches from noun group mode to normal mode, and so immediately considers all active requests. By recency, REQ12 is considered first, and triggers. Now C-LIST = (CON1 CON5) where CON5 =

    (PP CLASS (PHYSOBJ)
        TYPE (MARIJUANA)
        AMOUNT (UNIT TYPE (LB)
                     NUMBER (NUMBER VAL (1500))))

REQ6, which was activated to fill the OBJECT slot of the subordinate PTRANS, is triggered; CON5 fills the OBJECT slot, and C-LIST = (CON1) again. There are no more active requests.

CONSIDER REQUESTS LOOKING FOR SPECIFIC WORDS: (There aren't any.)

LOAD THE REQUESTS FROM THE DICTIONARY ENTRY: The entry for "crash" is:

```
(DEF CRASH
 (REQUEST REQ14
     [TEST: T]
   [ACTIONS:

    "Set STR0 to (PROPEL ACTOR (NIL)
                        OBJECT (PP CLASS (PHYSOBJ) TYPE (GROUND))
                        PLACE (NIL))
     Add STR0 to C-LIST"

    "activate
     (REQUEST REQ15
         [TEST: "find a PP which is a physical object
                   preceding STR0 on the C-LIST"]
       [ACTIONS: "put it in the ACTOR slot of STR0"])
     (REQUEST REQ16
         [TEST: "find a PP which is a location on the C-LIST"]
       [ACTIONS: "put it in the PLACE slot of STR0"]]]
```

This is REQ14, activated in POOL-11. (The filler of the object slot of the PROPEL (ground) is a default that can be overwritten.)

CONSIDER REQUESTS IN NORMAL MODE: REQ14 is triggered, and the C-LIST = (CON1 CON6) where CON6 is the representation for "crash". Also, two new requests, REQ15 and REQ16 are activated in POOL-12. These are considered, and REQ15 is triggered, which places CON1 in the ACTOR slot of CON6, so that C-LIST = (CON6). REQ16 is not triggered.

GET THE NEXT ITEM: "10". Switch to noun group mode.

CONSIDER REQUESTS LOOKING FOR SPECIFIC WORDS: (There aren't any.)

LOAD THE REQUESTS FROM THE DICTIONARY ENTRY: Again, the literal atom *10* is used in place of the number 10, and the following entry is constructed:

```
(DEF *10*
 (REQUEST REQ17
 [TEST: T]
 [ACTIONS: "add (NUM VAL (10)) to C-LIST"]]
```

This is REQ17, activated in POOL-13.

CONSIDER REQUESTS IN NOUN GROUP MODE: REQ17 is triggered, so C-LIST = (CON6 CON7) where CON7 = (NUM VAL (10)).

GET THE NEXT ITEM: "miles".

CONSIDER REQUESTS LOOKING FOR SPECIFIC WORDS: (There aren't any.)

LOAD THE REQUESTS FROM THE DICTIONARY ENTRY: The entry for "mile" is:

```
(DEF MILE
 (REQUEST REQ18
     [TEST: T]
  [ACTIONS:

    "Set STR0 to (UNIT TYPE (MILE)
                       NUMBER (NIL))
     Add STR0 to C-LIST"

    "activate
     (REQUEST REQ19
         [TEST: "find a number preceding STR0 on C-LIST"]
     [ACTIONS: "put it in the NUMBER slot of STR0"]]]
```

This is REQ18, activated in POOL-14.

CONSIDER REQUESTS IN NOUN GROUP MODE: REQ18 is triggered, so C-LIST = (CON6 CON7 CON8) where CON8 is the representation for "mile". Also, REQ19 is activated in POOL-15, and then also considered. It fires, so that the C-LIST = (CON6 CON8) where CON8 = (UNIT TYPE (MILE) NUMBER (NUM VAL (10))).

GET THE NEXT ITEM: "south".

CONSIDER REQUESTS LOOKING FOR SPECIFIC WORDS: (There aren't any.)

LOAD THE REQUESTS FROM THE DICTIONARY ENTRY: The entry for "south" is:

```
(DEF SOUTH
 (REQUEST REQ20
      [TEST: T]
    [ACTIONS:

     "Set STR0 to (LOC PROX (NIL)
                       DIR (SOUTH)
                       DIST (NIL))
       Add STR0 to C-LIST"

     "activate
      (REQUEST REQ21
           [TEST: "find a distance unit preceding
                     STR0 on the C-LIST"]
        [ACTIONS: "put it in the DIST slot of STR0"])
      (REQUEST REQ22
           [TEST: "the next word is OF"]
        [ACTIONS:
         "activate in the next pool, marked as high priority:
          (REQUEST REQ23
               [TEST: "find a structure representing a location
                         following STR0 on the C-LIST"]
            [ACTIONS: "put it in the PROX slot of STR0"]]]
```

This is REQ20, activated in POOl-16.

CONSIDER REQUESTS IN NOUN GROUP MODE: REQ20 is triggered, and now C-LIST = (CON6 CON8 CON9) where CON9 is the structure representing "south". Also, REQ21 is activated in POOL-17, and REQ22 in the special pool of requests looking for specific words. REQ21 fires, and so now C-LIST = (CON6 CON9) where CON9 =

```
(LOC PROX (NIL)
     DIR (SOUTH)
     DIST (UNIT TYPE (MILE) NUMBER (NUM VAL (10))))
```

GET THE NEXT ITEM: "of".

CONSIDER REQUESTS LOOKING FOR SPECIFIC WORDS: REQ22 is triggered, but waits until the next request pool is activated to add a request, REQ23.

LOAD THE REQUESTS FROM THE DICTIONARY ENTRY: Again, since the meaning of "of" will be locally changed, it doesn't matter what the dictionary request for "of" has in it. However, REQ23 is activated in POOL-18.

CONSIDER REQUESTS IN NOUN GROUP MODE: REQ23 is considered but does not fire.

GET THE NEXT ITEM: "here".

CONSIDER REQUESTS LOOKING FOR SPECIFIC WORDS: (There aren't any.)

LOAD THE REQUESTS FROM THE DICTIONARY ENTRY: In this case, the entry is:

```
(DEF HERE
 (REQUEST REQ24
    [TEST: T]
    [ACTIONS: "add (HERE) to C-LIST"]]]
```

This becomes REQ24 in POOL-19. (The representation for "here" is simply a place-holder. In a newspaper story understander, it would be replaced by information from the dateline.)

CONSIDER REQUESTS IN NOUN GROUP MODE: REQ24 is triggered, and changes the C-LIST to (CON6 CON9 CON10).

GET THE NEXT ITEM: "period". Switch to normal mode of the execution monitor. This means checking all requests. REQ24 is triggered and C-LIST = (CON6 CON9) where CON9 =

```
(LOC PROX (HERE)
     DIR (SOUTH)
     DIST (UNIT TYPE (MILE) NUMBER (NUM VAL (10))))
```

Then REQ17 is considered and triggers, filling the PLACE slot of CON6 with CON9. Since period signals the end of a sentence, there are no more active requests. The analysis has constructed one complete conceptualization, and we are done. C-LIST = (CON6) where

```
CON6 =
(PROPEL ACTOR (CON1)
        OBJECT (PP CLASS (PHYSOBJ) TYPE (GROUND))
        PLACE (CON9))
```

```
CON1 =
(PP CLASS (VEHICLE)
    TYPE (AIRPLANE)
    SIZE (SMALL)
    REF (INDEF)
    REL (PTRANS ACTOR (NIL)
                  OBJECT
                  (PP CLASS (PHYSOBJ)
                      TYPE (MARIJUANA)
                      AMOUNT
                      (UNIT TYPE (LB)
                              NUMBER (NUM VAL (1500))))
                  TO (INSIDE PART (CON1))))
CON9 =
(LOC PROX (HERE)
     DIR (SOUTH)
     DIST (UNIT TYPE (MILE)
                 NUMBER (NUM VAL (10))))
```

14 Micro ELI

INTRODUCTION

McELI is a micro version of the English Language Interpreter, ELI (Riesbeck, 1978). As such it is also a micro version of the Conceptual Analyzer described in the previous chapter. McELI is responsible for taking English sentences and converting them into CD forms.

McELI reads sentences one word at a time. Most words have associated with them small programs which specify what these words mean in different contexts, and how they combine with other words. The analysis of a sentence results from the execution of these programs.

The programs that are attached to words are called *packets*. Each packet is a list of *requests*, and a request has the form

```
((TEST expression)
 (ASSIGN variable expression variable expression . . .)
 (NEXT-PACKET request request . . .))
```

where

1. (TEST . . .) says when the request can be executed. When the test expression is true, the request is said to be *triggered*.
2. (ASSIGN . . .) assigns each variable to the expression following it. This is done only if the request is triggered. The variables hold the results of the analysis.

3. (NEXT-PACKET . . .) gives a packet of requests to be loaded if the request is triggered, after the variables have been assigned.

Any of these parts can be left out in a particular request.

When McELI reads a word, it looks up the packet for that word and puts the packet on top of a stack of previously loaded packets. Then it looks at the requests in the packet on top of the stack. If one of the requests in the top packet is triggered, it is executed, the whole packet is removed from the stack, and the next packet on the stack is looked at.

The flow of control in McELI is:

```
WHILE there is another word in SENTENCE
    DO remove the word from SENTENCE
        add the word's packet to STACK
        WHILE there is a packet in STACK
                AND a request in the top packet triggers
            DO remove the packet from STACK
                execute the assignments in the request
                save the request in the list TRIGGERED
                END WHILE
        WHILE there is a request in TRIGGERED
            DO remove the request from TRIGGERED
                add the request's next-packet to the stack
                END WHILE
END WHILE
return the CD built by the requests
```

Notice that as soon as a request in a packet with a true test is found, it is triggered and no other requests in that packet are looked at. Notice also that the NEXT-PACKETs of triggered requests are not loaded until the stack is emptied or the top packet has no triggered requests. This means that things are not added to the stack until packets that can be removed have indeed been removed.

Example Definitions

Definition packets are assigned to words in McELI with the function DEF-WORD. To be specific,

(DEF-WORD word request1 request2 . . .)

attaches to the word a packet containing request1, request2, and so on.

Here is the definition of the word "Jack":

```
(DEF-WORD JACK
  ((ASSIGN *CD-FORM* '(PERSON (NAME (JACK)))
           *PART-OF-SPEECH* 'NOUN-PHRASE]
```

There is just one request in the packet, and it has just an ASSIGN clause. This clause assigns the CD form for a person named Jack to the variable *CD-FORM*, and assigns the atom NOUN-PHRASE to the variable *PART-OF-SPEECH*. This says in effect that "Jack" is a proper noun that means a person named Jack.

Here is the definition of the word "went":

```
(DEF-WORD WENT
  ((ASSIGN *PART-OF-SPEECH* 'VERB
           *CD-FORM* '(PTRANS (ACTOR ?GO-VAR1) (OBJECT ?GO-VAR1)
                              (TO ?GO-VAR2) (FROM ?GO-VAR3))
           GO-VAR1 *SUBJECT*
           GO-VAR2 NIL
           GO-VAR3 NIL)
   (NEXT-PACKET
      ((TEST (EQUAL *WORD* 'TO))
       (NEXT-PACKET
          ((TEST (EQUAL *PART-OF-SPEECH* 'NOUN-PHRASE))
           (ASSIGN GO-VAR2 *CD-FORM*)))))
      ((TEST (EQUAL *WORD* 'HOME))
       (ASSIGN GO-VAR2 '(HOUSE]
```

Again, there is only one request in the word's packet, and it has no TEST clause. The ASSIGN clause says that "went" is a verb referring to PTRANS. GO-VAR1, GO-VAR2, and GO-VAR3 are variables used inside the PTRANS form. GO-VAR1 is assigned the value of the variable *SUBJECT*. Another request that we shall look at shortly sets *SUBJECT* to the CD produced by analyzing the first noun phrase of the sentence. GO-VAR2 and GO-VAR3 are set to NIL. Therefore this ASSIGN clause sets *CD-FORM* to a PTRANS where the ACTOR and OBJECT are both the subject and the TO and FROM are NIL.

The NEXT-PACKET clause has two requests in it, both of which have TEST clauses. The first request will be triggered if *WORD* is equal to "to". McELI sets *WORD* to the current word being processed, as it parses from left to right. If the first request is triggered, it sets no variables (because it has no ASSIGN clause) but it does add a new request, which tests for a noun phrase. If the new request is triggered, that is, if some other request sets *PART-OF-SPEECH* to NOUN-PHRASE, then this request sets GO-VAR2 to the value of *CD-

FORM* at that point in time. This should be the meaning for that noun phrase. In effect, this request is looking for a prepositional phrase starting with "to".

The other request in the NEXT-PACKET clause for "went" is simpler. If *WORD* is set to "home" then GO-VAR2 is set to the value of *CD-FORM*. This should be the meaning of "home" at that time. Both requests in "went" 's NEXT-PACKET are therefore concerned with finding a value for GO-VAR2. There are no requests to fill GO-VAR3.

The variables of special concern to McELI are:

1. *WORD*—McELI sets this to the word of the sentence currently being looked at.
2. *SENTENCE*—McELI sets this to the remainder of the sentence after *WORD*.
3. *CD-FORM*—Requests set this variable to the most recent CD form.
4. *PART-OF-SPEECH*—Requests set this variable to the most recent part of speech.
5. *CONCEPT*—Requests set this to the final meaning of the sentence.

Other variables are set and used by the requests in the dictionary. Almost all of McELI's knowledge about English is kept in the lexicon.

Example Analysis

When McELI starts to analyze any sentence, it initializes the stack to contain the following packet of one request:

```
TOP OF STACK:

((ASSIGN *PART-OF-SPEECH* NIL
         *CD-FORM* NIL
         *SUBJECT* NIL
         *PREDICATES* NIL)
 (NEXT-PACKET
  ((TEST (EQUAL *PART-OF-SPEECH* 'NOUN-PHRASE))
   (ASSIGN *SUBJECT* *CD-FORM*)
   (NEXT-PACKET
      ((TEST (EQUAL *PART-OF-SPEECH* 'VERB))
       (ASSIGN *CONCEPT* *CD-FORM*]
```

This packet comes from the definition of the pseudo-word *START* which is processed at the start of each sentence. The request in this packet clears some variables and adds to the stack a new packet containing a request looking for a noun phrase. That request when triggered sets the *SUBJECT* and adds another packet with a request looking for a verb. That request sets *CON-CEPT*.

Let us follow the analysis of "Jack went home" in detail. First, the packet for *START* is put on the stack. It has one request with no TEST. If a request has no TEST, then it is triggered immediately. Therefore the packet is removed from the stack, and the request is executed. The ASSIGN clause just clears the variables *PART-OF-SPEECH* and *CD-FORM* by setting them to NIL.

After the assignments are done, the stack is checked again, but it is now empty. Therefore, the NEXT-PACKET clause of the triggered request is put on top of the stack:

```
TOP OF STACK:

((((TEST (EQUAL *PART-OF-SPEECH* 'NOUN-PHRASE))
  (ASSIGN *SUBJECT* *CD-FORM*)
  (NEXT-PACKET
    ((TEST (EQUAL *PART-OF-SPEECH* 'VERB))
    (ASSIGN *CONCEPT* *CD-FORM*]
```

WORD is set to JACK and the packet for JACK is put on top of the stack:

```
TOP OF STACK:

((((ASSIGN *CD-FORM* '(PERSON (NAME (JACK)))
            *PART-OF-SPEECH* 'NOUN-PHRASE]
```

Since there is no TEST, the packet is removed and the request is executed. The ASSIGN clause sets *CD-FORM* to (PERSON (NAME (JACK))) and *PART-OF-SPEECH* to NOUN-PHRASE. Now the top of the stack is the initial packet again:

```
TOP OF STACK:

((((TEST (EQUAL *PART-OF-SPEECH* 'NOUN-PHRASE))
  (ASSIGN *SUBJECT* (CD-FORM*)
  (NEXT-PACKET
    ((TEST (EQUAL *PART-OF-SPEECH* 'VERB))
    (ASSIGN *CONCEPT* *CD-FORM*]
```

This time the TEST is true, so the packet is removed from the stack, and the request is executed. This sets the variable *SUBJECT* to the value of *CD-FORM*, i.e., (PERSON (NAME (JACK))).

Now the stack is empty, so the NEXT-PACKET clause of the triggered request is put on the stack:

```
TOP OF STACK:
  (((TEST (EQUAL *PART-OF-SPEECH* 'VERB))
    (ASSIGN *CONCEPT* *CD-FORM*]
```

WORD is set to WENT and the packet for WENT is put on top of the stack:

```
TOP OF STACK:
  (((ASSIGN *PART-OF-SPEECH* 'VERB
            *CD-FORM* '(PTRANS (ACTOR ?GO-VAR1)
                               (OBJECT ?GO-VAR1)
                               (TO ?GO-VAR2) (FROM ?GO-VAR3))
            GO-VAR1 *SUBJECT*
            GO-VAR2 NIL
            GO-VAR3 NIL)
    (NEXT-PACKET
       ((TEST (EQUAL *WORD* 'TO))
        (NEXT-PACKET
           ((TEST (EQUAL *PART-OF-SPEECH* 'NOUN-PHRASE))
            (ASSIGN GO-VAR2 *CD-FORM*))))
       ((TEST (EQUAL *WORD* 'HOME))
        (ASSIGN GO-VAR2 '(HOUSE]
```

Since the request has no TEST, the packet is removed, and the request is executed, setting the various variables. In particular, *PART-OF-SPEECH* is now VERB, *CD-FORM* has the PTRANS CD, and GO-VAR1 has the value of *SUBJECT*, i.e., (PERSON (NAME (JACK))). Note that the question mark indicates variables GO-VAR1, GO-VAR2 and GO-VAR3 in the CD form, but is not used when the variables are set to their initial values. McELI removes items with question marks from the CD form when the analysis is done.

Now the top of the stack looks like this:

```
TOP OF STACK:

  (((TEST (EQUAL *PART-OF-SPEECH* 'VERB))
    (ASSIGN *CONCEPT* *CD-FORM*]
```

The TEST is true, so the variable *CONCEPT* is set to the value of *CD-FORM*, i.e., to the PTRANS CD form, and the stack is empty.

Now the NEXT-PACKET clause for the triggered WENT request is put on top of the stack:

TOP OF STACK:

```
(((TEST (EQUAL *WORD* 'TO))
  (NEXT-PACKET
      ((TEST (EQUAL *PART-OF-SPEECH* 'NOUN-PHRASE))
       (ASSIGN GO-VAR2 *CD-FORM*))))
 ((TEST (EQUAL *WORD* 'HOME))
  (ASSIGN GO-VAR2 '(HOUSE]
```

Note that this packet has two requests in it.

Now *WORD* is set to HOME which in this lexicon has no packet associated with it. The top of the stack is unchanged. The second request in the packet on top of the stack is triggered, and the packet is removed from the stack. GO-VAR2 is set to (HOUSE).

The stack is empty and there are no more words. Hence the analysis is finished. Now McELI takes the value of *CONCEPT*, removes the variables, and returns the final answer:

```
(PTRANS (ACTOR (PERSON (NAME (JACK))))
        (OBJECT (PERSON (NAME (JACK))))
        (TO (HOUSE)))
```

Since GO-VAR3 was never set to anything other than NIL, it is omitted from the answer.

McELI Versus ELI/CA

Some of the differences between McELI and a real conceptual analyzer, such as ELI or CA (the Conceptual Analyzer), are trivial and easy to remove. For example, in CA, packages of requests can be named, so that similar words can be defined by just specifying the names of the desired requests.

Slightly more important is the lack of any morphological routines in McELI. In order to handle the sentence "Jack got the kites", a separate entry for "kites" would have to be added, even though an entry for "kite" already exists. Likewise, "Jack wanted to go to the store" would require an entry for "go" even though "went" is already defined.

ELI and CA both have a morphology routine, albeit a primitive one, that can handle regular plurals, regular and irregular tenses, and possessives. Such a facility would not be hard to add to McELI. Note, however, that tenses and the conceptual times they refer to are ignored totally in McELI.

McELI can only handle simple noun groups such as "Jack" and "the red lobster". Because McELI finishes a noun group as soon as it sees a noun, it can't handle noun-noun pairs, such as "the napkin holder" or "the cash register receipt''. In ELI, a fairly complex noun grouper was added by Anatole Gersh-man (1977), capable of handling sequences like ''Frank Smith, 23, of 593 Foxon Road, the driver of the vehicle.''

McELI's control structure is significantly different from that found in either ELI or CA. In McELI, packets of alternatives are kept on a stack and only the requests in the top packet are looked at. In ELI, all the requests are kept in one list and everything in the list is checked when new input arrives. In CA this list contains pools of requests, ordered by recency. Both ELI and CA keep a list of the variables that each request affects and is affected by, so that when variables change values only the appropriate requests need to be considered.

The restricted nature of McELI's control structure is intentional. By limiting how many requests are looked at, and treating them in a last-in, first-out manner, there is less chance of the wrong request being triggered. Thus, for learning purposes, it is better to have too little happen, rather than too much. In a real analyzer, however, this simplicity has to be traded for the greater power of an openly available set of requests.

The single most important difference, however, is the absence of top-down control in McELI. The last exercise in this chapter is but a slight step towards rectifying that. In ELI, almost everything is controlled by what has gone before. This is done by separating out the slots that are being filled, the constraints placed on those slots, and the requests that, if triggered, will satisfy those constraints. See Riesbeck (1978) for a discussion of how this top-down control is implemented. In CA, this top-down control is augmented by better bottom-up control so that more variable input texts are acceptable.

SAMPLE OUTPUT

The following is a log of the McELI program, applied to the sentences ''Jack went to the store. He got a kite. He went home.''

    [PH: Initiation. 7–Jan–80 4:28PM]

    · · ·

    (PROCESS-TEXT KITE-TEXT)

    Input is (JACK WENT TO THE STORE)

    Processing *START*

    Processing JACK
        CD-FORM = (PERSON (NAME (JACK)))
        PART-OF-SPEECH = NOUN-PHRASE
        SUBJECT = (PERSON (NAME (JACK)))

Processing WENT
    PART-OF-SPEECH = VERB
    CD-FORM = (PTRANS (ACTOR (*VAR* GO-VAR1))
                              (OBJECT (*VAR* GO-VAR1))
                              (TO (*VAR* GO-VAR2))
                              (FROM (*VAR* GO-VAR3)))
    GO-VAR1 = (PERSON (NAME (JACK)))
    CONCEPT = (PTRANS (ACTOR (*VAR* GO-VAR1))
                             (OBJECT (*VAR* GO-VAR1))
                             (TO (*VAR* GO-VAR2))
                             (FROM (*VAR* GO-VAR3)))

Processing TO—not in the dictionary

Processing THE

Processing STORE
    PART-OF-SPEECH = NOUN
    CD-FORM = (STORE)
    PART-OF-SPEECH = NOUN-PHRASE
    CD-FORM = (STORE)
    GO-VAR2 = (STORE)
CD form is
  (PTRANS (ACTOR (PERSON (NAME (JACK))))
         (OBJECT (PERSON (NAME (JACK))))
         (TO (STORE)))

Input is (HE GOT A KITE)

Processing *START*

Processing HE
    PART-OF-SPEECH = NOUN-PHRASE
    CD-FORM = (PERSON)
    SUBJECT = (PERSON)

Processing GOT
    PART-OF-SPEECH = VERB
    CD-FORM = (ATRANS (ACTOR (*VAR* GET-VAR3))
                               (OBJECT (*VAR* GET-VAR2))
                              (TO (*VAR* GET-VAR1))
                              (FROM (*VAR* GET-VAR3)))
    GET-VAR1 = (PERSON)
    CONCEPT = (ATRANS (ACTOR (*VAR* GET-VAR3))
                               (OBJECT (*VAR* GET-VAR2))
                              (TO (*VAR* GET-VAR1))
                              (FROM (*VAR* GET-VAR3)))

Processing A

Processing KITE
 PART-OF-SPEECH = NOUN
 CD-FORM = (KITE)
 PART-OF-SPEECH = NOUN-PHRASE
 CD-FORM = (KITE)
 GET-VAR2 = (KITE)
CD form is
 (ATRANS (OBJECT KITE)) (TO (PERSON)))

Input is (HE WENT HOME)

Processing *START*

Processing HE
 PART-OF-SPEECH = NOUN-PHRASE
 CD-FORM = (PERSON)
 SUBJECT = (PERSON)

Processing WENT
 PART-OF-SPEECH = VERB
 CD-FORM = (PTRANS (ACTOR (*VAR* GO-VAR1))
        (OBJECT (*VAR* GO-VAR1))
        (TO (*VAR* GO-VAR2))
        (FROM (*VAR* GO-VAR3)))
 GO-VAR1 = (PERSON)
 CONCEPT = (PTRANS (ACTOR (*VAR* GO-VAR1))
        (OBJECT (*VAR* GO-VAR1))
        (TO (*VAR* GO-VAR2))
        (FROM (*VAR* GO-VAR3)))

Processing HOME—not in the dictionary
 GO-VAR2 = (HOUSE)
CD form is
 (PTRANS (ACTOR (PERSON) (OBJECT (PERSON))
(TO (HOUSE)))

[PH: Termination. 7–Jan–80 4:29PM.
PS:<RIESBECK>FOURTE.LOG.1]

FLOWCHART

The flow chart in Fig. 14.1 shows the central function in McEli: PARSE.

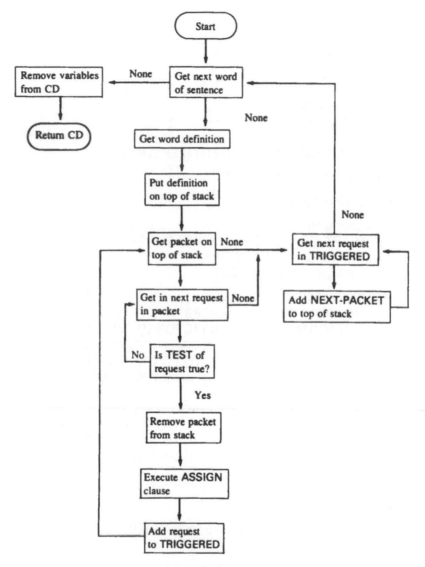

FIG. 14.1.   PARSE(sentence).

THE PROGRAM

```
-  ****************************************************************
-             McELI: THE ENGLISH LANGUAGE INTERPRETER
-  ****************************************************************
- PROCESS-TEXT takes a list of sentences and parses each one,
- printing the answer.
```

```
(DE PROCESS-TEXT (TEXT)
 (FOR (SENTENCE IN TEXT)
    (DO (MSG T "Input is " SENTENCE T)
       (LET (CD (PARSE SENTENCE))
            (MSG T "CD form is ")
            (SPRINT CD 2]
```

 ˜ PARSE takes a sentence in list form—e.g., (JACK WENT TO THE
 ˜ STORE)—and returns the conceptual analysis for it. It sets
 ˜ *SENTENCE* to the input sentence (e.g., (JACK WENT TO THE STORE))
 ˜ with the atom *START* stuck in front. *START* is a pseudo-word in
 ˜ the dictionary with information useful for starting the analysis.

 ˜ PARSE takes *SENTENCE* one word at a time, setting *WORD* to the
 ˜ current word, and loading the packet for that word (if any) onto
 ˜ *STACK*. Then it calls RUN-STACK which looks for and executes
 ˜ triggered requests.

 ˜ During the analysis, the variable *CONCEPT* will be set to the
 ˜ main concept of the sentence (usually by the packet under the main
 ˜ verb). Since McELI builds CD forms with variables in them,
 ˜ McELI has to remove these variables when the sentence is finished,
 ˜ using the function REMOVE-VARIABLES.

 ˜ To make debugging easier, *CONCEPT* and *STACK* are global
 ˜ variables. PARSE returns the CD with all variables filled in,
 ˜ while *CONCEPT* still holds the original CD, including unfilled
 ˜ variables.

```
(DE PARSE (SENTENCE)
 (SETQ *CONCEPT* NIL)
 (SETQ *STACK* NIL)
 (LOOP (INITIAL *WORD* NIL
                *SENTENCE* (CONS '*START* SENTENCE))
       (WHILE (SETQ *WORD* (POP *SENTENCE*)))
       (DO (MSG T T "Processing " *WORD*)
           (LOAD-DEF)
           (RUN-STACK))
       (RESULT (REMOVE-VARIABLES *CONCEPT*]
```

 ˜ RUN-STACK:
 ˜ As long as some request in the packet on top of the stack can be
 ˜ triggered, the whole packet is removed from the stack, and that
 ˜ request is executed and saved.
 ˜ When the top packet does not contain any triggerable requests,
 ˜ the packets in the requests that were executed and saved (if
 ˜ any) are added to the stack.

```
(DE RUN-STACK ()
 (LOOP (INITIAL REQUEST NIL TRIGGERED NIL)
       (WHILE (SETQ REQUEST (CHECK-TOP *STACK*)))
       (DO (POP *STACK*)
           (DO-ASSIGNS REQUEST)
           (PUSH REQUEST TRIGGERED))
       (RESULT (ADD-PACKETS TRIGGERED]
```

``` CHECK-TOP gets the first request in the packet on top of the stack
``` with a true test (if any).

```
(DE CHECK-TOP (STACK)
 (COND (STACK
         (LOOP (INITIAL REQUEST NIL PACKET (TOP-OF STACK))
               (WHILE (SETQ REQUEST (POP PACKET)))
               (UNTIL (IS-TRIGGERED REQUEST))
               (RESULT REQUEST]
```

``` IS-TRIGGERED returns true if a request has no test at all or if the
``` test evaluates to true.

```
(DE IS-TRIGGERED (REQUEST)
 (LET (TEST (REQ-CLAUSE 'TEST REQUEST))
  (OR (NULL TEST) (EVAL (CAR TEST]
```

``` DO-ASSIGNS sets the variables given in the ASSIGN clause.
``` The first POP gets a variable and the second POP gets the value
``` following it.

```
(DE DO-ASSIGNS (REQUEST)
 (LOOP (INITIAL ASSIGNMENTS (REQ-CLAUSE 'ASSIGN REQUEST))
       (WHILE ASSIGNMENTS)
       (DO (REASSIGN (POP ASSIGNMENTS) (POP ASSIGNMENTS]
```

``` REASSIGN sets VAR to the value of VAL and prints a message saying
``` it did it. Note that if VAL is NIL, then nothing is printed.

```
(DE REASSIGN (VAR VAL)
 (COND ((SET VAR (EVAL VAL))
         (MSG T 4 VAR " = ")
         (SPRINT (EVAL VAR) (CURRCOL]
```

``` ADD-PACKETS takes a list of requests and adds their NEXT-PACKETs
``` to the stack.

```
(DE ADD-PACKETS (REQUESTS)
 (FOR (REQUEST IN REQUESTS)
      (DO (ADD-STACK (REQ-CLAUSE 'NEXT-PACKET REQUEST]
```

``` REMOVE-VARIABLES takes a parsed CD from ELI and returns a copy
``` of the pattern with the variables replaced by values. NIL fillers,
``` and their roles, are left out of the final CD.

``` Note that ELI's REMOVE-VARIABLES is like INSTANTIATE in McSAM and
``` McPOL, except that LISP values rather than binding lists are used
``` to hold the values of variables.

```
(DE REMOVE-VARIABLES (CD-FORM)
 (COND ((ATOM CD-FORM) CD-FORM)
       ((IS-VAR CD-FORM)
         (REMOVE-VARIABLES (EVAL (NAME:VAR CD-FORM))))
       (T
        (LET (VAL NIL)
         (CONS (HEADER:CD CD-FORM)
```
```

```
(FOR (PAIR IN (ROLES:CD CD-FORM))
     (WHEN (SETQ VAL
                 (REMOVE-VARIABLES (FILLER:PAIR PAIR))))
     (SAVE (LIST (ROLE:PAIR PAIR) VAL)
```

```
~ *********************************************************************
~                           DATA STRUCTURES
~ *********************************************************************
```

~ McELI uses a stack for control. The top of the stack is the first
~ element of the list.

```
(DE TOP-OF (STACK) (CAR STACK)
```

~ ADD-STACK puts a packet at the front of the list of pending
~ packets.

```
(DE ADD-STACK (PACKET)
(AND PACKET (PUSH PACKET *STACK*))
PACKET)
```

~ Word definitions are stored under the property DEFINITION.
~ LOAD-DEF adds a word's request packet to the stack.

```
(DE LOAD-DEF ()
(LET (PACKET (GET *WORD* 'DEFINITION))
(COND (PACKET (ADD-STACK PACKET))
      (T (MSG "—not in the dictionary")]
```

~ REQ-CLAUSE gets clauses from the format
~   ((TEST...) (ASSIGN...) (NEXT-PACKET...))

```
(DE REQ-CLAUSE (KEY L)
(LET (X (ASSOC KEY L)) (AND X (CDR X)]
```

~ The sample sentences for McELI to test are:

```
(SETQ KITE-TEXT
'((JACK WENT TO THE STORE)
  (HE GOT A KITE)
  (HE WENT HOME)
```

```
~ *********************************************************************
~                           THE DICTIONARY
~ *********************************************************************
```

~ (DEF-WORD name request1 request2...) stores a definition
~ under a word consisting of the list (request1 request2...).

```
(DF DEF-WORD (L)
(PUTPROP (CAR L) (CDR L) 'DEFINITION)
(CAR L)
```

~ HE is a noun phrase that means a person.

```
(DEF-WORD HE
 ((ASSIGN *PART-OF-SPEECH* 'NOUN-PHRASE
          *CD-FORM* '(PERSON]
```

" JACK is a noun phrase that means a person named Jack.

```
(DEF-WORD JACK
 ((ASSIGN *CD-FORM* '(PERSON (NAME (JACK)))
          *PART-OF-SPEECH* 'NOUN-PHRASE]
```

" GOT is a verb that means someone ATRANSed something to the subject.
" GOT looks for a noun phrase to fill the object slot.

```
(DEF-WORD GOT
 ((ASSIGN *PART-OF-SPEECH* 'VERB
          *CD-FORM* '(ATRANS (ACTOR ?GET-VAR3) (OBJECT ?GET-VAR2)
                             (TO ?GET-VAR1) (FROM ?GET-VAR3))
          GET-VAR1 *SUBJECT*
          GET-VAR2 NIL
          GET-VAR3 NIL)
  (NEXT-PACKET
     ((TEST (EQUAL *PART-OF-SPEECH* 'NOUN-PHRASE))
      (ASSIGN GET-VAR2 *CD-FORM*]
```

" WENT is a verb that means someone (the subject) PTRANSed himself to
" somewhere from somewhere. WENT looks for "to <noun phrase>" or
" "home" to fill the TO slot.

```
(DEF-WORD WENT
 ((ASSIGN *PART-OF-SPEECH* 'VERB
          *CD-FORM* '(PTRANS (ACTOR ?GO-VAR1) (OBJECT ?GO-VAR1)
                             (TO ?GO-VAR2) (FROM ?GO-VAR3))
          GO-VAR1 *SUBJECT*
          GO-VAR2 NIL
          GO-VAR3 NIL)
  (NEXT-PACKET
     ((TEST (EQUAL *WORD* 'TO))
      (NEXT-PACKET
         ((TEST (EQUAL *PART-OF-SPEECH* 'NOUN-PHRASE))
          (ASSIGN GO-VAR2 *CD-FORM*))))
     ((TEST (EQUAL *WORD* 'HOME))
      (ASSIGN GO-VAR2 '(HOUSE]
```

" A looks for a noun to build a noun phrase with.

```
(DEF-WORD A
 ((TEST (EQUAL *PART-OF-SPEECH* 'NOUN))
  (ASSIGN *PART-OF-SPEECH* 'NOUN-PHRASE
          *CD-FORM* (APPEND *CD-FORM* *PREDICATES*)
          *PREDICATES* NIL]
```

" THE is identical to A as far as McELI is concerned.

```
(DEF-WORD THE
 ((TEST (EQUAL *PART-OF-SPEECH* 'NOUN))
  (ASSIGN *PART-OF-SPEECH* 'NOUN-PHRASE
          *CD-FORM* (APPEND *CD-FORM* *PREDICATES*)
          *PREDICATES* NIL]
```

¨ KITE is a noun that builds the concept KITE.

```
(DEF-WORD KITE
 ((ASSIGN *PART-OF-SPEECH* 'NOUN
          *CD-FORM* '(KITE]
```

¨ STORE is a noun that builds the concept STORE.

```
(DEF-WORD STORE
 ((ASSIGN    *PART-OF-SPEECH* 'NOUN
             *CD-FORM* '(STORE]
```

¨ *START* is loaded at the start of each sentence. It looks for
¨ a noun phrase (the subject) followed by a verb (the main concept).

¨ The following variables are English-oriented. They are used only
¨ by the dictionary entries, not by the central McELI functions:

¨ *PART-OF-SPEECH*—the current part of speech
¨ *CD-FORM*—the current conceptual dependency form
¨ *SUBJECT*—the CD form for the subject of the sentence
¨ *PREDICATES*—the list of predicates used in a noun phrase

```
(DEF-WORD *START*
 ((ASSIGN *PART-OF-SPEECH* NIL
          *CD-FORM* NIL
          *SUBJECT* NIL
          *PREDICATES* NIL)
  (NEXT-PACKET
   ((TEST (EQUAL *PART-OF-SPEECH* 'NOUN-PHRASE))
    (ASSIGN *SUBJECT* *CD-FORM*)
    (NEXT-PACKET
       ((TEST (EQUAL *PART-OF-SPEECH* 'VERB))
        (ASSIGN *CONCEPT* *CD-FORM*]
```

EXERCISES

1. Add the definitions needed to parse:

   (JACK WENT TO A RESTAURANT)
   (HE ORDERED A LOBSTER)
   (HE LEFT)

   The CD forms produced should match those expected for this story by the
   Micro SAM program.

2. Add RED to the dictionary so that (JACK GOT A RED KITE) will parse into

$$
\begin{aligned}
&\text{(ATRANS (ACTOR (PERSON (NAME (JACK))))} \\
&\qquad\text{(OBJECT (KITE (COLOR (RED))))} \\
&\qquad\text{(TO (PERSON (NAME (JACK)))))}
\end{aligned}
$$

HINT: Look at what the word "a" does with *CD-FORM* when it sees a noun. What should the variable *PREDICATES* be set to for *CD-FORM* to end up looking like the right thing?

3. Sometimes a word can disambiguate itself by looking at what comes next. For example, "John had an apple" normally means he *ate* an apple but "John had a newspaper" means he *possessed* a newspaper. Define the verb HAD such that (JACK HAD A KITE) becomes

(POSS (ACTOR (PERSON (NAME (JACK)))) (OBJECT (KITE)))

but (JACK HAD A LOBSTER) becomes

(INGEST (ACTOR (PERSON (NAME (JACK)))) (OBJECT (LOBSTER)))

4. Define BILL, CHECK and PAID so that (JACK PAID THE BILL WITH A CHECK) becomes

(ATRANS (ACTOR (PERSON (NAME (JACK)))) (OBJECT (MONEY))
    (AMOUNT (COST-FORM)) (FROM (PERSON (NAME (JACK)))))

PAID should look for "WITH" the same way that WENT looked for the word "TO".

Notice that the conceptual OBJECT of the ATRANS comes from the object of "with", not from the direct object of PAID. The direct object of PAID specifies the AMOUNT of money transferred. (NOTE: AMOUNT is a role we made up for this example. In actual practice the BILL would be a modifier of the OBJECT filler).

5. We just defined "check" to represent MONEY. But in a restaurant story, "check" can also refer to the COST-FORM, as in the sentence "Jack paid the check with a check." This uses both senses of "check" at once. That is, CHECK should be

```
(DEF-WORD CHECK
  ((ASSIGN *PART-OF-SPEECH* 'NOUN
           *CD-FORM* '(COST-FORM)))
  ((ASSIGN *PART-OF-SPEECH* 'NOUN
           *CD-FORM* '(MONEY]
```

This is ambiguous out of context, but in "Jack paid the check with a check", McELI could resolve the conflict, if it saved what kind of CD form the verb "paid" is looking for. That is, after seeing "paid", McELI should predict COST-FORM. After getting a noun phrase to be the direct object of "paid" (i.e., the COST-FORM), McELI should predict MONEY. The following exercises give McELI this capability, to some extent.

a. Define the function FEATURE so that (FEATURE CD-form predicate) will test whether the CD is of the form (predicate...) or not. Fix PAID so that the TEST of the request looking for the direct object of "paid" is

>   (AND (EQUAL *PART-OF-SPEECH* 'NOUN-PHRASE)
>   (FEATURE *CD-FORM* 'COST-FORM))

and the "with" request similarly tests for MONEY.

h. Define a function GET-NP-PREDICTION which looks for a request in the top packet of the stack with a test like the one given in (a)—i.e., the request looks for a noun phrase generating a particular type of CD. If it finds one, GET-NP-PREDICTION returns the predicate that FEATURE is looking for. Thus GET-NP-PREDICTION should return 'COST-FORM for the test in (a).

c. Redefine the articles "a" and "the" so that, in the variable *PRE-DICTED*, they save the CD form returned by doing a GET-NP-PREDICTION.

   You can check your definition by parsing (JACK PAID THE BILL). When THE is processed, McELI should print

>   *PREDICTION* = (QUOTE COST-FORM)

   If this doesn't happen, you have done something wrong. Note that COST-FORM should be quoted in the printout.

d. Define a function GET-CD-FORM which takes a request and returns the structure the request would assign to *CD-FORM* if executed. Assume that such ASSIGN clauses will have the form

>   (ASSIGN ... *CD-FORM* '(COST-FORM ...) ...)

e. Define a function called RESOLVE-CONFLICT which applies GET-CD-FORM to a list of requests, picking the first one that assigns to *CD-FORM* a structure matching *PREDICTED*.

   For example, if *PREDICTED* is set to (QUOTE COST-FORM), and CHECK has two requests, one of which assigns COST-FORM to *CD-FORM*, then RESOLVE-CONFLICT should choose this request over the other. Use EVAL to get rid of the QUOTEs.

f. Redefine the function CHECK-TOP so that it will look through all the requests on the top of the stack and pick the ones that can be triggered. If more than one can be triggered, CHECK-TOP should use

RESOLVE-CONFLICT to pick a request that satisfies *PRE-DICTED*.

g. Give CHECK the ambiguous definition written before (a) and parse (JACK PAID THE CHECK WITH A CHECK). The result should be

```
(ATRANS (ACTOR (PERSON (NAME (JACK)))) (OBJECT (MONEY))
        (AMOUNT (COST-FORM))
        (FROM (PERSON (NAME (JACK)))))
```

Bibliography

Abelson, R. P. (1973). The structure of belief systems. In R. C. Schank & K. M. Colby (Eds.), *Computer models of thought and language*. W. H. Freeman Co., San Francisco.

Barstow, D. R. (1979). *Knowledge-based program construction*. North Holland, New York.

Bartlett, R. (1932). *Remembering: A study in experimental and social psychology*. Cambridge University Press, London.

Berliner, H. J. (1974). *Chess as problem solving: The development of a tactics analyzer*. Ph.D. Dissertation, Computer Science Department, Carnegie-Mellon University.

Birnbaum, L. & Selfridge, M. (1979). Problems in conceptual analysis of natural language. Research Report #168, Computer Science Department, Yale University.

Bobrow, D. & Collins, A. (1976). *Representation and understanding: Studies in cognitive science*. Academic Press, New York.

Bobrow, D. & Fraser, B. (1969). An augmented state transition network analysis procedure. *Proceedings of the first international joint conference on artificial intelligence*, Washington, D.C., pp. 557–567.

Bower, G. H., Black, J. B., & Turner, T. J. (1979). Scripts in text comprehension and memory. *Cognitive psychology*, Vol. 11, pp. 177–220.

Buchanan, B. G., Sutherland, G., & Feigenbaum E. (1969). Heuristic DENDRAL: A program for generating explanatory hypotheses in organic chemistry. In B. Meltzer and D. Mitchie (Eds.), *Machine intelligence 4*, American Elsevier, New York.

Burton, R. (1976). Semantic grammar: An engineering technique for constructing natural language understanding systems. BBN Report No. 3453 (ICAI Report No. 3), Bolt Beranek and Newman, Inc., Cambridge, Mass.

Carbonell, J. G. (1978). Politics: Automated ideological reasoning. *Cognitive science*, Vol. 2, No. 1, pp. 27–51.

Carbonell, J. G. (1979). *Subjective understanding: Computer models of belief systems*. Ph.D. Dissertation, Research Report #150, Computer Science Department, Yale University.

Carbonell, J. G. (1979). The counterplanning process: A model of decision making in adverse conditions. Department of Computer Science Report, Carnegie-Mellon University.

Charniak, E. (1972). *Towards a model of children's story comprehension*. Ph.D. Dissertation, Report AI TR-266, Massachusetts Institute of Technology.

373

Charniak, E. (1977). A framed PAINTING: The representation of a common sense knowledge fragment. *Cognitive science*, Vol. 1, No. 4, pp. 355–394.

Charniak, E. (1977). Ms. Malaprop, a language comprehension program. *Proceedings of the fifth international joint conference on artificial intelligence*. Cambridge, Mass.

Charniak, E., Riesbeck, C., & McDermott, D. (1980). *Artificial intelligence programming*. Lawrence Erlbaum Associates, Hillsdale, N.J.

Colby, K. & Enea, H. (1973). Heuristic methods for computer understanding of natural language in context-restricted on-line dialogues. *Mathematical biosciences*, Vol. 1.

Cullingford, R. E. (1978). *Script application: Computer understanding of newspaper stories*. Ph.D. Dissertation, Research Report #116, Computer Science Department, Yale University.

Cullingford, R. E. (1979). Integrating knowledge sources for computer "understanding" tasks. *Proceedings of the 1979 international conference on cybernetics and society*. Denver, Col., pp. 746–752.

Davis, R. & King, J. (1975). An overview of production systems. AI Memo AIM-271, Department of Computer Science, Stanford University.

De Beaugrande, R. & Colby, B. N. (1979). Narrative models of action and interaction. *Cognitive science*, Vol. 3, No. 1, pp. 43–66.

DeJong, G. F. (1979). *Skimming stories in real time: An experiment in integrated understanding*. Ph.D. Dissertation, Research Report #158, Department of Computer Science, Yale University.

Duda, R. & Hart, P. (1973). *Pattern recognition and scene analysis*. John Wiley & Sons, New York.

Erman, L. D. & Lesser, V. R. (1975). A multi-level organization for problem solving using many diverse cooperating sources of knowledge. *Proceedings of the fourth international joint conference on artificial intelligence*. Tbilisi, USSR, pp. 483–490.

Feigenbaum, E. (1961). The simulation of verbal learning behavior. *Proceedings of the western joint computer conference*, Vol. 19, pp. 121–132.

Feigenbaum, E. & Feldman, J. (1963). *Computers and thought*. McGraw-Hill, New York.

Feigenbaum, E. (1977). The art of Artificial Intelligence: Themes and case studies of knowledge engineering. *Proceedings of the fifth international joint conference on artificial intelligence*. Cambridge, Mass., pp. 1014–1030.

Gershman, A. V. (1977). Conceptual analysis of noun groups in English. *Proceedings of the fifth international joint conference on artificial intelligence*. Cambridge, Mass., pp. 132–138.

Gershman, A. V. (1979). *Knowledge-based parsing*. Ph.D. Dissertation, Research Report #156, Computer Science Department, Yale University.

Goldman, N. (1975). Conceptual generation. In R. C. Schank (Ed.), *Conceptual information processing*. North Holland, Amsterdam.

Graesser, A. C., Gordon, S. E., & Sawyer, J. D. (1979). Recognition memory for typical and atypical actions in scripted activities: Tests of a script pointer and tag hypothesis. *Journal of verbal learning and verbal behavior*, Vol. 1, No. 8, pp. 319–332.

Greene, P. H. (1959). Problem-solving and learning machines. *Behavioral science*, Vol. 4, pp. 249–250.

Hayes, P. (1977). Some association-based techniques for lexical disambiguation by machine. Technical Report #25, Department of Computer Science, University of Rochester.

Hayes-Roth, F., Mostow, D. J., & Fox, M. S. (1978). Understanding speech in the HEARSAY-II system. In L. Block (Ed.), *Speech communications with computers*. Springer-Verlag, Berlin.

Hays, D. G. (1964). Dependency theory: A formalism and some observations. *Language*, Vol. 40, No. 4, pp. 511–525.

Hewitt, C. (1970). PLANNER: A language for manipulating models and proving theorems in a robot. Research Report AI 168, Massachusetts Institute of Technology.

Johnson-Laird, P. (1974). Memory for words. *Nature*, Vol. 32, No. 3.

Kaplan, R. (1975). On process models for sentence analysis. In D. Norman & D. Rumelhart (Eds.), *Explorations in cognition*. W. H. Freeman Co., San Francisco.

Katz, J. & Fodor, J. (1963). The structure of a semantic theory. *Language*, Vol. 39.

Kintsch, W. & Monk, D. (1972). Storage of complex information in memory: Some implications of the speed with which inferences can be made. *Journal of experimental psychology*, Vol. 94.

Kuno, C. & Oettinger, A. (1962). Multiple path syntactic analyzer. In C. M. Popplewell (Ed.), *Information processing 1962*. North-Holland, Amsterdam.

Lehnert, W. G. (1978). *The process of question answering*. Lawrence Erlbaum Associates, Hillsdale, N.J.

Locke, W. N. & Booth, A. D. (Eds.) (1955). *Machine translation of languages*. The Technology Press of The Massachusetts Institute of Technology and John Wiley & Sons, Inc., New York.

Marcus, M. (1975). Diagnosis as a notion of grammar. In R. C. Schank & B. L. Nash-Webber (Eds.), *Theoretical issues in natural language processing*. Bolt, Beranek and Newman, Cambridge, Mass.

Marcus, M. (1979). A theory of syntactic recognition for natural language. In P. Winston & R. Brown (Eds.), *Artificial intelligence: An MIT perspective*. The MIT Press, Cambridge, Mass.

Meehan, J. (1976). *The metanovel: Writing stories by computer*. Ph.D. Dissertation, Research Report #74, Computer Science Department, Yale University.

Meehan, J. (1979). *The new UCI LISP manual*. Lawrence Erlbaum Associates, Hillsdale, N.J.

Minsky, M. (1961). Steps toward artificial intelligence. *Proceedings of the IRE*. Also in E. Feigenbaum & J. Feldman (Eds.) (1963). *Computers and thought*. McGraw-Hill, New York.

Minsky, M. (1975). A framework for representing knowledge. In P. H. Winston (Ed.), *The psychology of computer vision*. McGraw-Hill, New York.

Nelson, K. & Gruendel, J. (1978). From person episode to social script: Two dimensions in the development of event knowledge. Paper presented at the biennial meeting of the Society for Research in Child Development, San Francisco.

Newell, A. (1973). Production systems: Models of control structures. In W. Chase (Ed.), *Visual information processing*. Academic Press, New York.

Newell, A. & Simon, H. A. (1961). GPS, a program that simulates human thought. In H. Billing (Ed.), *Lernende automaten*. R. Oldenbourg KP, Munchen.

Newell, A., Shaw, J., & Simon, H. A. (1958). Chess-playing programs and the problem of complexity. *IBM journal of research and development*, Vol. 2, No. 4, pp. 320–335.

Norman, D. & Rumelhart, D. (1975). *Explorations in cognition*. W. H. Freeman Co., San Francisco.

Oettinger, A. G. (1960). *Automatic language translation*. Harvard University Press, Cambridge, Mass.

Quam, L. H. (1969). LISP 1.6. Technical Report SAILON 28.3, Stanford Artificial Intelligence Laboratory, Stanford University.

Reddy, D. R. (1976). Speech recognition by machine: A review. *Proceedings of the IEEE*, IEEE.

Rieger, C. (1975). Conceptual memory. In R. C. Schank (Ed.), *Conceptual information processing*. North Holland, Amsterdam.

Riesbeck, C. (1975). Conceptual analysis. In R. C. Schank (Ed.), *Conceptual information processing*. North Holland, Amsterdam.

Riesbeck, C. (1978). An expectation-driven production system for natural language understanding. In D. A. Waterman & F. Hayes-Roth (Eds.), *Pattern-directed inference systems*. Academic Press, New York.

Riesbeck, C. & Schank, R. C. (1976). Comprehension by computer: Expectation-based analysis of sentences in context. Research Report #78, Computer Science Department, Yale University. Also in W. J. M. Levelt & G. B. Flores d'Arcais (Eds.) (1979). *Studies in the perception of language*. John Wiley & Sons Ltd., Chichester, England.

Rumelhart, D. E. (1975). Notes on a schema for stories. In D. Bobrow & A. Collins (Eds.), *Representation and understanding: Studies in cognitive science*. Academic Press, New York.

Schank, R. C. (1975). *Conceptual information processing*. North Holland, Amsterdam.

Schank, R. C. & Abelson, R. P. (1977). *Scripts, plans, goals, and understanding*. Lawrence Erlbaum Associates, Hillsdale, N.J.

Schank, R. C. & Carbonell, J. G. (1979). Re: The Gettysberg Address: Representing social and political acts. In N. Findler (Ed.), *Associative networks: Representation and use of knowledge by computers.* Academic Press, New York. Also Research Report #127, Computer Science Department, Yale University (1978).

Schank, R. C. & Colby, K. M. (Eds.) (1973). *Computer models of thought and language.* W. H. Freeman Co., San Francisco.

Schank, R. C., Goldman, N., Rieger, C., & Riesbeck, C. (1973). MARGIE: Memory, analysis, response generation and inference in English. *Proceedings of the third international joint conference on artificial intelligence,* pp. 255–261.

Schank, R. C., Goldman, N., Rieger, C., & Riesbeck, C. (1975). Inference and paraphrase by computer. *Journal of the association for computing machinery,* Vol. 22, No. 3, pp. 309–328.

Schank, R. C. & Lehnert, W. G. (1979). The conceptual content of conversations. Research Report #160, Computer Science Department, Yale University.

Schank, R. C. & Nash-Webber, B. (Eds.) (1975). *Proceedings of the conference on theoretical issues in natural language processing.* Distributed by the Association for Computational Linguistics.

Schank, R. C., Tesler, L., & Weber, S. (1970). SPINOZA: Conceptual case-based natural language analysis. AI Memo AIM-109, Computer Science Department, Stanford University.

Schank, R. C. & Kolodner, J. L. (1979). Retrieving information from an episodic memory, or why computers' memories should be more like people's. Research Report #159, Computer Science Department, Yale University.

Schank, R. C., Lebowitz, M., & Birnbaum, L. (1978). Integrated partial parsing. Research Report #143, Computer Science Department, Yale University.

Selfridge, O. (1959). Pandemonium: A paradigm for learning. In D. V. Blake & A. M. Uttley (Eds.), *Proceedings of the symposium on mechanisation of thought processes,* held at the National Physical Laboratory, Teddington, England. H.M. Stationery Office, London.

Shortliffe, E. H. (1976). *Computer-based medical consultations: MYCIN.* American Elsevier, New York.

Small, S. (1978). Conceptual language analysis for story comprehension. Technical Report #663, Department of Computer Science, University of Maryland.

Smith, E. E., Adams, N., & Schorr, D. (1978). Fact retrieval and the paradox of interference. *Cognitive psychology,* Vol. 10, pp. 438–464.

Smith, D. C. (1970). MLISP. AI Memo AIM-135, Department of Computer Science, Stanford University.

Stutzman, W. J. (1976). Organizing knowledge for English-Chinese translation. *Proceedings of the sixth international conference on computational linguistics.* Ottowa, Canada.

Thorne, J., Bratley, P., & Dewar, H. (1968). The syntactic analysis of English by machine. In D. Michie (Ed.), *Machine intelligence 3.* American Elsevier, New York.

Wilensky, R. (1978). *Understanding goal-based stories.* Ph.D. Dissertation, Research Report #140, Computer Science Department, Yale University.

Wilks, Y. (1973). An artificial intelligence approach to machine translation. In R. C. Schank & K. M. Colby (Eds.), *Computer models of thought and language.* W. H. Freeman Co., San Francisco.

Wilks, Y. (1975). A preferential, pattern-seeking semantics for natural language inference. *Artificial intelligence,* Vol. 6, pp. 53–74.

Wilks, Y. (1975). Seven theses on Artificial Intelligence and natural language. Research Report #17, Istituto per gli Studi Semantici e Cognitivi, Castagnola, Switzerland.

Wilks, Y. (1976). Parsing English I and II. In E. Charniak & Y. Wilks (Eds.), *Computational semantics.* North-Holland, Amsterdam.

Winston, P. H. (1975). *The psychology of computer vision.* McGraw-Hill, New York.

Winston, P. H. (1977). *Artificial intelligence.* Addison-Wesley, Reading, Mass.

Winograd, T. (1972). *Understanding natural language*. Academic Press, New York.

Wish, M. (1975). Comparisons among multidimensional structures of interpersonal relations. Unpublished manuscript, Bell Laboratories, Murray Hill, N.J.

Woods, W. A. (1970). Transition network grammars for natural language analysis. *Communications of the association for computing machinery*, Vol. 13, No. 10, pp. 591–606.

Woods, W., Kaplan, R., & Nash-Webber, B. (1972). The lunar sciences natural language information system: Final report. Bolt, Beranek and Newman Report No. 2378, Cambridge, Mass.

Author Index

INSIDE COMPUTER UNDERSTANDING
R.C. Schank and C.K. Riesbeck

Numbers in *italics* denote pages with complete bibliographic information.

A

Abelson, R.P., 7, 8, 37, 40, 76, 82, 89, 136,
    137, 197, 259, 260, 268, 273, 278, 281,
    293, *373*, *375*
Adams, N., 8, *376*

B

Barstow, D.R., 291, *373*
Bartlett, R., 84, *373*
Berliner, H.J., 1, *373*
Birnbaum, L., 9, 284, 321, 325, *373*, *376*
Black, J.B., 8, *373*
Bobrow, D., 319, *373*
Booth, A.D., 2, *375*
Bower, G.H., 8, *373*
Bratley, P., 319, *376*
Buchanan, B.G., 2, *373*
Burton, R., 319, *373*

C

Carbonell, J.G., 8, 26, 269, 273, 282, 284,
    292, 293, 296, 309, *373*, *376*
Charniak, E., 41, 66, 67, 69, 73, 75, 82, 125,
    136, 143, 153, 179, *373-374*
Colby, B.N., 199, *374*
Colby, K.M., 8, *374*, *376*
Collins, A., 142, *373*

Cullingford, R.E., 83, 136, 179, 273, 278,
    295, 324, *374*

D

Davis, R., 340, *374*
De Beaugrande, R., 199, *374*
DeJong, G.F., 7, 76, 276, *374*
Dewar, H., 319, *376*
Duda, R., 1, *374*

E

Enea, H., 8, *374*
Erman, L.D., 82, *374*

F

Feigenbaum, E., 2, 176, *373*, *374*
Fodor, J., 334, *374*
Fox, M.S., 295, *374*
Fraser, B., 319, *373*

G

Gershman, A.V., 284, 321, 328, 335, 342,
    344, 361, *374*
Goldman, N., 4, 75, 84, 89, 198, *374*, *376*
Gordon, S.E., 8, *374*
Graesser, A.C., 8, *374*

Greene, P.H., 1, *374*
Gruendel, J., 8, *375*

H

Hart, P., 1, *374*
Hayes, P., 334, *374*
Hayes-Roth, F., 295, *374*
Hays, D.G., 2, 334, *374*
Hewitt, C., 88, *374*

J,K

Johnson-Laird, P., 84, *374*
Kaplan, R., 271, 319, *374, 377*
Katz, J., 334, *374*
King, J., 340, *374*
Kintsch, W., 84, *375*
Kolodner, J.L., 9, *376*
Kuno, C., 153, *375*

L

Lebowitz, M., 9, 325, *376*
Lehnert, W.G., 8, 79, 89, 97, 264, 304, *375,
376*
Lesser, V.R., 82, *374*
Locke, W.N., 2, *375*

M

Marcus, M., 319, 334, *375*
McDermott, D., 41, 66, 67, 69, 73, *374*
Meehan, J., 41, 197, 202, *375*
Minsky, M., 1, 11, 82, 136, *375*
Monk, D., 84, *375*
Mostow, D.J., 295, *374*

N,O

Nash-Webber, B., 271, *376, 377*
Nelson, K., 8, *375*
Newell, A., 1, 291, 326, *375*
Oettinger, A.G., 2, 153, *375*

Q,R

Quam, L.H., 202, *375*
Reddy, D.R., 261, *375*
Rieger, C., 4, 82, 84, 89, *375, 376*
Riesbeck, C.K., 4, 41, 66, 67, 69, 73, 75, 83,
84, 89, 153, 165, 166, 265, 283, 284, 318,
319, 321, 325, 334, 337, 354, 361, *374,
375, 376*
Rumelhart, D.E., 82, *375*

S

Sawyer, J.D., 8, *374*
Schank, R.C., 4, 7, 8, 9, 13, 17, 26, 29, 31,
37, 40, 75, 76, 82, 83, 84, 89, 136, 137,
197, 260, 265, 268, 269, 273, 278, 281,
283, 284, 293, 318, 319, 321, 325, 334,
337, *375-376*
Schorr, D., 8, *376*
Selfridge, M., 284, 321, *373*
Selfridge, O., 153, *376*
Shaw, J., 1, *375*
Shortliffe, E.H., 2, 291, *376*
Simon, H.A., 1, *375*
Small, S., 334, *376*
Smith, D.C., 202, *376*
Smith, E.E., 8, *376*
Stutzman, W.J., 89, *376*
Sutherland, G., 2, *373*

T

Tesler, L., 318, 319, 321, *376*
Thorne, J., 319, *376*
Turner, T.J., 8, *373*

W

Weber, S., 318, 319, 321, *376*
Wilensky, R., 136, *376*
Wilks, Y., 319, 334, 336, 343, *376*
Winograd, T., 319, *377*
Winston, P.H., 1, 41, *376*
Wish, M., 198, *377*
Woods, W.A., 271, 319, *377*

Subject Index

INSIDE COMPUTER UNDERSTANDING
R.C. Schank and C.K. Riesbeck

A

ACTION, 11-13
ACTOR, 11-13
AI research, 1-4, 11, 197
Ambiguity (*see* Disambiguation)
Anaphora (*see* Reference)
Antiplanning, 140
Applier (*see* Scripts)
ATN (*see* Augmented transition network)
ATRANS, 16-17
ATTEND, 18-19
Augmented transition network, 334

B

BABEL, 75, 78, 89, 97, 198, 202
Backbone (*see* Scripts)
Backwards inferences (*see* Preconditions)
Belief system, 8, 259-260
Binding form (*see* Scripts)
BORIS, 9

C

CA (*see* Conceptual Analyzer)
Causal chains, 7, 29-30, 76-77, 207
Causal connections, 28-29
  of texts, 6, 29
Causal types

enablement, 28-29
initiation, 29
reason, 29
result, 28
CD (*see* Conceptual Dependency)
Coherence, 199
Computational linguistics, 2
Conceptual Analyzer, 318-353
  annotated example, 344-353
Conceptual Dependency, 4-5, 10-26, 320-321
  forms in LISP, 60-61
  functions in LISP, 63-64
  LISP code, 69-70
Condition-action pairs (*see* Requests)
Conscious Processor, 18-19
Consequences, 207, 214, 221-222
Context, 27-28, 75, 222
  use in SAM, 78-79
Control structure, 83, 86-87, 145-146, 175,
  198-199, 223-224, 271
Counterplanning, 261, 264-265, 268, 280-282
  strategies, 290-299
CP (*see* Conscious Processor)
CYRUS, 9

D

D-CONT (*see* Goals)
Demons, 153, 200, 214
DENDRAL, 2

Determinism, 334-335
Dictionary entry, 283-285
Direct header, 106-107
DIRECTION, 11-13
Disambiguation, 324-325, 333-334, 342-343, 370-372
Discrimination net, 148, 187
D-KNOW (see Goals)
D-PROX (see Goals)

E

ELI, 75, 78, 83-85, 283, 321, 334, 337, 354, 360-361
Episodes, 76, 107-108
Expectation-based analysis, 284-285
Expectations, 318-319
EXPEL, 18
Explanation-driven understanding, 136, 140, 143-144
Event, 11
  assertion of, 220
  key, 278

F

Forward inference (see Consequences)
Frame hypothesis, 142-144
Frames, 125, 197
FRUMP, 6-9, 276
Function, 87-88, 104, 115

G

Gaps, 165, 171, 173-175, 336-337 (see also Suggestions; Requests)
  dummy, 177
Garbage collection, 222
Generation, 198, 217, 225-226
Global script, 88
Goals, 7, 37-39, 150-154, 202
  analysis, 287-290
  calculus, 107, 203
  competition, 138, 140
  concord, 138
  conflict, 138, 141
  subsumption, 137-138
  trees, 8, 261, 268, 278-280, 285-286
  types
    Achievement goals, 39, 299
    D-goals, 35-37, 197
      D-CONT, 35-36, 156, 201, 205-206, 209, 210-211
      D-KNOW, 35-36, 158-159, 198, 201, 205, 211, 223
      D-PROX, 37, 157, 198, 201, 206, 209, 211-212, 223, 236
    Enjoyment goals, 39
    Preservation goals, 39, 299
      P-CONT, 161
      P-HEALTH, 38, 162
    Satisfaction goal, 38
      S-HUNGER, 38, 165, 167, 205, 209, 213
      S-REST, 214
      S-SEX, 38, 214
      S-SLEEP, 38
      S-THIRST, 213
Goldwater machine, 259-260
GRASP, 18, 24

H

HEARSAY-II, 261, 295
Hypothesis testing, 148-149

I

Ideology, political, 260, 278
Inference, 4-6, 140, 222-223
  bottom-up, 146, 148-149
  constraining, 6
    with scripts, 32-33
  explosion, 5, 222
  goal-directed, 262-263, 265
  rules, 16, 275-276
  types, 76-77, 214, 224-225
INGEST, 23-25
Instantiation, 88
Instantiator, 86-88
  in LISP, 72-73
Instrumental header, 106
Instrumentality, 22-24, 76, 106, 150, 264, 280
  acts of, 18
Intentions, 136-137, 148, 202
IPP, 9

L

Language, theory of, 10-11, 25-26
LISP
  AND, 54
  APPEND, 47, 54
  APPLY, 54

ASSOC, 55
ATOM, 49, 55
atom, 41-42
binding list, 62-64, 122
branching, 45
CADR, 48
CAR, 48, 55
CDR, 48, 55
comments, 42
COND, 45, 55
conditional, 45
Cons, 46,55
CONS-END, 54
  LISP code, 69
CONSP, 49, 55
DE, 44, 55
defining functions, 44, 55-56
  nonstandard, 64-74
DEFPROP, 55
DF, 55
DIFFERENCE, 55
DM, 56, 73-74
DRM, 56
empty list, 43
EQUAL, 49, 56
EVAL, 52, 56
evaluation, 43-44
EXPANDMACROS, 73
EXPLODE, 56
expression
  definition, 41
  evaluation of, 42-44
false (see NIL)
FEXPRs, 73-74
FILLER:PAIR, 63
  LISP code, 69
FILLER:ROLE, 63-64
  LISP code, 70
FOR, 52-54, 56-57
  implementation functions, 65-66
  LISP code, 67-68
FUNCTION, 65
GET, 50, 57
HEADER:CD, 64
  LISP code, 69
Identifiers
  definition, 42
  properties on, 50, 55, 57, 59
input, 52, 59
INSTANTIATE, 64
  LISP code, 72-73

IS-VAR, 64
  LISP code, 70
iteration, 50-53
keywords, 51-54
LAMBDA, 65
LAST, 57
LENGTH, 50, 57
LET, 57
  implementation functions, 65-66
  LISP code, 68-69
LIST, 47, 57
lists, 42
  data structure, 46
LOOP, 51-52, 57
  implementation functions, 65-66
  LISP code, 66-67
macros
adding, 73
  expanding, 73-74
MAPC, 65
MAPCAN, 65
MAPCAR, 65
MATCH, 61-64
  flowchart, 71
  LISP code, 70-72
MEMBER, 46, 57
MINUS, 45, 57
MINUSP, 45, 57
MSG, 57-58
NAME:VAR, 64
  LISP code, 70
NIL, 43
NOT, 49-50, 58
NULL, 49-50, 58
NUMBERP, 58
numbers, 41
OR, 58
output, 52, 57-58
parentheses, 42
pattern matching, 61-63
PLUS, 43-44, 58
POP, 49, 58
  LISP code, 69
PRINT, 52, 58
PROG, 65-66
PROG1, 58
PROGN, 44, 58
PUSH, 47, 59
  LISP code, 69
PUTPROP, 50, 59
QUOTE, 43, 59

READ, 52, 59
readmacros, 56
recursion, 50-51

REMOVE, 59
REMPROP, 59
REVERSE, 59
ROLE:PAIR, 64
   LISP code, 69
ROLES:CD, 64
   LISP code, 69
SELECTQ, 59
SET, 60
SETQ 43, 60
Setrole, 64
   LISP code, 70
SOME, 66
special characters, 42
SPRINT, 60
strings, 41
SUBST, 60
T, 43
TIMES, 44, 60
true (see T)
variables
   local, 44
   pattern, 62
ZEROP, 60
Locale header, 106
LUNAR, 271

M

Machine translation (see Translation,
   mechanical)
MARGIE, 4-6, 321, 334
MBUILD, 25
Memory, 9, 31, 85, 215, 224, 325
   short-term, 326
MOVE, 18, 24
Ms. Malaprop, 125-126, 136, 144
MTRANS, 18-20
Multi-module programs, 82-83
MYCIN, 2, 291

N

NGP (see Noun Group Processor)
Nodes, 166, 279 (see also Gaps)
Noun Group Processor, 321
Noun groups, 341-342

O

OBJECT, 11-13

P

Packet (see Requests)
PAM, 7-9, 136-179
   annotated example, 155-163
Paraphrase
 in MARGIE, 5
 in PAM, 139-140
 in SAM, 89
Parsing, 318-372
Partial-order comparisons, 201-202
Pattern
   definition, 103
   matching, 61-63, 86-88, 103-105, 114-119
      in Micro SAM, 123-124
      utility functions, 268
Pattern-directed function invocation, 88, 116
Pattern Matcher, 86, 123
   in LISP, 70-72
Patterns in LISP, 61-63
PECOS, 291
Permanent tokens, 85
Picture Producer, 11-12, 83-85
Planboxes, 35-36, 142, 206, 210-214
   ASK, 35-36, 157, 174, 201
   BARGAIN, 36-37, 154, 174, 175-177, 201,
      210, 226
   DO-$RESTAURANT, 168
   EXPLAIN, 36
   GIVE, 162
   OVERPOWER, 36-37
   PERSUADE, 201, 206, 212
   PROMISE, 210
   REFUSE, 159
   REQUEST, 210
   STEAL, 36
   TELL, 158-159, 201, 208, 211-212
   THREATEN, 36, 142, 154, 160, 206
   UNDO-PRECONDITION, 142
   USE-VEHICLE, 156
   WALK, 157
Plans, 7, 33-37, 152-154, 202
   theory of, 143-144
POLITICS, 8-9, 33, 259-307
   annotated example, 299-307
PP (see Picture Producer)
PP-MEMORY, 83-85

Precondition header, 106
Preconditions, 293-294
  in plans, 207, 210-214, 264-265
  in scripts, 86, 106
Prediction, 137, 148, 294-295, 319-320
  inference-based, 77
  in plans, 150-154, 163-170, 181
  removing, 149
  in scripts, 116-117, 273
  top-down, 154
Primitives, 13-25
Problem solving, 1, 198-199, 202-203,
  210-214
Process model, 2, 270
Productions (see Requests)
Pronominal reference, 178-179
PROPEL, 22-24
Props (see Scripts)
PSG system, 291
PTRANS, 21-22

Q

QUALM, 79, 89
Question-answering, 79-80, 89, 139-140,
  263-265, 272-273, 304

R

Reasoning, 136
  common-sense, 260-261
  integrated, 261
  interpretive, 294-295
Recency rule (see Requests)
Reference, 85-86, 95, 178-179
Representation
  of events, 11-13, 102-103
  of ideology, 260
  of knowledge, 4
  of meaning, 11, 16
Requests, 145, 153, 165-166, 172-175, 321,
  325-369
  active, 166, 271
  chain, 171
  condition-action pairs, 142, 148, 290-291
  consideration, 326
  gap-filling, 336-337
  in Micro ELI, 354-355
  packet, 354
  in PAM, 150-153, 166-170
  pool, 340-341
  recency rule, 339-341

  removing, 173-175, 327, 338
  selection, 333-334
  testing, 177-178, 335-336, 338-339
  types, 172-173, 327
Roles (see Scripts)
Role instantiation, 76-77, 302
  in Micro SAM, 124-125
Role merging, 76-77, 100
Rules (see also Requests)
  context-dependent, 268, 276
  context-switching, 268, 271, 276-278
  goal analysis, 285

S

SAM, 6-9, 75-119, 273, 276, 295
  annotated example, 89-100
Scenes (see Scripts)
Scripts, 6-7, 30-33, 101-109, 121, 260, 277
  active, 86-87
  application, 30, 31-33, 109-119, 273-275
  Applier, 83, 86-89
  backbone, 87, 101, 114
  binding form, 122
  context, 85-87, 111-112
    of active script, 86-87
  header, 105
  instantiation, 30-31, 124
  management problem, 86, 88
  in Micro SAM, 121
  props, 85, 101-102
  roles, 77, 80, 101, 121
  scenes, 32, 76, 109
  setting, 80, 101
  situational, 268
  tokens, 84-85
    permanent, 85
  tracks, 30-31, 125, 273
  variables, 87, 101, 103-105
Setting (see Scripts)
Simulation, 197, 203
  hypothetical, 222-223
  of ideology, 259
Situations, 76
Slot-filling, 11-13, 84, 197, 331-332, 341-342
Social ACTs, 26, 269, 284-285
Social relations, 210, 214
Space, representation of, 198, 216, 221
SPEAK, 18
Stories
  classes, 141
  content, 145

theory of, 198, 202-203
  understanding, 81-82
Suggestions, 165-166, 174-175
Summarization (*see* Paraphrase)
Symbolic arithmetic, 201-202, 216
Syntactic parsers, 2, 319, 321, 334-335
Syntax, 10-11, 331-333

T

TALE-SPIN, 7-9, 197-226
  annotated example, 203-210
Test-action pairs (*see* Requests)
Themes, 39-40, 150
  FONDNESS, 156

Tokens (*see* Scripts)
Tracks (*see* Scripts)
Translation
  mechanical, 2, 321
  simultaneous, 89
TRIAD, 269
Turning points, 76, 108

U

Understanding
  integrated, 270
  subjective, 259, 261, 268
  theory of, 10